QUEER JUDAISM

Queer Judaism

LGBT Activism and the Remaking
of Jewish Orthodoxy in Israel

Orit Avishai

NEW YORK UNIVERSITY PRESS

New York

NEW YORK UNIVERSITY PRESS
New York
www.nyupress.org

Library of Congress Cataloging-in-Publication Data
Names: Avishai, Orit, author.
Title: Queer Judaism : LGBT activism and the remaking of Jewish Orthodoxy in Israel /
Orit Avishai.
Description: New York : New York University Press, [2023] | Includes bibliographical
references and index.
Identifiers: LCCN 2022027522 | ISBN 9781479810017 (hardback) |
ISBN 9781479810031 (paperback) | ISBN 9781479810055 (ebook) |
ISBN 9781479810048 (ebook other)
Subjects: LCSH: Homosexuality—Religious aspects—Judaism. | Sexual orientation—
Religious aspects—Judaism. | Sexual minorities—Religious life—Israel. | Social
movements—Israel—History—21st century. | Orthodox Judaism—Israel.
Classification: LCC BM729.H65 A95 2023 | DDC 296.3/664—dc23/eng/20220709
LC record available at https://lccn.loc.gov/2022027522

New York University Press books are printed on acid-free paper, and their binding materials
are chosen for strength and durability. We strive to use environmentally responsible suppli-
ers and materials to the greatest extent possible in publishing our books.

Manufactured in the United States of America

10 9 8 7 6 5 4 3 2 1

Also available as an ebook

Dedicated to Kadag, the Proud Religious Community

CONTENTS

GLOSSARY

BAT KOL Orthodox Lesbian and queer women's organization founded in 2005 whose name literally means "the voice of God." Officially changed its name to the more inclusive Lesbian, Bisexual, Transgender, and Queer Orthodox Women in 2021. Part of the Proud Religious Community.

BEIT HILLEL A Torah leadership organization associated with liberal factions of Israeli Jewish Orthodoxy and made up of over 170 religious-Zionist Rabbanim and Rabbaniot (women religious authorities) located throughout Israel.

HALACHA Jewish law and jurisprudence.

HAVRUTA Orthodox gay men's organization founded in 2007 whose name refers to the practice of Jewish learning, typically conducted in pairs; the practice alludes to a sage's observation juxtaposing human sociability and life with loneliness and death. Part of the Proud Religious Community. As of July 2022, Havruta is considering expanding its mission and name to be more inclusive of more diverse gender and sexual identities.

HOD Now-defunct conservative gay men's organization that operated between 2008 and 2016.

HOMMO Hebrew vernacular term preferred by many Orthodox gay men. Given the term's fraught cross-cultural resonance, I italicize it to mark it as a foreign/native term.

KADAG Hebrew acronym for the Proud Religious Community, a loose amalgam of several organizations that serve Orthodox LGBT persons.

KAMOHA Now-defunct conservative gay men's organization. A Havruta breakaway that operated between 2011 and 2020.

NOAM Über-conservative homophobic and transphobic nationalist party that first ran in the September 2019 elections and later merged with the Religious Zionist Party.

PESACH SHENI The marking of a Jewish day of religious tolerance that occurs a month after Passover; literally "second Passover." Previously a fringe folk Hasidic tradition that was harnessed by progressive Jewish groups in the United States to advance a broad vision of social justice centered on the inclusion of marginalized groups.

SHOVAL Israeli Orthodox LGBT outreach organization founded by Bat Kol and Havruta activists in 2006.

ULPANA Orthodox girls-only high school.

"We Exist"

Volunteers with Shoval, an Israeli Orthodox LGBT outreach organization, frequently encounter claims that LGBT lives and religiously committed ones are incompatible.[1] Shoval runs two-hour workshops that begin with volunteers telling their Orthodox LGBT story—a narrative arc revolving around a normative Orthodox childhood interrupted by a painful realization that the protagonist was "different." The Shoval story then relays a period of reckoning that often includes violent ruptures on the path to normative Orthodox adulthood, culminating with a declaration, "My name is ____ and I am a lesbian/*hommo*/trans Orthodox person. (*Hommo* is the Hebrew vernacular term used by many Orthodox gay men.) Volunteers have come to expect objections along the lines of, "How can you call yourself Orthodox when the Bible/*halacha* [Jewish law] says . . . ?"

On the face of it, skeptics are on solid ground. A dominant thread in Jewish thought holds that scripture and tradition prohibit not only male-on-male anal sex but also all forms of intimacies, identities, relationships, desires, and families that fall outside the heteronormative and cisnormative order. (Heteronormativity and cisnormativity imply, respectively, that being heterosexual and cisgender is superior to other manifestations of gender and sexuality and mark deviations as nonnormative.) This position renders religious LGBT persons as paradoxical at best, more likely transgressive, pathological, or sinful, and, until recently, all but invisible. Rabbi Shlomo Aviner, a conservative Orthodox stalwart and founder of a defunct conversion therapy organization, captured this sentiment at the turn of the twenty-first century when he declared that "there is no such thing as a religious homosexual."[2]

"We have *hommos*. They are more numerous than you can imagine," countered Nati Epstein, cofounder of Havruta, an Orthodox gay men's organization, writing anonymously in 2001.³ Moreover, the Jewish tradition is much more pluralistic and ambiguous vis-à-vis same-sex love, lives, attraction, and families than Orthodox conservatives allow. It has become even more so since the mid-aughts as a result of the activism of organizations and individuals affiliated with Kadag, the Proud Religious Community.

This book tells the stories of Orthodox lesbians and *hommos* and the movement they built: how they came to tell new stories and remake their dreams; how they fought to make their lives visible, legible, palatable, and livable—first to themselves and then to their communities; how Jewish traditions, symbols, sensibilities, and mythologies, intertwined with a rhetoric of nationalist belonging, helped them articulate new scripts for living Orthodoxy; how in the process they challenged dominant ideas about a divinely ordained cisgender and heterosexual social order; how this process culminated in a broad recognition that Orthodox LGBT persons do, in fact, exist. Their lived experiences reveal a rich complexity: LGBT persons of faith who embrace their sexual identity not in spite of—*but because of*—their commitment to the Jewish tradition.

Three lines of inquiry run through this volume. First, Orthodoxy asserts itself as a timeless heterosexual and cisgender social order. But who gets to decide who—and what—is authentically Orthodox? Orthodox LGBT persons and their allies do not think that rabbis, theologians, and the community at large should have the final say. To claim that "Orthodox LGBT persons exist" is at once a statement about visibility—making visible the invisible—and a statement about who can legitimately claim this label. When Orthodox LGBT persons lay claim to the Jewish tradition, they reveal religious identities and LGBT ones as social, cultural, and political artifacts. Orthodox conservatives consider these identities an existential threat.

A second line of inquiry ponders how a once-hegemonic stance—one that pathologizes and silences homosexuality and that had been so taken for granted that it hardly needed to be articulated—has come to play defense. How did same-sex-attracted Orthodox Jews in Israel, within the space of a decade and a half, forge new identities, create a Proud Orthodox community, and win over (some) Orthodox families, communities, educators, and leaders? The analysis points to a movement that strove to "make space" for the marginalized by drawing on political logics of authenticity and moderation. Kadag insists that it intends not to rock (let alone destroy) the Orthodox boat, just to make space for marginalized Jews. But Orthodox LGBT persons' presence and visibility within families, synagogues, neighborhoods, schools, and on social media—*in and of themselves*—destabilize taken-for-granted positions on "authentic" forms of Jewish bodies, desires, and family life. What to make of an LGBT movement that enlists religious language, heteronormative frameworks, and a nationalist stance as it pursues inclusion and equality?

A final line of inquiry asks what it takes for LGBT persons to achieve psychological well-being (in social scientists' parlance) or livable lives (queer theory's take) in a conservative social context. Religion is often portrayed predominantly as a source of conflict and anguish in the lives of LGBT persons and an obstacle to LGBTQ+ agendas. This book documents how the Jewish tradition is also a site of comfort, guidance, and support for Orthodox LGBT persons, thus highlighting the dynamic process by which religious and sexual identities are made.

This book is thus at once a tale of LGBT activism and the making of livable LGBT lives, and one about negotiated boundaries: what does it mean to be "us"? What does it take to be afforded group membership? Who creates the rulebook and polices its boundaries? And what happens when pressure from the bottom challenges faith traditions' stories about themselves? At the local level, this volume documents how a social movement that sought to make space for marginalized members of society unmasked the unsteady foundations of a purportedly timeless religious tradition. But this local story has broader resonance: as homegrown religious LGBT movements proliferate across faith traditions and geographical locations, the battle over Orthodoxy's straight soul may be instructive as to how communities of faith create and patrol boundaries, how minority groups define themselves within and against these boundaries, and how an analytic lens that sees the nuanced and complex realities of religious LGBT lives beyond that of conflict and shame and through the lens of queer worldmaking can help us make sense of identity journeys and struggles for social change.

A NOTE ON TERMINOLOGY

The glossary provides a roadmap for readers not familiar with the local context, but three linguistic choices are of particular significance. First, to mark intra-Orthodox discourse, I refer to Orthodox liberals and Orthodox conservatives. The latter are *not* synonymous with Conservative Judaism; in fact, they are far from this strand. I use conservative in its general definition to refer to those who hold traditional values and are averse to change or innovation. Second, I use LGBT in the context of Jewish Orthodoxy since most of my respondents use a Hebrew acronym that does not include queer; I use LGBTQ+ to refer to gender and sexual variance in other contexts in line with scholarly linguistic norms. However, a shift is under way among the youngest Orthodox LGBT persons, some of whom identify as queer. Q is increasingly becoming more central to the communal narrative, but at the time of this writing the discourse focuses on lesbian, gay, bisexual, and trans identities. Finally, I use the term *hommo* because many Orthodox gay men in Israel identify as homosexual, *hommo* in Hebrew. I recognize that in English the term may read as pejorative, rife with internalized homophobia, but in the context I discuss *hommo* is subversive: mainstream Orthodoxy refers to homosexuality as an "inverse tendency" that can be "cured," while "gay" is associated with secular culture. Asserting "I am an Orthodox *hommo*" is an act of defiance toward traditional orthodoxy that signals religious and sexual self-affirmation. Given the term's fraught cross-cultural resonance, I italicize it to mark it as a foreign/native term.

Introduction

Kippa Battles

For a couple of weeks in July 2019, in the midst of the second of three parliamentary elections held in close succession against the backdrop of mounting dissatisfaction with Israel's prime minister Benjamin Netanyahu, and with no end in sight to the Israeli-Palestinian conflict, Orthodox public figures in Israel zeroed in on the "LGBT agenda." An interim education minister representing the ultranationalist and religious Jewish Home political party, Rabbi Raffi Peretz, voiced support for purportedly "benign" forms of conversion therapy.[1] As heart-wrenching testimonials from the front lines of such interventions flooded mainstream, Orthodox, and social media, Rabbi Peretz tried to walk back his comments, but a chorus of his supporters stood firm. One rabbi reduced homosexuality to unbridled lust that could be disciplined with staunch observance, directing his most damning comments at Orthodox same-sex-attracted persons: throw away your *kippa* (yarmulke), he demanded.[2] Another rabbi turned to the animal kingdom: one does not find same-sex pairings among beasts, he claimed (implying, presumably, that homosexuality was not "natural," though same-sex pairings do in fact exist among nonhuman animals).[3] Later that week an Orthodox newspaper distributed a pamphlet, authored by LGBT foe Rabbi Yigal Levinstein. *Family Values in the Face of Postmodernism* told a familiar if demographically unsubstantiated tale about the precarity of Jewish family values. The pamphlet's cover featured a house perilously perched on a cliff and held back by a shabby rope and a couple of stakes, ostensibly representing the likes of Rabbi Levinstein.[4] Meanwhile, a founder of Noam, an über-conservative nationalist party that ran in the September 2019 elections, laid out its raison d'être: the eradication of the "LGBT phenomenon," which Noam deemed to be "a virus," from Israeli society.[5] (Noam dropped out in 2019 but won a parliamentary seat in March

2021 as part of the Religious Zionist Party.) Leaders of two other right-wing parties, both Orthodox men, posed for a joint photograph with the *Family Values* pamphlet. The photo-op ended months of disunity with an announcement that the two parties had signed a cooperation agreement; homophobic and transphobic Jewish family values was apparently something they could agree on (the agreement fell apart after a poor showing in the polls, but one of the men in the photo, Naftali Bennett, became prime minister in March 2021).

Orthodox LGBT persons and organizations responded to the episode with characteristic speed and wit. Shai Bramson, a longtime activist, conversion therapy survivor, and Havruta board member, appeared on seemingly every news channel and social media platform. Other Orthodox LGBT persons flooded social media with painful personal stories. Some took their protests to the streets, where they trolled Noam booths, showing up with pride flags—and, naturally, their kippas. LGBT ally Rabbi Ronen Lubitch dismissed conservative rabbis' focus on LGBT persons as an unhealthy and unproductive obsession,[6] while Bat Kol, the Orthodox Lesbian women's organization, contextualized Rabbi Lubitch's tolerance in battles hard-fought and won by Orthodox LGBT persons themselves. A joint statement by several Orthodox LGBT organizations known as Kadag, the Proud Religious Community, zeroed in on the battle's essence: Orthodoxy's rules of belonging. "It is not clear to us where the Rabbi draws his power to push us away from Judaism. Where does he get the courage to ask us to give up Shabbat and therefore our Orthodox identity?"[7]

Other materials and initiatives circulated during this period: podcasts with Orthodox LGBT leaders; invitations to public outreach events featuring Orthodox LGBT persons;[8] and a snazzy public visibility campaign depicting Orthodox LGBT families, *Our Faces*.[9] These initiatives were grounded in Kadag's politics of authenticity, which mobilizes Jewish values, language, and sensibilities to advance the movement's key goal: making space for Orthodox LGBT persons in their communities. That the circulation of these materials coincided with the Peretz incident was pure happenstance (they had been in production for months), but such coincidences have been frequent since the mid-aughts, when Orthodox LGBT allies and foes became locked in a choreographed dance: a battle for Orthodoxy's straight soul.[10]

The episode also captures the deep polarization among Orthodox Jews in Israel. Orthodoxy's troubles did not begin with nor do they center on LGBT issues, but they coalesced here: on the one side a liberal Orthodoxy (reluctantly and belatedly) coming to terms with reality—Orthodox LGBT persons were living in their midst—on the other a reactionary Orthodoxy erecting ever more stringent boundaries to protect itself from this reality.[11] While the liberal faction accepts LGBT persons as a challenge that Orthodoxy must resolve, the reactionary one views LGBT people as confused at best, more often a "phenomenon" or condition to be either contained or severed. This episode left no doubt that Kadag and its allies had won the framing war. An activist marveled, "We are so threatening that they need a whole political party organized against us." Another said that such homophobic protests were the final gasps of a bygone—if vocal—world (the mood was less joyous when a Noam representative was elected to the Israeli Parliament).[12]

Caught in the middle are people who want to live their lives: attend educational institutions of their choice; find a partner to whom they are attracted emotionally, physically, and romantically; align their physical body with their gender identity; send their children to neighborhood schools; live among their friends and family; feel welcome in the synagogue and *beit midrash* (learning community). They seek to make their own and their Orthodox LGBT peers' lives fully human, fully Jewish, or, to use queer theorist Judith Butler's terms, livable.[13] Most of them do not take to the streets, join Kadag organizations, subject themselves to the prying questions of reporters and researchers, or come out on Facebook. But through the choices they make about whom to love, how to live in their bodies, where to locate their families, and how to worship, they, too, partake in the grand experiment of queering orthodoxy: disrupting taken-for-granted ideas about authentic Jewish identities, families, bodies, and manifestations of love.

These are remarkable developments. Fifteen years earlier Orthodox persons could not imagine embracing their sexual or gender identity while staying within the Orthodox fold, let alone sharing their stories publicly and receiving love and support. Orthodox LGBT persons did not partake in Israel's gay revolution of the 1990s, and those who came of age before the close of the aughts had few visible alternatives to heterosexual marriage or celibacy if they were to remain Orthodox. Few persons over thirty-five identify as Orthodox LGBT, virtually none over forty. Then, within less than fifteen years, Orthodox LGBT persons articulated new identities (lesbian Orthodox, trans Orthodox, etc.); forged social networks and communities; and persuaded families, rabbinic authorities, congregations, and communities to make space for them. They have gone from chatrooms and backrooms, from being fearful, anonymous, and closeted, to crafting and disseminating personal and collective narratives through viral Facebook posts that proudly feature their faces, names, families, and stories. How did this happen?

Kadag activists followed a well-honed LGBTQ+ movement arc: they came out, educated communities, reframed old conversations and told new stories, made allies, and engaged in public protests running the gamut from "respectable" to playful to subversive. They also mobilized strategies less common in LGBTQ+ activism, enlisting religious language, sensibilities, and rhetoric, ones deeply intertwined with nationalist sentiments. In the annals of LGBTQ+ struggles, religious people are more likely to be foes rather than fellow travelers, and religious rhetoric is more likely an obstacle to overcome rather than an archive to be mined for comfort, guidance, support, and activation of unexpected allies.

This religious LGBT movement and the experiences of LGBT persons of faith who compose it thus provide unique insights into the intersection of activism, religion, and LGBTQ+ lives. It also poses some challenges. Kadag does not wish to "destroy the institution of the straight family," but rather seeks for LGBT persons "a room of our own within the Jewish home."[14] Not only does this stance leave heteronormative systems in place, but the "home" to which Orthodox LGBT persons lay claim is political as much as religious. Orthodox LGBT persons criticize religious communities' and political parties' homophobia and transphobia, but many align with their nationalism (this alignment, or homonationalism, characterizes most Israeli LGBT movements and interest groups).[15] Kadag's campaign to make space for some marginalized groups leaves intact social structures and institutions that privilege men, cisgender persons, normative families, and Jewish citizens of the state. What to make of a seemingly complicit LGBT movement?[16]

Other insights emerge from engaging a social science literature that depicts religion predominantly as a source of conflict and anguish in the lives of LGBTQ+ persons and my findings that the Jewish tradition provides comfort, guidance, and support for Orthodox LGBT persons seeking new scripts. This book makes a case for shifting the emphasis from individual identity conflicts to the dynamic, lived, and culturally and historically contingent process by which religious and sexual identities are made. Making LGBTQ+ lives "livable" entails the transformation of everyday spaces, practices, and discourses—a process of (religious) queer worldmaking.[17]

Finally, this is a story about a community negotiating its rules of inclusion. One need not be familiar with the idiosyncrasies of Orthodox Judaism to recognize the implications of denying group membership to those deemed un-Jewish, un-Orthodox, corrupted by "modern," "secular," and "postmodern" values. Viewed through the lens of the politics of belonging,[18] the case can be read as a contest over the Jewish tradition: Orthodox LGBT persons who claim Jewish authenticity (and their allies) are locked in a battle over Orthodoxy's straight soul with Orthodox conservatives who seek to write them out of existence.

The Politics of Authenticity

Kadag promotes monogamy, marriage, a family, and a home within the community.[19] Departing from the simple claim—"we exist"—Orthodox LGBT persons seek to make space for themselves, their relationships, and their families within Orthodoxy.[20] While Kadag deploys the standard LGBTQ+ activist playbook, it also leans heavily on religious and political affinities. Its activism is anchored in claims to a shared Orthodox experience, and its activists come to the table not as revolutionary warriors but as Orthodox persons who happen to be LGBT. But in Israel religious and nationalist sentiments are deeply intertwined; the Jewish Home, in which Kadag seeks a room, was also the name of a nationalist, right-wing political party (Rabbi Peretz, mentioned earlier, was a onetime party head; though the party dissolved, its vision lives on in other nationalist parties, including Noam). Orthodox traditionalists label LGBTQ+ movements, Kadag among them, as radical "terrorists" who threaten both Jewish Orthodoxy and the state. But is Kadag radically queer?

Students of social change distinguish between transformative politics that consider all facets of the existing social order suspect and liberal politics of inclusivity that work within this existing order. The radical impulse in queer activism embraces and celebrates difference, demands solidarity with other marginalized groups, and prefers dissidence to working methodically from within the system.[21] Its goal is to unmask and "transform the basic fabric and hierarchies that allow systems of oppression to persist and operate efficiently."[22] But not all LGBTQ+ persons envision or desire a fundamentally altered society, and many LGBTQ+ movements pursue a liberal politics of "normalcy," tolerance, and inclusivity premised on claims of sameness between LGBTQ+ persons and dominant groups.[23] Queer critiques of such liberal politics center on two areas of complicity: the incorporation of heteronormative ideals and constructs into LGBT culture and identity (homonormativity),[24] and the association between LGBTQ+ rights and nationalism (homonationalism).[25]

Homonormative movements emphasize inclusivity and integration, focus on issues such as monogamy, marriage, procreation, and acceptance in state institutions (the workplace, the military, or, in the case of religious groups, the synagogue, the church, the mosque), and collaborate with dominant social institutions. Homonormative agendas rattle, but stop short of upending, oppressive gender systems, sometimes even entrenching gender binaries. Critics of marriage equality in the United States claim that the normalization of same-sex marriage resulted in such retrenchment,[26] and religious acceptance movements that seek to normalize the presence of (some) LGBTQ+ persons in religious congregations seem to be having the same effect.[27] Homonormative agendas thus tend to benefit more privileged dissident groups (such as educated gay white men) while preserving existing discriminatory institutions (for example, a transphobic health care system). In contrast, queer politics actively work to destabilize such heteronormative logic and its associated social institutions and power structures, thereby benefitting a range of disenfranchised groups.

Though LGBTQ+ movements oscillate between collective identities that celebrate and suppress differences from the cis/straight majority,[28] the pursuit of "normalcy" has proven to be a particularly apt strategic choice in contexts where LGBTQ+ people are invisible, denied basic rights, stigmatized as deviant, and persecuted.[29] The logic of sameness has proven to be a particularly viable strategy for achieving cultural change (e.g., reshaping values, beliefs, ideologies, frames, public discourse, social practices and norms, institutional logics and practices, and creating new networks, organizations, communities, and identities).[30] By drawing on claims of sameness, movements can alter taken-for-granted ideas about how an institution operates (who can partake in the institution of marriage?) by creating new logics, introducing new images (two brides in white), making the previously impossible seem plausible and previously normative behavior seem suspect. Alignment with an institution's mission ("love is love") increases their chances of success.

Kadag's politics of authenticity seems like a textbook example of sameness. Kadag transforms taken-for-granted ideas about who can "be" an Orthodox Jew by creating new logics and introducing new identities and images—Orthodox LGBT—while working from *within* the Jewish tradition and insisting that it merely intends to make space. These sentiments render Kadag a conservative LGBT movement.[31]

But the politics of authenticity is more than a mere variation on the theme of sameness. Orthodox LGBT persons' demand that their communities make space for them rests on claims not that they are "like" their heterosexual counterparts but rather that they *are* Orthodox. This claim, in and of itself, presents a radical challenge to a social order that, until recently, claimed that "religious homosexuals" do not exist. In other words, the very claim to Orthodoxy—a resistance located in everyday lives—poses a grave existential threat.

The second form of LGBTQ+ complicity is captured by the concept of homonationalism, or the association of LGBTQ+ rights with nationalist projects that conceal other forms of oppression.[32] Here a state's treatment of LGBTQ+ persons serves as an index of tolerance, and support for LGBTQ+ rights is enlisted as part of a nationalist narrative of progress that portrays the state as tolerant while obscuring other human rights violations.[33] LGBTQ+ movements' cooperation with the state thus compromises activism's transformative potential. The result is not only a hierarchy among LGBTQ+ constituencies but also an inherently deradicalized politics that does not disavow (or supports) larger systems of oppression, including nationalist ones.

Israel, with its prolonged occupation of Palestinians and state-sponsored violence toward them, juxtaposed with Tel Aviv as a gay mecca, is the paradigm for such critiques.[34] As gay rights took off in the 1990s, Israel began to brand itself as a gay-friendly nation in a homophobic region: the villa in the jungle, per former prime minister Ehud Barak.[35] Kadag allies enlist this logic as they develop a Jewish theology of tolerance; one liberal rabbi, critical of pride parades on theological grounds, asserted that he was nevertheless proud to live in a country where such parades are allowed "and not in a country where LGBT people are thrown off a high-rise building."[36] Although the Israeli LGBTQ+ movement has seen moments (or, more correctly, pockets) of radicalism, it has forsaken solidarity in favor of working with the state and its dominant social institutions. This is especially true of Kadag: while some Orthodox LGBT activists are mum about Israel's geopolitical conflict, most Orthodox LGBT persons subscribe to right-of-center nationalist visions.

Where do these debates leave religious LGBT activism? Kadag does not subscribe to queer ideas such as sexual experimentation and the dissociation of love, intimacy, and desire and emphasizes tolerance and inclusivity, not a transformational agenda of solidarity.[37] On the face of it, Kadag appears to be a deradicalized, complicit, homonormative, and homonationalist movement. Yet, in the social context in which it operates, it is precisely its assimilationist, complicit impulse that allows it to exist and thrive. Its presence in a queer space that stands in solidarity with Palestinians would be hard to imagine while allegiance to the nationalist project makes claims of Orthodox authenticity plausible. The case thus complicates ideas about assimilationist and liberationist queer projects.

Some scholars caution against deploying homonormativity and homonationalism as totalizing and universalizing frameworks to assess LGBTQ+ movements.[38] All movements craft goals, strategies, and rhetoric in dialogue with local cultural and political norms and in response to the needs and desires of their constituents. Some contexts are not conducive for radical queer messages and visions. For example, studies of LGBTQ+ activism in various African contexts suggest that visibility, coming out, and other staple LGBTQ+ tactics and terminology need to be adapted to contexts where LGBTQ+ identities are considered foreign.[39] In addition, assimilationist movements may adopt only some aspects of homonormative agendas (monogamy and domesticity) but reject others (consumption, individualism);[40] localized and contextualized homonationalist politics may contain kernels of resistance to nationalism.[41] But above all, totalizing frameworks ignore culturally and politically specific complexities and gloss over the messiness of everyday life where identity categories, daily experiences, and the desires of the marginalized rarely align with critical theory and radical political frameworks.[42]

Critical transnational studies of sexuality can provide direction for assessing religious LGBTQ+ movements' potential for disruption, resistance, and queering. Per queer theorist José Esteban Muñoz, for those located outside sexual and racial mainstream cultures, the most viable path to livable lives might be "disidentification," a strategy that recognizes the importance of local context, locates resistance in everyday lives, works on and against dominant ideology, and seeks to transform cultural logics from within.[43] Geographer and queer scholar Natalie Oswin is wary of the radical queer versus complicit sellout binary, suggesting instead that complicity is both ambivalent and porous, simultaneously enabling resistance and capitulation.[44] Seemingly complicit figures and movements can thus pose a threat to heteronormativity and normalization by virtue of their very being—even if (they claim that) this is not their intention. More broadly, critical transnational studies of sexuality suggest that evaluations of queerness, radical politics, or complicity are best made in local contexts. However, this scholarship has mostly focused on national contexts, and the Kadag case provides an opportunity to move from national debates about complicity versus radicalism to religious ones. Doing so hinges on interrogating LGBTQ+ activism and queer scholarship's secularist biases.[45]

Taking Religion Seriously

Religion is often either absent from analyses of LGBTQ+ activism and lives or depicted as a villain in stories of LGBTQ+ struggles. It is not only the high priests of religious communities who believe that religion and homosexuality are incompatible; many queer intellectuals and activists also view religious actors as adversaries rather than fellow travelers.[46] For example, when the Jerusalem Open House, which organizes the Pride Parade in the city, announced its 2017 theme "LGBT and Religion," the backlash was swift. A furious Facebook commentator captured a widely shared sentiment: "Instead of saying that secularism and sexual and gender freedom have room in this city, you focus on propaganda that claims that 'Orthodox are allowed to be *hommo*.'"[47]

Undoubtedly, religious (and especially conservative) traditions have earned their bad reputation: the historical record is replete with examples of injuries sustained by LGBTQ+ persons at the hands of religious institutions and authorities.[48] High rates of disaffiliation from such traditions by LGBTQ+ persons serve as a reminder that faith communities historically had little to offer them; as noted, this was the near-universal route that Orthodox LGBT persons took until the turn of the twenty-first century. But some LGBTQ+ people of faith take other paths. Dignity, a Catholic LGBTQ+ affirming group, has recently celebrated its fiftieth anniversary, and starting in the early aughts religious LGBTQ+ persons across *conservative* faith traditions began to articulate their claims to these traditions and sought to make them more accepting by changing them from within, à la "making space" (LGBTQ+ presence in mainline Protestant denominations and congregations dates much earlier). Thus contextualized, Kadag is part of a global trend of activists who call out LGBTQ+ movements' secularist bias.[49] Nevertheless, the needs and concerns of religious LGBTQ+ persons are still largely invisible in scholarship about LGBTQ+ activism.

The intellectual secularist bias also cedes hold on religion to conservatives and traditionalists, thus downplaying religious pluralism and the transgressive potential of subversive religious voices. Orthodox LGBT activists take much delight when they describe themselves as "on the spectrum" and "Queer Orthodox," by which they refer to a *religious,* not a gender or sexual, spectrum. Herein, then, lies another way that a politics of authenticity complicates queer critiques of assimilation and complicity: the lives, struggles, goals, and desires of LGBT persons of faith may not check all the usual queer boxes. Their politics may not be sufficiently progressive, and their visions certainly fall short of queer utopias that call for the dismantling of *all* systems of oppression. And yet, when they lay claim to religious spaces, texts, and families in defiance of religious authorities who write them out of existence, aren't Orthodox LGBT persons engaging in a quintessential queer project? At the very least, the case suggests that we might find "queering" in unexpected places and among actors who do not adopt a full-on gay, secular, antias-similationist, radical stance.[50]

As noted, a vast archive documents how local histories and contexts shape movements' goals, strategies, and tactics,[51] including the translation into local vernaculars of ideas about LGBTQ+ rights, dignity, and acceptance,[52] and the transgressive possibilities of complacent movements.[53] In other words, transnational queer and sexuality studies have well-developed frameworks that privilege the local. But *religiously* motivated hesitations about radical queer visions seem to get less of a pass. The case of Orthodox Jewish LGBT activists in Israel is saddled with the additional burden of being aligned with nationalist violence and injustice. Taking religion seriously invites us to ask who can claim the label "queer" (Is there a checklist? Who defines it?) and consider the transgressive potential of assimilationist LGBTQ+ movements.

Taking religion seriously also means recognizing that no less than gender and sexuality, religion can be a core aspect of people's lives and identities. Coined by legal theorist Kimberlé Crenshaw,[54] intersectionality refers to the interconnected nature of multiple social positions. Crenshaw's original articulation emphasized the workings of social oppressions, but subsequent scholarship considered how the intersection of multiple identity dimensions turns productive, in the sense that they make a diverse range of realities plausible and socially legible. In the context of religion, intersectionality implies that religiosity is contingent on other dimensions of identity (such as gender and sexuality) and that these social categories co-constitute one another. Thus, "how to be gay" is context specific,[55] shaped by one's geography, history, and other demographic characteristics as well as, this book argues, religion. Though intersectionality is a central concept in feminist, gender and sexuality, and queer studies, the concept has been underutilized in studies of religious identities.[56] "Taking religion seriously" implies that religion should be added to the long list of identity attributes considered through the lens of intersectionality. Doing so also helps challenge a dominant framework in scholarship on the lives of LGBT persons of faith.

Orthodox LGBT Livable Lives

Eitan, a *hommo* man in his thirties, responded to a call for participants posted on my behalf on a Facebook group for Orthodox *hommos*. He agreed to be interviewed but told me over a WhatsApp exchange that the intense interest in his life baffled him. "Another seminar paper about the conflict? I think this is my fourth interview on this. What's so hard to understand? I am Orthodox and I am *hommo*." When his partner came home during the interview the joke continued: "This one is a real professor, we're going to be in a book." Eitan referenced a popular and scholarly frame that posits that religious LGBT lives are paradoxical—marked by an "identity conflict." At an outreach event, when the inevitable question came up—"how can you be Orthodox and a lesbian?"—a Bat Kol activist rejected this frame: Orthodox LGBT persons, she said, were simply "a variation" on Orthodoxy.

The reality is more complex. Like LGBTQ+ persons of faith from other religious traditions, many same-sex-attracted Orthodox Jews pass through a period where they are convinced that their sexuality, romantic desires, practices, attachments, and realities are incompatible with Judaism, regardless of whether they act on their sexual desires. Their experiences are consistent with a large body of scholarship that documents the enormous toll that incongruence takes on psychological and emotional well-being.[57] This research implies that LGBT people of faith live perennially paradoxical, conflictual lives, and it is in their best interest to "reconcile" these conflicts into a so-called integrated identity.

I heard plenty of stories about conflicted identities during my research for this book, snippets of which are woven throughout the volume. Interviewees said they were tortured, experienced dissonance, or tried their hand at celibacy (all concluded the latter was not a viable long-term life path). Still others sought a route of self-acceptance, sometimes after years of denial. But their narratives suggest that experiences of exclusion, conflict, and shattered dreams were a product of a heteronormative social order, not an individual identity conflict that they could resolve on their own.

As for the other side of the coin, some disaffiliated from Orthodoxy altogether. Others found their way into LGBT-affirming Conservative, Reform, or (for now) fringe über-liberal Orthodox congregations, though the sting of rejection continued long after disaffiliation from Orthodoxy.[58] But many took a different route: they injected new meanings into what it means to be an observant Jew and embraced a religiosity that was inherently ambivalent and fluid and existed on a spectrum. These religious experiences did not differ much from those of non-LGBT Orthodox persons; contemporary Orthodoxy is characterized by such a vibrant splintering that some observers claim that it is no longer a legible category.

I argue that identity conflict flattens these experiences of identity fluidity, ambiguity, and ambivalence and fails to capture how in the process of coming out of the shadows, LGBT persons did not merely reconcile religiosity and sexuality—they produced new Orthodox identities. To do so, they changed their dreams, their stories, and their understanding of what it means to be Orthodox. "My dream is still to have a Jewish home," one participant told me. "It won't be the same home that I imagined. But it will be a Jewish home and God will be a part of it. You see, I had to change the story."

Queer theory, which rejects the possibility of a comprehensive, stable, core "self," provides a framework for analyzing such splintering, fluidity, and seemingly fleeting and contradictory identity formations. The process of making *religious* LGBT lives livable thus entails contending with religious traditions, communities, texts, and institutions. In this reading, the encounter between LGBT persons of faith and their religious tradition—or, in queer theory parlance, the process of queer worldmaking—turns productive, with religion as *both* a source of conflict and pain as well as a potentially productive force. To fully appreciate this dynamic, this book dispenses with claims of identity conflict, instead examining journeys of self-acceptance, a politics of authenticity, and an LGBT battle centered on making space for those whose lives were previously not livable.

Lived Religion and Queer Worldmaking

One reason the "paradox" or "identity conflict" approach dominates scholarly, popular, and religious conversations about LGBT persons of faith is that "religion" is often narrowly defined as both organized and the domain of the powerful and authoritative. For the time being, the dominant authoritative positions within Jewish Orthodoxy view homosexuality through the lens of transgression, but the Jewish tradition is far more pluralistic and ambiguous vis-à-vis same-sex love, lives, attraction, and families. Rather than inquiring about a faith tradition's official archive—documents, scripture, religious authorities—my point of entry is through the lived religion tradition in the sociology and anthropology of religion, which inquires how people of faith—*in their multitude of variations*—live and make sense of their religiosity. The "lived religion" frame assumes that religious lives, beliefs, and actions are inherently messy, fluid, and ambiguous and that people do not uncritically absorb authorized versions of religious doctrines.[59] Thinking about religious LGBTQ+ persons through this framework further shifts us away from paradox and identity conflict to meaning-making through mundane, everyday actions. In doing so, this frame emphasizes the connection between lived realities, dissent, and social change.

I am suggesting that to understand Kadag's impacts we must think beyond the usual subject matter of social movement activism (goals, visions, tactics, frames, strategies, recruitment) and interrogate the connection between lived realities and politics. Collective action is rooted in social relations—joint struggle often begins with and is embedded in the mundane structures of everyday life. Thus, while research on contentious politics and political action often removes these arenas from everyday life, this book is anchored in the seemingly mundane, taking as its point of departure that contentious politics and political action are continuous with everyday life.[60]

Queer scholarship offers a slightly different take on the relationship between the mundane and the political through the concept of queer worldmaking, or the idea that making LGBTQ+ lives livable is rooted in transforming everyday spaces. Queer worldmaking suggests that in addition to more formal routes of collective action in the political sphere, LGBTQ+ persons resist and reshape hegemonic institutions, discourses, practices, and identities through a bottom-up engagement with the everyday, involving any number of places, spaces, and people. Per queer theorist José Esteban Muñoz, queer worldmaking is a "mode of being in the world that is also inventing the world."[61]

Gender and sexuality scholars' focus on queer worldmaking and religion scholars' focus on lived religion converge in their attempts to understand how queerness—or religion—is experienced by ordinary people going about their lives in the context of social systems and institutions outside of their control, and how new forms can emerge from the cracks.[62] These frameworks are rarely brought in dialogue with one another—yet another legacy of the fraught place of religion in feminist, gender and sexuality, and queer studies.

Bringing the various threads together, this book argues that examining the experiences of Orthodox LGBT persons through the lens of the politics of religious authenticity disrupts conventional understanding of queer worldmaking while revealing how Orthodox LGBT persons are queering Orthodoxy. Since this battle for recognition has unfolded at a time that Orthodoxy itself has been experiencing a seismic shift, the case is instructive on how thinking about religious communities from their margins reveals the ideological, cultural, and historically contingent work that goes into producing (and protecting) the collective.

Jewish Orthodoxy in Israel

This book focuses on a demographic group known in Israel as "religious nationalist" (*dati-leumi*) or religious Zionist, which loosely tracks the modern Orthodox in the United States. "Orthodox" is a misnomer in the Israeli context, but I use it because "religious" in English does not have the same register as the Hebrew term.[63] For my purposes, Orthodox includes disaffiliated persons who were raised Orthodox (in Israel ex-Orthodox, or *datlash* in Hebrew, is a distinct demographic category) and those who subsequently reaffiliated with other Jewish denominations. Many such disaffiliated/reaffiliated LGBT persons are involved with Kadag. In addition, the experience of growing up Orthodox shapes one's identity regardless of adult religiosity. Finally, Orthodoxy is a sociological and demographic boundary marker: LGBT persons threaten Orthodoxy because they destabilize it from within, in the process exposing Orthodoxy's fissures. As groups of Orthodox persons refuse to take off their kippa and demand to be seen, heard, embraced, and recognized as Orthodox, the battle over the right to claim this label exposes Jewish identity for what it is: a figment of history.[64]

"Orthodoxy" implies adherence to a correct or accepted theory, practice, or doctrine. Various streams of Jewish Orthodoxy claim to be (sole) true heirs and authentic representatives of a timeless tradition, its rituals, and divine authority: an imagined premodern Judaism. But before the eighteenth century there were no "Orthodox" Jews—Jews were Jews. Living in their own political units, they were marked by ethnoracial differences from gentiles. "Orthodoxies" emerged in nineteenth-century Europe in tandem with (and in response to) urbanization, Enlightenment, and nationalism. Orthodox Judaism(s) are thus a modern phenomenon that developed, and continues to evolve, as multiple reactionary movements.[65]

All Jewish Orthodoxies share an adherence to traditions and strictures of rabbinic law as codified in the sixteenth-century legal code *Shulchan Aruch* and subsequent commentaries. The most visible strictures concern gender and sexuality, food consumption, and the Sabbath, but the Jewish legal code—the *halacha*—is elaborate and touches all domains of religious and secular life. All Orthodox movements claim fidelity to Jewish laws, texts, and rabbinic authorities, but they differ in their interpretations of Jewish law, their perspectives on proper Jewish conduct and the role of rabbinic authorities, their integration in the secular state, and their perspective on the Israeli state. Some distinguish between various forms of Orthodoxy to express gradations of practice and belief, as nodes on an imaginary range with modernity (and secular Judaism) at one pole and tradition (Ultra Orthodoxy) on the other, but for my purposes "Orthodoxy" is a product of a philosophical, theological, and sociological discursive process. What is considered "correct" adherence is up for deliberation, negotiation, and change even as these processes are couched in terms of adherence to a tradition. Orthodox LGBT Jews' claims of authenticity add to this archive yet another case that reveals the extent to which Orthodoxy is a permeable and unstable category.[66]

The nationalist-Zionist Orthodox movement revolves around three key characteristics: religiosity, Zionism, and a certain openness toward modernity. Like Modern Orthodoxy in the United States, this movement strives to balance transformation and continuity. While Orthodoxy positions itself as a return to an "original" Judaism, it also prides itself on openness to the modern world. Accordingly, its ethics, morality, and jurisprudence reflect a duality that is grounded in scripture but adapted to new realities.[67] Another distinguishing feature of the movement is its approach to Zionism. In the nineteenth century, most observant Jews and their leaders rejected Zionism, but a small strand was fueled by the messianic theology of Rabbi Abraham Isaac Kook, which combined a theological vision and a distinct political identity. Barely registering at the beginning of the twentieth century, religious national Zionism would grow into prominence after Statehood, ascending politically and culturally from humble roots as a marginal movement: Orthodox persons now occupy strategic positions in all major social institutions. It has also grown, constituting around one-fifth of Israeli Jews, thanks to a high birth rate and porous boundaries; group membership is associated not only with religious observance and spiritual belonging but also with a way of life and political identification.[68]

Orthodoxy had never been homogeneous, but in recent decades it has come to encompass such a broad range of beliefs, communities of practice, and ideologies that it almost defies a clear definition. Observers note that Orthodoxy is marked by tribalism and fragmentation and is coming undone to the point it may no longer be a meaningful category. Some observers refer to a divide between liberal and conservative (*Haredi-leumi*, or *hardal*) factions—this book leans on this distinction as shorthand—but this categorical schema obscures more nuanced processes of fragmentation. Tensions between liberal, mainstream, and conservative Orthodox groups are not new, and neither liberal nor conservative groups are growing in number. While conservatives have grown more conservative over the decades, what is particularly striking is that debates have moved closer to Orthodoxy's core. Past issues of contention were directed at the state and civil society (e.g., the settlements) and could therefore be compartmentalized, but current disagreements go to the core of religious practice: how people pray, get married or divorced, consume *kosher* food, observe modesty and purity, have sex, and interact with Jewish law, traditions, and authorities. There is no longer a clear agreement, one standard way (if there ever was one) to be Orthodox, and while the list of differentiating practices is long, the process boils down to the decline in traditional authority structures, the increasing embrace of "secular" language and values (self-determination, identity, fulfillment, rights discourse) in the pursuit of religious practice, and the privatization of religious practice.[69] The Orthodox feminist revolution accelerated many of these tensions, but Orthodox LGBT persons' claims to authenticity seem to have brought them to a breaking point.[70] Furthermore, precisely at the juncture where a rights frame is ascendant—

the "right" to pursue Jewish religious practice and belonging—the old religious monopolies (rabbinic authorities)[71] have collapsed and power has shifted from institutions (the rabbinate, yeshivas) to religious entrepreneurs and individuals.

This individualistic rights framework not only is foreign but also directly contradicts traditional Jewish jurisprudence, which is committed to the collective over the individual, is totalistic in its demands, and strives to draw clear boundaries between insiders and outsiders. To put it bluntly: the halacha does not explicitly care about individual, let alone collective, rights. In the past those who felt that they were outcast or viewed as transgressors had to either bow out or accept their inferior status, but now a range of Others—LGBT persons among them—demand to be seen, heard, and embraced. In the process, they vie with established authorities (rabbis) over the authority to define, interpret, and deploy Jewish law.

A robust sectorial media, and especially social media, accelerated these processes by obscuring existing hierarchies, democratizing access to rabbinic authorities and their materials, and creating a public dialogue between rabbis and individuals. Facebook in particular has been a game changer because it allows a range of public figures (or influencers) to speak directly to the masses. The digital age has also changed the nature of halachic making, taking it from private consultations with rabbis to online, mostly public and anonymous venues. This shift has democratized the process of building the Jewish legal archive—a more diverse range of rabbis can partake in the action—and has opened up conversations about previously silenced issues, including sexuality: it is easier to ask intimate and embarrassing questions anonymously. But these shifts have also exacerbated the gulf between people's realities and Jewish jurisprudence, revealing an elite class threatened by eroding relevance and tribalism.[72]

Disagreements have reached such a boiling point that some observers believe that Orthodoxy is collapsing from within, fragmenting into demographic, cultural, religious, and political camps, some barely distinguishable from Ultra-Orthodox counterparts, others distant from the core organizing ideologies, theologies, and practices of yesteryear's Orthodoxy. Liberalizing Orthodoxies differentiate and distance themselves from Conservative and Reform Judaism, both marginalized in Israel's religious landscape. Nevertheless, in conservative Orthodox circles "reform" is an epithet lobbed at liberalizing voices (Rabbi Lubitch, mentioned above, is one such target). Thus, Orthodox LGBT persons who demand a room of their own within the Jewish home are not satisfied with the already-existing rooms in other Jewish denominations. Even when they join such congregations, they continue to demand that Orthodoxy recognize and accept them. In doing so they engage in a battle over Orthodoxy's boundaries and over the authority to define them. Their demands are threatening not only because they undermine the existing social order but also because they expose Orthodoxy's constructed nature. This is the radical potential of the seeming assimilationist goal of "making space."

The Study

I was born and raised in Israel and identify as neither Orthodox nor LGBT. I am a sociologist of religion, a gender scholar, and a faculty member at a Jesuit university. I am also a secular Jew who has been studying Jewish Orthodoxy for almost two decades. I have been blessed with excellent teachers: undergraduate students who attend this Jesuit university, many of them raised Catholic, who grappled with their own gender and sexual identities. As my students shared with me their struggles with the Church I began to think more globally about the intersection of religion and LGBTQ+ identities and landed on this project.

Researchers who are outsiders to the communities they are working with contend with the ethics of doing such research—who am I to tell their story? How to do it justice? On the flip side, such researchers can be strategically useful. One activist hoped that "having an outsider, a professor, at an American university study us and write a report will help further our cause, give us legitimacy." Another said that she agreed to talk to me despite feeling "like a monkey in a lab" because "there's a calling, the desire in publicity, to have people like you write as many studies as possible so that women like me would be able to feel more comfortable." Acutely aware that my interlocutors sought to enlist me as an ally, my outsider status provided a buffer, but as I spent time with some of the activists featured in this book (or lurked on their Facebook pages) I came to admire many of them. How would I keep personal sympathies from clouding analytical judgment? At the same time, I break with some of them politically. I am critical of Israeli occupation and the settlement project and am frustrated by the movement's thunderous silence about Israel's poor human rights legacy on the Palestinian question. This critique does not frame my analysis, since I approached the study as one of lived religion and the making of unlikely queer worlds but the silence did inform my analysis of the limitations of LGBT activism in conservative social contexts.

At each juncture, I returned to the tradition of grounded ethnography: an inquiry that begins, from the ground up, with a focused interest on the lived experience: *what does it mean to be you?* Ethnographers strive to decipher, contextualize, and translate these experiences into a relatable tale that tells us something about how the world works. A successful ethnography humanizes our interlocutors—warts and all—thereby, one hopes, moving the needle on pressing social issues. These tensions shaped decisions throughout the research process. Some decisions were practical: What kind of data was I going to collect, and what kind of data would I *not* collect? Who was I going to talk to, and who would be willing to talk to me? What kind of spaces would I try to enter, and what about spaces I could not enter? (Ethnographers like to be a fly on the wall, but there are many spaces that I could not access as a cis/straight, middle-aged, secular Jewish Israeli woman.) What kinds of questions would I ask, and what questions would I consciously avoid asking? I had additional ethical concerns. How would I preserve my interlocutors' anonymity when the field is so small, while at the same time honoring some activists' expectation that I identify them?

I also had to make decisions about the particular story I would tell and the intellectual traditions I would tap to tell this story. Who was my audience? Orthodox LGBT persons? Jewish studies scholars? A general public interested in the Jewish experience? Social movement scholars? Queer theorists? Readers are served by a comprehensive, neat thesis—mine revolves around the idea of "queering Orthodoxy." But grounded ethnography does not begin with a thesis—we start with a series of hunches, a sense that interesting stories lurk precisely in fissures, tensions, and silences. Working from the ground up means that we are constantly articulating new questions even as we attempt to make sense of what we are learning in the field.

When I began my research, I was primarily interested in document-ing everyday lives of those whose experiences of gender and sexual iden-tity defied Orthodox teachings. These questions frame chapters 2 and 3. But my research suggested that questions of identity and lived expe-riences are intertwined with activism: identities are not negotiated (or lived) in a vacuum. Activism thus turned out to be a central thread in my research. To tell the activist tale I brought the Kadag case into con-versation with a range of debates about LGBT activism (chapters 4–6). I also expanded my inquiry to include the many stakeholders who par-took in this negotiation: Orthodox LGBT persons, activists, and allies; Orthodox clergy, educators, and theologians; and Orthodox communi-ties. I ran into another problem: the cultural history of the movement had yet to be written; I was the first to be piecing it together. Chapter 1 provides an overview of Kadag's trajectory and maps the activist field.

One of the most consequential decisions I made was to focus my analysis on sexual, rather than gender, identity, specifically on the same-sex-attracted. Divergent histories, politics, and Jewish jurisprudence meant that I could not do justice to all the categories under the LGBT umbrella. Despite Kadag's genuine commitment to all members of its coalition, bisexuals, transgender persons, genderqueer persons, those who identify as nonbinary, and others are just starting the process of coming out of the shadows and articulating their own versions of LGBT Orthodox identities. In addition, the public conversation remains fo-cused on the same-sex-attracted. In choosing to focus on Orthodox les-bians and *hommos*, I honor activists and scholars who caution against extrapolating from their lives to other populations;[73] by focusing on sexual but not gender diversity I affirm that history, contemporary poli-tics, and theological stances vary across identity categories. At the same time, when I speak of activism I do use "LGBT," mirroring my interlocu-tors' own terms. I hope that this volume, with its particular historical and topical focus, will serve as a starting point for charting Kadag's next phase of questioning the very categories it fought for in its first decade and a half of activism.[74]

This book is the product of more than four years of fieldwork in Israel and related research activities. I used a multipronged approach, combin-ing interviews, physical and digital ethnography, and archival research, all of which were supplemented by analysis of media content. Because I spent a long time in the field I was able to track and assess changes over time and build relationships with activists.[75] I conducted over one hundred twenty interviews with Orthodox LGBT persons, activists, allies, educators, therapists, family members, and rabbis.[76] I was struck by the ease with which I found willing participants as well as by the number of interviewees who suggested we meet in public spaces (cafés, parks, or libraries), though I caution that my sample includes few deeply closeted persons. (Several interviewees were reluctant to meet face-to-face, and these interviews took place over the phone or email.) To preserve privacy, I provide little contextual background information on participants and sometimes produce composites; the field is so small that attempts to mask one participant might inadvertently implicate others who did not partake in this study. Exceptions are activists who insisted that I identify them; I distinguish these participants by including their full names (otherwise I refer to respondents by a first-name-only pseudonym).

The ethnographic component includes digital data and more conventional objects of ethnographic inquiry. I observed ritual spaces, political activism, social gatherings, and community engagement. I also conducted a digital ethnography on the Facebook pages of Orthodox LGBT persons and allies who invited me to join their networks and those of Kadag organizations and high-profile organizations and religious authorities. My digital data include thousands of threads and complement the observational and interview data. (I also followed several anti-LGBT accounts.) A key source of digital data is a Facebook Confessions Page for Religious LGBTQ (the page's name in Hebrew does not include Q), which was launched in April 2018 and is a hub of activity. The page invites "gay, bi, and trans Orthodox or ex-Orthodox. Or in between. Or ultra-orthodox. Or queer. Or traditional" to "tell their stories, ask questions you've always wanted to ask and never dared to. Anonymously respond to other posts." To date, the page has published more than eight thousand posts. Since these conversations are more accessible to the public (pages are accessible to anyone with a Facebook account), they provide insight into study participants' words that are typically held on password-protected files. I supplemented interviews and fieldwork with archival research into Kadag organizations' documents that I was given access to and media accounts. Whenever possible, I use publicly accessible information rather than propriety data I collected as illustration.

Though a sizeable portion of my data are digital, I do not frame this study as a digital ethnography. Digital spaces are indispensable for studying dispersed, marginalized, or closeted communities; they are often a replacement for, and a precursor to, creating and participating in in-person social spaces. In addition, as more of us spend more time in such spaces, our ethnographies should train our focus there.[77] I thus treated virtual spaces as ethnographic field sites; I observed them in real time, noting content that is added, edited, or removed. I visited sites and pages several times weekly, took screenshots for coding, made notes about evolving conversations. When significant episodes broke, I monitored the virtual field more closely, often in conjunction with setting up formal interviews or, more often, informal communications with key informants.

Overview

Chapter 1, "Making a Social Movement: From Anonymous Chatrooms to the Synagogue and Streets," maps key milestones in LGBT Orthodoxy's journey from reviled, maligned, and marginalized to normalized. The chapter describes a dizzying array of initiatives that sprung from a modest beginning of anonymous, online spaces that drew a few dozen closeted participants at most and grew, within less than a decade, into a visible online and offline presence. LGBT persons' willingness to emerge from the safety of anonymity, the founding of activist organizations in the mid-aughts, the numerous initiatives undertaken by individuals and organizations, along with broader processes in Orthodoxy and the strategic use of social media to support activist endeavors have coalesced into a sophisticated activist program that navigates a range of strategies, visions, and goals. But the movement reflects the fault lines of Israeli society, LGBTQ+ activism, and Orthodoxy: the privileging of Ashkenazi, heterocis men; Orthodoxy's hegemony over other strands of Judaism; and nationalism over solidarity with other marginalized groups.

The next two chapters focus on everyday lived experiences, charting a journey from a shattered picture and its chaotic aftermath (chapter 2, "Unlivable Lives: Shattered Pictures and the Desire to Be 'Normal'") to the futures made possible when a group of previously silenced Ortho-

dox Jews reenvisions what it means to be Orthodox (chapter 3, "Orthodox Queer Worldmaking: Everyday Theologies of Life, Sex, and God").
Chapter 2 discusses experiences of shame, secrecy, denial, repression,
spiritual harms, and family drama that result in a shattered life plan,
social death, crises of faith, and a yearning to be "normal." Chapter 3
considers the new scripts of everyday life that same-sex-attracted Orthodox Jews devise, in part by drawing on the same religious tradition
that harmed them. As Orthodox LGBT persons mine, harness, and mobilize the tradition's own logics, language, and sensibility to make sense
of themselves, they also produce new theologies of God, sex, and what
it means to be Orthodox. The backdrop to these chapters is a social science scholarship that frames religious LGBT lives around the notion of
identity conflict and reconciliation. The construction of new scripts and
everyday theologies to live by troubles the categories of Orthodoxy and
queerness, suggesting that religious same-sex-attracted persons are not
so much looking to "reconcile" "conflicting" aspects of their identity as
they construct new modes of being.

The next three chapters elucidate the unique modality of a politics
of authenticity. Chapter 4, "Educating Our Rabbis: From a Theology
of Transgression to a Theology of Tolerance (and Beyond)," considers
the halacha as a realm of activism. Theological debates and religious
jurisprudence hardly seem like an arena for LGBT battles, more likely
to focus on freeing sexuality from regulation rather than seeking new
forms of surveillance. But for religious LGBT persons, the path toward
equal rights, full personhood, and acceptance passes through the religious system's own logics, institutions, and sensibilities. The theological
disputes at the center of this chapter reflect a deeper chasm between
those who view modernity as an existential threat and those who embrace the challenge to propel Orthodoxy forward. The debates covered
in this chapter bear a striking resemblance to those in Catholicism and
Evangelical Christianity.

The final two chapters consider how activists mobilize Orthodox values, language, and sensibilities, blending assimilationist and homonationalist rhetoric with a radical politics of difference that challenges what
it means to be an "authentic" Orthodox Jew. Chapter 5, "Telling Stories,
Making Space: Politics of Authenticity," discusses outreach initiatives intended to educate Orthodox communities about LGBT persons with the

intention of making space. The chapter considers how activists' strategic storytelling, messages of authenticity ("we are of you"), and claims to a politics of moderation ("we come in peace") navigate the tension between complicity and liberation, laying the foundation for the argument in the book's final chapter about the radical potential of the politics of authenticity. Chapter 6, "The Battle for Judaism's Straight Soul: Queer Antics, Religious Restraint, and Respectability Politics," centers on public visibility and protest in the context of polarization between conservative and liberal Orthodoxy.

The conclusion summarizes Orthodoxy's journey from the unfathomable to the possible, ponders what religious LGBT movements teach us about queer activism and how to study it, and considers how the case complicates our understanding of the encounter between LGBT persons of faith and their religious traditions.

1

Making a Social Movement

From Anonymous Chatrooms to the Synagogue and Streets

Orthodox LGBT identities, consciousness, and activism can be traced to now-defunct and lost online forums and chatrooms. From 2002 to 2005, same-sex-attracted Orthodox persons flocked to an online Walla forum, one of the first public spaces where they could congregate and interact anonymously with like-minded people. Yishai Meir launched the forum because he was tormented by a "dark secret" and wanted to connect with others who shared his existential conflict,[1] though per one participant, conversations covered much ground: "People wrote poems, told painful stories; we debated religion, what it means to be religious *hommo*, the conflict." Many forum participants did not identify as *hommos* or lesbians—an Orthodox lesbian or *hommo* was an oxymoron at the time. Some were heterosexually married and had planned on remaining so; one man, then in his early twenties, said he found the space "a little creepy." But for many the forum was life changing: before they found the forum, participants thought that they were alone in their pain, suffering, and shame. "From my perspective ten years ago, there wasn't another lesbian in the world," Avigail Sperber reflected in 2008.[2] She helped change that reality by founding Bat Kol, an Orthodox lesbian organization.

Participants knew they were taking risks when they moved from the anonymity of the web onto email or phone, then to meeting face-to-face, but the payoff was worth it: friendships that began online spilled into the real world, and conversations helped participants articulate new identities, a vision, organizations, a movement. By 2005, this nascent consciousness would be mobilized—several Bat Kol members marched in pride parades that year, flanked by a homemade banner. But the forum would be lost to history.[3] It was plagued by conservative trolls but was undone by disagreements about the essence of same-sex attraction, whether one could truly be Orthodox and gay, and how to engage homophobic Orthodox families, leaders, and communities. These debates continue to this day.

"We had no idea that we were launching a movement," one activist told me, but forum participants were following a social movement script: safe spaces that empower individuals also encourage them to develop a shared political consciousness ripe for mobilization. In a 2003 group interview with journalist Vered Kelner several anonymous forum participants articulated a bold goal: acceptance by their Orthodox communities.[4] They charted the course of the movement they were about to launch: it would engage rabbis and other thought leaders and ground demands for empathy, love, and legitimacy in science ("homosexuality is immutable") *and* Jewish values ("my hope is that every religious *hommo* or lesbian who reads this knows that [God] loves them"). They dared to imagine "a community in which two religious men could live together." And they charted the course of Orthodox LGBT organizing: "It'll start with the Americans in Jerusalem, go through the liberals, and end up in [mainstream and conservative Orthodox locales]." Their aspirations and timeline proved to be prescient.

Several of Kelner's interviewees would soon assume leadership roles in the movement. Ze'ev Shvidel began a storied activist career as forum moderator; by 2006 he was publishing under his own name. Avigail Sperber went on to found Bat Kol. Ron Yosef founded the conservative *hommo* organization Hod. Within a decade and a half, Orthodox *hommos* and lesbians achieved many of the goals they had laid out in 2003: they founded organizations and launched initiatives that educated Orthodox communities about Orthodox LGBT persons in their midst. More than that, they created the very category "LGBT Orthodox." Early in my research I observed an inverse relationship between age and identification as Orthodox; there were few self-identified Orthodox LGBT persons over thirty-five. The history of LGBT Orthodoxy makes plain the cutoff: Israel's gay decade of the 1990s was predominantly a secular affair; Orthodox LGBT persons who came of age before the close of the aughts had no visible alternatives to heterosexual marriage or celibacy if they were to remain in the Orthodox fold. In the aughts some began to ponder the previously unthinkable: that they could be Orthodox and LGBT. This chapter begins to tell the story of the making of LGBT Orthodox identities and a collective consciousness—the Proud Religious

Community (Kadag)—though this is an overview, not a comprehensive social history. The chapter focuses on the movement's first decade, key milestones in LGBT Orthodoxy's journey from the unfathomable to possible, from reviled, maligned, and marginalized to a normalized and visible presence. Like other tales of movements agitating for social change, that of Kadag is not free of internal tensions. Despite claims of inclusivity, Kadag replicated Orthodoxy's gender and ethnic dynamics that privilege Ashkenazi men: most of its founders, leaders, visionaries, and vocal activists—certainly in the early years—are cisgender graduates of esteemed Orthodox schools and yeshivas, and many grew up in elite Orthodox neighborhoods and families. Their priorities and experiences continue to shape the movement and its vision of authentic Orthodoxy, although in recent years younger activists have been agitating toward a more expansive lens that prioritizes both sexual and gender diversity. But first, a brief history of LGBT activism in Israel.

LGBT Activism in Israel

In the 1990s lesbian and gay activists, with the support of left-wing parliamentary allies and liberal courts, acquired an array of rights and protections. Some histories of this "gay decade" situate it between a silencing (through 1988) and mainstreaming (mid-aughts) of lesbian and gay identities, agendas, and rights, but others caution that the silenced era was not so silent and that mainstreaming was not all conformity. The gay decade itself left much to be desired: the struggles and gains of the 1990s (and subsequent chronicles of the era) paid scant attention to transgender persons.[5]

The gay decade launched with an air of optimism with the repeal of sodomy laws in 1988. Homosexuality was reframed as a human rights issue, a framework later extended to other LGBTQ+ issues. Activists deployed increasingly sophisticated sociopolitical, legal, and mass media strategies, and some were willing to put a public face on the movement in interviews, public hearings, and lobbying. Sexual orientation became a protected employment category and same-sex partners were recognized for some welfare benefits (same-sex marriage is still not legalized though). Also, the Tel Aviv Pride Parade became prominent on the international pride circuit, LGBT organizations proliferated, and gay characters began to appear in mainstream movies and popular TV shows. In 1998, transgender singer Dana International, representing Israel, won the Eurovision contest. Her celebrity is credited with shining a positive, corrective light on LGBT persons.

The late 1990s and the aughts also saw a significant expansion of identity and spatially based organizations and those that focus on outreach or support. Many are networked under the Aguda, or the Association for LGBTQ Equality in Israel. Founded in 1975, the Aguda remains Israel's most influential LGBT advocacy organization.[6] Orthodox LGBT organizations were launched at the tail end of this era, working from both within existing LGBT movement infrastructure and outside of it: in LGBT circles, just as in Orthodox ones, the idea of an LGBT Orthodox person, agenda, or movement was, at best, a curiosity.

The proliferation of organizations was accompanied by fragmentation and deradicalization. Visibility, too, was a mixed bag: as the Tel Aviv Pride Parade grew in popularity, enjoyed municipal support, and drew hundreds of thousands of Israelis and tens of thousands of tourists, it was criticized for commercializing and pinkwashing the gay scene.[7] With a multitude of organizations representing a range of identities, political agendas, and interests, checkered public support, a commodified thriving gay scene, and a common external enemy (Israel's strong Orthodox communities and their representatives in Parliament), in the aughts Israel's LGBTQ+ community ran into the queer dilemma:[8] a tension between identity politics, which empower individuals and mobilize them into imagined political collectives, and the queer impulse to disrupt identity categories and politics as usual. There was also the perennial problem of gay cis men who dominated LGBT organizations yet purported to represent all groups. Add to the mix infighting among factions of the coalitions that make up LGBTQ+ communities, a simmering tension between radicals and liberals, and a desexualized gay legal revolution and lines of inclusion and exclusion formed, with Jews, urban, secular, cis, and gay men gaining an easier foothold in the consensus. The mainstreaming tactics that helped usher judicial, legislative, and public support came with a high price tag.

On August 1, 2009, a perpetrator entered a space operated by the Aguda and opened fire, killing two and injuring twelve. (A third victim died by suicide years later.) Victims were young: the space was hosting a weekly meeting of an LGBTQ+ youth group, Bar Noar. Still unresolved, this hate crime marked a turning point in LGBTQ+ politics in Israel. A spiteful act that could have united activists instead exposed fault lines dividing liberal LGBTQ+ and radical queer activism and accelerated processes of centralization, institutionalization, and assimilation. The episode also drew LGBT activism into national politics: it provided the state an opportunity to signal support for LGBTQ+ persons and causes without angering their Orthodox coalition partners. The result was a homonationalist discourse that dissociated LGBTQ+ activism from broader human rights agendas. As battles and realignments between radical and liberal, critical and assimilationist factions continue, the LGBTQ+ landscape is fragmented across over thirty organizations and initiatives, dominated by urban centers, and characterized by heightened identity politics.[9]

Such tensions are not unique to the Israeli LGBTQ+ landscape, though they do have a local flavor. Israel's human rights revolution of the 1990s was a product of broader cultural, political, and economic shifts that embraced pluralism, individualism, and free market ethos. But the country was also entering its third decade of occupying the West Bank and other territories. The gay decade's achievements hinged on a homonationalist, Zionist rhetoric that brought (some) gender and sexual minorities into the Israeli mainstream but excluded others—namely, Palestinians.[10] Homonationalism does not necessarily imply a deliberate collusion with the state, but in some contexts—including in Israel—this is the case. Critics term this pinkwashing, a political strategy that promotes products, people, and entities through an appeal to their gay-friendly status. In the Israeli context, the tactic meant that public embrace of gay rights and the fun façade of Tel Aviv's thriving gay scene concealed systemic human rights violations. "There is no pride in the occupation," declared a banner carried by a group of radical activists in the 2001 Tel Aviv Pride Parade, but the "black-pink" coalition never took off. Pockets of radical, antiassimilationist groups have had little impact on the mainstream. Law professor and queer scholar and activist Aeyal Gross argues that Israeli LGBTQ+ activists struck a devil's bargain with the state, accepting support for their cause by a broad coalition of political allies in return for making the enhancement of gay rights a fig leaf for Israeli democracy. Per geographer and queer scholar Gilly Hartal, these dynamics continue to shape LGBTQ+ activism in Israel.[11]

Mainstreaming of LGBTQ+ rights and the nationalist ideology underlining them undermined the movement's ability to advocate for a truly progressive agenda and diminished its alliance with other marginalized groups; meanwhile, the state co-opted the movement's gains to position itself as liberal, progressive, and democratic. The mainstreaming of lesbians and gays also came at the expense of solidarity and revolutionary queer politics: Israel's LGBTQ+ movements succumbed to homonormative impulses with an emphasis on issues such as marriage, adoption, and surrogacy over others, such as access to gender confirmation surgeries. The inclusion of some privileged groups who can easily blend into the existing social order (Jewish, mostly urban, secular, mostly Ashkenazi gays and lesbians) marginalized others—trans, bisexuals, Arabs, and those living on the periphery. The result is a split between radical queer and assimilationist politics, a fragmented LGBTQ+ activist field, and a deradicalized queer politics.[12] At the same time, this chasm provided an opening that allowed new groups, including Orthodox LGBT organizations, to lay claim to an LGBT identity and pursue sectoral agendas.[13] These new groups emerged and operated both within and outside this existing fragmented LGBT space.

Though *individuals* from Orthodox backgrounds had been involved in LGBTQ+ politics—some Kadag key activists got their start in organizations such as the Aguda or the Jerusalem Open House (JOH)—the movement had been largely a secular affair, and Orthodox persons were viewed as adversaries, not fellow travelers. Same-sex-attracted Orthodox persons and those questioning their gender identity were marginalized, silenced, and vilified by both Orthodox communities and LGBTQ+ politics. This was the landscape that early Orthodox LGBT activists faced.

"There Is No Such Thing as a Religious Homosexual": Invisibility through the Early Aughts

In 2001, Havruta cofounder Nati Epstein published an anonymous letter in a popular daily newspaper in response to an Orthodox journalist's claim that homosexuality did not exist in Orthodox circles.[14] Nati frequented an IOL chatroom populated by Orthodox *hommos* and knew full well that religious *hommos* existed: they just feared exposure.

> We do have *hommos*. They are more numerous than you can imagine. . . . I invite you to our post-Shabbat chat in our room, religious gays. My name there is Dan. I invite you to hear the heartbreaking confusion of seventeen-, eighteen-year-olds who don't understand where God abandoned them. Listen to soldiers who seek an outlet with those like them. . . . And listen to bachelors like myself who wonder what kind of future they have. . . . You can also join a conversation of the married . . . some of whom have come to terms with the lies they tell their wives, others less so. They're all looking for someone who will understand.

After the letter was published, Nati told me, "From a chat of six or seven people, that night we had fifty, sixty, and everyone looked for Dan from the letter. The forum blossomed. Suddenly there were a *lot* of religious *hommos!*" A couple of years later, thirty-five people showed up for an early in person meeting.

Interviewees who had come of age in the late nineties and early aughts shared versions of this story—secrecy, fear, loneliness, the joy of discovering others. A lesbian remembered how, in the late 1990s, "the taboo was so strong that nobody even said *hommos* are perverts. There was just this silence." An activist spoke of a secret religious *hommo* group in the 1990s explaining that "they didn't imagine coming out. They were thankful that they weren't lined up in front of a firing squad." Another man, in his late thirties when we met in 2017, said that he had been falling apart before he discovered the online forum and found out he was "not the only one in the world! When you find others . . . you see that you're not a demon and not a monster and that people like you aren't whores, promiscuous, perverts."

Part of the problem was that Orthodoxy at the time shrouded all things sexual in secrecy, though by the early aughts Orthodoxy adopted a boundary marking rhetoric: "There is no such thing as a religious homosexual," the conservative stalwart Rabbi Shlomo Aviner announced.[15] Just to make sure, in 2001 he founded the much reviled (and now defunct) conversion therapy operation Azat Nefesh. The new rhetoric was necessitated by the gay decade and homegrown tensions. By the turn

of the twenty-first century, the Orthodox feminist revolution, brewing since the 1980s, had forced open conversations about sexuality.[16]
Yet, lacking visible role models for living as religious *hommos* or lesbians, and with messaging from rabbis, educators, and families drawing
clear lines in the sand, same-sex-attracted Orthodox Jews had to make
choices that continue to haunt them. Many left the Orthodox fold—
thereby confirming Aviner's stance.

Lack of public visibility does not mean that Orthodox persons did not
experience (and act on) same-sex attraction. Some ex-Orthodox LGBT
persons were associated with secular LGBT organizations, and several
organizations and initiatives operated just below the surface. Steven
Greenberg, an American gay man later ordained as a rabbi (and founder
of Eshel, an organization that serves Orthodox LGBTQ+ persons in the
United States), led a study group for men through the JOH in the 1990s.
The Aguda and JOH both sponsored support groups targeting Orthodox
persons but these groups were unappealing because their members were
older, were often married, and skewed Ultra-Orthodox. "We wanted to
meet people like us," said an activist who briefly attended a JOH group.
But knowing that these groups had existed provided a sense of anticipation, leading would-be activists to seek out online forums. These quickly
became gateways to articulating identities, fomenting friendships, and
organizing.

Similarly, in the mid-1990s, one woman was introduced to the lesbian
organization Orthodykes, one of several groups in Jerusalem's vibrant
LGBT scene in the 1980s and 1990s.[17] She sought assurances that she
could be *both* Orthodox and lesbian but found little solace in the group:
many participants were married to men; some were Ultra-Orthodox,
most had children; and few were able to sustain long-lasting lesbian relationships. Worst of all was the closet: "You couldn't say hello if you saw
each other on the streets."

There were other signs that something was brewing. In 1995, a young
rabbi advocated compassion, tolerance, and acceptance toward homosexuals in a paper published in an obscure Jewish education journal.
The original paper did not get much traction, but when a more polished
version appeared in the heady journal *Deot* in 2001 people noticed.[18] By
then the author, Rabbi Ronen Lubitch, had begun to make a name for
himself as a liberal Orthodox thought leader. The piece struck a nerve:

Orthodox LGBT persons sent letters to *Deot* calling out rabbis for their thundering silence despite being aware of their struggles. Many interviewees told me about anonymous letters, email exchanges, and phone and in-person consultations with rabbis. But at the time even the most empathetic rabbis had little to offer: they had no framework to talk about homosexuality outside Orthodoxy's dominant stance of blanket prohibition. The same-sex-attracted were assured by rabbis that they could change, and some were referred to conversion "therapists." (The theological discourse would change within a decade.)

Two other events helped break the silence: the launch of the conversion therapy organization Azat Nefesh and the release of the documentary *Trembling Before G-d*, about the experiences and rabbinic responses to Jewish lesbians and *hommos* (Rabbi Greenberg, the American gay Rabbi mentioned earlier, was one of the subjects). A massive public education effort accompanied the film's release: trained moderators held screenings and discussions in communities and educational institutions across the country, with the official blessing of the Ministry of Education. Standing in for experiences that Orthodox same-sex-attracted persons dared not yet discuss publicly at the time, screenings helped audiences develop empathy toward those living (secretly) in their midst. The public outreach organization Shoval would later build on this approach. The film also mobilized activists and allies. Bat Kol founder Avigail Sperber, filmmaker by profession, had worked on the film. Tzachi Mezuman, under whose editorialship *Deot* published the Lubitch piece, was a facilitator on the project (he was also a Shoval cofounder and worked at the JOH, under whose auspices the group that later became Havruta was launched). Rabbis Yuval Cherlow and Benny Lau had helped facilitators shape their messaging years before these rabbis identified publicly as prominent allies.

In contrast to *Trembling*'s case for acceptance and tolerance, Azat Nefesh emphasized perversion and sin. Nevertheless, it inadvertently helped mobilize Orthodox LGBT persons because, per one activist, at the time "there were no [Orthodox] LGBT organizations. And they put this on the table. They were homophobes. But, suddenly, it's a topic that's talked about. . . . When you create space for dialogue you don't know where it's going to go. Many of us started our way there. . . . Perhaps you wanted to change. BUT, you also met people." More often, the organization caused a lot of pain. And it was the harbinger of the moral panic to come.

Rabbi Aviner's staunch conservativism also created the space—and need—for more liberal approaches to homosexuality. The rabbi was among the first to publish halachic answers (responsa) about homosexuality online; not long after, Rabbi Cherlow also began posting online responsa, taking a more tolerant tone. This interplay between conservative foes and progressive allies has shaped the movement ever since.[19]

Still, even those who dared to name their same-sex attraction could not fathom *living* as an Orthodox *hommo* or lesbian. In this sense, Rabbi Aviner was right to claim that there are no religious *hommos*. Prior to the twenty-first century Orthodox same-sex persons were invisible, living in the shadows. Within a decade, however, they would develop individual and collective consciousness, and some would be marching openly in pride parades. A confluence of factors helped them to imagine a different future: the internet, Israel's gay decade, and the path blazed by Orthodox feminists. But the movement was their own making.

Coming Out of the Shadows: ~2002–9

In May 2005 Yael Orian and Tzachi Mezuman, representing the JOH, testified in a parliamentary hearing about the lack of support for same-sex-attracted students attending Orthodox public schools. The picture was bleak: Orthodox youth struggling with sexual orientation were met with ignorance, silence, and referrals to conversion therapy. (My interviewees shared similar stories.) Yael Orian indicted her community's silence: "I come here as a lesbian and Orthodox woman, activist in a group called Bat Kol. I grew up in Orthodox schools, and when I recognized that I was lesbian I was silent. There was nobody I could turn to. When I came out to my family, they were silent. The Orthodox school system has to begin to recognize that we exist."[20] In the aughts activists such as Orian and Mezuman and organizations such as Bat Kol and the JOH urged the state, LGBT organizations, and Orthodox communities to take action by moving the conversation about homosexuality and Orthodoxy from the anonymity of the internet into the public eye.

The Walla religious gays forum launched in September 2002, marking the dawn of a new era. Replacing an earlier IOL chatroom, the forum expanded the visibility of and access to anonymous online spaces. During its three-year run, the forum facilitated individual and collective coming out of the shadows. Participants formed friendships and networks, articulated new identities, and charted an activist agenda.[21] By the decade's end silence had been replaced by a mind-boggling array of organizations and initiatives. Bat Kol was founded in 2005 (the group had begun meeting a couple of years earlier), followed by Havruta, the Orthodox *hommo* organization founded in 2007. Hod, one of two conservative *hommo* organizations, was founded in 2008. Shoval, an outreach organization that promotes tolerance toward and awareness of LGBT persons within Orthodox communities, was launched in 2006, and an initiative advocating religious tolerance, Pesach Sheni (second Passover), commenced in 2009 (the latter two initiatives are discussed in chapter 5). General LGBTQ+ organizations began to recognize the needs of Orthodox populations. The parent support group Tehila opened a religious group in 2007, founded by Avigail Sperber's mother. IGY, an LGBTQ+ youth organization, launched groups targeting Orthodox youth in 2009. Also in 2009, the Proud Minyan prayer group began operating in the LGBT Center in Tel Aviv on the High Holidays and the first inclusive synagogue, Yachad (Together), opened in the heart of Tel Aviv. These organizations and initiatives provided Orthodox LGBT persons with safe spaces where they found support and camaraderie (and, if they were lucky, love). It was here that they dared to dream about a future as Orthodox LGBT persons, engaged in Jewish ritual, and were mobilized into activism.

Avigail Sperber brought together Bat Kol's founding members and was the organization's early visionary and public face. Some founding and early members found each other online; others knew each other from feminist circles. Word began to spread. One early member had read about Sperber in the newspaper and tracked down her number. Another early member joined after she "ran into this woman on a bus who I knew from college, she knew I was Orthodox, and she gave me a phone number and said 'I think you'll find this useful.'" From eight attendees in the first meeting, "quickly we were several dozen."

One early member was drawn by the "desperate need to alleviate the sense that you are alone in the world . . . there is no one like you." Another said that they each "needed a home. Many of us didn't feel comfortable in other lesbian spaces." In the beginning, the small group of mostly closeted women preferred to keep a low profile. Sperber had originally thought that "if the women would meet it would solve the problem." She later realized that the group would have to engage in outreach—otherwise how would other women find them? An organization was born, one with a website and a public presence, though since its founding days Bat Kol has sought to balance privacy, community, and a family-like atmosphere with public visibility. This combination was a lifeline when public role models were lacking. Kadag activist Zehorit Sorek's experience was common (Sorek quickly became one such public role model):

> The day I understood that I'm an Orthodox lesbian I thought I was the only one in the world. One evening I googled "religious lesbians." The first result was "Bat Kol—Religious Lesbians." I started to read. The women were writing about my own uncertainties, my fears, the desire to mediate between religious identity and lesbian identity, fear of responses from parents, siblings and friends, and about how to move forward. I got in touch with the organization and a few days later I was invited to a meeting in someone's home. When I entered I felt that I had arrived home.[22]

A similar trajectory from anonymous online chatrooms to public visibility occurred on the men's side, though the tensions that began brewing in the online forums about the compatibility of homosexuality and Orthodoxy shaped the activist field: two men's organizations were founded in the late aughts—with a third in 2011. One participant recalled that Benni Elbaz, who later founded Havruta, shared his number in the IOL chat room: "I think he was the only one who was out. *Do you understand?* An Orthodox *hommo*, unheard of. He invited people to call him." Another participant described how he met religious *hommos*: "In the IOL chatroom, everyone was anonymous; then we started to exchange email addresses. . . . They talked about a meeting. . . . I came to a meeting in Tel Aviv . . . the first in my life. Ten people. Some of them older. It was scary. But for the first time you're with people who are like you."

A couple of years later, another man went to a gathering where he met a *hommo* couple (Benni Elbaz and his partner) at an underground meeting in Jerusalem. He was "hypnotized. For the first time I saw a *hommo couple.* Not a one-night stand. *A couple!* It was a revelation. I can't remember what was said in the meeting."

Havruta cofounders Benni Elbaz and Nati Epstein met online. Benni was asked to start a group for Orthodox *hommo* men by the JOH and invited Nati to join him. The original group was discreet—one early member recalled that "everyone was in the closet." But founders reached out to young men from Orthodox backgrounds. "Benni collected us," said another participant, describing the momentum as the group grew from "twenty to eighty, one hundred":

> We announced the first meeting in the forum and we hung posters all over Jerusalem. And thirty-five people came. Every religious *hommo*, thanks to the internet, got to know two or three more. They arrived lonely to the meeting, their legs shaking. [We] tell them it is possible, we sit, we talk to them, and slowly they brought their friends. And they met new friends. And their friends. We knew other activists through JOH, connected lots of groups to work together. Within a year we have something like a hundred fifty people pass through. We created a community. Within a year and a half or two, there are lots of religious *hommos*. . . . It created a reality that there's a big group that gives each other strength.

Eventually, group members decided to found an organization, Havruta, a name that references both the Jewish tradition and the LGBT experience. Havruta refers to the practice of Jewish learning, typically conducted in pairs; the practice alludes to a sage's observation juxtaposing human sociability with loneliness and death: "This is how we see our lives as Orthodox *hommos*. Either you're with someone or you are akin to dead."[23] (This idea would become a rallying cry in the late 2010s when Rabbi Lau declared "the closet is death.") Although Havruta began as a social group, its founders' goals were bold. Saving people "from the claws of Azat Nefesh," one early activist said, topped that list.

A third organization to emerge from the forum was Hod (the term is an acronym for Orthodox *hommos* but also refers to truth telling), founded by a group of about a dozen. Rabbi Ron Yosef, who came out publicly in a series of columns and interviews in 2009,[24] was the organization's only visible face during its eight-year run.[25] Hod shared some of Bat Kol's and Havruta's goals, but ideological differences and personal style resulted in Hod's marginalization. The organization ceased operations in 2016 when Yosef became mired in an embezzlement scandal.

The three organizations, and especially Bat Kol and Havruta, interwove inward-looking community building and social functions with a multipronged activist agenda that included dialogue with rabbis, educational outreach, and public visibility. These activist arenas are discussed in chapters 4, 5, and 6, respectively, but I preview some key milestones here to provide a holistic picture of the movement.

One feature that distinguishes religious from other LGBTQ+ movements is that they turn theology into an activist arena. However, Havruta and Bat Kol activists understood early on that Orthodoxy's theology of transgression was rooted in a culture that *couched* homophobia in theology. Activist efforts therefore emphasized outreach, education, and public visibility initiatives. One early activist said that when he and his peers began to public identify as *hommos* they were terrified but "understood that things won't change unless we work outward. Our communities needed to know that we exist." Kadag never made coming out a rallying cry, but activists recognized that visibility breeds empathy, a process well documented in social movement scholarship. "When people start coming out," one activist told me,

> their religious friends and families have to learn to accept them. Suddenly you get this straight religious cloud around religious *hommos*. . . . And from a world of slogans and stereotypes they see people, and suddenly they talk to them, they learn. My friends, siblings, family, they all went through a process. And this fans outwards because it causes them, when they talk about this topic with others, to speak differently, to bring a different perspective.

The emphasis on public education and visibility gave rise to the educational outreach organization Shoval, which was founded by Bat Kol and Havruta activists in 2006, and the Pesach Sheni (second Passover) initiative, which began in 2008 as a small gathering where Orthodox LGBT activists hosted public discussions about tolerance, acceptance, and the treatment of "others within" over the course of an evening. The initiative has since expanded into a countrywide effort that includes a variety of events under the title Making Space. As a result of these and other efforts, by the mid-aughts Orthodox *hommos* and lesbians were in the public eye first as objects of inquiry and later as authors of their own stories.

Mainstream and sectorial Orthodox media began to cover Orthodox LGBT topics with regularity. A 2003 book by Irit Koren provided an intimate portrayal of the lives of Orthodox lesbians and *hommos*. Koren, an Orthodox psychologist who did not identify as LGBT, traced the pain and suffering her book documented to a tension between Orthodox and Western values.[26] Ilil Alexander's documentary *Keep Not Silent*, released in 2004, followed three Orthodox lesbians' attempts to find space within Orthodox communities. The secular filmmaker won many national and international awards, but this film has not aged well within Orthodox LGBT circles.

The 2007 short feature *Will You Marry Me?* got more traction. The film, which troubled heterosexual marriage, began with a familiar plot line: a young Orthodox man tells his rabbi that he plans to marry a woman despite his attraction to men, reasoning that marriage would "cure" his same-sex attraction. Enter the plot twist. Actual conversations between rabbis and students often involve assurances such as "you are confused" and "it will pass," but the fictional rabbi implores his student to tell his fiancée that he was attracted to men. The rabbi left his student little choice, threatening that he would reveal the young man's secret. A predictable breakup ensues, but the movie ends on an ambiguous note: in its final frames the student is (modestly) flirting with another young Orthodox woman.

What the film lacks in nuance it makes up for in provenance: it was produced by one rabbi (Mordechai Vardi) and featured another (Ronen Lubitch, the Orthodox liberal thought leader, plays a fictional version of himself). Rabbi Vardi did not want to vilify the young man, he told an audience in 2019, but he did take an unapologetic moral stance: marriage is not the answer.[27] Alas, many rabbis and educators continue to insist that change is possible; one woman I interviewed was told in 2018 by a rabbi "you're not really a lesbian. You're just young." Vardi's movie remains on Kadag's list of conversation starting resources. In 2020 he released a documentary on the topic, *Marry Me, However.*

Orthodox lesbians and *hommos* also joined the field of commentators. In 2004 Ze'ev Dror (an alias) and Ruti (first name only) responded to Rabbi Aviner's assertation that "there is no such thing as a religious homosexual" with letters published in the popular Orthodox paper *Makor Rishon*.[28] Addressing Rabbi Aviner directly, Ruti writes, "I am lesbian and Orthodox . . . and I exist just like you and everyone else. We stood together at Sinai and we received the same Torah, it belongs to us equally." Ze'ev sought to refute the rabbi's claims about the efficacy of conversion therapy and hinted at what was coming: "Until now religious *hommos* and lesbians did not have the courage to respond directly, out of fear of exposure and social ostracism. . . . It is no longer possible to ignore." A year later, he published a groundbreaking article under his real name, Ze'ev Shvidel. "The Others Within: On the Place of Religious Homolesbians in the Orthodox Community" unpacked Orthodoxy's silencing of homosexuality and hinted at the existence, just below surface, of a vibrant if still discreet proud religious community.[29] Shvidel argued that Orthodoxy possessed the methodological tools and theological frameworks to normalize same-sex-attracted persons' status, adding that the battle centered on society's moral character. Shvidel has gone on to a storied activist career as a therapist, writer, and movement intellectual. His comments have proved prescient.

Bat Kol member Ziva Ofek was another movement intellectual who came out of the shadows that year. Prompted by a friend who had observed a dearth of resources, Ofek produced the first halachic overview of lesbianism, in which she argued that lesbian relationships and families were compatible with the halacha.[30] Controversial in the mid-aughts, Ofek's claims have since become reality: some rabbis now agree that a monogamous, same-sex relationship might be a plausible life path in some circumstances.[31] Like other early movement activists, Ofek has helped make this a reality; she has granted numerous interviews and participated, with her family, in several publicity campaigns.

Of lasting impact is Chaim Elbaum's *And Thou Shalt Love*, a 2007 short film about a closeted yeshiva student tormented by unrequited love for his best friend. The film's protagonist turns for help to a conversion therapy organization (modeled on Azat Nefesh). He fasts, repents, contemplates self-harm, and attempts a behavioral corrective measure involving a tight fitting bracelet. Reaching a breaking point, the protagonist confesses to his friend, only to be rejected, but the film ends on a hopeful note: the protagonist claims his rightful place within the synagogue, suggesting that Orthodoxy and same-sex attraction can be reconciled. A Havruta member who saw the film in the early 2010s said this message broke him to pieces because it implied that Azat Nefesh's message "is bullshit, you're not going to change. That was my lifeline! I was planning on changing. And the movie says no, you're not going to change, you either leave or you live as a *hommo*. . . . Like you don't have a choice other than to come out." The movie prompted him to examine his orientation, which he had ignored for years.

But in the early to mid-aughts there were few public models for living as an Orthodox *hommo*. "What kind of future was I looking at? It was bleak," one interviewee said. Elbaum, the filmmaker, did not know what life as an Orthodox *hommo* would be like when he made the movie in 2007. All he knew at the time was that he was gay and religious.[32] A decade later, emboldened by the movement he helped launch, Elbaum had found some answers and shared them with the world. In January 2019, he stood under a wedding canopy with his partner Yair Strauss. Among the guests was Kadag ally Rabbi Benny Lau, who used the occasion to explain, in an interview with an Orthodox media outlet, why he supports some forms of same-sex partnerships, if not Jewish weddings. Within a year Rabbi Lau would take an even more expansive stance toward normalizing same-sex unions and families, along the lines suggested by Shvidel and Ofek more than a decade earlier.[33]

Back in 2007, none of that seemed possible, but the movie was enthusiastically received. The film broke ground as the first depiction of an Orthodox *hommo* on the screen, and Elbaum won several awards. Elbaum took the film on the road, screening it in schools and communities and to groups of rabbis and educators. For a while, he was the public face of religious *hommos*. Like "Dan" from the chatroom before him, Elbaum became a contact point for young men seeking answers, inundated by "people who wanted to talk, and had no one to turn to. So they turned to me. And I just listened."

The early years of Orthodox LGBT activism, then, centered on coming out of the shadows. It bears keeping in mind that Orthodox LGBT activists' efforts were bolstered by processes outside their control, including the larger LGBTQ+ movement's successes, liberalizing trends within Orthodoxy, and the possibilities opened up by the internet and especially social media. But it all came together when enough same-sex-attracted persons from Orthodox backgrounds had concluded that, as one interviewee put it, "in the calculus between fear [of exposure] and the pain [of the closet] . . . my fear was big but the pain was bigger." Others, arriving at similar conclusions, began to find one another. At the start of this era, many Orthodox *hommos* and lesbians thought they were alone with their secret and the most audible voice was that of the homophobic Azat Nefesh. A mere six years later, Orthodox *hommo* men had two organizations to choose from (soon, three), activists were talking to rabbis and developing ambitious educational and public outreach interventions, and LGBT persons and their families had access to social and support groups. The initial group of activists was fairly small, but the infrastructure they built in the middle of the aughts—organizations, initiatives, networks, and guiding principles—has been the backbone of Orthodox LGBT activism ever since.

Establishing a Movement: 2009–15

The Orthodox LGBT movement expanded its reach in a six-year period bookended by two deadly homophobic incidents. The first violent act—the shooting spree targeting LGBTQ+ youth in Tel Aviv in August 2009—fractured alliance with other human rights campaigns but also provided an opening for Orthodox LGBT activism. The second violent act, perpetrated by a knife-wielding Ultra-Orthodox man at the 2015 Jerusalem Pride Parade, left teenager Shira Banki dead and several others wounded and resulted in widespread soul-searching among Orthodox leaders, individuals, and communities. After that, one activist said, "you could no longer sit on the fence. You were either with us or against us."

Other strands of activism also fell into place in 2009. In February, Havruta held a semipublic meeting hailed as a milestone. Several dozen *hommos* met with three rabbis: Rabbi Yaaqov Madan of the Har Etzion yeshiva, Rabbi Mordechai Vardi of the Ma'ale school, and Rabbi Yehushua Engleman of the Yakar synagogue, then considered a "gay-friendly" synagogue (that would change soon). In April of that year, *Uvda*, a prominent investigative journalist TV show, took on the conversion therapy organization Azat Nefesh; Rabbi Ron Yosef came out publicly in that interview. Later that month, Bat Kol activists launched Pesach

Sheni. The fall of 2009 saw the founding of two LGBT ritual spaces in the heart of Tel Aviv's gay scene. The year also marked Kadag's embrace by general LGBTQ+ organizations: LGBTQ+ youth organization IGY launched its first support groups for Orthodox persons. Many activists got their start at IGY, where they were schooled in radical activism and acquired a queer vocabulary. Reportedly, the Kadag "brand" itself also came into being that year.

Proud Ritual Spaces

The Proud Minyan, an inclusive prayer space that has operated in Tel Aviv's LGBTQ+ center since 2009, was born out of exclusion. In June 2009, Zehorit and Limor Sorek tied the knot and invited their Tel Aviv congregation to celebrate with them with a *Kiddush*, a luncheon and wine for blessing following Shabbat prayer services.[34] Their congregation, Yakar, revealed the limitations of gay-friendly tolerance and inclusivity. Marking a same-sex wedding was outside some congregants', and the rabbi's, comfort zone, and the Kiddush was held in a park outside the synagogue, sponsored by Dr. Hanna Friedman, an ally, and her husband Aviad. Zehorit was asked to leave the synagogue, but there was a silver lining: the episode accelerated the creation of two LGBT ritual spaces: the Proud Minyan and the LGBT-affirming egalitarian Yachad congregation, led by the Friedmans.

Spiritual spaces are a thorny subject for many LGBTQ+ persons of faith, a site where psychological and spiritual harms and violence are inflicted by coreligionists who mobilize religion to violate LGBTQ+ persons' relationship with God. (The next chapter discusses such harms.) But spiritual spaces do not have to be hostile to LGBT bodies. Faith leaders and communities across religious traditions have created welcoming and accommodating spiritual spaces accompanied by affirming theologies and practices that attempt to repair this harm.[35] For Orthodox LGBT Jews in Israel the turning point came in the late aughts.

The Proud Minyan was founded hastily by Zehorit Sorek and a handful of fellow Kadag activists who decided that "if you don't have a minyan to pray in, found your own minyan."[36] In the context of an increasingly diversifying Orthodox landscape, the time was ripe for radical experiments, though the minyan's location in secular (some would say anti-religious) Tel Aviv and its unapologetic embrace of gender and sexual diversity were a first. Boasting elaborate municipal supports for LGBT persons and community initiatives, and still reeling from the Bar Noar incident's aftermath, the center was ready to take on the challenge.[37]

Organizers were caught off guard in their first year: they expected fifty attendees at most but by Kol Nidrei (the final Yom Kippur prayer) more than three hundred people had gathered in the cramped space, and many more were standing outside. Per one founder, the group "realized that the need, desire, interest was much bigger than just us Bat Kol, Havruta, graduates of yeshivas and *ulpanas* yearning for community." Five years later, the Proud Minyan hosted communal prayers and celebrations marking additional holidays and events in the life of the Proud Religious Community. At the height of its success, in the early to mid-2010s, some would walk miles on Yom Kippur to attend services (travel by car and public transportation are suspended in Israel on Yom Kippur). One man's testimonial explains why:

> Mid-1990s, and in synagogue we hear the reading of [Leviticus chapter that includes the "abomination" verse], as happens every year. But this time I can't stand it. I leave and sit alone because there's no room for me inside.
>
> End of the aughts, the Proud Minyan on Yom Kippur. I'm surrounded by brothers and sisters, partners in the complexity and the spiritual journey. The prayer is beautiful and pure, and there's room for me.[38]

The minyan's practices reflected queer sensibilities borne of exclusions that it sought to redress. The minyan is egalitarian and nondenominational yet sensitive to the needs of Orthodox persons. Orthodox synagogues separate men's and women's seating, while Conservative and Reform synagogues have done away with spatial gendered separations; the Proud Minyan queered the synagogue spatially by creating three sections: a men's section, a women's section, and a mixed section—by far the most popular one. "The goal," a founder told me, "was to create a space where everyone would feel welcome, the feminist and the Orthodox, those who haven't been to synagogue in years and the traditionalist. There must be room for people all across the gender spectrum." "All [should] feel welcome here, this is a bridge between worlds," Zehorit told the gathered before prayers began in 2016.

And what a bridge. When I attended in 2016, it was clear that many attendees knew each other, talking, greeting, hugging, asking about kids, partners, and parents. Others came alone. I, like other "new faces," was invited to partake actively in the service. The crowd skewed young (late twenties and thirties) and male presenting, but the range was broad. Those seated up front seemed to know the prayers, the chants, and the bodily movements. They knew when to stand and when to sit. A couple helped me follow my *siddur* (prayer book). Many male attendees wore the customary Orthodox holiday "uniform" of slacks and a white button-down shirt, but others wore white cotton T-shirts. Most female presenting attendees wore pants rather than skirts or dresses. The mostly Orthodox prayers featured gendered adaptations and additions; a prayer memorializing those killed by LGBTQ+ hostilities and a healing prayer for AIDS sufferers.[39] There was a woman cantor. Better: her shirt read "smash the patriarchy." A rainbow flag covered the holy ark. Some women were wearing prayer shawls (in the Orthodox tradition, only men wear them). When I returned from a "bathroom run" (really, to take furious notes: writing and the use of electronics are forbidden on Yom Kippur), I realized that the real action was in the back of the room: there were people in flip-flops and shorts and heavily pierced and tattooed persons whom I could not imagine setting foot in an Orthodox synagogue.

Despite the minyan's success in disrupting some spiritual harms and exclusions, it replicated others, namely Judaism's ethnic divides and the privileged status of Ashkenazi ritual practices. In response to members' demands that the minyan be more inclusive of Sephardi practices, minyan leaders experimented with alternating between Ashkenazi and Sephardi prayers, but neither faction was ever fully satisfied with the solution, and the Sephardi version never achieved parity. The minyan has been plagued by broader tensions and dynamics in Kadag, whose leaders tend to draw disproportionally from prominent educational institutions, yeshivas, and networks associated with Ashkenazi elites. The year I visited, by the time we got to breaking the fast, the group had dwindled down to its core: about two dozen who seemed to know each other and revel in each other's company. This group did not include those in flip-flops, the heavily tattooed, and others who had by then had stopped attending altogether because, as one Mizrachi man told me, the space did not include the chants and prayers of his childhood synagogue.

In recent years the initiative has been scaled back to a handful of Yom Kippur prayers and a reading of the *megila* in Purim. Internal tensions explain part of its demise, but the minyan is a victim of its own (and the larger movement's) success. "People feel more accepted, they can go to their synagogue, in their neighborhood, they don't need us anymore," a longtime leader told me. Activists nevertheless hoped that the minyan would continue to provide a spiritual home for those lacking one.

Located in another of Tel Aviv's gayborhoods, Yachad (together) also emerged from the Sorek Kiddush debacle. It, too, has delivered on its promise of inclusivity. Congregation leaders Dr. Hanna and Aviad Friedman left a bourgeoise Orthodox settlement and relocated to Tel Aviv to do their part to redress divisions within Israeli society. Dr. Freidman characterizes Yachad not as an LGBT congregation but rather one as that "refuses to throw out those who should be in," but members say that the vast majority of its members are LGBT, and they like it that way. The congregation and its leaders do not probe people's sexual behaviors: such questions are irrelevant.[40] Members say the congregation is a corrective for years (or decades) of rejection and other spiritual harms. One told me that Yachad "is a synagogue where they don't tell you who's in and who's out. Anyone who wants to pray can come. There are lots of *hommos* and lesbians. *Families*. It's an open community. An egalitarian community." There is an additional, symbolic spatial layer. Lacking its own space, the Yachad congregation meets in a school, a traditionally fraught space for LGBT persons. Yachad is no longer unique in its inclusivity.[41] That inclusive congregations are thriving in the face of the minyan's declining fate reflects one of Kadag's greatest achievements: persuading Orthodox communities to make space for Orthodox LGBT persons and families.

Bat Kol's Feminist Ethos: An Inclusive Community

Bat Kol was founded in 2005 by lesbian women who grew up in Orthodox homes. Founders sought to create a safe, welcoming community and promote social change. The organization was a lifeline for Orthodox lesbians, one longtime member explained, because when a woman "realizes that she's a lesbian, her world rocks. Especially for someone religious. It's important to belong somewhere where they understand your language. For seculars it's a different world. The dreams are different." By 2022, the organization had over five hundred members, though a small group of volunteers does most of the heavy lifting. Finances have always been precarious, and Bat Kol has benefited from financial and strategic support from NGOs (including from the much derided, in Orthodox circles, the New Israel Fund). The organization has a strong feminist ethos, which has shaped its organizational structure and culture: for most of its history, it was run by an executive committee of equals (it first hired a paid CEO in 2019).[42] The organization prides itself on being more than a community—members say it is a family. And, like any family, Bat Kol navigates a host of tensions. Bat Kol had been accused of marginalizing and excluding bisexual and trans women.[43] It also tries to accommodate the religious needs of a broad membership that runs from the ex-Orthodox to Ultra-Orthodox women. As an organization with a broad activist agenda, volunteer labor often falls short of needs, especially when early members moved on even as more women joined. Other tensions are inherent to its multifaceted agenda: the emphasis on creating an intimate atmosphere and deep friendships can alienate newcomers, public visibility threatens safe spaces, a non-hierarchical structure gets in the way of decision making. One Bat Kol member described these tensions: "We want discretion [but] we have to talk to the media, to researchers like you, to rabbis and our communities, and generally have visibility. . . . We have some discreet evenings and then other events are open like Pesach Sheni; there are the parades, our campaigns, lots of places where we yell." Bat Kol has successfully navigated these challenges and turbulent times. Members told me that their lives had been touched, altered, repaired, and saved by Bat Kol.

In its early days, new members found Bat Kol through word of mouth. One recalled a postcard that her older sister, an ally, brought from a Jerusalem Pride Parade years before this member acknowledged her sexual orientation. Another was referred by an acquaintance. The majority found Bat Kol online. Zehorit Sorek, a prominent activist, often tells the story of how, after being told that "there is no such thing as an Orthodox lesbian," she turned to "rabbi google" who advised her otherwise.

Bat Kol strives to empower individuals, build community, and raise public awareness. According to its CEO Tehila Attias, Bat Kol first and foremost serves its members, some of whom "have been thrown out of their homes, who don't have any other place. . . . Their friendship circles are reduced. They come here and find a community. . . . They have a social space, where they can breathe. Be who they are." A longtime member likewise said that Bat Kol's "goal is . . . to build a community of Orthodox lesbians. . . . We do social events and build a network. So that if someone doesn't have a place to go for a Shabbat dinner, a holiday, she'll always find a home in Bat Kol." To do this, Bat Kol operates via a number of different channels: a newsletter that includes substantive content, Torah commentary, and information about events; a public-facing (and sometimes outdated) website; small groups meetings; social events and holiday celebrations; a yearly Shabbat; private Facebook and WhatsApp groups; study groups.

Bat Kol also seeks to raise public awareness through outreach, though it puts less stock in dialogues with rabbis, more prominent on the men's side, because, per one member, men "have the halachic problem and they are more invested in finding a halachic solution." Nevertheless, Bat Kol has cultivated rabbinic allies and remains in close dialogue with them.[44]

Bat Kol members also recognize the importance of public visibility. The organization maintains a list of media-tested members who can, per one activist, "hop on air at a moment's notice." One such member told me that these appearances get "tiring and repetitive but we have to do it, otherwise they [Orthodox critics] go unchallenged." Bat Kol has also maintained a presence in both the Tel Aviv and Jerusalem parades since 2005. Visibility raises public awareness but also serves to communicate to closeted women that they are not alone. One member recalled that as an adolescent in the aughts, newly aware of her attraction to women, she assumed that "LGBT people lived in communities of LGBT people, and religious people lived in religious people communities." An unexpected encounter in a synagogue expanded her horizon:

> It was one of the first places where they started Torah reading for women in Simchat Torah. This woman comes to read in the Torah and next to her is a woman with a rainbow-colored belt. And next to her two small girls. It took me a couple of minutes to understand the situation. After the prayer I looked for them. That was the first LGBT family that I met. And I met them in the synagogue!! Of course they were in Bat Kol.

Bat Kol is aware of the life-changing potential of such encounters and has striven to formalize them through a mentorship program. Many Bat Kol interviewees spoke about specific women or couples, referencing a shared LGBT experience: lack of positive role models that is combatted through the building of homegrown networks. One woman reflected how "Avigail [Sperber] sent us to this couple from Bat Kol. We sat down to talk to them. I was blown away. Finally, women I could identify with. . . . It opened this door, to a possibility, of where I'm heading." One young woman said an older member had become "like my second family. No, my first. I went to her parents' home for the Seder [Passover]." Another found solace in Bat Kol when, during a rough patch, she ran into an old acquaintance; "she said 'come to our *Sukkah*, every year we have all the women from Bat Kol.' I was going through divorce. I came, saw happy women, smiling. Kids. I'd never seen anything like this! It was transformative." Another member is now paying it forward by trying "to be [a role model] for other women. . . . It's very helpful to have those who are older than you, ahead in life. To see LGBT families." But, she conceded, involvement comes at a price: "We have this 'open doors' policy but it is sometimes exhausting, to always have to be there for others."

Unlike the situation on the men's side, where, by 2011, three organizations vied for members touting distinct theological, ideological, and strategic visions, Bat Kol had no competitors, a relief according to one longtime member because the donor base was such that it could not sustain competition. An attempt to start a more halachic organization never came to fruition. Instead, Bat Kol developed a pluralist, inclusive, and fluid vision of Orthodoxy. Bat Kol, one member said, "embraces lots of different groups: study groups . . . A Haredi group *and* the Proud Minyan. There are lots of paradoxes but we are somehow able to embrace everyone." Another member conceded that while the majority were "on the *ex*-Orthodox spectrum" Bat Kol also has a place for Haredi women and those who are married to men. Embracing this plurality required taking a stance about heterosexual marriage and the closet while developing seemingly conflicting activism streams. Accepting closeted women and guarding their interests hinged on commitment to insularity and secrecy, while working "outward, to help those not in the closet" entailed, as one member put it, "making lots of noise." Navigating this plurality also hinged on creating what one member called "a safe space to be religious," achieved through "bylaws, rules about observing Shabbat in public during our gatherings . . . all food served and shared at our events is *kosher*. We don't want anyone to apologize for their religiosity. Even though the majority aren't very religious."

Still, the space was hard to navigate. One member joined when she was a highly observant twenty-year-old. "They joked with me, okay, okay, you're very observant. Soon you won't be." Another young woman first experienced Bat Kol's atmosphere and language as "too gay" and "foreign." She found a home in its study groups and the Pesach Sheni initiative. Though some members say that there are now more observant women in Bat Kol, tolerance has its limits: "I always wonder how comfortable *hardal* [highly observant] women . . . could feel in Bat Kol, and the answer is clear—they don't really come to us or just test out the water and don't stay." Still, for others, the organization was *too* religious. One woman discovered Bat Kol in her early twenties, in the primary stages of a divorce. Miserable and disillusioned by rabbis who told her that her "feeling toward women will pass, that I will get used to married life," she rejected Bat Kol because "they were all about being religious."

Ironically, women's marginalization within Judaism partially accounts for Bat Kol's ability to successfully navigate these tensions. Some questions that men just could not avoid—rabbinic acceptance, interpretations of the abomination clause, inclusion in synagogue ritual—are less pressing for women. But Bat Kol's inclusive religiosity and pluralism is also a product of its proud feminist ethic. Inclusivity and safe spaces have a long feminist history, while Orthodox feminists have led challenges to Orthodox hegemonic practices and institutions. (There are overlaps: many Bat Kol members had attended educational institutions at the forefront of the Orthodox feminist revolution.) Doubly excluded from the center of Orthodoxy, the women of Bat Kol followed the path of other marginalized groups: they criticized dominant culture, structure, organizations, and leadership while demanding that they make space for others in their midst. Thus, by demanding acceptance Bat Kol members were also challenging Orthodoxy itself. One member told me that "most of us don't stay Orthodox in the same way we were when we first joined, the way we grew up. They don't stay with their skirts, and sleeves, you know, the ulpana (seminary) look. But they're committed."

As opposed to the relative ease with which members embraced religious diversity and inclusivity, for several years in the 2010s Bat Kol was consumed by fierce battles over gender inclusivity, similar to those that have plagued other feminist and lesbian organizations. Bat Kol originally defined itself as an organization of Orthodox lesbians; in 2019, it updated its bylaws to include "those who are challenged by integrating of religious identity or religious nuclear family and their sexual identity," and in 2021 it officially changed its name to the more inclusive "Lesbian, Bisexual, Transgender, and Queer Orthodox women." The road had not been smooth. For several years it seemed that debates about expanding the organization's constituency would tear it apart. Debates spilled from membership meetings and closed Facebook groups and into public domains. The issue, as one longtime member put it, was deciding "Who's Bat Kol for? Only for lesbians?" Part of the problem was religious breadth: "We had new members who come to us from IGY [the secular LGBT youth organization], where they didn't have to self-define, and now they feel confined. But on the other end of the spectrum we have Haredi women who are afraid to come to events. Think of what a girl from an ulpana in Shomron would think." (Shomron is an area in the West Bank, home to settlements and communities considered to be highly observant and nationalist.)

When attempts to change the bylaws came up short in 2016, opinions were fierce on both sides; an Orthodox trans organization had just been founded by a member fed up with Bat Kol. One member who supported the changes was optimistic in 2016 because the debates, fierce as they were, were marked by a feminist ethic of negotiation: "We're slowly getting there. It'll happen with the right dialogue, which we are having. There are already trans and bi women in Bat Kol. It's just that when it was founded, this wasn't in the forefront of conversation. Things have changed, and our community is constantly changing." Another was more forceful: "We have to change or we won't be relevant. But it's a process. It used to be that the girls from ulpana didn't know what lesbians are and now they do. So in five years they'll know about trans." Members were optimistic that the disagreements had not torn the organization apart, although some original and older members were furious with newcomers. Ultimately, the voices of change won.[45]

Havruta versus Conservative Hommo Organizations

For several years during the 2010s, entering the terms "religious" and "*hommo*" in Hebrew in a Google search box would return, in addition to a slew of hateful headlines and Azat Nefesh, three organizations vying to represent the interests of same-sex-attracted Orthodox men: Havruta, Hod, and Kamoha, a Havruta breakaway faction.[46] Tensions between these organizations date back to the online forums, where participants debated the plausibility and permutations of same-sex Orthodox identities, lives, and families. In time, these debates came to center on the meaning of Orthodoxy itself. That the Havruta/Kadag pluralist vision won was not a forgone conclusion in the early 2010s, and this outcome reveals as much about Orthodoxy's trajectories as about the effectiveness of Kadag's activism.

Havruta began under the auspices of the JOH as a discreet group of men seeking to support one another; many were ex-Orthodox. By 2011, the group was "a real community, [with] hundreds of email subscribers, dozens of participants in various events and thousands of people who enter its website every day."[47] Still, discretion abounded; a 2011 article about a Havruta affiliated group referred to its founder only by his initial; by the time I began my research in 2016 such anonymization was rare. Havruta sponsors holiday celebrations and other social events and its volunteers still staff an anonymous help line. But Havruta was not just a support group: "We were never an Alcoholics Anonymous," one activist said, "our goal was acceptance." To that end, Havruta's activism engages in conversation with Orthodox journalists, politicians, rabbis, and other thought leaders.

Many Havruta founders and early activists were ex-Orthodox; as the organization grew, its membership diversified, though it continues to skew less observant. Havruta experienced tensions surrounding religiosity: the organization's stance vis-à-vis hegemonic interpretations of halachic positions toward homosexuality, dialogues with and expectations of rabbis, participation in non-Orthodox initiatives such as pride parades and the Proud Minyan. That halachic issues were more prominent for men reflects women's marginalized status in Jewish thought, ritual, and communal life as well as in scripture: the abomination clause in Leviticus references men. Divergent educational experiences also meant that men were generally more familiar with halachic rhetoric and more accustomed to talking to rabbis; as former students, they tended to have access to rabbis. These tensions, apparent in rivalries between the three organizations vying to cater to Orthodox *hommos*, helped Havruta brand itself as a pluralist Orthodox organization. More recently, younger activists have begun to advocate for an even more pluralist and expanded vision in response to changed reality: many trans, queer, bisexual, and binary members, or potential members, find the Havruta focus on *hommos* exclusionary.

But that came later. In its early days, Havruta was stretched thin, attempting to find its footing within a network of Orthodox and general LGBT organizations reeling in the aftermath of the Bar Noar shooting. Some of its early members were also involved in initiatives such as the Proud Minyan and Shoval.[48] The multipronged strategy and broad vision would pay off later, but for several years (~2008–12) Hod competed for the spotlight as a spokesperson for Orthodox *hommos*. During this time, Hod founder Ron Yosef had a prolific media presence through which he sought to normalize religious *hommos*.[49]

Hod shared Kadag's goals of visibility and tolerance and opposed conversion therapy but differed on strategy, rhetoric, and vision: Havruta's approach blended public visibility, community outreach, and sometimes public meetings with rabbis, while Hod preferred to meet privately with rabbis and work with legislative and professional bodies. The organizations developed vastly different visions of what it meant to be an Orthodox *hommo* and the place of the halacha in their activism. Kadag held that centering acceptance on private sexual practices was demeaning, whereas opposition to anal sex was foundational to Hod's identity as a halachic organization. These positions, along with personality differences, hampered collaboration.

In 2008 Yosef invited dozens of rabbis to sign a document intended to serve as a moral and practical guide for Orthodox rabbis, educators, and communities; a similar document was circulating among Orthodox rabbis in the United States.[50] The "principles document," as Yosef called it, posited that homosexuality was immutable; distinguished between practice (forbidden) and identity (permissible); and made a case for tolerance, including toward those who engaged in male-on-male anal sex. It also criticized pressure to enter heterosexual marriage and seek conversion therapy. The document was negotiated with rabbis for a couple of years before its release in 2010. Hod claimed that over 160 rabbis endorsed the document, but the number of public endorsements is much smaller (the list does include prominent rabbis including Yuval Cherlow, David Bigman, and Haim Navon).[51] Per Hod's telling, the organization, with Ron Yosef at its helm, was the document's initiator, engine, and author,[52] but I was not able to corroborate this claim. Either way, Hod benefitted from the broader activist field. Kadag activists agreed with some of Hod's principles but resented its rhetoric, which portrayed same-sex-attracted men as miserable, centered on same-sex intercourse, and was premised on a narrow vision of Orthodoxy. Kadag also disagreed with Hod's refusal to cooperate with secular organizations and its privileging of dialogue with rabbis over other modes of activism.[53]

Like Havruta, Hod sponsored social events, community Shabbats, and support groups and was a significant waystation on many men's journeys of self-acceptance, especially for Mizrachi men who found Havruta unwelcoming. I interviewed around a dozen men who had subsequently left but shared a version of one man's reflection that "Hod was a good place to have when I was coming to terms. It was comforting to know there are people like you, who understand you, who speak your language." The organization began to fall out of favor by the early 2010s. One man found Hod's social gatherings "boring, busy writing letters to rabbis, trying to write a manifesto." Another did not agree with Hod's strategy that favored "lobbying rabbis. . . . I didn't think that this is how you move along social processes. I didn't care what rabbis thought and what the halacha says." Others noted the organization's undemocratic nature: Yosef was the organization's sole public face. With Kadag organizations streamlining operations, securing funding, and successfully collaborating with one another, they became attractive alternatives to Hod's undemocratic style, the large number of closeted and heterosexually married members, and its narrow vision of Orthodoxy. Along with philosophical, theological, and ideological differences, interpersonal strife was brewing.[54] Many members left, and Hod lost prominence even before a scandal brought the organization to a halt in 2016, when Ron Yosef was the subject of a criminal investigation (he was accused of embezzlement). Kadag activists were rightly concerned that his fall from grace would have ripple effects on their movement: publications in the

Orthodox press predictably appropriated personal lapses in judgment to promote a broader homophobic agenda. But the tide had shifted to such an extent that Hod's downfall did not reverberate other than confirming the obvious: Kadag was the de facto face of Orthodox LGBT activism. By the time I began working on this book, Hod's domain's name had been bought, its Facebook page had been mostly silent since the scandal broke out, and few Kadag activists mentioned it, though when asked about Hod's legacy one activist angrily told me that the organization should be written out of Orthodox LGBT history.

Hod had presented itself as the sole authentic voice of halachically committed same-sex-attracted men but faced competition from Kamoha—"Like You"—a Havruta breakaway.[55] Kamoha founder Amit (an alias) charged Havruta with religious inauthenticity and its website claimed that (unnamed) "other organizations" compromised rabbinic support and alienated same-sex-attracted men.[56] Kamoha touted its members as singularly "highly observant," specifically when it came to prohibitions against same-sex relationships and intercourse (not so, according to interviewees who had passed through Kamoha).

During its nine years of existence—the organization ceased operations in 2020—Kamoha was Kadag's foil: "They're the Catholics. We [Havruta] are the Protestants, more accepting of ex-Orthodox, secular, Conservative, Reform Judaism," a Havruta member told me. Another said that "Havruta and Kamoha are two separate worlds. One tells you: 'you can change'; the other marches in the parades." Kadag members reviled Kamoha. They were angered by its secrecy ("You can't call yourself an activist yet operate under an anonymous name," one Havruta activist said) and its association with homophobic rabbis who supported conversion therapy, celibacy, and heterosexual marriage (at one point Kamoha and its affiliated rabbis promoted a homo-lesbian marriage project, marriages between gay men and lesbians; the initiative fizzled, reportedly with little to show for it). Nevertheless, they respected Amit's desire to maintain anonymity and most referred to him by his alias in their conversations with me.

But many men struggling with same-sex attraction were drawn to Kamoha—the organization held communal Shabbats and monthly or bimonthly get-togethers (some of these meetings featured allied rabbis and other public figures). Amit, the founder, is also a skilled archivist:

Kamoha's website includes many documents, interviews, photos, summaries of conferences and meetings pertaining to Orthodox LGBT persons and matters—as well as a series of blog posts and other content the organization and its allies generated. Men traveled between organizations; some Havruta activists got their start in Hod or Kamoha. Others were oblivious to ideological differences. One man went to a Kamoha Shabbat simply because it was on the calendar; he did not care about ideological differences: "I just wanted to meet people like me." Others were more deliberate, preferring Hod or Kamoha because Havruta was perceived as too secular, "reform," overrun by ex-Orthodox; in the mid-2010s, Kamoha's commitment to the closet was especially appealing to the young and the heterosexually married. Also appealing was the message that homosexuality can be overcome. One ex-Kamoha member said Havruta had initially repelled him:

> They supported coming out of the closet, that wasn't my thing. I didn't want to come out. I wanted to make this thing go away, find a solution. I went to a Kamoha Shabbat. There were fifty people there, mostly closeted. They were all across the religious spectrum. It was empowering to see so many people like me in one place, who are going through the same thing, understand how you feel.

In the end, empowerment turned out to be double-edged sword. Kamoha rejected the plausibility of a political identity based on sexual orientation and yet members found the sociability it offered comforting; interviewees reported meeting friends, fellow activists, and, predictably, romantic partners at Kamoha activities. Thus, in its desire to give people a lifeline through community, Kamoha inadvertently encouraged members to develop an identity as Orthodox *hommos*, which, in turn, made continued affiliation with Kamoha unsustainable. One former Kamoha member said that the outcome was inevitable: "Once people start talking, they develop ideas, and some start thinking 'maybe this isn't so bad,' 'maybe *I'm* not the problem.'"

Another deal breaker was Kamoha's insistence on celibacy and heterosexual marriage, messages that, one man said, "crushed" him when he could not abide by them: "After going to a couple of Kamoha events I decided I was going to check out this aspect of myself, and I went back to dating girls. You know, the Kamoha line is conversion, marriage. If you can't succeed stay celibate or marry someone. . . . But I couldn't live it." A man in his thirties who was married to a woman reached out to Kamoha seeking a referral to a psychologist "who speaks my language." He deliberately reached out to Kamoha because at the time he found Havruta to be "too liberal . . . I wanted a conversation, I wasn't really looking for a miracle cure." What he got instead was a rabbi whose message was "stay married and have stints on the side." Worst of all, said another man, was "the self-pity that went on there. You've probably heard Nadav's line 'oy, I'm *hommo*. Oy, I'm an Orthodox *hommo*.' I didn't like this whining." He, too, left for Havruta, drawn by its message of self-acceptance.

Kamoha's membership dwindled. The closet was oppressive, and celibacy and heterosexual marriage were unappealing, while Kadag presented more viable alternatives. Some members were asked to leave after coming out publicly or getting involved in LGBT activism. By 2020, Kamoha ceased to operate (though as of this writing its website remains active). Yet, even Kadag activists concede that "there's a place for an organization like Kamoha. Men who are married, with kids, they can't change that but they need a place to go. Havruta is too much for them. Kamoha allows that." Another Havruta member observed that "Kamoha is a place where people go in the beginning, when they're still in the closet and they're afraid. They have to work through this fear, thinking 'I'm the only one in the world.'" But Kamoha's support for conversion therapy precluded redemption. "Kamoha," one activist said, "has blood on its hands."

In the mid-teens, while Kamoha was still active and vying for members and a cultural foothold, it forced Havruta to articulate its ideology, boundaries, and identity. In response to Kamoha's break with it, Havruta CEO Daniel Jonas touted his organization's bona fide Orthodox credentials alongside a religious pluralism:

> Havruta was founded by yeshiva graduates for anyone who considers himself a homosexual with an affinity for Orthodox Judaism . . . [it] remains committed to the Orthodox Jewish halacha, and promises its members the best possible considerations to live according to the halacha, with and despite their orientation. Havruta does not encourage halachic transgression, but it nevertheless attempts to provide a home even

to those who are less observant. Havruta is in communication with rabbis and Orthodox public figures to address the religious needs of all its members.[57]

In the early to mid-teens, Havruta was walking a fine line: it sought to pose an alternative to organizations promoting conversion therapy and heterosexual marriage. This would demand a lower profile and a more wholesome public image. One man said he initially avoided Havruta because "they seemed REFORM. That was a pejorative . . . I was a good yeshiva boy, I hardly seemed like their target audience." Another was repelled by Havruta's support for coming out. On the other hand, with some of its founders approaching their thirties, long ex-Orthodox, and losing patience with the Orthodox establishment, its members "wanted to make noise . . . we were eager for progress, recognition, legitimacy, acknowledgment."

With Kamoha as its foil, Shoval and Bat Kol as its allies, and its membership losing patience, Havruta came to take a bolder stance vis-à-vis visibility, religious pluralism, and what it meant to be *hommo* and Orthodox. By the mid-2010s, these messages found an audience among a range of same-sex-attracted men, and Havruta began to register a shift in demographics; more observant men joined, and membership age began declining (both trends would become more pronounced later in the decade). Some of this shift was deliberate: as other organizations folded, Havruta leaders discussed how to accommodate and make room for "Kamoha refugees." It also made some inroads on the Ashkenazi/Mizrachi ethnic divide, though many still experience it as a predominantly Ashkenazi space.

During this time Havruta also articulated its stance vis-à-vis rabbis and the place of the halacha in its activism. In contrast to conservative Orthodox rabbis who centered on the halachic ramifications of same-sex love, Havruta and Kadag viewed their predicament as social rather than theological. One Havruta leader explained that the organization "decided not to rely on rabbis . . . we target social issues, we are not a halachic organization." This does not mean that Havruta ignored rabbis, but rather it harnessed allies to advance visibility and legitimacy. A few days before the 2015 Jerusalem Pride Parade, Havruta posted a photo of activists with Rabbanit Malka Puterkovsky. "My takeaway," one attendee said, was "that we should stop waiting for the rabbis to make the revolution. She said, 'You will not receive a stamp of approval from them. Build homes. Have children. Dictate a reality on the ground.'" Referencing the photo, Havruta's post about the meeting concluded, "For the first time in history, fifteen *hommos*, Havruta members, exposed faces." It was a few days after this meeting that a knife-bearing Ultra-Orthodox man, Yishai Shlisel, wounded several participants in the Jerusalem Pride Parade; a teenage ally, Shira Banki, died two days later.

A Proud Religious Community: Kadag as a Bridge

By the early 2010s, Havruta and Bat Kol had honed community-building and activist agendas along with operational strategies that combined online and offline engagements: meetings, holiday celebrations, newsletters, blogs, writing workshops, study groups, and Facebook groups, all aimed primarily at their members, and a public presence achieved through participation in parades and other protest arenas, events targeting Orthodox audiences, and a media and social media presence. Both organizations boasted hundreds of members though the burden was carried by a relatively small number of activists.

Collaboration made this activism possible: by the late aughts various initiatives, agendas, and organizations came together under the umbrella of Proud Religious Community—Kadag. (There are various origin stories of the term, but many attribute it to Zehorit Sorek circa 2009.) Some activists envisioned a single, unified organization working on behalf of all Orthodox LGBT persons. Others preferred a looser coalition, recognizing the varied needs of Kadag's constituent groups. Either way, transcending narrow agendas was key to achieving shared goals. Kadag hosts events for Orthodox LGBT persons—Shabbat dinners after the Jerusalem Pride Parade, a yearly communal Shabbat—and has a savvy media presence; it generates content and rapidly responds to unfolding events; its leaders recognize the power of speaking in a unified voice. Kadag cosponsors events with other LGBT organizations while also focusing on events targeted at Orthodox audiences. Its constituent organizations have varied; core organizations include Havruta, Bat Kol, and Shoval, but at times the coalition has also included Pesach Sheni, the Proud Minyan, Tehila, and IGY Religious Groups. One Kadag leader told me that the coalition, years in the making, "came together after the 2015 parade. That's when we became a real community. Before, each organization worked with their own audience. . . . A lot of it comes from friendships, our own networks. It made much more sense to work together." The coalition was also more attractive to funders.

Kadag's affiliates also expanded their collaborations with general LGBT organizations, which had previously been oblivious, and occasionally hostile, to the needs of Orthodox persons. These collaborations included using LGBT spaces (the Proud Minyan was housed in Tel Aviv's LGBT center), working together on campaigns and other events, including on college campuses, and recognizing Orthodox persons' unique needs. A Bat Kol member who attempted to join IGY in the early 2010s was alienated: "It's like they were speaking a different language." By the mid-2010s, IGY understood that "there's a special community that needs its own space, especially when it comes to young people." IGY, this volunteer added, "has learned to translate its materials to 'Orthodox.' Like they translate to Arabic."

Personal relationships helped facilitate collaboration,[58] but it was the sense of shared struggles that made these collaborations inevitable. Positioning themselves as fellow travelers, Orthodox LGBT persons asserted that the general organizations can no longer ignore them:

> When there are meetings of the LGBT organizations, Bat Kol, Havruta, Shoval will be part of the conversation. You can't ignore us in campaigns or parades. We have earned our place. We will be in the parade, even if you don't like the *Hasidic* music. We also participate in LGBT communication agenda. If you're going to do a story about LGBT people, you'll have to talk to a religious lesbian, *hommo*. If you're doing an ad campaign, you're going to have to feature a religious lesbian and *hommo*.

Sticking points remain. Kadag is reluctant to cosponsor campaigns it deems too sexual or too political because, one leader explained, "we are talking to our parents, families, neighbors, rabbis." Another explained that in each instance, Kadag organizations had a decision to make: "How provocative do we want to be in rallies, parades? What kinds of signs do we carry? How close do we remain to the religious, more conservative world?" Another said that nevertheless Kadag expected to be taken into account "in planning events. Don't have a major demonstration on a fast day. Don't have parties on Shabbat. We're constantly educating them."[59]

Kadag thus positions itself as a bridge between Orthodox and LGBTQ+ communities. A Kadag member explained that "many seculars think it's a problem, Orthodox LGBT people who don't give up their Orthodox identity. Sometimes it's real hatred, it comes up every time some rabbi says something about LGBTs." In the face of such attitudes, Kadag's task is "to say not only that it is possible [to be Orthodox and LGBT], but also to show that Orthodoxy is a broad concept." Kadag, another activist said, puts a different spin on Orthodoxy: "Our voice is no less important than that of the more conservative Orthodox. . . . We are creating a different reality, showing that Judaism is *also* about other things, that there are different voices within Orthodoxy." At the same time, Kadag brings "a different voice [to the LGBT] landscape. When you come to a pride parade, and there's a large religious community, and then a truck with Hasidic music, it's unexpected. People can't imagine that there's a relationship between religious and LGBT people, and suddenly we make this connection. *In the parade.*"

To successfully maintain this bridge, Kadag activists engage in code switching. One activist said that she has learned to speak "to the secular organizations in their language, and to the Orthodox in their language. That's what you learn as an Orthodox LGBT person: to be flexible with your mind, language, expectations." She found this liminal position to be a "blessing." Liminality would prove invaluable in the aftermath of the violence at the 2015 parade, when Kadag helped organize two impromptu rallies. One activist recalled that "Jonas [Daniel, then Havruta CEO] called Rabbi Benny [Lau] and told him 'you have to come to the rally, people need to hear you speak.'" But it comes at a price:

Kadag is always torn, always in the middle. We owe A LOT to the secular LGBT community. In Shoval workshops people often say, "But why do you have to march with the seculars, you're not like them." They like to put us on a pedestal, an ideal *hommo*. I'm not going to bite the hand that feeds me! I am here thanks to those who came before me. I owe them. If it weren't for the secular LGBT activists who were here a decade ago I wouldn't be here to talk to you, I wouldn't be *able* to talk to you. But we are torn because we are also committed to an Orthodox dialogue. On the other hand, I sometimes feel that Orthodox LGBT persons are like children with cancer . . . it's sexy, it sells, and the secular organizations sometimes like to make use of us.

A one-minute video inviting participants to march with Bat Kol in the 2013 Tel Aviv Pride Parade set to Hasidic pop music captures the making of Kadag in the late aughts and early 2010s.[60] The video scrolls through photos from previous parades. In 2005, a few women in white shirts carried purple balloons and homemade signs declaring "Tolerance Parade." More homemade signs were carried in 2006: "Bat Kol for Tolerance in the Orthodox Community" and "Love Thy Neighbor." Bat Kol here rebranded the Tel Aviv parade; though it has certainly seen its fair share of political protests, it is mostly a carnivalesque street party—not a demonstration of tolerance. By 2008, Bat Kol had a logo and a professional banner. In 2009, there were kids and babies galore, as well as new faces. A coalition arrived in 2011: a banner listed Bat Kol, Havruta, IGY, and the Proud Minyan, along with their logos. In 2012, there were Proud Religious Community banners and associated merchandise. The rolling images capture how, within less than a decade, Orthodox *hommos* and lesbians had established themselves as a bridge between Orthodox and LGBT communities; how they navigated the politics of the secular, sacred, and profane; how they built a coalition of organizations, expanded public visibility, and confronted the tyranny of the closet.

There were many more initiatives, events, and firsts during this half-decade (I elaborate on some of these in chapters 4–6): the late aughts and early 2010s saw the rapid establishment of organizations and networks of activists and allies and the articulation of strategic goals and tactics. Kadag politicized and mobilized newly identifying Orthodox *hommos* and lesbians into action—their ranks were growing. However, like secular LGBT organizations, Kadag's demographics favored the privileged: Bat Kol and (especially) Havruta membership and activists skewed Ashkenazi and hailed from Orthodoxy's core. This elitist status left those from less privileged backgrounds alienated and excluded from Kadag's agendas, social circles, and vision. Also left unexamined was alignment with Jewish nationalism, a point I return to in the conclusion.

Those who could, pursued Rabbanit Malka Puterkovsky's advice: they just lived their lives. They found love, got married, had children, and came out to their families and friends, thereby expanding the "straight religious cloud around religious *hommos*." But this "religious cloud" itself was transforming: the break between liberal and conservative Orthodox factions was becoming more pronounced. These tensions all came to a head at the 2015 Jerusalem Pride Parade.

Violence, Soul Searching, Polarization: 2015–20

A six-minute speech that Rabbi Benny Lau gave at a hastily organized rally in Jerusalem following Shira Banki's death marked Kadag's arrival on the national stage. By 2016 Rabbi Lau was a reliable ally, but for Kadag activists "it mattered that he finally said the words *publicly*." Rabbi Lau denounced homophobia, called on Orthodox leaders to eradicate hate, and invited *hommos* and lesbians to come out of the closet because, he said, "a closet is death . . . and you should choose life." Rabbi Lau called on like-minded Orthodox people to "release Israel's Torah from the shackles of unenlightened people."[61]

Activism and acceptance accelerated after the 2015 parade though it would be wrong to attribute Kadag's successes to the murder; the violence and its soul-searching aftermath hastened processes a decade and a half in the making: ground-up activism, a growing circle of allies, a community increasingly willing to acknowledge and address homophobia, and rabbis willing to take a stance. In December 2015, several dozen Orthodox *hommos* and lesbians came out collectively through the Our Faces campaign, while others, including Walla forum founder Yishai Meir, came out in viral Facebook posts.[62] In April 2016, the liberal Beit Hillel rabbis released a halachic paper advocating tolerance and acceptance of same-sex-attracted persons. The rabbis had invited Kadag members to weigh in on drafts. In July 2016 conservative Orthodox Rabbi Yigal Levinstein called LGBT persons "perverts." A week later, the Jerusalem Pride Parade boasted over twenty-five thousand participants, the largest turnout ever, including thousands of Orthodox allies. Kadag confronted polarization head-on. Some Kadag marchers carried signs with Rabbi Lau's face accompanied by his words "a closet is death." Others carried posters featuring the words and images of Kadag foes Rabbi Shmuel Eliyahu ("an unhealthy phenomenon, like obesity, smoking, and prostitution") and Rabbi Yigal Levinstein ("perverts who have lost normalcy"). In October 2016, days before Yom Kippur, Shoval released a video featuring messages of penitence from prominent rabbis.[63] In November 2016 Havruta members met with a group of rabbis, Orthodox educators held a first public conference on improving services for same-sex-attracted youth, and the Rabbanit Malka Puterkovsky met with several dozen Kadag (mostly Havruta) members and their parents. Meanwhile, a pride flag hung outside Havruta activist's Moshe Argaman's (then Grossman) home in a conservative West Bank Orthodox settlement, drawing the ire a local rabbi associated with the conservative *hommo* organization Kamoha. This list does not include numerous articles, op-eds, viral Facebook posts, and interviews.

As Orthodox LGBT activism enters its third decade, Orthodox LGBT persons are more visible than ever. Their agenda is queerer than ever, the landscape they navigate more polarized. In April 2018 Michal Schonberg, an Orthodox bisexual activist in her twenties, launched a Facebook Confessions Page for Religious LGBT persons, inviting them to share their stories, ask questions, and respond to other posts. People have much to say. The page has published over eight thousand posts: confessions of lost love, frustration, and suicidal ideation along with heady halachic ruminations and political contemplations. A community has formed around the page, and people praise it as a sane oasis of wisdom and generosity. Since Facebook pages (unlike groups) are accessible to anyone with a Facebook account, the initiative brings LGBT Orthodoxy the combination of broad accessibility and visibility along with safety and anonymity that had been lacking since the demise of the forums. And like the forums before it, the page spills into the physical world: friendships and romances have blossomed. Quotes from the page were made into stickers distributed during the 2019 and 2022 Jerusalem Pride Parades. And page administrators collaborated on a collection of prose and poetry that first appeared on the page, the first literary collection by and for Orthodox LGBT persons with a wide reach.

Within a few months, Schonberg's Confessions Page had a competitor: Confessions of the Struggling Community. ("Strugglers" experience same-sex attraction but do not act on it.) Perusing the pages side by side reveals that disagreements that began on the online forums in the early 2000s about the essence and mutability of same-sex attraction and whether same-sex relationships are compatible with Orthodoxy are far from settled. But despite lingering discords within its ranks, Kadag's vision—inclusivity, tolerance, emphases on community outreach, education, and dialogue, alongside insistence on Orthodox authenticity—has won the day. As of June 2022 the Strugglers page has published about one-eighth of the posts on the LGBT affirming page. And it is the "strugglers" and their allies who are now on the defense, with posts justifying decisions to remain closeted or to reject Kadag's path. In the process, these strugglers confirm the obvious: Orthodox LGBT identity has become a reality.

* * *

This chapter has provided a broad overview of the Orthodox LGBT movement. Kadag replicates tensions that already existed within LGBT activism in Israel but the movement also introduced nuances and new agendas as it sought to create space for Orthodox LGBT persons within Orthodoxy, while educating both LGBTQ+ organizations and Orthodox communities that Orthodox LGBTQ exist. Chapters 4 to 6 consider the activist tale, namely how a marginalized group demanded recognition and how the larger community responded by patrolling its boundaries to fend off threatening insiders. But the activist tale does not fully capture the experiences of those living within a society that frames them as nonexistent, sinners, deviants, an oxymoron, nor the generative potential of negotiating and asserting new forms of identity. Before they began to challenge their reality Orthodox LGBT persons surmised that it was not possible to be both LGBT and Orthodox. As they came together to change these perceptions they also created a new set of social identities and imbued them with meanings and possibilities. The next two chapters consider how they went about this.

2

Unlivable Lives

Shattered Pictures and the Desire to Be "Normal"

"So, what is it like to be an Orthodox *hommo*?" This is the opening line of a lengthy poem posted on the Facebook Confessions Page of Religious LGBTQ in June 2019.[1] The young anonymous poet's situation initially seems bleak, as "black holes of uncertainty" engulf him and consume (imaginary) family photos featuring a wife and children. The poet recounts a journey through denial, fear, secrecy, loss, shame, theological angst, and a quest to be "normal." The tale then takes an optimistic turn. New images of a husband and children replace the void in the photos, and the poet is surrounded by a supportive family and a newfound community. The poem ends on a sanguine note: "To be an Orthodox *hommo* . . . is to know that you have gone through a lot, that you have a lot more to go through . . . that there are those who will make the journey with you." The next two chapters follow the poet and his fellow travelers on their journey from shattered pictures and their chaotic aftermath to the lives made possible when a previously silenced group reenvisions what it means to be Orthodox.[2]

Same-Sex Journeys

When I first met Ayelet (names and identifying information have been changed to protect privacy) in 2017, she was mourning the "picture of what life is supposed to look like." Closeted and in her late twenties, Ayelet occasionally dated men. She held on to a glimmer of hope that she will marry a man and have "a real wedding with a *huppah* [wedding canopy] and a shattered glass [part of the Jewish wedding ceremony], rather than shattered dreams." Ayelet had known from a young age that "something was wrong. That I was different." Her friends would speak endlessly about boys, but she experienced a series of crushes on female teachers and youth movement counselors. She kept her predicament secret and "prayed for this to change. That I'll be normal. 'Please, please, make it change.'"

When I caught up with her two years later, Ayelet was mostly closeted, celibate, and "stuck." Her high school, *midrasha* (seminary), and college friends were married with (several) children. Friends and family had stopped trying to set her up with eligible men; she had declined too many offers. She was growing distant from her married friends, who were juggling careers, motherhood, and busy lives in Orthodox communities. Many ended up settling in the same type of tight-knit Orthodox neighborhoods where they grew up. This had been part of Ayelet's life plan too, but Orthodox spaces were not hospitable to single women or single mothers—never mind a same-sex couple. Besides, she had already drifted away from Orthodoxy; her status as a single woman, she said, shut her out of what she had liked most about Judaism—community, home, rituals. The main reason she was stuck, however, was that *she* could not imagine building a life with another woman. Lifelong messages from family, teachers, and rabbis ran too deep. People like her, Ayelet bitterly observed, were collateral damage in a war between Orthodox conservatives and progressives. She would know: her father was a rabbi.

Benni realized that he was *hommo* in early adolescence. By his Bar Mitzvah (at thirteen) he was acutely aware of the hypocrisy of being invited into a Jewish male adulthood he would never be able to fully realize. Benni figured that he would never be a true God-abiding Jew. One of the first calls he placed when he got a cell phone in the late aughts was to Azat Nefesh, the conversion therapy organization. Benni's contact told him that it was possible to change and assured him that he will change, but there was time—Benni was only fifteen at the time. So he waited. In the meantime, he was subsumed by unrequited crushes—a best friend, a classmate, a youth group counselor. During his military service, Benni contacted an Orthodox therapist rumored to help men in his situation.[3] Years later he would meet several men who had been scarred by "therapeutic" interventions—which by then he knew to be conversion therapy—and was relieved that he followed his gut and avoided "therapy." But in hindsight, Benni recognized that the episode had accelerated a crisis of faith: a trusted rabbi had referred him to the therapist, a common experience among Orthodox LGBT persons. Benni joined Kamoha, the conservative *hommo* men's organization, hoping to find solace among peers who, like him, were staring down an uncertain future. The group brought him no closer to making "this thing" go away, but he met his first boyfriend there. Meanwhile, the matter became urgent: his friends and *younger* siblings were getting married and having children.

> My sister got married at nineteen. My brother at twenty-three. Another at twenty-one. There are eight of us. . . . My friends had this running joke, "Benni was going to be the first to get married." But there's this dark secret, and I'm trying to figure out exactly how this [marriage to a woman] was going to happen. Will I be able to live in [the settlement where Benni grew up] and teach at the local school? Because that was my plan.

When we crossed paths again a few years later, Benni was in a monogamous relationship with an ex-Orthodox man (they had met through Kadag). The two were considering starting a family and said that they would send their children to Orthodox schools. A preposterous proposition a decade earlier, when Benni placed his first call to Azat Nefesh, now seemed feasible. Benni's family, too, had come around, save for a couple of siblings and their partners. His extended family was less accepting, but, Benni said, "you just have to move on."

Benni was at peace with where he had landed, although it had taken the better part of a decade to get to this point and there had been some dark times. The turning point came when Benni recognized that "this thing" was *never* going away and he had to decide how he was going to live his life, though first, he casually said, he decided that he was going to live. He was far from an outlier: suicidal ideation is alarmingly common among LGBTQ+ youth, and even more widespread among LGBT persons of faith.[4] Benni made another decision: his primary commitment was to himself—not his parents, rabbis, siblings, or community. This decision may sound like a logical route to achieving well-being, but prioritizing one's well-being belies a communally oriented Jewish ethics. Benni also knew that he would need to find an alternative Orthodox congregation, one composed of progressive Orthodox Jews who not only were "accepting" of LGBT persons but also embraced personalized forms of worship and religious commitment, questioned rabbinic authority, and challenged the primacy of the *halacha* as Orthodoxy's organizing principle (see chapter 4). It was in the context of worshipping in such a community, along with his involvement with Kadag, that Benni came to identify as an Orthodox *hommo*.

How do people like Benni come to define themselves as Orthodox *hommos*? Why do people like Ayelet feel stuck? How do Orthodox same-sex-attracted persons navigate a religious tradition that has historically denied their existence and vilified them? The narrative arc that emerges from the dozens of stories I collected and masterfully captured by the anonymous Facebook poet include recurrent waystations:[5] a shattered life plan, a chaotic aftermath, and a new life plan that entailed a reimagining of what it meant to be Orthodox. The next two chapters sketch these journeys of faith and meaning-making, beginning, in this chapter, with the dark side of this tale—shattered pictures and the desire to be normal.

Operating in the background is a social science literature that depicts these experiences predominantly through the lens of identity conflict and reconciliation. The stories recounted in these chapters suggest that while Orthodox LGBT persons experience conflict, as a conceptual framework this lens misses the dynamic, lived, and culturally and historically contingent process by which religious and sexual identities are made (and remade). To shift the emphasis from individual experiences to larger social dynamics that structure and constrain them I draw on the notion of "queer worldmaking,"[6] or the idea that making LGBTQ+ lives "livable" entails the transformation of everyday spaces, practice, and discourses.

A Shameful Secret, a Problem with No Name

The Facebook poet writes that "[to be an Orthodox *hommo* . . .] is to be afraid of yourself. To hate yourself. To be sure that under the mask there's a monster and hope that it will never be revealed." Many interviewees echoed these words, and the aggregate picture was overwhelming: being same-sex-attracted was shameful and the secret had to be managed.[7]

Regardless of gender, closet status, heterosexual marital/dating status, and age (though more common for those who came of age before the mid-2010s), study participants talked about a gnawing sense that something was different about them *and* that this difference, that as young kids and adolescents they could not name or articulate, deviated from community norms and expectations. Coming of age thus entailed managing a shameful trait that they neither wanted nor could do much about. Of this they were sure: the monster under the mask must be kept hidden. Efrat, who was in her early thirties and ex-Orthodox when we met in 2017, said she had been attracted to girls for as long as she could remember. She played "mom and mom" when she was little. In middle school, she tried to kiss a friend. In high school, she realized that she was looking at her friends "differently." She knew that "mom and mom" was a silly game and that she was going to marry a man. It would take years to acknowledge that she was attracted to women. David's experience was similar. When he realized in high school that he had a crush on a classmate, he surmised that something was wrong with him though the problem had no name. He explained his predicament this way: "Since you're a kid, you know that you're going to one day marry a woman. And then you realize that this conflicts with your reality. You also know this: the Torah is never wrong. It has answers for everything. So if you can't find a way within the Torah the problem is with you. That's what I always knew: the problem was me."

It made sense that the problem had no name: Orthodox educational institutions offer little (formal) sex education, and, until recently, representations of homosexuality and same-sex relationships were either absent or vilified, neither option providing viable role models.[8] Ayelet was familiar with the term "lesbian" but did not see how it could possibly apply to her: the only LGBT characters she knew were from television and film, foreign and detached from her reality. Since she had never met a lesbian who was religious like her, she could not identify with the concept nor fathom living as one. "It wasn't even 'how am I going to deal with this, how am I going to tell my family, my friends.' It seemed unrealistic."

Younger cohorts report more diverse experiences which can be traced to Orthodox LGBT visibility. One woman credited an award-winning television show with offering a horizon. *Srugim*, which aired from 2008 to 2012, centered on the lives of young Orthodox Jews living in Jerusalem's hip Orthodox bubble. The show offered the first instance of Orthodox LGBT visibility on prime-time television but for most Orthodox Jews the show's Orthodox bubble was as unrealistic as the notion of an Orthodox *hommo* or lesbian.

Eventually, the problem acquired a name: inverse tendencies (per Orthodox traditionalists), same-sex-attracted or struggling (terms used by some Orthodox LGBT persons), or lesbian and *hommo* (more common in activist Kadag circles—the move from same-sex-attracted, a descriptor, to an identity-based label involves developing a political consciousness). And when it did, the problem needed to be managed. For many Orthodox LGBT persons, sexual awareness was associated with confusion, pain, shame, fear, and denial, a sense of being an outsider and an interloper—always in danger of being found out and outcast. Managing these emotions consumed much of my respondents' adolescence and young adulthood. The anonymous Facebook poet reports the minutia of managed interactions: "Looking for too long at someone is to expose myself. But if I avoid looking at them they may suspect there's a reason." One man told me that he stopped going to the *miqveh*, a cleansing spiritual practice that some Orthodox men cherish, fearing erections that would give his secret away.

Denial and Repression: "I Was Closeted from Myself"

Einat told me that her life began at twenty-five. By which she meant: that was when her story began to make sense. By twenty-five, she had been a youth group counselor, served as an officer in the military, graduated from college with honors, and landed a spot in a prestigious training program. She had also experienced a string of intense adolescent crushes on girls and women and had been in a committed relationship with a woman. Although the two were involved for three years, they knew that eventually they would split up and each marry a man. Einat's ex-lover had followed that path, but for Einat dates with men went nowhere, and when the latest of these men attempted to kiss her, she "freaked out." Einat initially attributed her reaction to the fact that her boyfriend had violated the behavioral modesty code that forbids all forms of physical intimacy before marriage but eventually conceded: she was attracted to women. "I fell apart. It took me two years to climb out of a mild depression." Looking back, Einat realized that she had been "closeted from herself." Her teenage diary provided clues: "I write about a friend and our time together. But I don't use any word that might, God forbid, indicate that I was attracted to women. And then I write a prayer, to the God all mighty, asking that he send me a husband. . . . This is within five minutes of writing that other thing. You see how deep my repression was?"

When I met Leah in 2017, she was at a juncture. She had just emerged from several years of an on-again-off-again relationship with a woman, a "real, true, pure love." Her love object was engaged to be married to a man (the two never called themselves girlfriends or partners, and in her conversation with me Leah referred to this woman by name, so I will call her Michal). Coming from a very observant family, Leah had never really given much thought to her sexuality. She just knew that she was going to have to marry a "good yeshiva boy" in her early twenties, though she had a vague sense that she was not remotely interested in doing so. Marriage, she said, had struck her as "suffocating." Nevertheless, Leah kept dating men. There was no other path to adulthood.

Meeting Michal in college had sent Leah off that path. The two became fast friends, spending most of their free time together. Both were dating men and as they rejected the offering they more or less lived as a couple—they would spend some nights at Leah's home, others at Michal's (both lived with their parents). They rationalized that with no men in their lives, they diverted their attention toward women; Leah was certain she had heard this in some lesson she had attended (I heard similar stories from other women). Leah knew that "women who love women" existed, but could not see how the term "lesbian" could apply to someone like her: a religious, normative girl who had "always followed the path. I was a good girl, I was normal. I never got into trouble, I was never different in any way." Leah and Michal occasionally tried to "stop loving, to stop touching. We knew that this was wrong." At other times they would fantasize: "What if we got married? How would our parents react? Our friends? But we knew that this was something that could not happen." For years the two vacillated between denial, breakups, and fleeting moments of fantasy.

Leah pondered: was she not attracted to men, or was she was attracted to Michal? If that was the case, could she resume a normative life course? Leah was navigating these waters alone: having not yet resolved to identify as a lesbian or bisexual, she had no peer group, though she occasionally read entries on an archaic message board populated by mostly married Ultra-Orthodox women.[9] Meanwhile, there was that steady stream of invitations to friends' weddings. Her parents were growing impatient although it seems that they, too, were in denial: by that point, Leah had been introduced to or dated (and rejected) dozens of men.

Denial, repression, and their adverse outcomes are not unique to LGBTQ+ persons raised in conservative religious communities, but conservative settings do exacerbate what social scientists call minority stress.[10] Members of stigmatized minority groups face high levels of stress that can be traced to poor social support and prejudice; in the case of LGBTQ+ persons, well-being is tied to a communities' ideological positions about and policies regarding gender and sexual diversity.[11]

Queer scholars are understandably troubled by internalized homophobia, but for LGBT persons who want to remain affiliated with a faith community, adhering to its rules, norms, and logics, including those regarding gender, sexuality, and family life, makes denial and repression more likely and, in some sense, easier, the path of least resistance. Orthodox educational institutions and youth groups are overwhelmingly segregated by sex and provide little meaningful sexual education (this is beginning to change). Modesty norms, which forbid intimacy before marriage, and *niddah*, menstrual purity rules that regulate marital sexuality, facilitate denial because all forms of premarital intimacy are forbidden and marital intimacy is reduced to periods when the woman is ritually pure, approximately two weeks of every month.[12] The consequences can be dire. For years, Shlomo had a close "friend" but said that "only in hindsight did I understand that I fell in love with him . . . we didn't call it a relationship. It was very hidden. And during that time I dated girls. I got engaged, then married." It would be more than a decade until he finally recognized that he was attracted to men. The divorce, involving children, was messy. Likewise, Yaniv was certain of his sexual orientation by his early twenties. At that point, he had been in gay chat rooms for years, although he had not been in a relationship. Nevertheless, he started dating girls: "Some continued to a second or third date. Most didn't. I would say 'I'm taking it slowly' or 'I observe modesty rules.'" He did not fully appreciate the depths of his denial until his wedding night when, he said, "I was not able to perform. I didn't have an erection. . . . We didn't touch before then. But I just used modesty as a crutch. It was never really a religious thing. I just didn't want to touch her." Yaniv was emphatic that he did not deliberately mislead his ex-wife: he had simply followed the normative path.[13]

Some suppressed their sexuality altogether. Uri, who had no intimate relationship "with a man or a woman" until he was twenty-six said he erased his sexuality. Heterosexual dating sometimes brought temporary relief. Reut's teenage boyfriend "was like a security blanket. . . . I thought 'great, I have a boyfriend and I can stop fantasizing about women.' But I didn't get it until four or five years later. That just goes to show you how much I repressed it." Aaron diverted his energies: "When you take your studies seriously you have no time to think about . . . sexual things. I would start at 7:00 AM and continue until late at night. And I thought 'There, I succeeded, I'm no longer thinking about it, I'm not there.' And really, I *wasn't* there. I was in a very pure place of studying Torah. I didn't have sexual thoughts, I didn't have sexual needs." It all came crumbling down when he left the yeshiva for his military service: "When you can't study all the time, you have to live. And in real life, you have sexual needs and you fall in love." Dor, who had crushes on boys since middle school but "knew" that he was going to marry a woman, waited to fall in love with a woman. Until then, "I was just going to repress, make my sexuality disappear."

Strategic denial occasionally had a silver lining: getting through adolescence without having to manage a shameful secret. Na'ama appreciated that she "didn't grow up as a girl in the closet. I just ignored sexuality, I just didn't think about it. Nothing. I wasn't interested in men or women. So I didn't grow with a feeling that I was hiding something." Only in hindsight did her strategy become clear: she had "put this thing on hold" until she could safely deal with her attraction to women. Predictably, denial took a huge emotional toll, keeping people in a state of liminality and anxiety that often led to depression and, occasionally, to suicidal ideation.[14] Denial also produced collateral damage: heterosexual spouses and children. Eventually, denial was not feasible. Life cycle events, scorn for inability to meet social and familial expectations—or, alternatively, a suffocating marriage—along with emergent Orthodox LGBT visibility triggered a rude awakening of shattered dreams.

Shattered Pictures: The Loss of a Normative Adulthood

Dor's world came crashing down in high school: "In twelfth grade, the rabbi starts talking about relationships, home, family. And I realized, to be religious means to marry a woman. To build a normative family. But I knew that I'm not there, I can't be there. I HAVE NO FUTURE!" Uri had been in a state of deep denial until his late twenties—he rejected date after date but refused to admit his same-sex attraction. But denial was wearing him down, and once he was set on a professional path he decided to "sort out" his personal life. Working with a therapist, Uri slowly acknowledged "the truth." He began telling his close family and friends that he was gay. Doing so brought to a halt the endless stream of introductions to potential dates and nagging questions about his late singlehood, though it plunged him into a different form of distress. Uri described this period as one of "mourning. Because it is a death. There was a dream, a big dream. And it was gone."

This dream was caught up in a utopic idea about normative Ortho- dox families: a mother who wears a head covering (and possibly hates it—the practice is fraught in progressive Orthodox circles) and blesses over the candles, a father who does *Kiddush* (a ceremony that marks the beginning of the Sabbath) and takes the children to synagogue. The fam- ily might reside in a settlement or another Orthodox community. Uri likened the men and women, families and communities that populate this idealized version of Orthodox life as scenery in a play: "When you grow up in such a home, in such a community, there is this scenery all around you. What the home is supposed to look like, the family. And that rubs off on you." The tragedy was that he subscribed to this vision but (hetero)normative Orthodox adulthood was out of reach.

Einat said that "what was supposed to happen was that I was going to marry a yeshiva boy at twenty-two or so." When it became clear that the plan would not become a reality, Einat had to rethink every aspect of her adult life:

> Growing up I had this idea of what Shabbat, holidays, religious rituals, and celebrations were going to look like in my home. And then there is that point where you understand. I understood that that was not going

to happen, I would have to let go of that dream. The home that I had been seeing in front of my eyes all these years, a learned, halachic home, where religion is at the center, where children *of course* attend single-sex schools. All gone. I wasn't going to have that wedding. I wasn't going to have that Shabbat table. That school. I mourned the loss of that home.

"To be an Orthodox *hommo*," writes the anonymous Facebook poet, is "to discover how hard it is to think about the future. How it's unclear. How in the place where once there were photos of you with a wife and children, there are only black holes of uncertainty." These holes were dark and violent; respondents said that the picture of their lives had been shattered, torn, broken, irreparably, leaving in its place a frightening void, an unknown, death. Efrat tried to mend the hole: "Every once in a while I meet someone and think, wow, he seems perfect, like if you took a picture and glued him in, it could be perfect . . . but that's not real life."

In real life, the future was unclear. Benni said he did not know how he "was going to live. I always knew I was going to live with a woman and lead a religious life." Efrat was terrified: she had imagined raising a large family in the settlement where she grew up, but she would need to move away. Though "the verse" (Leviticus 18:22, which instructs, "You shall not lie with a male as with a woman, it is an abomination") cast a long shadow, the shattered picture is as much a product of cultural messages, representations, and norms as of scripture. Reut, who had been married to a man briefly a decade earlier, got married because she wanted to have children and did not see any other option. She associated self-actualization with having a large family: "They always tell you that family life and children are central." Another woman said, "Growing up in an Orthodox family you are constantly surrounded by children. Siblings and cousins and nieces and nephews. . . . This grief. How would I have children? You're probably thinking 'what's the rush she's only twenty-four.' You see, a lot of my friends, even the less devout, are married or on their way to being married. Some have kids."[15]

Making matters worse, it was impossible to escape the onslaught of heteronormativity. Ayelet felt trapped by "all this matchmaking. My aunt drives me crazy. I work in a place with lots of religious women so they're constantly trying to set me up. My parents' neighbors. Not only do I have my own difficulties, but you also have to deal with these reactions from all sides 'why aren't you getting married'? 'You need to be a little more flexible.'" Uri stopped picking up the phone "so many people were calling to offer a *shiduch* [match]. I was tired of making excuses."

On the flip side, Orthodoxy does not offer alternative visions: respondents cited lack of context, role models, education, and cultural representations. Ayelet said that Orthodox messages were so deeply ingrained that she could not even imagine "life with a woman. What would it look like? In my family, my siblings, all the families I know, in the settlement, I don't have a single example where I can look and say 'this is what I want my home to look like.'" Efrat could not imagine a future because, in her mind, the family sitting at the Shabbat table included a man and a woman. "That's what you know." A few weeks before her doomed wedding to a man, Reut was doing homework and drew a picture of her wedding. She wrote "no, never" and tore up the page. The picture depicted two women. She was divorced within a year.

Family Crises: "Have You Heard about Cohen's Daughter?"

The anonymous Facebook poet spends considerable time reflecting on family dynamics. He brings his parents into the picture early in the process, suffers no negative consequences, and is assured of unconditional love (his father continues to bless him under the *tallit*, a prayer shawl). His parents denounce conversion therapy. A man I interviewed shortly after the poem was published bitterly pointed out that compared with other family stories, the anonymous poet's entry is the stuff of fairy tales. But even fairy tales have a dark side. The poet reports sheltering his younger sibling and his extended family from "the truth" and is pained when his mom lies on his behalf.

Family dynamics are central nodes in many LGBTQ+ narratives, but Orthodoxy presents a particularly rough terrain. Many Orthodox families are large and offer a steady stream of family obligations—weddings, funerals, bris, Bar Mitzvahs, holiday gatherings, Shabbat dinners. Thus, even in the fairy-tale version, same-sex-attracted persons have to account for a large cast of characters: grandparents, aunts and great aunts, nephews and cousins. Negotiations over who to tell, when, and how unfold over a long period of time—months, years, sometimes decades.

David, who said that his family was "typical," explained the dilemma: "My mom has five siblings, my dad four. We are all very close. Coming out was . . . family drama. When to tell the grandparents? What will the Haredi [Ultra-Orthodox] faction of the family say? Maybe delay until after this cousin's wedding? My sister is getting engaged. Why ruin Passover?" LGBT persons and their family members who are aware of their same-sex attraction strain under the weight of a web of truths, partial truths, and lies. To make matters worse, some Orthodox LGBT persons seek to shelter their families from the prying eyes of the community.

Nurit's story is instructive of complex family dynamics. Nurit realized that she was attracted to women in her late teens. By her mid-twenties, she was in a settled relationship with a same-sex partner, and when we met in 2017, the two—both in their early thirties—were living just a few miles from Nurit's parents. Though they had been together for nearly a decade, Nurit's partner had never been to the family home, and Nurit does not frequent it much either. Nurit told her parents that she was attracted to women several times but was repeatedly rebuffed: "It was like talking to a wall." Nurit's mother demanded that she "change" because having a lesbian daughter "was just not okay with her." Less combative, Nurit's father had assured her that "it was just a stage."

Though she had hoped that the strained relationship would improve once she was financially independent and out of the house, familial obligations weighed her down. Nurit was expected to join her family for Shabbat dinners and holiday gatherings and to attend extended family events. When she broke up with her first girlfriend and turned to her mother for support, Nurit again hit a brick wall: "She was actually *glad* we broke up, said it was an opportunity for me to be normal." The two did not speak for months after this exchange. Nurit vowed to never bring the topic up again. But secrets have their way. Several years later, Nurit forgot a bag at her parents' home, sending her mother into a rage: the bag held a telltale sign of her life, a rainbow sticker. "My mom called me and said are you still with this nonsense? She said she thought that I was done with this. That I had changed. That she doesn't want this in her home. And I said it's not nonsense, it's my life, my identity. I tried to explain that's who I was."

Nurit occasionally comes for Shabbat dinners and other events, but she has grown distant from her family, and the relationship with her mother never recovered. She does not think it ever will. "My mother's issue isn't that it [same-sex attraction] is forbidden, so she doesn't care that some rabbi says that there's nothing in the Bible about this. Her issue is 'what will people say.' It's not normative."

Concerns about such family dynamics led many respondents to avoid the topic for as long as possible. By the time Aaron moved in with his boyfriend he was in his late twenties. His parents must suspect, he said, but he never brings up the topic and they stopped asking about marriage. The parents know that the two are roommates, "so they can't come to visit, because if they do they'll realize that we share a bed." Aaron kept putting off telling them: "My life seems fine. I'm doing well in school, working. We have a good relationship. Why introduce stress?" This was a common sentiment: wait until you are financially independent, preferably also in a stable, long-term relationship, to bring parents into the picture. A stable relationship, one interviewee explained, is a shield: "When they say, oh, you just haven't met the right man. You can say, yeah, but I *really* know."

But stalemates cannot continue forever—parents probe, secrets spill out of bags, a crisis forces a conversation. Deciding when, how, and in what order to tell family members is exhausting. Conversely, delays further entrench limbos, denial, and repression, exacting a heavy mental toll. One woman in her early twenties had been in limbo since early adolescence. She had wanted to join an LGBTQ+ youth group as a teen but lacking transportation she could not do so without her parents' support. She was literally stuck.

Family responses varied. Though rare, long-term estrangements were sufficiently common to serve as a cautionary tale. A woman in her late thirties who had a child with her same-sex partner said that her parents had never met her child, adding that she no longer cared. One man's siblings all cut him off when he came out: "I went from being the favorite uncle . . . to an outcast." Estrangements were typically temporary, as in the case of a man whose parents reached out after several years: "They didn't sit *shiva* [Jewish mourning of the dead], but it wasn't far from that." Another was thrown out of the house and didn't talk to his parents for several years, a rupture never fully mended; he still felt like he was the black sheep of the family. Determined to avoid this outcome, Yael decided to stay at home during a long and agonizing coming out process.

She is certain that her relationship with her parents would have suffered irreparable damage if she had left the house during this period.

Other parents defied expectations. Hod was so certain that his parents would ask him to leave home upon learning about his sexual orientation that he had made plans to stay with a friend for a few weeks. "My parents were sad but didn't even think about kicking me out." Einat learned that her paralyzing fear was unwarranted only after enduring years of limbo. By the time she told her family—she was in her mid-twenties by then—none were surprised. "We've known for years," one sibling said. Another was hurt that Einat did not trust her enough to talk to her earlier. A third, she bitterly recounted, responded "with lots of empathy. Like you would when someone tells you about a horrible illness."

Conditional recognition was a common experience. Yael's parents accept her new family grudgingly "because they want to have a relationship with her [child]." But they did not attend Yael's commitment ceremony. For Na'ama "it's never at the same level as my siblings, where their spouses just became part of the Shabbat table. Every step took much longer for us, and I still dread spending a whole Shabbat with them" (observant Jews do not travel on the Sabbath). Einat's family settled on "a simmering armistice": her parents refused to engage the topic.

> The result was that I came out but remained in the closet. I live my life here in [large city] and go home for the weekend and then we just don't talk about my relationship. I broke up with my girlfriend, I was hurting and crying and I couldn't talk about it. . . . Now I've been with my new girlfriend for several months. And I try to bring it up every once in a while. But every time I broach the topic they're inflicted by selective deafness. I would say "[girlfriend] and I went to this play." Nothing. Conversation over.

Such armistices and partial acceptance meant that homophobia continued to simmer, often in plain sight. At another Shabbat table, when talk turned to politics (a common occurrence), a sibling voiced support for the religious, right-wing Jewish Home party. "I said 'Just not Bennett. He's a homophobe and a person like that can't represent me.' And then my brother said 'He's not a homophobe and I happen to think he's right.' I'll never forgive him for what he said next: 'Letting them get married is like letting someone marry their dog.' And he knew [about sexual orientation]!"

Such random conversations informed decisions about coming out to families. One man decided to delay telling his parents after he heard his father rant about a pride parade. Another cried when he realized he was *hommo* because his family was "unenlightened. My father would say things like 'I prefer my son to marry an Arab woman and not be a *hommo.*'" One woman was dissuaded from coming out after an unrelated conversation with her father about upcoming elections:

> He said, "We have to pray and pay attention to these elections, because some of these parties, if they have control of the government, they'll pass laws where a man will marry a man and that's something horrible that we can't allow." My bubble burst. His homophobia was so blatant and he was so scared of this thing that I wanted to happen—proud marriages that'll make life easier for me. It would make it easier for me to think about myself as a married woman. But for that to be a reality I would need my family on board.

Family dramas—real and anticipated—resulted in an acute sense of loneliness and a sense of being stuck. At a time when they would most benefit from family (especially parents') support, young people had to hide the sources of their discontent. They faced alone the trials and tribulations of unrequited love, unsettled adolescence, precarious young adulthood, and, sometimes, sexual violence. Ayelet went through a rough patch in her early twenties—work, medical issues, and "dealing with this thing" converged but kept her parents out of the picture. "They realized that I was going through something but they didn't help. I would come home and cry. It was awful that I couldn't rely on them." Years of censoring key life events often resulted in an irreparable chasm between adult children and their parents.

And yet, there were good arguments to be made for delaying coming out; almost everyone had a story about family friction, tensions, drama. A mother who found out about her teenage son's chatroom interactions told him he was going to kill his father with grief. A father told his daughter that if she "stuck with it" (being lesbian), she would be responsible for her parents' divorce: the father anticipated that the mother would eventually come around, but he could not fathom having a lesbian for a child. One man's sister demanded that nieces and nephews not be told "to not give them ideas." (They found out anyway when they friended him on Facebook.) Another had to reassure his seventeen-year-old sister that his coming out would not imperil her own marriage prospects. Parents, siblings, and grandparents warned that they would not attend weddings, commitment ceremonies, *Brit*, and other lifecycle celebrations. Some changed their minds eventually. Others did not: "My parents had a very hard time accepting in the beginning. They just couldn't handle it. They didn't come to the wedding, but my sister came." A father who promised to protect a daughter from her siblings' wrath later changed course: a rabbi he consulted convinced him that sexual orientation can be changed and started to press her to explore therapeutic interventions.

Concerns and tensions extended far beyond the nuclear family, introducing a web of lies, record keeping, and secrets into extended family networks. One woman "knew that it would be okay with my parents. . . . But I had my extended family to worry about. My grandmother's sisters. And my aunt. And this cousin who's very observant. He always comes for holidays." Dor's parents embraced him but his grandfather's reaction was harsh:

He said "Don't bring this to my family." That's the only thing I remember. "Don't bring this to my family." The family doesn't need to know. And I said grandpa, I am your family! My mom tried to be supportive but was caught between myself and her parents. We left there in shock . . . I still cry when I recall this conversation.

Many parents insisted that their sons and daughters see a therapist, a rabbi, or a counselor for spiritual guidance and emotional support, often making clear that they hoped that this process would result in heterosexual marriage. Even when parents did not insist on reparative therapy, the line between conversion therapy and "just therapy" was fine. Einat's parents suggested she consult a therapist who might coach her on how "despite this attraction, I can still marry a man." Shlomo's parents encouraged him to seek therapy to address vague "unresolved issues," but he knew: "What they really wanted was for me to change." In some cases the pressure to seek "help" was relentless. Benni met with half a dozen rabbis at his parents' urging. One father accused his daughter of not trying hard enough, engaging her in lengthy conversations that she likened to a poor man's version of DIY conversion therapy. "To this day he says 'You haven't tried enough, you don't really know, you just connect with women emotionally but really, you could be with a man if you just tried, you're not up to the challenge.'" Hadar's parents told her that "there's a treatment for this. There are psychologists who can help. They kept saying that it's an illness that I can treat. My father said it's just like any other condition. . . . It's not something you're born with, you're not a lesbian. So if you want that will be your choice. But still, it's an illness." Hadar did not relent, nor was she upset with her parents: "I grew up in that world. With stigmas about *hommos* and lesbians. I almost feel sorry for them."

Such sympathies are quite common: many respondents were protective of their families. Reut, who felt "trapped" in her marriage and cried during sex with her husband, delayed starting divorce proceedings out of concern for her family. She knew that leaving would make her happy "and then I would think about my parents and I knew that for them it'll be death. There'll be a stain on them. It'll hurt my siblings. The entire extended family." Uri, who mourned the death of his own dream, also dreaded bursting his parents' bubble: "I knew it was going to be a rupture. They won't know how to see my world and it'll be painful. It'll be hard for them to see how I'll have children." Hadar summarized these sentiments, explaining that having a child come out was a "social crisis for parents. A crisis of the hopes that they had had for you. They support, watch you grow, and have an image of what they hope for you. And then there's the concern, what your life will be like, it'll be hard, you'll be different." The social piece—the one that Kadag and its allies try to combat—was often in the background: "As much as my parents might say, 'All we care is about your well-being,' the social pressure will be huge." "My parents are very open people. I knew that. So there wasn't fear to tell them. I never thought I'd be thrown out of the house. I just didn't want to put all this on their plate. This closet. When you come out you put your entire family in the closet." Na'ama summarized this dynamic:

I feel sorry for them. When a child comes out of the closet they have to take care of their family. There's a bit of role reversal. That's why I waited, that's why I accept that I'm the one who has to provide support. I waited to tell them until I was in my own space, stable, confident. Through my work in the community, school, friendships I've made in Kadag I'm at a place where I can be there for my family when people start gossiping, "Have you heard about Cohen's daughter?" And not cry. Because it's hard to be there for them and expect support. It's funny. You need support . . . but instead, you have to support them.

Fifteen years of Kadag activism, helped by allies such as Rabbi Benny Lau and Tehila, the parent support organization, rendered experiences of embrace and support more common (and experiences of estrangement less common). Occasionally, the Confessions Page posts a request for feel-good family stories. Readers oblige with stories that run the gamut, from a fairytale version similar to that of the anonymous poet to more somber stories of partial acceptance and alternative families. Yael Mishali, a writer, life coach, and Orthodox influencer, often shares snippets from her own family's journey with homosexuality—two sons had come out, over a decade apart—with thousands of Facebook followers. These interventions provide families with concrete tools for responding empathically but also target larger cultural narratives that make Orthodox LGBT lives unlivable. Family responses are socially conditioned; like their children, parents mourn the shattered picture and suffer repercussions of its aftermath. The best response to families' fears, one activist said, comes in the form of depictions of same-sex persons surrounded by loving families (chapter 5 describes a public outreach campaign that follows this blueprint). These images provide the reassurance that many LGBT persons seek: that they too would be embraced, rather than shunned, by their communities.

A Social Death

Einat was one of those girls who had always planned her wedding. When she realized that she was not going to have the wedding she had envisioned, she "fell apart." Same-sex weddings did not measure up, she said. "Sure, I still can call it a wedding. But it'll look different. My father won't believe it's a wedding, because for him a wedding is a religious ritual. He'll think it's a joke. And it won't be a real wedding anyway because it'll be so small. Some of my closest friends already told me they won't be able to come." Einat knew that she was really mourning not her wedding but rather what it stood for: the knowledge that she belonged.

Well-versed in the messaging and sentiments of the world they came from—and which many desperately wanted to hold on to—Orthodox LGBT persons I talked to anticipated and tried to manage social rejections. One strategy was to carefully select a supportive circle of friends to accompany them on their journey. Einat expanded her circle of friends in college but let high school friendships lapse because she knew that she could not reliably count on their support once she came out. One friend told her that she would not be able to welcome Einat to her home with a female partner.

Almost everyone had stories about such exclusions and slights reaching into every aspect and stage of life, both ritual and secular domains. Benni took anticipatory measures: "I would tell people who invited me over for Shabbat or to a wedding that I was gay, so they know who they're dealing with, if they have a problem with it." Few revoked invitations, but as he drifted away from his old life invitations naturally slowed down to a trickle. Others carefully managed information about their relationships. One man said he did not share news of his engagement to his longtime partner on social media, and he never talks about his romantic life in his Jerusalem neighborhood. One woman was still angry, years after the fact, that none of her midrasha (seminary) teachers came to her wedding. Another described a near-paralyzing fear that "everyone will look at me and talk about me and say, 'Oh, her.' And there'll be gossip. I come from a small *yishuv* (village). Everyone knows my family."

One outcome of exclusions—real and anticipated—is having to weather some of life's most momentous events alone: respondents couldn't talk about broken hearts, the miseries and humiliations of single life, crushes and new loves. They endured sexual assaults alone. The internet was a lifesaver for Efrat, who turned to friends she met in online chatrooms for advice and information. But this meant that she was excluded from her circle of friends, from "small talk, excitement, bonding over things with girlfriends." Ayelet was upset that her romantic life was invisible:

I was hanging out with friends and one of them said, "Wow, I haven't dated anyone in seven months." And later another said, "Oh it was so hard to hear her pain." And I said "Well that's not much different than me" but she said "It's totally different." And I said "You don't even have anyone for me to meet. And I also haven't been dating." I wish they would suggest someone. But all they have to introduce me are men. I don't want a man.

Respondents shared stories of being kicked out of their high school or higher yeshivas and feeling unwelcome in synagogue. Rejections were often subtle. David was not told to leave his yeshiva "but rabbi X made it very clear I should leave." One young woman's acceptance to a prestigious midrasha was effectively rescinded when she shared with its leaders that she was questioning her sexual orientation. When Na'ama and her partner had moved from a Tel Aviv suburb, where their family never thought twice about attending the local synagogue, to a town in the periphery, they "thought people were going to stone us." One man, rumored to be *hommo*, was honored with an *aliya* at his childhood synagogue (the calling of a member of a congregation to read a portion of the Torah and recite blessings; Orthodox conservatives argue that as transgressors *hommos* are ineligible for this honor). His brother overheard a fellow congregant cast doubt on whether *hommos* deserved this honor. Another man was genuinely surprised when he was called for an aliya in similar circumstances: "I wouldn't have believed this ten years ago, being called to aliya in my childhood synagogue. With my husband present!"

These slights, exclusions, invisibilities, and erasures amounted to a message that Orthodox LGBT persons do not belong—a social death per a disaffiliated *hommo* in his thirties: "the Orthodox world . . . gives you a community. You're born into a community, you grow into a community, synagogue, friends in your youth group, yeshiva. . . . And you need this community at every step. But to be Orthodox means to marry a woman. To build a normative family." Little wonder that many experienced a chasm between their religious and social, emotional, and sexual lives.

Theological Angst

Orthodoxy's purported incompatibility with same-sex attraction comes up frequently on the anonymous Confessions Page. One young man writes, "No matter how hard I try to convince myself that it is pure love and that there's nothing wrong with it, I still feel blemished, degenerate, uncouth."[16] Another writes that his attraction to men makes him feel "disgusting, like a cheat, I can't go into synagogue." Like LGBTQ+ persons of faith from other religious traditions, many same-sex-attracted Orthodox Jews pass through a period where they are convinced that their sexuality, romantic desires, practices, attachments, and realities are incompatible with Jewish teachings, theology, doctrine, and norms, regardless of whether they act on their sexual desires. This is especially true for men who say that they cannot reconcile Orthodoxy with male-on-male sex. Many view "the verse" (Leviticus 18:22, which includes the abomination reference) as the main source of conflict. But the turmoil can be traced to the broader cosmology of Jewish life.

The anonymous Facebook poet traces his burdens to daily Jewish life. In one example, a rabbi's routine talk about the weekly portion of the Bible (*dvar torah*), leaves him "breathless, as if you were punched in the gut." Experiences such as this amount to feeling that "slowly, against your will, you are being pushed out of the religion. Because everything they say, they're not saying to you. Because if they knew, they wouldn't be willing to talk to you."

Leah's disconnect implicated Judaism's heteronormative social order in its entirety: "When I open the Bible and read verses like 'and thy desire shall be to thy husband, and he shall rule over thee' there's no place for me because there's no recognition of other kinds of relationships. I feel completely out of the picture, I can't be connected. This conflict is too big." (The reference is to Genesis 3:16.) Leah's conflict was less about identity and more about a stinging sense of exclusion: "I love the religion. I love the practice, I like the feeling." Staying connected, she said, hinged on "rising above the anger. Because you are very angry about all these things that say that I'm out of the camp. I don't belong."

Leah experienced this exclusion vis-à-vis Jewish philosophy, ethics, and values, not just in reference to specific verses or even scripture. Leah thought that heterosexual marriage would suffocate her but knew that she could experience joy in a relationship with a woman. In her reading, the Jewish sources do not ban such relationships.[17] But a lack of an outright halachic ban did not imply permission to do so. The sticking point was an amorphous Jewish value system that had taught her that "there are things that are bigger than me, it matters less whether I fulfill my dreams, whether I am happy." The goal of intimate relationships, she had been taught, "is not happiness, finding joy in not being alone, or growing old together but in starting a family." Partnering with a woman defied the Jewish value system because it was egoistic: "I'm choosing me. Because it's either that or choosing all the rest, I can't have both. There are my parents. They won't be able to leave the house because of the shame I'll bring upon them if I come out. And there are these kids of two moms who encounter an Orthodox world but don't really belong to it."

Leah chose her own happiness, but she was not sure whether she could reconcile it with Orthodoxy—doing so would require embracing a new vision of Orthodoxy, one that prioritized the well-being, needs, and fulfillment of the faithful, and she was not ready to make this leap. Leah still held on, for now, but in many cases, this struggle resulted in a crisis of faith.

A Crisis of Faith

At his suggestion, I meet David in a trendy gastropub in one of Tel Aviv's vivacious gayborhoods. He lives right across the street. His job, at a high-tech company, is a short bike ride away. The inclusive Yachad congregation is within walking distance, but he does not frequent it often these days. Handsome, fit, gregarious, David has made a comfortable life here. During our conversation, several friends stop by to say hello. He knows all the cool parties, though recently he has slowed down a bit because he is in a monogamous relationship. David was still trying to figure out what that means for two gay men. David implores me to imagine him as a yeshiva boy, which he had been until a few years earlier. When I admit that it's hard to do so he pulls out his phone to show me photos. The photos were not offered for their shock value but rather to illustrate who David "really is"—or sought to be. Throughout high school, David had been in touch with Azat Nefesh, hoping to be "normal," to change, "to be like everyone else." His failure landed him in this life. David hates the party scene. He is here, in this neighborhood, in this restaurant, in this relationship, and in this life because Orthodoxy pushed him out. It gave him no other option.

David's friends and family had been supportive for the most part. David lays the blame for his disaffiliation with rabbinic authorities who rendered him invisible, an undesired interloper. The Jewish legal system—the halacha—comprises elaborate rules that organize and regulate every aspect of life, including intimate relationships. On same-sex relationships, however, it has little to say beyond interpreting the notorious Leviticus abomination clause to forbid all forms of same-sex desires, intimacies, and relationships (see chapter 4). Upset that the halacha has "nothing for *hommos*," David surmised that Orthodoxy had effectively expelled same-sex-attracted Jews. His faith has remained strong, but he no longer feels part of the community and doubts he ever will. Hence his new life in Tel Aviv.

Na'ama and her wife also felt excluded. The two were committed to building a Jewish home, one grounded in Jewish laws and customs. They sought guidance regarding modesty and sexual intimacy from rabbis known to be allies, but these rabbis had "no answers for us. I want to live a halachic life. It's like I don't exist." The two, with the support of a circle of learned friends from Kadag and beyond, have begun charting their own path.

Unlike social deaths and exclusions, which could be managed via expanding one's social networks, crises of faith, grounded in Judaism's core philosophical roots, interpretive dynamics, and authority structures, were more difficult to contain. A woman in her mid-twenties said she disaffiliated because she worried that her future children would be confused by a home life inconsistent with theological dictates. Some respondents, mainly though not exclusively men, believed that same-sex desire, sexual relations, or relationships were inherently and irreparably incompatible with Orthodox values, traditions, and teachings. This was David's stance, although he ultimately laid blame for his crisis of faith on rabbis. Like a growing contingency of LGBT Orthodox persons, David believed that by taking a series of brave interpretive steps, rabbis *could* create a truly inclusive halachic space within Orthodoxy (in October 2020 Rabbi Benny Lau charted a halachic framework for monogamous same-sex relationships).[18] For people like David, the crisis of faith amounted to a crisis of authority. He disaffiliated because he refused to accept that he was a "sinner," but he maintains a personal faith and his own set of practices. David, who resented the rabbis' message that he was "dirtying the world," who could no longer set foot in a synagogue, excused himself when his food arrived: he had to wash his hands and say a blessing before he could begin eating in that (non-Kosher) Tel Aviv gastropub. Other crises of faith went directly to the source, faulting God for his misguided creation. One man suggested that remaining Orthodox amounts to sullying the religion. "Call it internalized homophobia if you like, I know it sounds awful, but I felt that I couldn't continue living like this [having sex with men] and calling myself Orthodox." This man could not forgive God "for creating me this way."

Leah, David, and many others were angry at God, often drawing on imagery and language from the Jewish tradition to express this anger. Why did God create an ugly vessel? (The reference here is to a Talmudic story in which an ugly man challenges his critics to blame "the craftsman" who created him.)[19] Why did he banish them to a desert? Leave them "outside the camp"? Remaining religious was contingent upon finding satisfactory answers to such questions or finding peace with an unsettled score (the next chapter elaborates on theological answers my respondents found). Leah did not know she had it in her in the long term: "My relationship with God has gone through ups and downs in the past few years. These days I'm pretty upset with him. I haven't left yet. I'm not oblivious to him. I'm still very religious and very connected. But angry."

For some, then, the crisis of faith was focused on a God who rendered the faithful as social outcasts, theologically invisible subjects and constitutionally barred from fulfilling one of Judaism's central *mitzvot*: having children. For others, the crisis of faith is more of a social crisis: the social death of those banished from the community. Ayelet said that for many years she had been "angry. Livid. At God. How did he screw me over like this? How did he bring me into the world like this? If at least he'd brought me into a secular family." Others, like David, blamed not God but religious authorities and Orthodox communities.

Either way, it is easy to see why many lesbians and *hommos* disaffiliated (or considered disaffiliating) from Orthodoxy, even if their faith remained strong. What they describe is not only, and definitely not exclusively, an internal identity crisis but rather a social one: there was literally no way for them to remain Orthodox. Ayelet said that "life would be much easier if I would become ex-Orthodox, if I were willing to give up my religious world. But I felt that I couldn't give it up. I really, really believe. I belong to the religious world, no matter what. But I also feel that I can't be with men." For Leah, the tension seemed unsurmountable. Fulfilling her desires hinged on developing a new vision of Orthodoxy, one that prioritized the well-being, needs, and fulfillment of the faithful. Leah was not ready to embrace this new—shall we say queer?—vision of Orthodoxy.

Others, as we will see in the next chapter, were prepared to do so. Thus, while crises of faith resulted in the loss of faith, disaffiliation, or both, they also bred creative, productive interventions—what queer scholars (if they cared to pay attention to religion) would call queer worldmaking. Surveying the crises of faith he witnessed around him, one man said, "You can become 'weaker' in your faith. I'm not judging! Or: You can come out stronger. . . . Realize that there's another way to be Orthodox. That's what happened to me, that's what I've been working to get people to recognize." Chapter 3 expands on how the crisis turns productive, while chapters 4 and 5 consider the vibrant movement intent on making space for the banished vis-à-vis their communities of faith and God. What should be readily clear is that these were not identity crises that individuals can resolve on their own. Likewise, other responses to these crises—conversion therapy, celibacy, heterosexual dating, and marriage, often described in the literature as alternatives to identity reconciliation—are better viewed as part of a quest "to be normal," milestones in the journey from shattered dreams to forging a new path forward.

The Quest to Be Normal: "I Just Wanted to Make This Thing Go Away"

The anonymous Facebook poet writes that he prays every day "to be different. To be normal." He reports how he is always making "plans. How to get rid of it. What to do about it. How to solve this problem without anyone finding out, so that the day will come and it won't have any impact on my life." His experience is painfully common.

Dor knew that one day he would be "normal." His crushes on boys, which began in middle school, did not weaken his conviction that he was going to marry a woman because, he reasoned, his attraction to boys was a life stage. That's what his rabbi told him when he shared his fears with him in eight grade: "Things can change until age twenty. And that's just what I believed. I thought it'll pass, it'll be okay, I'll grow up and get married." Reut had a crush on a girlfriend at school. When the pressure became too much to bear, she confided in a teacher whose response bought her several years of relative solace: "She said not to worry, that it happens a lot to young girls like us. We are separated from boys, the hormones kick in. She told me it would pass once I start dating. I'll fall in love and somehow I will want to touch him. It would happen after the wedding."

From the perspective of an adolescent or young adult Orthodox person, the idea that same-sex attraction was fleeting is not preposterous. In some ways, this stance, espoused by many Orthodox conservatives, is much better aligned with critical theories of sexuality than Rabbi Aviner's blanket denial of yesteryear ("there is no such thing as an Orthodox homosexual"). Recall that Orthodox schools provide poor sexual education. Add to the mix messages that same-sex desires are sinful, shameful, and deviant or, conversely, that sexual "confusion" was both common and typically resolved by young adulthood; the emphasis on marriage and children as the exclusive path to authentic Orthodox adulthood, the basis of Orthodox communities, and the embodiment of one's religiosity; and the lack of public visibility of Orthodox same-sex couples and families, and these narratives make sense. Dor summed it up: "The message is that this is a passing phase, like any other rebellious streak that a teenager might have, and the question is how to change it quickly so you don't suffer too much."

Though Dor and his peers believed their rabbis and teachers (and the occasional parent) who said that change was likely, for the most part, they also recognized that "this thing" may not just pass on its own. Many respondents engaged in a project of transformation, willing to invest time, energy, money, and devotion. "Working at it" sometimes meant turning to God. Respondents reported that they prayed and pleaded, adding, for good measure, a more stringent observance. For a couple of years, David pursued a regimen of intense study, prayer, fasts, to no avail. God's refusal to make him "normal" ultimately accelerated his crisis of faith.

But "working at it" was mostly an earthly project. At its most benign, this project targeted gendered traits. Told by his father that he should man up, Benni tabled his love of theater and singing for several years. Einat, who blamed her lesbianism on "defective femininity," ceased playing sports and began wearing dresses and jewelry reasoning that enacting normative femininity would eventually transform her sexual orientation. Both failed at this normalizing project, conceding defeat only after it had consumed their adolescence and early adulthood.

The most common normalizing intervention was dating heterosexually, a near-universal experience ranging from a string of failed first dates to decades-long marriages. In some cases, dating was a conscious decision that operationalized rabbis', teachers', and parents' advice: "You will change when you meet the right person." Benni said he took the classic Orthodox approach: "Date, date, date intensively until you get married." Some rejected a long string of suitors, reasoning that they had "high standards." In other cases, heterosexual dating was undertaken as a probe. Na'ama wanted "to be sure before I committed myself as a lesbian. So I broke up with my girlfriend and decided I was going to date men for a while." Ayelet concluded that she was indeed attracted to women exclusively, but not before she dated several men, mired herself in a web of lies, and generally felt that she had acted egoistically.

In many cases, same-sex attraction was so repressed that dating a member of the other sex was not much of a decision but rather a religious duty. One man described this journey from confused adolescence to a *hommo* man who made a conscious decision to marry a woman whom he had told about his attraction:

> As you grow older you realize that you're attracted to men. You realize that you're *hommo*. But you don't know what this means, the implications. By high school, you realize that there are implications. By twelfth grade I was asking, "What am I going to do with this thing?" You try to put aside the complexity. And just focus on your *yetzer* [per Jewish teachings, the evil impulse or inclination with which humans are endowed]. . . . At the yeshiva you are *expected* to make decisions: "How are you going to live

your life?" I got to know myself and my sexuality. I became very religious. I studied the topic. And I decided that I was going to marry a woman.

Once ubiquitous among the same-sex-attracted, such mixed-orientation marriages are still common in faith communities. Such marriages often fail because they are fragile to begin with, although some couples can arrive at relative stability with pastoral and professional support.[20] Among Orthodox Jews, support for such marriages was unshakeable until the turn of the twenty-first century, but two decades of Kadag activism has changed the landscape. Mixed orientation marriages have come under intense public focus in recent years, with a documentary film, long-form journalist investigations, a book, and personal testimonials unraveling the dramas and collateral damage to unwitting spouses and children. Thus, while most Orthodox traditionalists still promote this route (some propose celibacy as a viable alternative),[21] Kadag-allied rabbis no longer support them. Allies trace their change of hearts to their exposure to the pain and suffering of all parties involved in such marriages.[22]

But the vast majority of same-sex-attracted Orthodox Jews still pursue this path of least resistance. Even in my sample, skewed toward those who identify as lesbians and *hommos* (a label that implies a political consciousness, as opposed to the more descriptive label same-sex-attracted), heterosexual dating was ubiquitous and marriage not uncommon. As noted, contextualized in Orthodoxy's messaging about normative gender, sexuality, families, and adulthood, lesbians' and *hommos'* decision to date and marry heterosexually makes sense. Respondents genuinely believed the message that "this" could change, that they hadn't found "the one," or that forming a normative family was a Jewish duty. Leah, brokenhearted, still closeted, and with several-dozen failed dates in her history, nevertheless held off "making a big announcement" (coming out) because there was still a "voice in the background saying 'you may be able to join sexually with a man.'" Benni genuinely thought that if he tried hard enough, dated enough girls, "things will change." He also reasoned that a large enough dating resume would help convince his parents, "the world," and, ultimately, himself that "it won't change." Yaniv, who had been previously married to a woman said he was not trying to make excuses, but insisted that "what everyone misses when they point fingers at us is the level of repression. Yes, some men get married knowing that they are attracted to men. But in my experience, many of us aren't really aware. For me, denial was so deep that it wasn't that I didn't tell my wife, that I hid something from her. I didn't even know myself until much later! I didn't understand. How would I?"

In other cases, the normalizing project also involved therapeutic interventions in the form of conversion therapy, though I offer the following observations with a caveat: this volume cannot do justice to this topic. I suggest, however, that there is no clear boundary between those who are subjected to such interventions and those who are not. Rather than thinking about individual interventions, it might be helpful to think about how talk of conversion therapy impacts LGBT persons of faith who reside in a homophobic culture that promotes it.

While Orthodox organizations in Israel display an array of homegrown organizations such as the now-defunct Azat Nefesh and Bikdusha or imported programs such as "Journey into Manhood," their rhetoric and strategies track those of Evangelical Christian organizations in the United States, suggesting cross-fertilization. Proponents of conversion therapy claim that interventions can help clients explore and overcome sexual fluidity or that clients are merely "confused" or are "struggling" with same-sex attractions; many same-sex-attracted persons use this terminology to discuss their experiences and their identities ("struggling" rather than *hommo* or lesbian). The scholarship does not support claims of successful therapeutic interventions, finding instead that conversion therapy is ineffective and likely to cause significant harm.[23]

Still, over half of the men and a third of the women I talked to sought some type of intervention intended to change their orientation (more sought therapeutic assistance to help them navigate and negotiate their lives as same-sex-attracted). They turned to licensed therapists, rabbis, and a variety of organizations, often at the referral of a rabbi (some yeshivas have funds available to support such interventions). The treatments and interventions varied in their intensity—some had only a couple of conversations by phone, others sustained years-long therapy. None achieved the desired outcome in terms of changed orientation. My sample is self-selected, but these findings are consistent with those of other research.

Conversion therapy has long been a focal point of LGBTQ+ activism in Israel, and Kadag activists have played a central role in battles to ban such practices.[24] Activists point out rightfully that heterosexual marriage, touted by proponents of conversion therapy as evidence of its efficacy, is hardly a measure of therapeutic success, since many graduates of these interventions report a diminished sexual desire, while others continue to seek sexual liaisons on dating apps. Many of these marriages end in divorces several years or decades down the line.[25] My interlocutors were emphatic: conversion therapy, at best, does not work but more commonly leaves its subjects scarred. Some spoke of irreparable emotional damage, unable to commit themselves romantically. Others had been left with a stunted sexual drive. Even those who escaped mostly unscathed did not mince words: conversion therapy was evil.

The efficacy of therapeutic interventions is a key focal point in contemporary debates about LGBTQ+ lives. One result of these debates is that they have forced activists, along with their allies and foes, to draw clear lines in the sand. Orthodox conservatives now tout dynamic theories of sexuality, while progressives insist on a born/made that way theory of sexuality that is grounded in the Jewish tradition (often drawing on the Talmudic story about the ugly man who challenges his critics to blame "the craftsman who made me"). Ironically, a backlash against stricter forms of conversion therapy led Orthodox conservatives to accept more fluid and dynamic theories of sexuality and "softer" versions of conversion therapy. The most dominant forms of interventions practiced today are grounded in the idea that most people are rated as neither Kinsey 0 (exclusively heterosexual) nor Kinsey 6 (exclusively homosexual), and can therefore achieve and be content in heterosexual marriages if their other-sex attraction can be encouraged to prevail. One man in his thirties was pondering "giving it a try because I'm still trying to understand where it came from. And what it means about me. . . . In the Orthodox community, there's this idea that sexual orientation is not something inborn, that it can change. It's a series of events that led you to be this way. Plus, many of us aren't fully one way or the other. So it might be worth a try." Reut, who had been married to a man in her twenties and saw a therapist to address an ensuing depression, came to think of herself, with the therapist's assistance, as a fluid bisexual: "I couldn't accept that I was a lesbian, so I concluded that I was 70/30. And I thought, with 30 percent I can live with a man." Leah, whose girlfriend left her for a man, reasoned that if her ex-girlfriend "could date men, why can't I? I'm not even repulsed by men. It's just that I've never really connected with a man. And I was still young." Ruti took the idea of fluidity to its logical conclusion: when she concluded that she was attracted to both men and women, she decided to choose to partner with a man, seeing it as the easy option.

While dynamic theories of sexuality better reflect the realities of human attraction, what has not changed is the idea that living one's same-sex sexual desires is inherently and irreparably immoral. Thus, despite growing Orthodox LGBT visibility, the desire to be "normal" has not lost its allure. At the same time, as testimonials from the field and research continue to document conversion therapy's harms, allied rabbis are slowly embracing less dynamic theories of sexuality. In the past couple of years, several longtime rabbinic allies have publicly voiced their support for committed, long-term, same-sex monogamous relationships. But there is a caveat: this support is reserved solely for those whose same-sex attraction is both stable and exclusive.

Having worked through denial, having processed Orthodox messages about sexual malleability, and having put immense efforts into changing their orientation, many emerged from their quest to be normal with a stark realization that "this thing" was not going to change. To be an Orthodox *hommo*, writes the anonymous poet, is "to understand one day that it won't disappear. That maybe it's something that will remain unchanged."

Moving Forward: "I Chose Not to Live My Life as a Problem"

Netta gathered the courage to divorce her husband of over twenty years, with whom she had several children, after bouts of mild depression. Several years of therapy helped her identify the source of her discontent: her marriage was suffocating her, she felt an emptiness. Netta divorced and started over in a new town. The relationship with some of her children was fraught, but the price was worth it. She could finally breathe. It helped that by the time she took this step she knew that she was not alone: early in her divorce process, she connected with Bat Kol.

Reut, who had been assured by rabbis and teachers that she will change once she is married, could have well ended up in the same boat. Reut experienced married life as traumatic. Month after month, she pretended to enjoy sex with a husband, whom she felt she was failing and betraying despite being honest with him. The pair had consulted several conservative rabbis who are known for their work with same-sex-attracted persons but none of their suggestions worked.[26] Reut felt that she was locking herself up in a prison. She became depressed and anxious, and a psychiatrist prescribed medication. "That's what I took upon myself: to live with a man and take pills that will help me not screw up." But eventually she concluded that the "70/30" theory was a lie, got divorced, and came out of the closet. Two episodes helped push her toward a decision. A friend's giddiness in anticipation of her wedding drove home to Reut the extent of her misery. Then, she ran into an acquaintance who was rumored to be a lesbian. In the casual conversation that unfolded—the two had caught each other up on their lives since they parted ways in high school—the acquaintance shared that she was involved with Bat Kol. Reut, who had been lurking in an anonymous chat room for years but had never met an Orthodox lesbian, suddenly faced a real-life alternative. Three years later she caught me up: she was off antidepressants, no longer considered herself Orthodox, and had recently ended a long-term relationship with a woman. She thought that she was now falling in love with a man but had made peace with this twist of fate: involvement with LGBTQ+ spaces had led her to accept that sexuality really did exist on a spectrum.

Benni's epiphany that he was losing the battle with same-sex desire came very slowly and then all at once. Benni had spent his late teens and early twenties willing for change, to no avail. For years, Benni had put thinking about his sexuality on hold: he just couldn't deal with it. Meanwhile, he was dating women and grew increasingly miserable. "Then I was twenty-three, twenty-four, almost twenty-five, and I thought, '*this has to STOP!*'" The final push came after a conversation with a heterosexually married man about his life as a closeted gay man. A rabbi Benni consulted had made the connection, thinking that Benni would benefit from hearing firsthand from someone who had weathered the storm and "successfully" settled down. Benni's takeaway was starkly different from the one the rabbi had in mind: "Listening to his story, how he's happy with a woman etc. etc.—I believed him!—made it clear to me what I *didn't* want. I don't want to live with a woman. I don't want to whisper that I'm *hommo* for the rest of my life. And I realized: I did not have to suffer."

Einat's unraveling began when a boyfriend tried to kiss her. The floodgates let loose; in short order, she broke up with him, came out to her family, and opened accounts on all the online dating apps marking herself as a woman seeking a woman. Hod had returned home from the *n*th date with a "lovely young woman" and could no longer bear the lies. He felt like a failure. Disgusted with himself, he stared reality in the face: "It has not changed, I was not going to change. I had dated women and concluded that I was not capable of marrying a woman. What are you going to do about it?" Na'ama, who initially thought that she had just "fallen" into same-sex relationships, was quite methodical about her inquiry. She broke up with her girlfriend and began dating men until she came full circle to acknowledge that she was exclusively attracted to women. She, too, forced the question: "Okay, so I can't live with a man. What are my options?"

Nir described a showdown with his parents when a cousin invited him to his wedding. When he informed his parents that he would be attending with his husband, his "mom said, 'What do you mean he's coming? I've never met him.' And I said, 'Mom, this is my life. I'm moving on. You can be a part of it, or not. But there's a limit to how much I'm willing to live for you. That's the reality, I'm an adult.' We were already married by then!"

A longtime activist who was familiar with such stories said that she became determined to move forward when she realized how many around her were miserable. She had met "people who are stuck in the closet for years. And I saw how it screws them up, they can't lead a normal life. I'm not judging. But still. They're in their thirties, have no job, living with their parents. That's not what I want." The Confessions Page is full of such narratives, of people who ached to move on yet were immobilized by fear, unable to imagine what life might look like if they were to be true to their desires.

Though they differed on their triggers, their pathways, and where they landed, what unites these stories is that their protagonists reached a decision point at which they stared reality in the face and consciously deliberated "what are you going to do about it." Taking stock of their options, some decided that their only choice to move forward, toward a fulfilling life, while preserving their emotional and psychological well-being, was to honor their sexual, romantic needs and desires even before they figured out what that would entail. "I decided I was not going to live my life as a problem." "I was not going to be tortured." "I don't have to suffer." "I didn't doubt my sexual identity. It was more about how I want to live."

These decisions, it must be emphasized, do not pertain to the *state* of being same-sex-attracted. This, they insisted, was neither a choice nor a decision—to the contrary, the entire premise was that one's sexual orientation was *not* a matter of choice—as noted, the vast majority of my respondents subscribed to the "born this way" (or, rather, God made me this way) theory of sexuality (I return to this in the next chapter). Rather, the breakthrough was grounded in the realization that given this reality, one needed to make a decision about how to live. "You can't choose how you're born," Benni said, "but you can choose if you want to face yourself or stay buried forever."

There are, of course, excellent psychological reasons to move forward, to elevate happiness, and to reject suffering. But for Orthodox Jewish persons these decisions hinged not just on making sound psychological choices but also on making sense of them in the context of a Jewish cosmology in which the alleviation of suffering or the promotion of personal happiness is not necessarily the most important value, where the word of God and his interpreters carry weight, and which (still) encouraged conversion therapy, celibacy, and mixed-orientation marriages over assuming homosexuality as a social label. How they do so is the subject of the next chapter.

So, What's It Like to Be an Orthodox *Hommo*?

This chapter sketched the darker side of tales same-sex-attracted Orthodox Jews shared with me. At some point in adolescence, they became aware of sexual desires and romantic attractions that belied messages about normative Orthodox adulthood. Perplexed, the vast majority repressed and denied their desires. They sought to be normal. Some fell into a depression, experienced suicidal ideation, sought therapeutic interventions, and took pills. They hid the monster under the mask and hoped for the best. The journey reached a violent crescendo: a torn, shredded, broken picture, image, vision—a life plan that fell apart with no immediate alternative to take its place. This is a narrative arc, a journey across waystations, not a linear story of progression across stages. Travelers may skip waystations or visit them more than once. Others get stuck. Either way, to be an Orthodox same-sex-attracted person is to deal with a shameful secret; to spend precious years in denial and repression; to endure a shattered life plan without clear alternatives; to experience familial dramas, social deaths, and crises of faith; to spend years seeking to be normal. Here is what it's not: a raging, deliberate rebellion intended to challenge and dismantle traditional ways of life (per Orthodox traditionalists), nor an experience that can be summed up as an identity conflict that one may reconcile on one's own accord (per social science scholarship). Rather, these experiences amount to what queer scholars term unlivable lives, which are shaped by larger social structures, institutions, and dynamics. Orthodox LGBT lives were rendered unlivable by communal messages, expectations, and structures that offered only one path to Jewish adulthood (being straight and cisgender). Little wonder respondents reported feeling stuck, anxious, lonely, and depressed.

But the picture is not *all* bleak, and these are not the *only* stories same-sex-attracted Orthodox Jews tell. The next chapter recounts how the anonymous poet and his peers get unstuck and move forward. What distinguishes the narrators of the stories I tell here—for the time being, they are outliers—is that when they hit that wall, when they realized that they were stuck, that they couldn't live 70/30, that "this thing" was not going to change, they decided to figure out how to be Orthodox and gay, thereby creating a blueprint for Orthodox LGBT livable lives. As the next chapter reveals, the antidote to harmful Orthodox messages about same-sex attraction and gay identities draws from the same fount of Orthodox scripture, wisdom, tradition, and philosophy, a thoroughly local project of queer worldmaking.

3

Orthodox Queer Worldmaking

Everyday Theologies of Life, Sex, and God

Your whole life, you know what it means to be Orthodox.
Then, you find out that you're a lesbian and you need a new story.
—Efrat

Around Hanukkah, Jewish Facebook feeds fill up with photos of family, friends, and other groups who gather to light menorahs and eat oil-drenched latkes and *sufganiot* (doughnuts). In December 2020 a photo of one such get-together went viral in Kadag and progressive Orthodox circles.[1] The accompanying caption read:

> The sixth night of Hanukkah, six families.
> The Proud Orthodox community in Ariel. We will multiply and spread out!
> Lighting a Hanukah candle and publicizing the miracle at our place.
> #weareheretostay

Hanukkah commemorates the recovery of Jerusalem by a group of Jewish warriors whose second-century BCE uprising against the Greeks led to the rededication of the Temple. The holiday's underlying themes of nationalism, rebellion, and internecine struggle (the rebels' initial targets were assimilating Jews) and, especially, the miracle of Hanukkah—that a small bottle of oil was able to keep the lights on in the Temple for eight nights—make it a natural site to celebrate Jewish rootedness, perseverance, and devotion. Jews are called to not only commemorate the miracle but also publicize it—hence the tradition of displaying menorahs on windowsills. The photo in question depicted people, not menorahs or candles, and the Jewish forbearers referenced were not Hanukkah's Jewish heroes (the Maccabim) but rather Jewish slaves who had spread out and multiplied under their Egyptian oppressors' thumb. The caption refers to Exodus 1:12: "But the more they oppressed them, the more they multiplied and the more they spread out, so that they dreaded the sons of Israel." By replacing the Bible's third-person "they" with the first person "we," the post asserts the existence, visibility, persistence, and perseverance of a group of Jews that until recently had been shunned and silenced. These Jews had already multiplied: there were almost a dozen children in the photo.

Insisting that Orthodox LGBT persons are "here to stay" alludes to a harsh reality: disaffiliation rates among LGBT persons of faith are high. Conversely, LGBT persons of faith who do not disaffiliate often suffer adverse outcomes including suicidal ideation and depression.[2] These outcomes are often attributed to unresolved identity conflicts, but as noted in the previous chapter, such explanations overlook social dynamics.[3] Rather than asking how LGBT persons of faith navigate—and potentially resolve—tensions between their religious tradition and their sexual identity, this chapter considers how they mobilize religion in their search for, in the words of the opening excerpt, "a new story."

There was another twist in the announcement that LGBT Orthodox Jews were "here to stay." Ariel is among the largest settlements in the West Bank, a vibrant college town that offers middle-class families affordable housing within driving distance of the country's major cities. While Orthodox Israeli Jews are hardly alone in supporting the settlement project (and some Orthodox Jews are critical of this vision of Zionism), nationalism and religiosity are deeply intertwined, and ancestral claims to the land are grounded in biblical stories and other scripture.

The Hanukkah photo—and the story of Orthodox authenticity and belonging it tells—captures the essence of this chapter: Jewish traditions, symbols, sensibilities, language, and mythologies, intertwined with nationalist sentiments, are central to Orthodox LGBT persons' attempts to reframe, reimagine, and rewrite stories of self and community.[4] Undoubtedly, Orthodox LGBT persons articulate new narratives of self to achieve psychological well-being (in social scientists' parlance) or livable lives (queer theory's take). But the personal is famously political: narratives of self are constructed through dialogue with social scripts. These new narratives of self thus conjure an alternative vision of Orthodoxy, one that emerges from within the tradition itself. Religion, in this reading, is not *only* an obstacle to overcome but also a source of knowledge, empowerment, and self-understanding.

Rewriting the Script: How to Be Orthodox and Gay?

An anonymous seventeen-year-old asks for advice on the Confessions Page. Is it really possible to be Orthodox and lesbian? A respondent assured her,

> You can have a good life, and if you want, it can be utterly boring and conventional, even if you'll have a woman (in hair covering and skirt) instead of a man with *kippa* and *zizit* [tassels, or fringes on clothing, part of a ritual garment worn by observant men] at your side. There are accepting religious congregations, there are [religious authorities] who say that there's no prohibition against a same-sex relationship for women (I'm waiting for them to say this publicly . . .), and a lesbian family is entirely possible. This is my reality. You don't have to choose, you don't have to be ripped [from Judaism]. You can and you should build a good religious life from the challenge that God has given us.

Questions whether "one can be" Orthodox and gay reverberated across my data, with some participants questioning their very right to exist, others rejecting the question as moot in the face of their own lived realities. What stumped them was how to articulate this reality. A *hommo* man who had recently become engaged to his longtime partner said that when he was younger it had never occurred to him not to be religious, but he just did not know what life would be like because he didn't know any Orthodox LGBT Jews at the time. "But taking off the kippa? That didn't even cross my mind." The key to keeping the kippa on (a metaphor for remaining religious), he said, was to make conscious decisions about concrete aspects of his life, such as where to live, how to get married, whether and how to start a family, how to interact with his mostly religious family, where to seek schooling for his future children, and how to practice Judaism. Each of these arenas entailed negotiating with Judaism's heteronormative life scripts.

The new stories and scripts that he and others devised cover a broad terrain, and what follows barely scratches the surface. I highlight choices in two arenas, lifecycle events and Jewish ritual life, to demonstrate how Orthodox LGBT persons "build a good religious life from the challenge." There is a subtext that I pick up later up in the chapter: belying conventional wisdom that traces social change to public protest and collective mobilization, rescripting of (Orthodox) everyday life along with "conventional ordinariness"—such as that conveyed by a group of friends gathered to celebrate a holiday ritual—are potent political tools.

Lifecycle Events: Weddings and Family Formation

In January 2018, photos and videos of longtime Havruta activist Chaim Elbaum and his now-husband Yair Strauss, standing under the *huppah* (the Jewish wedding canopy), went viral. Helen Elbaum (Chaim's mother) captivated guests and internet audiences with a blessing that mixed the stuff of traditional weddings with reflections on maternal love and religious devotion. Helen Elbaum had always accepted her son, but she fretted that Chaim would not find love. With God's assurance—"I created Chaim differently, but he is my son like all my sons. He will find a life partner"—Elbaum concluded that "no evil comes down from above, even if we don't understand. God's ways are mysterious . . . his plan will be carried out."

Weddings are public events; families, communities, and the state, via proxies, are invited to witness and certify the transformation of certain personal bonds and romantic attachments into socially, legally, and religiously meaningful forms. Same-sex weddings—especially ones marked within a community that denies them legitimacy—are at once personal declarations of love and commitment and political acts. Helen Elbaum wove these two aspects into a rhetoric of acceptance and signaled that the reimagining and rescripting of weddings was not so much a subversive act as an alignment with a preexisting divine plan.[5]

Same-sex couples have been rescripting weddings and the institutions of marriage and family for decades, though family formation, monogamy, and, especially, marriage remain contentious within LGTBQ+ communities. But what critics dismiss as a capitulation to heteronormativity is an entry point to reclaiming an authentic life course for LGBT persons of faith: Orthodox *hommos* and lesbians seek acceptance and recognition of monogamous relationships and family units as (Jewishly) legitimate.

But even as they sidestep the question of "whether" they should enter into monogamous, publicly recognized marital bonds, LGBT persons of faith ponder how to do so. As a legal institution, marriage imbues some personal bonds (but not others) with rights and responsibilities vis-à-vis the state, while religious, cultural, and social norms imbue these bonds with additional significance vis-à-vis one's family, community, and deity. Same-sex marriages in Israel are legally ambiguous. Blatantly homophobic policies are intertwined with a legal landscape that cedes all matters of personal status, including marriage and divorce, to religious authorities; the Chief Rabbinate, which has exclusive authority over marriages of Jews in Israel, is among the more than a dozen religious authorities licensed by the state to conduct marriages. In 2006 the Israeli Supreme Court ruled that same-sex couples who were married in jurisdictions where such marriages are legal can register as married in Israel, but this registration has little impact on same-sex couples' legal status since registration serves predominantly statistical purposes. Instead, same-sex couples' status is regulated by Israel's patchwork cohabitation case law, which provides some financial protections but does not address family matters. Nevertheless, many same-sex couples opt for commitment ceremonies that infuse marriage, weddings, and monogenous commitment with new rituals and meanings.

The terrain is more fraught for Orthodox same-sex persons who seek recognition not only from the state but also from a faith community that largely views same-sex love as transgressive. Traditional Orthodox Jewish weddings are highly structured, ritualized, and gendered. The couple, a man and a woman, stand under the wedding canopy in gender-coded clothing: a kippa (and sometimes tassels) for the man, a wedding dress and a veil for the woman. The wedding ceremony is conducted by a male rabbi. The man signs a Jewish wedding contract, a *ketubah*, which outlines the groom's rights and responsibilities concerning the bride, blesses the woman with a ring, and then shatters a glass. The ceremony is laden with nationalist references: the wedding canopy symbolizes the new Jewish home that will be built by the couple, while the broken glass serves as a reminder of foundational and traumatic events in Jewish history: the destruction of the Jewish temples in Jerusalem,. There is a string of ceremonial blessings involving families and others in the community. Additional celebrations, prayers, and blessings in familial and synagogue settings vary per local traditions. In more observant communities, men and women are spatially divided during the ceremony and celebrations. Orthodox feminists and other contemporary influences have introduced numerous variations, but traditional Jewish weddings remain gendered affairs.

"When we decided to get married—not a commitment ceremony, but a *real* Jewish wedding," one interviewee told me, "we realized we had to make all these decisions. Can we stand under a huppah? Which of the traditional blessings can we include? Who would bless us? Do we just tweak the language (Hebrew is highly gendered) or are there some blessings that simply don't make sense for two women? Shattering the glass was very important to us—'if I forget you Jerusalem and all that'—but can a woman do this?" As they negotiated their way, the couple did what Jews traditionally do when they encounter hard questions: they dove into Jewish archives and sources. "We asked ourselves, and then our rabbis, our teachers, our families, our friends: what makes a wedding 'Jewish'?" The huppah, they decided, was essential, and incorporating it into a same-sex wedding was unproblematic. And while they were not able to disassociate the breaking of the glass from its gendered origins, they found other ways to weave its symbolism into a blessing that a family member read at the wedding. The Jewish marriage contract had to go for other reasons: "Neither one of us cared for the ketubah, so that was an easy one; it would have been a stumbling block for both of us had we married men." They replaced the ketubah with a declaration of mutual commitment.

The result was a ceremony that was as deeply meaningful as it was Jewish: "My hetero friends were jealous. One said that we were fortunate to have been forced to write our own ceremony. They have borrowed some elements from it!" But a question loomed: "How much can you push the envelope without alienating your loved ones? At what point is the ceremony just a parody?" One interviewee would have preferred a more radical departure from Orthodox practice but compromised because she wanted her parents to attend and knew that "there was only so much I could expect of them." Appeasing family members led another couple to dispose of most of the traditional rituals and blessings. The original and repurposed poetry they used communicated that their ceremony was Orthodox-adjacent but not "Orthodox."

Predictably, investigations into the essence of "real Jewish weddings" modified, rather than duplicated, traditional weddings. Gendered rituals were remade—one example is of having both grooms shatter the glass—and blessings and ceremonial chants were rewritten. Couples reminisced and consulted with family members, rabbinic authorities, and friends. Some said that this was a rewarding and healing journey. One woman, who had disaffiliated over a decade earlier, was so moved by this process that by its end she recommitted herself—delving into the sources and meeting with progressive rabbinic authorities had helped her reidentify with the "beautiful parts of the tradition."

Thus, while weddings and marriage remain fraught for Orthodox LGBT persons who would like to have their love and commitment be witnessed, acknowledged, and embraced by their community—Helen Elbaum, for now, is somewhat of an outlier—this arena has emerged as a vibrant area of rescripting. Photos and videos of Orthodox same-sex engagement parties and wedding ceremonies often go viral by design: couples encourage their guests to share photos, videos, and reflections on their social media accounts. But even couples who refrain from turning their private ceremonies into public spectacles are agents of change: meaningful and recognizably Jewish wedding ceremonies are a product of weeks, months, and sometimes years of consultations and negotiations with family members, friends, rabbinic authorities, and other LGBT persons. Couples also seek guidance on planning Orthodox (or Orthodox-adjacent) same-sex weddings on social media, resulting in lively semipublic exchanges about writing personal vows and what makes a ceremony meaningfully Jewish. Couples who had spent months compiling resources share them with others. Rewritten scripts, which may begin as private, subversive acts, were thus normalized and mainstreamed for all to witness.

Family formation is another arena undergoing creative rescripting. The gendered nature of Orthodox family life means that the absence of a member of the other sex creates unique obstacles, but until recently Orthodox LGBT persons have had few role models for imagining alternative families. One lesbian said that she could imagine herself in an intimate and sexual relationship with another woman but family life stumped her: "What kind of house will I have? Who will bless the Sabbath? Who will do *Kiddush*, take the children to synagogue? Who will do all these tasks that in the *halacha* and in the Orthodox community are the tasks of the man?" Conservative forces within Orthodox communities capitalize on such fears with campaigns that castigate families that deviate from the cis and heteronormative script as non-Orthodox, non-Jewish, foreign, and menacing. Thus, Orthodox LGBT persons say that their decisions about family formation take into account not only their own well-being and desires but also those of their future children— "Will there be a school that accepts them? Will we be able to celebrate their birth in a synagogue? Would they be able to be bar mitzvahed there?"[6] On the flip side, having children is so central to Orthodox Jewish life—reproduction is a *mitzvah* one is expected to fulfill. So central is this mitzvah that some rabbinic authorities have used it as an entry point to support *monogamous* same-sex unions.

Regardless of whether they arrived at satisfactory answers to these questions, the reproductive impulse—and the desire to achieve normative Orthodox adulthood—is such that many Orthodox LGBT persons decide to have children. The path to parenthood—both biological and social—has always been easier for lesbians as compared with *hommos*, but, as one Havruta member told me in 2018, "we are in the midst of a baby boom." In the course of my fieldwork I encountered Orthodox LGBT persons who shared custody of children born during a previous, heterosexual marriage, sometimes with a new, same-sex partner; lesbian couples who had children using both anonymous and known sperm donors; *hommo* single men and couples who had children using foreign surrogates or had children with lesbian or single women (sometimes Orthodox, often not);[7] and LGBT persons who had created alternative family structures, with—or more often without—the blessing of their parents, families, and rabbinic authorities. Jewish law trails these emergent social arrangements, resulting in an ambiguous theological terrain. "In the end," one respondent said, "we just decided to go ahead and have children. The community will just have to catch up. It took some wrangling but our synagogue figured out how to celebrate the birth and I am sure that when the time comes, the school principal will just have to deal with two moms. She may not be comfortable with that but I am not here to make people comfortable." One Bat Kol activist often tells audiences in public events that much of her activism comes down to her family's presence in Orthodox spaces—going to syna-

gogue, sending her children to school, being visible in the community—
the everyday corollary to the menorah on the windowsill. Indeed, one
of my observations was, to use the words of the Facebook respondent
mentioned earlier, that such alternative families' lives were "utterly
boring and conventional." The Facebook pages of many of my new acquaintances were filled with the usual stuff of everyday life: photos of
children in their Purim costumes, complaints about school closures
during COVID-19, recipe requests, home renovations, and, occasionally, a photo from a pride event or a reposting of Havruta announcement. These depictions of "utterly boring and conventional" everyday
lives serve a political purpose: making space for the previously invisible
and thereby remaking Orthodoxy.

Worship and Study

For many observant Jews, the "essence" of Judaism resides in everyday communal ritual practices: praying in the company of other men
in the synagogue; attending a postgraduate institute of Jewish learning
(yeshiva for men, *midrasha* for women); studying with one's study com-
panion, or Havruta in the yeshiva or *beit midrash* (study hall). But for
many LGBTQ+ of faith, spiritual spaces are also sites of exclusions and
psychological and spiritual harms.[8]

Stories about exclusions from Jewish rituals and spaces reverberated
across my data. The anonymous Facebook poet is relieved when his father blesses him under the prayer shawl (*tallit*); one man was surprised
to be honored with an *aliya* at his childhood synagogue (the calling of
a member of a congregation to read a portion of the Torah and recite
blessings); interviewees had been asked to leave educational institutions or refrain from attending a communal study or prayer session or
have been excluded from blessing a family member on the occasion of
their wedding, Bar Mitzvah, or birth of a child; many recounted sitting
through Torah readings, prayers, and lessons where same-sex attraction
and LGBT lives were vilified. Ritual spaces, in other words, were experienced as painful and exclusionary, as summarized by one man's reflections on walking out of the synagogue during Yom Kippur prayers that
include the Leviticus "abomination" verse: "I leave and sit alone because
there's no room for me inside."[9]

Until the early aughts, there was indeed no room for Orthodox LGBT persons in congregations and communities. But in the late aughts they began to rethink Jewish ritual, learning, and spiritual spaces, resulting in the creation of accepting spaces and a vibrant scene of queer-friendly— and sometimes queer-controlled—ritual spaces, including synagogues, prayer halls, and study groups. These spaces provided solace because, as one interviewee said of the Tel Aviv congregation Yachad (together), "you could bring your whole self without even thinking about it."[10] Importantly, these spaces proved to be fertile ground for spiritual creativity and experimentation: queer interpretations of old texts, new blessings fitting for new family forms, new sociabilities where heteronormativity did not rule, and rethinking gendered language and spatial arrangement.

The section began with a young lesbian woman seeking assurance that she could make an Orthodox life for herself—but her inquiry turned out to be not so much about whether one "can be" Orthodox and gay, but rather *how to be* Orthodox and gay. Orthodox LGBT persons answer this question by creating new pictures (à la the Facebook poet) and telling new stories about what makes a life "Orthodox," in the process interrogating taken-for-granted practices, rituals, categories, and definitions. The result is a new way of being Orthodox, a new way of doing Orthodoxy, and an Orthodox LGBT identity that resides at the intersection of these categories. What makes this LGBTQ+ rescripting process unique is that in addition to the usual suite of resources (allies, therapists, LGBTQ+ communities), LGBT persons of faith lean into religious sensibilities. Thus, LGBT persons of faith experience their religious traditions both as a source of traumas and spiritual harms *and* as a resource for rewriting it from within. The rest of this chapter elaborates on this process of Orthodox queer worldmaking.

Creating and Mobilizing Community

Many posts on the Facebook Confessions Page (and on various closed groups) include requests for guidance and support. In one instance, a young man writes to ask for help navigating family matters. He had just come out and his parents were having a hard time. Would group members be willing to connect his parents with their own? Invitations to do so poured in, along with advice and referral to additional resources.

Such requests reflect the extent to which LGBTQ+ lives are constructed, negotiated, and lived in community; self-making and community making are deeply intertwined. "To be an Orthodox *hommo*," writes the anonymous Facebook poet, "is to know that there are those who will make the journey with you." On the one hand, my interviewees looked around in their social circles to identify sources of harm, weeding out those who would not be supportive. Hod's experience was typical: over the course of several years, before he even contemplated coming out, he had half-consciously "pushed away people who I thought wouldn't be accepting, and only left those who would be." Other efforts were constructive: participants described how they deliberately remade their social networks and identified positive role models. Respondents knew that exposure to new people, ideas, and ways of life was crucial to developing a new language, lens, vision. Doing so entailed stepping outside the Orthodox cocoon; respondents said friends and acquaintances they met during their military service or when they moved to a college town helped them construct and navigate their new lives, though social media played a central role in this process. The single most important factor, however, was access to Orthodox LGBT spaces.

To those shunned by families, Kadag and adjacent initiatives, such as the Facebook group described above, provided a social safety net and support system. "People think that we go to these groups because we're looking for sex," one man told me. "No! I wanted to get to know the LGBT community. Hod, Havruta, the online forums were ways to just get to know people." Reut was able to see beyond a depressing heterosexual marriage after a chance encounter brought her to a welcoming religious lesbian space. "It was the first time that I saw . . . pairs of women, happy, smiling. Some kids. I'd never seen that before." Nir, who said he was sure he was going to marry a woman despite his attraction to men, began to imagine a different way of being as he met people "like him" and was open with them. His entry point into the community had been the anonymous Confessions Page—contacts he made there took him to Havruta. Another woman said that her same-sex attraction made no sense until she "found out that Orthodox lesbians existed. . . . Until then it didn't belong to me, lesbians were characters in American films and TV shows." A man who had come of age in the 1990s had struggled with his homosexuality for over a decade. In the early days of the internet, he

connected with other men, an experience that "changed everything. . . .
You've probably heard about Hod. I googled '*hommo* dati' (Orthodox
hommo) and found them. Hod was my first safe space. I also found the
tapuz [online forum], I was a celeb there, dispensing advice, people
came to me with questions." For a pair of lesbians, the community at
congregation Yachad became "a central part of our lives. It's a community that embraces *hommos*, lesbians, enables a broad range of people.
That's a real Jewish community. It's like a *shtetel* [Yiddish for village,
denoting communal familiarity and belonging]. This is who you have
[in your community], and you have to love everyone." Another Kadag
member now in his forties recalled how decades earlier he overcame fear
to attend a meeting at the beach organized by someone he knew from
the early online forums, years before public visibility would become routine. Meeting others who were just like him ("*mamash*") blew his mind
away. "That's how I met the first group with whom I went through a
period of growth. . . . You can't understand what this did for me. These
new friends, connections replaced the old ones . . . to know who you are
you have to have a community that will support you."

These narratives reflect insights gleaned from decades of research:
finding community is a lifeline for those struggling in the dark. Safe
spaces are crucial to mobilizing community and undoing the harms
of social stigmas.[11] But there is a context-specific layer here. Orthodox LGBT persons work against claims that nonnormative gender and
sexual identities are un-Orthodox, non-Jewish, foreign. When my respondents say that meeting others like them helped them make sense
of themselves, they indicate that they began to believe that they could
"be" Orthodox and LGBT without assuming foreignness. Nir described
an iterative process: the more he felt comfortable with himself, the more
he was able to integrate himself in his newfound community (Kadag),
further boosting his self-confidence and willingness to take on a new
identity, along with its scripts. Shortly after joining Havruta, Nir also
became involved in queer scriptural study spaces (beit midrash), and
within a year of coming out he began volunteering with LGBTQ+ youth.

Community and safe spaces were necessary but not sufficient ingre-
dients to undo years and decades of spiritual harms, and respondents
mobilized additional resources. Finding a good therapist was key to
moving forward, creating a new narrative, accepting oneself. For some,

therapy was a corrective on more harmful interventions they had previously endured, but in all cases positive therapeutic interventions supported a search for an authentic self, a space to try out and rebuild a vision of self and community. Others said that they could not embark on this path until they had some semblance of financial independence. For still others, it took falling in love: "You know what changed things? When I really fell in love, the first time I had a girlfriend. It really confused me. It confused her. I told her I was in love with her, she said she was in love with me. And I said okay, what does this mean now? That I'm a lesbian."

Some of the resources my respondents mobilized to move forward are not surprising: friends and new communities that provided support, friendship, and role models to weather tough times; accepting family and friends; therapy; safe spaces. But articulating new life scripts—the process of queer worldmaking—also entailed negotiating Jewish traditions, ethics, philosophy, and theology.

Mobilizing Religion

Dina, a semicloseted lesbian in her late twenties, was deeply invested in Jewish learning and was a graduate of a prestigious seminary for women. Her devoutness and knowledge mediated and shaped all aspects of her life, including, she said, her identity as an Orthodox lesbian. Dina found meaning in one particular well-known story in Jewish folklore, that of Rabbi Nachman and the rooster. The story, which is attributed to Rabbi Nachman of Breslov, founder of an important Hasidic sect, tells of a prince who comes to believe he is a rooster and begins to act like one, sitting naked under the table and pecking for food. A wise man (thought to be Rabbi Nachman) offered a curious cure: he too claimed to be a rooster and joined the prince naked under the table. Once the wise man gained the prince's trust, he convinced the prince that roosters, too, can wear clothes, dine at the table, and so on. The parable is often used to demonstrate how forging a spiritual connection with God can uplift those who are lost. But Dina used the parable to make a case for an embracing, forward-thinking God at whose tables lesbians too are welcome. More than that: the connection she forged with God was the very vehicle that helped Dina make sense of herself and claim her (legitimate) place in the world. The parable, Dina said, provided an opening to imagine herself within Orthodoxy because it showed her how the Jewish tradition, which for years had haunted and taunted her with its messages that lesbianism was incompatible with Orthodoxy, was not only a source of angst but also a path to articulating an Orthodox LGBT identity. "After years of denying and crying and praying to God that he would change me, this story helped me accept my lesbianism. From this story, I felt that God accepts me as I am. My lesbianism became real once I stopped denying it." In the face of popular and scholarly narratives that portray religion as an obstacle to overcome, Dina describes religion as a vehicle of LGBT self-making.

Na'ama also deployed seminary teachings about religiosity to first question and then embrace her sexual orientation. During her time in the seminary, she said, there was a lot of talk about belief, "There are some people who have never had doubts about their belief, they just knew. There's something enviable about it but also a little naïve. Because how do you just know? The takeaway is that those who have doubt, who go out and study are ultimately more devout. I used that analogy to think about my sexual identity." Sexuality, she said, was not unlike religiosity: a process of discovery and reflection that results in embracing one's true self.

Hadar took this logic one step further: she rejected the very notion that she would need to come to terms with herself. Making decisions in the face of ambivalence and ambiguity and debating one's path was not only part of the general human condition, she said, but also precisely where the Jewish tradition excelled: guiding humans through chaos, helping them make tough decisions. How is dealing with one's sexuality, she wondered, different from dealing with any other life challenge?

In contrast, Tamar had emerged from a two-year stint at a prestigious women's seminary angry and confused. Her learning opened up a world of Judaism that she relished but also led her to doubt her place in this world—lesbianism was hushed even in that progressive space. As friends began to get engaged and to marry, Tamar, who had put her own sexuality on hold until her early twenties, knew that it was time for honest inquiry. Leaning into a long tradition of heretics, she made a deal with God: "I gave him a year to show me why I should remain Orthodox." In that year Hadar joined a study group, volunteered, and took a deep dive into Jewish philosophy and ethics. Her reading opened up a new way to connect with and bring God into her life. The irony was not lost on her: her seminary training facilitated this deep dive. As Tamar began testing the waters, confiding in people—first telling them she was questioning her sexual orientation, then coming out as a lesbian—the sky did not fall. On the contrary: she made new friends and found accepting religious spaces. When I met her, a few months after the year was up, she surmised that the deal had paid off, with God delivering on his part. Tamar had emerged from this year confident in her sexual orientation and with a deeper connection with God. This was not *in spite of* her sexual orientation but *because of it*: her doubts, pain, search for answers, engagement with Jewish texts and philosophy had deepened her commitment. After all, God had shown her the way. She was now ready to pay in kind: having recommitted, she began to volunteer with Kadag to help others on their path. Volunteering to repair the world, she said, was as Jewish as it gets.

Ariel likewise recommitted to God after meeting his partner (now husband). Ariel described years of "ups and downs" during which he was angry at God, then rejected him. Finding a life partner brought him closer to God and helped him develop a "real love for the almighty, real love for the religion." The reason? Through his anger, Ariel continued to pray to be made whole, that he would find happiness, that the torturing would cease. Miraculously, God delivered: "It was almost thankfulness to God about our relationship, that I met him, saying thanks for being able to live a full life. To be content with myself." This process also led Ariel to reassess the halacha's hold on LGBT persons, especially men. Though he was unable to resolve the purported halachic ban on same-sex relationships of Leviticus (a reading that some dispute), Ariel realized that he *need not* be tortured by this halacha because it represented only a sliver of authentic Jewish life. Finding one's way to God thus did not hinge on making peace with the halacha: "The sex? I just decided not to let it torture me."

For mainstream Orthodox Jews the idea that the halacha can be set aside is heretical. And yet, time and again my interlocutors shared stories of self and sense-making that were deeply embedded in the Jewish tradition yet had little to do with "the verse" (Leviticus 18:22, which includes the abomination reference) or other matters of scripture. To do so they drew on other traditions in Jewish philosophy and thought that questioned the primacy of the halacha in Jewish life.

Tamar brings together these various threads of leaning into and mobilizing the tradition to make sense of self, making space within Orthodoxy, and deepening one's religiosity. For Tamar, religious training, belief, and identity were not just sources of sense-making or making amends with God. Thinking about her sexual identity through the lens of the Jewish tradition and her training led her to conclude that sexuality and religion co-constitute one another. She recognized that religious training brought much spiritual harm, but she could also see how it helped her maintain a relationship with God despite her anger. Moreover, precisely because her lesbianism forced her to look inward, Tamar had to do the hard work of developing a religious language and forging an authentic connection to God—a thoughtful, reflexive, deep religiosity. "Unlike my straight friends, I couldn't just *be* religious. I had to think and reflect. What I learned in the process is that God is part of my life. I am in conversation with him all the time. God's existence is not metaphysical, it is real. I am constantly asking: what does he want from me." Not only were her sexual and religious identities not in conflict: they were inseparable, having developed in tandem. "It was through my lesbianism that I developed this religious language, my connection to God. This connection is inseparable from my lesbianism." She too credited seminary training with providing tools to articulate a legitimate alternative to a halachically focused religiosity: "So even if I don't abide by some parts of the halacha, I believe that this [life with a female partner] is what he wants, what he intended. Even though I can't remain within the halacha, I still feel that God is very much with me. That's how I get over the conflict. I want a lesbian religious life."

Thus, while religion remains a source of much anguish for LGBT persons, faith traditions can *also* be sources of solace and support, providing the faithful tools to make sense of themselves and their place in the world. This makes sense. Religion is a discipline. Years of religious training provide one with a language, a frame of mind, a way of thinking. Orthodoxy's messages, Ariel said, "are deeply entrenched. You are bad, sinful, deviant. There's no place for you. So the question is, how do you rewrite that narrative?" For many, the answer was to mine the tradition for an alternative theology to live by.

Everyday Theologies

Everyday Theologies of God, Orthodoxy, and the Good Jewish Life

Effi had been tortured by his sexuality since early adolescence. His sexual orientation, he said, did not weaken his religious commitment in the sense that he continued to think of himself as an observant Jew who was connected to God and the Jewish people. But his sexuality made him wonder about his "*right* to be in this world." For several years Effi had been "miserable, trying to understand, desperate to change." Effi traced this misery to a concern that he would not be able to partake in *tikkun olam*—world repair. Many Jews fulfill this expectation by having children, but, Effi reasoned when he came out in the early aughts, he likely was not going to have children (at the time the idea of alternative families of the sorts described above seemed preposterous). The angst was existential: observant Jews consider world repair essential. If he would not be able to fulfill one of Judaism's key mitzvahs, did Orthodoxy even have a place for him? Effi concluded that he was destined to suffer unless he could change.

Over the years Effi had met with rabbis and therapists until he slowly came to terms with the fact that he was not going to change. Sometime in his mid-twenties, just as Kadag began to take off, Effi had an epiphany: "I realized I DON'T HAVE TO SUFFER! Maybe there are other ways." As a committed Jew, finding these other ways hinged on developing his own take on God, sex, life, and what it meant to be an observant Jew: everyday theologies born out of the scars of human existence, rather than (exclusively from) the learned study of scripture. Effi's definition of a committed Jewish life was less reliant on adhering to halacha, grounded instead in a personal commitment to God and the ethics of *tikkun olam*. Effi summarized the theological insights he gleaned in his journey from a tormented teenager to Kadag activist:

> God is good and has your best interest in mind and doesn't want to screw you over. He created you in a way that you cannot change and gave you a social challenge that you will be different and the Other, that you will force society to deal with you. It's not easy and it's not fun. But if you choose faith you choose this job, and that's how you can repair the world.

On the face of it, Effi's theological outlook defied what he had learned in the yeshiva, but Effi and his peers insist that quite to the contrary, their theology, born out of lived experience, was quintessentially Orthodox. One aspect of this theology lay in its definition of God and one's connection with him. Effi's God was "loving and good," a God who understood that his love for a man "ruins nothing in the world," and a God who "has your best interest in mind and doesn't want to screw you over." Along the same lines, Ariel thought that God did not intend for his people to be tortured: "I said, this is who I am. You made me this way. I love you. And I want to observe your mitzvahs [commandments]. But you need to be patient with me, and help me out a little, to not be tortured."

This perspective—faith does not hinge on suffering—belies a key Jewish theological principle: religious commitment demands sublimation. The theology of binding, or *Aqedah*, holds that accepting the halacha as a way of life is tantamount to subordinating oneself to a higher normative order; people who submit to God's will sublimate individual desires, needs, and values. Per this logic, same-sex attraction is not a special challenge: doing as God instructed means that one will at times endure trials and make sacrifices.[12]

Effi initially accepted this logic: "I had in my mind that this is just what you do. You're an observant Jew, you're *hommo*, you suffer. I didn't even feel sorry for myself. I said okay, I'll deal with the hardship." The realization that he did not need to suffer was as much a theological breakthrough as it was a psychological one: sublimation (and therefore suffering) did not have a monopoly on true devotion. Effi thus reframed God's challenge. Per Aqedah theology, homosexuality is God's trial, a challenge to endure and overcome.[13] Effi reasoned that the challenge was not about sublimating one's desires nor about "dealing" with the challenge of same-sex attraction but rather "to be how God made me, to find my way in the world through God. And it's a different way." His takeaway was that in creating gender and sexual variation, God was challenging *society* to deal with minority groups. Effi accepted the challenge of being a vessel for positive social change: "It's not easy and it's not fun. But if you choose faith, you choose this job." The job of world repair, he added, was much more meaningful than suffering.[14]

By reframing God's trial in these terms, Effi placed it squarely within the cosmology of Jewish values—specifically the notion of repairing the world. If he could not do his part of repairing the world by having children, he would do so through activism. Accordingly, going to the Pride Parade with his kippa, coming out, and educating his community about Orthodox LGBT lives were not political acts that furthered LGBT rights but rather acts that furthered a social good and Jewish ethics: "So that both Orthodox and secular Jews will see that Orthodox gays existed. . . . Once I come out, and people start talking with me about coming out of the closet, the circles will broaden. Because if I can impact my family, and they accept me, maybe they'll impact their friends." Participation in pride parades and other acts of public visibility are often a flashpoint for Kadag allies who prefer that Kadag take a more muted, "respectable" route to make their grievances public (see chapter 6). But here Effi uses the logic of the tradition to develop a theology of Jewish life that renders such participation not only a net social good but also one that is legitimated by—indeed *necessitated* by—Jewish ethics.

Deciding to not be tortured and suffer, to not live one's life as a problem references other theological questions: What renders a Jewish life fulfilled? Does individual happiness and self-fulfillment have a place in the Jewish cosmology of a well-lived life? Recall Leah's concerns in the previous chapter, that choosing happiness defied Jewish teachings that "there are things that are bigger than me, it matters less whether I fulfill my dreams, whether I am happy" and therefore egoistic, un-Orthodox. But others insist that they deserve to be happy *and* that self-fulfillment and self-realization do not contradict Jewish principles but rather embody them. Starting in adolescence, Dor had dialed down his romantic and sexual needs to the point that they were "extinguished." Embracing his sexuality resulted in his flourishing: "I went from being a very closed person to a very open one." But, he made clear, the freedom he had found was not about sex in and of itself—Dor did not have his first sexual encounter until two years later when he was in his late twenties; rather, the flourishing was rooted in a reordering of one's purpose and values: "A happy and content person can contribute much more to others. Others around us choose to be tortured and put themselves in a corner, alone. They don't live to their full potential. That's not how God intended us to live. That's why I chose [to embrace homosexuality]." With his right to be content firmly grounded in Jewish cosmology, halachic sticking points fell to the wayside. Unlike Leah, who viewed her own happiness as egoistic and contradictory to Jewish values, Dor viewed happiness as *essential* to living a Jewish life.

Hadar had come alarmingly close to attempting suicide. Hearing Rabbi Benny Lau's oft-repeated refrain that the closet is death, and you should choose life, helped shift her perspective. "Choosing life" is a key principle in Jewish law and ethics. When Kadag allies elevate this principle, placing it on the same plain as halachic principles that produce spiritual harm, they free LGBT persons to, quite literally, live. Hadar said that when she decided that she was "just going to live—I started to live." The conflict and angst did not disappear but she was able to reframe them: "Religious people just have conflicts. That's just the way it is. Sure, there are ways to explain, justify how you can be Orthodox and lesbian but really, it doesn't matter. The halacha is just one perspective to think about life. So even if I don't abide by halacha, I still feel that God is very much with me. I chose life! So that's how I get over the conflict. I want a lesbian religious life with what God has given me."

Everyday Theologies of Sex

The theological moves described thus far rest on existing theological and ethical traditions within Jewish thought, although they do represent minority voices that challenge hegemonic traditions. But these challenges rest on the assumption that same-sex attraction is a fixed, nonmalleable trait. Although human sexuality is the subject of much debate, with contemporary theories embracing explanatory mechanisms that strike a delicate interaction of "nature" and "nurture,"[15] Kadag and their allies, like persons of faith across religious traditions, reject theoretical ambiguity in favor of a "born this way"—or, rather, "made this way"—theory of sexuality.[16]

God, Effi said, "created you in a way that you cannot change." Many of my respondents, often unprompted, reached into early childhood to offer evidence of a long history of same-sex crushes, sexual experimentation, and fantasies, presumably to support claims of an inborn and fixed same-sex attraction. Almost universally they rejected claims that same-sex attraction was a choice. David remembered looking at men in the showers as early as six years old. Another man traced his epiphany about his sexual orientation to illicit porn consumption with friends in middle school: "I was definitely not interested in the girls." Ayelet remembered thinking of her middle school friends, who would "all be sitting there and talking about boys and I'm thinking, 'This is so boring.'"

The stakes are high: Orthodox conservatives, who claim that homosexuality is neither "natural" nor fixed, support conversion therapy and similar "therapeutic" interventions that activists and most mental health professionals agree to be dangerous. In a twist of irony, it is conservative Orthodox rabbis, not Kadag activists and their allies, who are aligned with poststructural theories of the socially constructed nature of sexuality. A "made this way" theology serves as a buffer against Orthodox conservatives, a platform from which to critique conversion therapy (why doubt or change God's creation?), and a path toward developing tolerant and affirming theologies. As Effi explained, "This [homosexuality] is not supposed to exist. Religious, gay is something that's not supposed to exist. *But it does exist!* We exist! So what does that tell you? To me, it means that God made us this way and has a purpose for us in the world." As Tamar put it, "If God created me this way and all his creation is good, why would I even need to change?"

One of the reasons Kadag promotes this theory of sexuality—and its theological underpinnings (for example, the story of the ugly vessel and the craftsman in the Babylonian Talmud)—is that it logically leads to affirmation (rather than mere tolerance, see next chapter) of LGBT persons, relationships, and families while avoiding thorny halachic questions. I was reminded of Kadag's investment in this framework in July 2019, when I was asked to speak at a book launch for Dr. Eyal Zack's volume on mixed-orientation marriages (composed of a same-sex-attracted man and a heterosexual woman).[17] Wanting to impress the audience with the author's theoretical sophistication—Dr. Zack is a clinical social worker—I took a detour to place his work within the scholarship on human sexuality. Wrong move for an audience composed of *hommo* men whose sense making hinged on a "God made me this way" theology of sexuality! The speaker after me, longtime Kadag ally Rabbi Yuval Cherlow, set the record straight. Rabbis, he said, reside in a world of essence, not a social construction. And rabbis such as himself, who support same-sex-attracted persons in their struggles, are increasingly on board with the claim that homosexuality is not an ideology, a "phenomenon," a way of life, or a social construct, but rather an essence.

But the "God made me this way" theology of sexuality is inconsistent with theories of sexuality. It also erases bisexuality. Rabbinic support for same-sex relationships and families, still nascent but no longer closeted, is grounded in the idea that same-sex-attracted persons did not choose this state of being. Accordingly, rabbinic support is reserved for those who have no choice in the matter—that is, they are exclusively same-sex-attracted.[18] In addition, this theological pivot does not displace one of Kadag's key critiques: rabbinic authorities and the Orthodox community should cease looking into the bedroom in the first place. The issue, they say, is not sex but social norms that render some sexualities more vulnerable than others (chapter 5 revisits these tensions).

These lingering tensions notwithstanding, the key point is that same-sex-attracted Orthodox Jews engage, rather than reject, Jewish theologies, concepts, and values. They do not get bogged down asking, "Can you be Orthodox and gay?" (the language of conflict): they know that they *are* Orthodox and gay. Instead, they ask foundational theological questions: What does it mean to believe in God? Who is this God that I believe in? What does it mean to be an observant Jew? To answer these questions, they draw on their own religious training and traditions within Jewish thought. To respond to a nagging question, "How did God create me this way?," they develop a new theology of God. To combat Orthodoxy's homophobic messages—"you are bad, sinful, deviant"— their new stories involve an understanding of God as "loving and good," a God who understands that one man's love for another man "ruins nothing in the world," and a "God that is good and has your best interest in mind and doesn't want to screw you over." Effi and his peers know full well that these theologies undermine hegemonic Jewish teachings. But, they say, they are not out to start a revolution. As one early Bat Kol activist put it in a public outreach event, "My intention was never to start a movement. All I wanted was to make space for my family." As the next three chapters make clear, however, this seemingly modest request to make space—and Orthodox LGBT persons' very presence in Orthodox spaces—did indeed start a revolution of sorts.

Orthodoxy on the Spectrum

So, what is it like to be an Orthodox *hommo*? Per the anonymous Facebook poet, the answer is a moving target. Chapters 2 and 3 chronicle a painful and uneven journey from shattered pictures to new images, from disorienting, derailed life plans to new scripts. The stories recounted in these chapters make clear that while LGBT persons of faith certainly experience conflict, this conflict does not exist in a vacuum. When religious communities mark LGBTQ+ persons as sinners, deviants, transgressors, it is little wonder that many people of faith experience their religious traditions as incompatible with nonnormative gender or sexual identities, disaffiliate, get stuck, or decide to bury their secret under a veneer of heteronormative life.

But a small—if growing and increasingly visible and vocal—minority of LGBTQ+ persons of faith choose a different path: they build a life-affirming narrative of self by devising new scripts about themselves, their God and their relationship with him, and the community to which they belong. At that juncture, a curious thing happens: religion emerges as a productive force.

In the literature on the experiences of LGBT persons of faith, religious and sexual identities are often assumed to be inherently conflictual, with a hyphenated, or integrated identity, as the best possible outcome—one that is possible *in spite of* religious messaging. But this reading does not account for the nuanced ways in which religious LGBT persons of faith mobilize their traditions. As we have seen, the encounter between faith traditions and LGBTQ+ lives is far more nuanced than a conflict lens would have us believe. Kadag activist Rafael J. Kelner Polisuk rejects the idea that identities such as his *bridge* conflicts and gaps, arguing instead that religious LGBT identities create and define new things: "I feel this in my personal life, in this hyphen, this Orthodox-LGBTQ. There are questions, some of them very difficult and existential, but in the end, this identity isn't a conflict, and nor is it a solution to a conflict. It is what it is, whole in its complexity. Not also LGBTQ and also Orthodoxy but LGBTQ Orthodoxy, not despite of but because of, as simple as that."[19]

To arrive at this new identity, script, and story, to redefine families and weddings, and to invigorate ritual and study spaces, Orthodox LGBT persons actively mine, lean into, and mobilize the Jewish tradition.[20] I read this as an unconventional process of queer worldmaking: resisting and reshaping hegemonic institutions, discourses, practices, and identities through a bottom-up engagement with the everyday, a "mode of being in the world that is also inventing the world."[21] And as they assert "#weareheretostay"—spiritually, within Orthodoxy, spatially, within the religious Zionist project—they chart their path forward and produce new ideas about Orthodoxy itself.

My respondents insist that they are not out to start a revolution, but their intentions aside, in refusing to cede Orthodoxy to conservatives, the making of Orthodox livable lives and the queering of Orthodoxy are intertwined: the very existence of Orthodox LGBT persons in Orthodox spaces is revolutionary. Social movement scholarship tends to focus on contentious politics as the locus of social change, but ethnographies of queer life and worldmaking on the one hand, and ethnographies of lived religious lives on the other, demonstrate that the "stuff" of social change is very much embedded in small, mundane, boring moments of daily life. Faced with the daunting question of how to be Orthodox and gay—a question with psychological, familial, cultural, legal, and theological ramifications—many Orthodox LGBT persons ultimately conclude that they are just going to live their lives as they see fit. Contentious politics seems to follow, rather than precede these decisions.

What makes the experiences of Orthodox LGBT persons unique is that they mobilize religion in the process of rewriting their stories and devising new scripts. To be an Orthodox *hommo*, to return to the Facebook poet, is to draw on the tradition to expand the boundaries of Orthodoxy itself, "to understand that you don't need some rabbi who will approve of you; that to be Orthodox is your own decision." The battle goes to the heart of orthodoxy: who is Orthodox and who gets to decide the bounds of Orthodoxy? As one man put it—with a wink and a nod—his own journey led him to conclude that he is a queer Orthodox—

"queer" referring not to fluid gender or sexual categories but rather to Orthodox fluidity.

Orthodox LGBT persons, long silenced and shunned by Orthodox authorities, assert themselves as legitimate, authentic conversation partners, and the next three chapters consider a dynamic process that engages Orthodox LGBT persons, their allies, and Orthodox conservatives who are alarmed by a changed (or queered) Orthodoxy that threatens (and exposes the constructed nature of) foundational categories, mythology, and authority structures.

4

Educating Our Rabbis

From a Theology of Transgression to a Theology of Tolerance (and Beyond)

I stand before you as . . . a messenger of a society that is
stuck, frightened, confused, and bewildered. The Torah
stands here beside me and says, "Men shall not lie with
men, it is an abomination." And my brother, who is standing here on the other side of me, says, "Do not cast me
aside, I am your brother." You hold the Torah in one hand
and your brother in the other, and you try to find a way.
—Kadag ally Rabbi Benny Lau

When we left David at the Tel Aviv gastropub in chapter 2, he was angry
with the tradition and its interpreters, rabbis who had rendered him and
his fellow same-sex-attracted Jews invisible at best, more commonly as
transgressors, unwelcome interlopers in Orthodox communities. David
was living a much-fulfilled life but felt as an outsider both in the Orthodox community in which he was raised but left behind and in the secular
gayborhood he could not fully embrace. David yearned for institutional
acknowledgment, an Orthodoxy that included same-sex couples. He
wished rabbinic leaders were more creative and courageous—utterances
of empathy and calls for "tolerance" that had proliferated in progressive
Orthodox circles by the mid-2010, he said, did not quite cut it. David
believed that rabbis were reneging on their fundamental duty to align
Jewish lived realities with the *halacha*. Even as he laid out this vision,
the idea of real embrace seemed preposterous to David when we met in
2016, but that would soon change. This chapter chronicles how theology
turned into an arena of LGBT activism, embroiling Orthodox *hommos*
and lesbians in battles over the meanings, boundaries, and future of
Orthodoxy.

A Historical Encounter with Rabbis Trying to Find a Way

Every fall, Havruta hosts a Shabbat retreat. Several dozen men gather to mingle, talk, and pray. Some come with spouses; others hope to meet someone. Occasionally, they do: several couples in the community met at Havruta functions. The November 2016 retreat was one for the history books: a group of liberal Orthodox rabbis affiliated with the religious Kibbutz movement gathered at the venue that same Shabbat. Eyal Liebermann, a former Havruta CEO, described the scene: "A big circle in the evening. Men and women, half of them *hommos*, sitting together. Leading the circle is a student and his rabbi. Avichai introduces himself and talks about his experience and process of coming out, and Rabbi Yehuda Gilad . . . completes the part of the story in which he was involved."[1]

Avichai Abarbanel has shared this story with multiple audiences: after he was publicly outed as a teenager, Rabbi Gilad had helped set a tone for his community's response. "In the midst of the emotional turmoil associated with the public outing . . . I am seated in synagogue between my father and grandfather and feel all eyes on me. . . . The rabbi approaches me, shakes my hand, and wishes me Shabbat Shalom and communicates with his eyes, no words—you are just fine."[2]

Liebermann's post continued to narrate the evening's events, turning to the request of Daniel Jonas, then Havruta's CEO, that rabbis "stop looking at us through the lens of transgression." Per the lens of transgression, homosexuality is pathological, mutable, unnatural, and unequivocally prohibited. In liberal Orthodox circles, the lens of transgression, which was hegemonic until the early 2000s, is being displaced by a theology of tolerance that assumes homosexuality to be a natural, innate, and immutable trait. Proponents of tolerance encourage Jewish communities to embrace *hommos* and lesbians but have yet to fully reconcile same-sex relationships with the halacha, leaving Orthodox same-sex-attracted persons in a bind (in October 2020 Rabbi Lau released an overview of what such halachic recognition might look like, but it is far from achieving widespread support nor does it address the needs of all LGBT persons).[3] Facing a decree of celibacy, many disaffiliate. Others, like many of the men gathered that Shabbat, demand that religious authorities and communities change their rhetoric, messages, and theological frameworks. Such dialogues are not unique to Jewish Orthodoxy but given the halacha's foundational force in organizing Jewish life, theological ambiguity is a painful, daily reminder of exclusion.

The theological reckoning discussed in this chapter began with an emphasis on tolerance, acceptance, and embrace, and the linkages between some of the ideas to emerge in liberal Orthodox Jewish, Evangelical, and Catholic contexts are striking.[4] Tolerance is often regarded as an unqualified achievement of modern political thought but critical scholars are wary of its dark undercurrents: tolerance is premised on dislike, disapproval, and regulation. To tolerate is not to affirm but to conditionally allow what is unwanted or deviant; tolerance leaves systems of knowledge and power intact. Queer scholar and political theorist Wendy Brown argues that tolerance consolidates power relationships and sustains the abjection of the tolerated by establishing a hierarchical relationship between a dominant center and its margins.[5] Since only "the tolerant" are marked as normative and hegemonic (in this case, authentically Orthodox), tolerance is an inadequate antidote to hatred, discrimination, and violence. Kadag activists are unlikely to have read Brown's text, but their lived experience led them to a similar conclusion: tolerance is enough. But what might come in its stead is less clear. Making space (Kadag's key goal) could be a request for tolerance; it can also be read as a demand for a joyous embrace and affirmation of marginalized groups and their experiences and perspectives, along the lines associated with Christian queer theology.[6]

The limits of tolerance were on display that November. Eyal Liebermann describes how a yeshiva student summarized for the rabbis Orthodox *hommo* men's options: entering a relationship with a man "with some constraints," undergoing conversion therapy, remaining celibate, and marrying a woman while possibly cheating on her. Closeted at the time, Yehonatan Gill Rossen Maman would soon emerge as a leading Kadag figure.

An educator pondered a solution: a committed relationship with another man. But there's a catch: without halachic principles to guide them, same-sex relationships not only lack theological and social legitimacy but also compromise Jewish subjecthood. The Jewish legal codex—a sprawling collection of guidelines that claims mandate over all of life's domains—has little to offer to those in same-sex relationships. The exclusion of entire categories of Jews from halachic purview compromises Jewish personhood in the same way that marriage laws restricting marriage (and its benefits) to heterosexual couples compromise citizenship status of non–heteronormative or cisnormative couples. Seeking recognition, Yehonatan asked the rabbis to formulate halachic principles for same-sex couples. As noted, four years later, Rabbi Lau released a document outlining such principles—lightning speed for a tradition accustomed to a glacial pace.

On Shabbat morning, Eyal Liebermann's post continues, "one of us was invited for an *aliya*" (the calling of a member of a congregation to read a portion of the Torah and recite blessings; Orthodox conservatives argue that as transgressors *hommos* are ineligible for this honor). In doing so, the rabbis practiced the tolerance that they preach, as if saying, "You are just fine."

Fate may have brought the groups together that Shabbat, but it was hardly providence that facilitated a dialogue that, per one attendee, was "unimaginable not a decade, but a year earlier." That Orthodox *hommos* could talk to rabbis as equals and rabbis' willingness to listen and engage them are direct outcomes of more than a decade of activism—including the work of many retreat participants. It certainly helped that the majority of the participants were cisgender men hailing from the heart of Orthodoxy; with yeshiva education and family and social ties to Orthodox elites, their representatives could hold their own in halachic speak. These same ties would prove as an obstacle: the most prominent allied rabbis are Ashkenazi, and Mizrachi *hommos* continue to feel marginalized, including in the spaces that organizations such as Havruta have opened up. Nevertheless, a breakthrough: Havruta had earned a seat at the halachic table. Eyal Liebermann concludes,

> For the first time *hommos* and rabbis are sitting together and talking about the issues eye to eye. Not another rabbi who comes to hear *hommos* or to talk at them, not to mention preach to them. Not rabbis who gather for a conference on LGBT issues, where the LGBT side is mediated by psychiatrists and other therapists. For a while we've been saying, talk with us, not just about us. This time it happened.

The 2016 Havruta Shabbat encapsulates how far the Orthodox Proud Community has come and the distance it has yet to travel because tolerance is not enough: it leaves same-sex couples and persons lacking clear rules of conduct and marks their continued exclusion from Jewish life. Little wonder that many continue to be tormented by the specter of transgression: "No matter how hard I try to convince myself that it is pure love and that there's nothing wrong with it, I still feel blemished, degenerate, uncouth," reads a 2019 entry on the Confessions Page.[7]

Theological debates hardly seem like an arena to wage LGBT battles, more likely to focus on freeing sexuality from religious oversight and regulation than seeking new forms of surveillance. But for LGBT persons of faith, theology is *precisely* the domain in which to wage these battles: it is the place one goes to look for new answers, contest and stretch the tradition, and demand to be seen. The path toward equality, full personhood, and affirmation passes through religious logics, institutions, and sensibilities, entailing heady philosophical dialogues about theology, interpretive methods, theological expertise, and history.

Halacha: A Brief Primer

The halacha, an elaborate codex of rules of conduct, holds jurisdiction over Jewish individual, family, and communal life. These rules, developed by rabbis since biblical times, regulate both religious observance and everyday conduct. The code of conduct pertaining to intimate and sexual relationships is notoriously elaborate: the halacha has something to say about dating through weddings and everything in between. It also regulates physical intimacy and conduct of married couples. Since the halacha does not recognize same-sex relationships, these rules leave same-sex persons abandoned by, or, depending on one's perspective, free from, halachic strictures.

Halachic rules derive from biblical commandments that were subsequently codified and modified by religious authorities. For millennia, Jewish rabbis have interpreted and debated biblical and other canonical texts, adapting them to specific contexts, eras, and circumstances. The result is a sprawling system comprising biblical rules and rabbinic stipulations, explanations, and nuanced interpretations, which continue to be debated.

On the one hand, the halacha is a symbolic arena. Not all Orthodox Jews follow every aspect of the halacha—in fact, the vast majority do not—but the halacha is an aspirational system, an ideal against which Jews are measured and against which they measure themselves. Halachic observance, in other words, is a boundary marker that separates the observant (Orthodox) from other Jews. Precisely because the halacha claims jurisdiction over all of life's domains, some Orthodox LGBT persons experience lack of jurisprudence (halachic exclusion) as a painful reminder of their marginal status, an affront to their very Jewish belonging and being. One lesbian was relieved to be exempt from regulations surrounding menstruation, a source of much disdain and anxiety among heterosexually married Orthodox women. Nevertheless, she said, "the lack of halacha tells me that there's no place for me."

As a legal discourse, the halacha develops through case law. Jews uncertain about conduct can seek guidance from a *decisor*—a learned scholar, an expert in Jewish law—who issues an answer (*responsum*). This exchange can happen in a meeting, over the phone, in a letter, by email, and, increasingly, online. Decisors reach into the vaults of Jewish scripture and responsa to provide guidance. One theory of halachic decision making aspires to insulate these deliberations from contemporary values, debates, and practices, but legal adjudication does not operate in a vacuum. This dispute transcends the issue at hand, but note that the halacha is cis and heteronormative, as are the Jews who populate its canonical texts and the generations of learned Jews who deliberated them. Little wonder that historically the halacha did not acknowledge the existence and needs of modern-day LGBT persons.

Nominally, a rabbi's response is case-specific but in aggregate responsa constitute a binding halachic archive. Private, case-specific halachic making allows decisors more wiggle room, but rabbis are cautious because private decisions can and do enter the public domain either through systematic expositions, as part of a collection of responses, or piecemeal. The internet has dramatically reshaped the making and disseminating of halacha.[8] When this process occurred through halachic books, rabbis were insulated from their audience: there is no medieval equivalent to the immediacy of a Facebook thread or to the comments section on a blog. The internet has also democratized halachic making: more rabbis can partake in the action. Anonymity also removed a barrier for consulting rabbis on intimate matters, resulting in unprecedented halachic public discourse on all things sexual. At the same time, the shift from private consultations to public forums undermined a delicate ecosystem. As halachic discourse shifted from an aggregate of context specific private consultations to a public spectacle (questioners' anonymity is preserved), responsa have been recast as generalized directives. Private, personal adjudications lend themselves to leniency and less grandstanding, while generalized pastoral guidance tends to focus on preserving an imagined Jewish community and its social order. Halachic discourse and online responsa have thus become sites of fierce battles between Orthodox liberals and conservatives and the proliferation of stricter and moralizing responsa.[9]

As rabbis began to confront the urgency and salience of same-sex attraction in their communities, halachic silence was replaced by a lens of transgression and denial followed, in the aughts, by the emergence of a lens of tolerance without legitimacy.[10] As they reckon with the limits of tolerance, some rabbinic authorities are now going a step further as they attempt to reconcile the halacha with lived of realities of same-sex-attracted Orthodox Jews.

Early Same-Sex Halacha: Silence, Transgression, Denial

Many Jews and Christians view the Bible as the source of a comprehensive and irrefutable ban on all things homosexual—acts, desires, identities[11]—though scholars of gender and sexual cultures argue that religious interpretations often *followed* attempts by states and religious groups to control morality and enforce group boundaries.[12] The Bible mentions only male-on-male anal sex, and even that reference is neither explicit nor conclusive,[13] and says nothing about homosexual relationships and identities (nor could it: the classificatory system of desire is a nineteenth-century invention). It is silent on women.[14] Earlier generations of Jewish authorities considered transgressions in this domain on par with lapses in other realms such as the Sabbath or dietary laws. Only more recently has homosexuality's immorality been elevated.[15] Indeed, until the latter half of the twentieth century, few *published* responsa addressed same-sex attraction, gender and sexual diversity, and LGBT persons' status within Jewish communities.[16]

Jews in antiquity through medieval times engaged in what we call today homosexual practices, but most Talmudic sages did not view sexual attraction between males as either exceptional or unnatural and there were persistent gaps between the halacha's forbidding ideal and everyday practices that normalized *some* same-sex encounters.[17] In addition, there was a wide variation between Sephardi and Ashkenazi jurisprudence. Sephardi rabbis were aware of the ubiquity of same-sex practices and desire and generally did not view same-sex encounters as *religious* transgressions. In contrast, Ashkenazi rabbis framed a variety of sexual practices, including sexual intimacy between men, as grave transgressions, likely a result of fears of ethnic contamination. This forbidding stance evolved into a monolithic account of the halacha of homosexuality, presenting it as normative, inflexible, historically linear, unequivocal, and oblivious to sociopolitical contexts.[18]

Until the 1970s decisors were relatively silent about homosexuality. When he wrote about the topic in the early 1990s—virtually a lone voice—Rabbi Ronen Lubitch attributed this silence to a profound disease—disgust, really.[19] When rabbis began to address same-sex attraction, their point of departure was that homosexuality was rare among the Orthodox ("Of course it was rare," one interviewee bitterly said. "We all left"). They also saw homosexuality as a transgression that could and must be fixed—not a social identity.[20] Many decisors viewed *attraction*—not just acts—as deviant and pathological: "persons afflicted in this manner are homosexuals even if they remain celibate," Rabbi Bleich wrote in 1981.[21] Rabbi Feinstein declared same-sex desire "a deviation from the path of nature."[22] This 1976 responsa continues to guide contemporary authorities.[23] Rabbi Shlomo Aviner, a stalwart of conservative Orthodoxy, captured this emerging consensus in the late twentieth century with a declaration that "there is no such thing as a religious homosexual."[24] Some authorities view homosexuality as disordered desire and thrill seeking; others cite corruptions of the modern world; still others are more lenient on the question of attraction itself.[25] Either way, this approach denies homosexuality as an authentic sexual expression that warrants halachic recognition and paved the way for corrective interventions (conversion therapy) or curbing (heterosexual marriage or celibacy).[26]

The majority of sources address sexual contact between men, reflecting women's historical invisibility in the tradition.[27] Although biblical silence and Talmudic ambiguity could have been leveraged by later decisors to develop more lenient halacha for lesbians, they instead expanded the ban on male homosexuality to cover women, ascribing similar gravity to both.[28] The idea that lesbian relationships are prohibited has become so entrenched that many Jews, including Orthodox lesbians who participated in this research, consider the ambiguous provenance of this ban irrelevant.

Orthodox Jews surely consulted with rabbis in earlier eras, but a smaller portion of responsa made it into the *public* archive before the twenty-first century.[29] By then, rabbinic authorities could no longer contain the truth: Orthodox persons were experiencing same-sex attraction and turning to rabbis for guidance. Until recently, this guidance had been almost universally harmful or dismissive. Nearly each of the dozens of Orthodox lesbians and *hommos* I talked to was told by at least one rabbinic authority—more commonly by several—that change was possible, necessary, a moral and religious obligation. One woman was assured by her *ulpana* teacher that same-sex attraction "happens to a lot of girls." A well-known conservative rabbi assured another, "You're not really a lesbian, you're just young." A *hommo* in his late twenties was advised by a rabbi to "meet a delicate woman to show masculinity, study lots of Torah, work out. . . . He promised that eventually I will be attracted to a woman . . . fall in love, marry." The rabbi also referred him to conversion therapy. Kadag has sought to shield Orthodox LGBT persons from such emotional and spiritual harms in part by identifying rabbis who were willing to be educated about Orthodox LGBT realities.

A Theology of Tolerance: Compassion and Recognition without Legitimacy

In the early aughts, an alternative halachic line emerged: *tolerance without legitimacy*.[30] First and foremost, the theology of tolerance recognizes that same-sex-attracted Orthodox Jews exist.[31] The theology of tolerance advocates compassion, empathy, and acceptance; assumes that same-sex attraction is a natural inclination (not an illness or perversion); and is grounded in and sensitive to lived experience. Rabbi Ronen Lubitch's 1995 article was an early harbinger of this stance, but it took him a while to find a venue willing to publish the piece; obstacles included taboos and journal editors who dismissed the topic's significance.[32] Rabbi Lubitch argued that homosexuality was proxy for other debates: tensions between the Torah and science, the halacha and modernity, and the halachic treatment of marginalized members of society.[33] Allied rabbis, per this view, approach the theology of homosexuality as a case of a larger category, the ethical treatment of "the Other."[34] Tolerance continues to be marked by a nod to such larger rhetorical debates. While this frame has opened up possibilities for inclusion, it also marginalizes the needs of LGBT persons.

When a more polished version of Rabbi Lubitch's article appeared in the heady Jewish journal *Deot* in 2001 it elicited much attention. Conservatives dismissed the rabbi as "Reform" (an epithet that evokes battles over religious authenticity and authority), while Orthodox *hommos* and lesbians responded with qualified praise, noting its failure to recognize same-sex relationships.[35] "Compassion is not enough," a reader named Avigail wrote.[36] She sought "a stance of pride, a stance of respect, even joy that someone who in the past was destined to a life of loneliness finds a way to live happily, find love . . . build a family . . . be part of a community."[37]

Revisiting the topic in 2010, Rabbi Lubitch noted progress: many Orthodox communities, rabbis, and educators now viewed homosexuality through the lens of tolerance. But the rabbis would not budge: "Compassion does not entail legitimacy," the young rabbi wrote in 1995, reiterating as recently as 2019 that compassion and empathy cannot "allow that which is banned."

Another milestone is the 2010 Principles Document drafted by the now-defunct *hommo* organization Hod with input from rabbinic authorities (see also chapter 1).[38] This aspirational ethical code distinguished between orientation and practice, declared that Orthodoxy and same-sex attraction were not incompatible, characterized mixed-orientation marriages (heterosexual marriage between a *hommo* man and heterosexual woman) as a moral injustice,[39] and subtly discouraged conversion therapy. (An earlier draft had been more critical of conversion therapy, but the language was softened over rabbinic objections; allied rabbis had their own tightrope to tread.) The document also encouraged inclusion, acceptance, and tolerance; denounced humiliation, hatred, and violence; and demanded full ritual recognition: homosexuals should be counted for *minyan*, recite priestly blessings, be called to the Torah, and serve as witnesses. Respect, the document posited, was a Jewish moral obligation: "Blaming or insulting homosexuals on account of their orientation violates commandments governing interpersonal relationships."

Kadag members "hated" the document because, a Havruta member told me, all it offered was "a lonely, miserable life. To be accepted you have to hide your relationship." The document did encourage acceptance even of homosexuals (this is the term the document uses) who acted on their orientation, but its version of tolerance still branded them as transgressors. Worse: this rhetoric turned "the homosexual" from a sinner into a tragic figure, a religious person grappling with a situation that cannot be remediated.[40] Homosexuals, the document stated, confront an "ordeal that must be overcome," their lives a great "trial." It encouraged homosexuals to "devote themselves to the greater goals that God has set the Jewish people." In contrast, Kadag sought full legitimacy for same-sex relationships. "My love is not a problem," a Bat Kol member told me. "God loves me as I am."[41]

Yet the document was a breakthrough of sorts: its very existence suggested a halachic field open for negotiation. It also indicated a changed environment: that two-dozen rabbis were willing to *publicly* sign on to these principles in 2010 is a huge feat[42]—Rabbi Lubitch was rebuked for advocating tolerance less than a decade earlier.

The Hod principles, and those articulated by Rabbi Lubitch, with minor variations, continue to inform the theology of tolerance: homosexuality is not a pathology but rather a natural orientation that warrants tolerance and acceptance. But this stance is plagued by internal inconsistencies. Those who frame same-sex attraction as pathological can prescribe a corrective course. But liberal rabbis who believe that same-sex attraction is authentic but are unwilling to give halachic legitimacy to same-sex relationships leave the same-sex-attracted in halachic limbo, inadvertently imposing a lifetime of celibacy. A harsh penalty for individuals, this stance also defies Jewish sexual ethics that do not advocate aesthetic celibacy. It also produces a tension between religious commitments and human morality; ideally, the two should align.

To justify their stance liberal rabbis have turned to the concept of binding, or *Aqedah*, which refers to Abraham's willingness to sacrifice his son. The theology of Aqedah holds that accepting the halacha as a way of life amounts to subordinating oneself to a higher normative order; people who submit to God's will sublimate their own desires, needs, and values. Per this logic, same-sex attraction is not a special challenge: doing as God instructed means that one will at times endure trials and make sacrifices, even when divine demands clash with moral values.[43] "Sometimes human beings are called on to bind themselves on the altar of God's commandments," wrote Kadag ally Rabbi Yuval Cherlow.[44]

Orthodox LGBT persons cry foul: they do not wish to be poster children for sacrifices. They do not want to be put on a pedestal; they seek to lead normative, pedestrian, "boring" lives, as one interviewee put it. They want to be wed under the Jewish wedding canopy, live and pray among their families and friends, send their children to Orthodox schools, and be part of the Orthodox body politic. For that to be a reality, one lesbian said, rabbis "need to see us and make halacha." In 2010, Rabbi Benny Lau was angered when he was asked whether Orthodox *hommos* were allowed to have sex. "Why do they need to ask this question? What do they want, a note [permission slip] from the rabbi?" "I want a halachic answer, Rabbi Lau. I don't want a note from a rabbi; I want God," responded Havruta member Eliq Oster.[45]

An improvement on transgression, tolerance does not amount to full Jewish subjecthood: tolerance offers acceptance in return for martyrdom and excludes same-sex-attracted persons from the business of halacha—in Wendy Brown's terms, replicating the hierarchy between the tolerant and its others. Wanting in, activists and their allies turned the halacha into a battleground. They challenged interpretive traditions, the primacy of the halacha as an organizing religious framework,[46] and traditional authority structures. Deploying the activist slogan "talk with us, not about us," Kadag insisted that the halacha could develop only through dialogue, not by rabbinic authorities who were removed from the daily realities of their flock. Activists also traced the lens of transgression to cultural biases. Displacing these biases through outreach and education and maintaining open dialogue with rabbis were thus central to Kadag's work in its first decade and a half.

Educating Our Rabbis

In 2016 activist Nadav Schwartz invited a rabbi to join him for an evening of cruising. A group of rabbis affiliated with the liberal Beit Hillel organization was putting the finishing touches on a halachic position paper that advocated tolerance toward *hommos* and lesbians. An early draft alarmed activists because it created halachic equivalency between one-night stands and committed relationships. "A decisor cannot make halacha before he knows the reality," Nadav said at a conference about the paper, "so I invited the rabbi for an evening of cruising for casual sex. So that he can see reality."[47] The rabbis changed their position and acknowledged Kadag's input.[48]

Despite a decline in status,[49] rabbis remain key stakeholders in Orthodox communities. They provide religious, legal, ethical, and pastoral guidance and support to individuals, families, and communities. They set, interpret, and mediate halachic principles. Some young people, and especially young men studying in yeshivas, develop strong mentoring relationships with their rabbis, whose approval, support, and guidance they seek on spiritual and personal matters. Families, parents, and spouses also turn to rabbis for guidance and pastoral support. Kadag activists are of two minds about rabbinic authorities. While they view rabbis as representatives of an archaic legal codex and a homophobic culture, they are keenly aware that rabbis are gatekeepers to and bellwethers of change. Engaging with—educating—rabbinic authorities is thus central to advancing the goal of making space.

The theology of tolerance began with a relatively small (and closeted in their support) cadre of rabbis but has grown to encompass a broad swath of mainstream Orthodox rabbis. Kadag activists refer to a loose network of allied rabbis and women halachic experts as "our rabbis."[50] These allies speak publicly about LGBT persons' needs and meet with, listen to, and guide LGBT persons and their families. They also meet with groups of Orthodox LGBT persons and their representatives. Some of "our rabbis" are known to provide lenient halachic guidance in *private* consultations. A few have a public profile.[51]

At times, "educating our rabbis" is a deliberate strategy. One lesbian woman recalled a long conversation with her high school rabbi. "I told him I was struggling, that they have to help us. He said, 'We have to think about this more.' And he has! He was part of the group that wrote that Beit Hillel paper." Another woman recalled an exchange with an allied educator who had said at a conference that she would prefer to not be invited to same-sex weddings. Unwilling to play along, this Bat Kol member told her former teacher that she should expect to receive an invitation to her wedding. "I told her: if you don't want to come don't come and I'll understand but I'm not going to let you not struggle with this."

Such interactions help explain why Orthodox rabbis take positions that can result in significant reputational damage: they are personally invested in the lives of people they had come to know.[52] But until fairly recently, activists and allies walked a fine and playful line between symbolic public visibility and strategic discretion. A typical engagement went something like this: Havruta or Bat Kol would host a meeting with a rabbinic figure and later post on Facebook a photo featuring attendees and their interlocutor, with an accompanying text summarizing the exchange. The posts were sometimes cryptic, divulging little details other than that a meeting had taken place. At other times, interactions are public, such as Pesach Sheni events (chapter 5). Targeted rabbis include former teachers, thought leaders, and halachic authorities. The occasion might be a rabbi's statement, publication, or social media post; a brewing debate (conversion therapy, the ethics of heterosexual marriage, pride parades are staples); or the Jewish calendar (many conversations occur around the High Holidays, Hanukkah, and Passover). A group of rabbinic authorities began meeting with activists in 2018 to learn about the lives, needs, and urgent questions of Orthodox LGBT persons (by 2021 activists said they grew tired and disillusioned of these conversations). The foregoing discussion may be frustratingly vague, but it captures a reality of guardedness. Activists will sometimes hint at such meetings on their social media accounts but avoid sharing details; they fear that disclosure might jeopardize rapport and a still fragile trust. At any rate, the details matter less than the fact that these interactions are taking place. While some activists are frustrated by the glacial pace of halachic change, others are encouraged that these conversations are happening.

Activists recognize that some rabbis were not ready to come out of the closet as allies and that in some cases discretion served Kadag's purposes. Rabbis who were not identified with Kadag maintained credibility with more conservative Orthodox communities. Rabbis for their part fear that publicly aligning themselves with Kadag would compromise their ability to advocate on behalf of not only LGBT persons but also other, "delicate" and highly contentious causes such as sex abuse and divorce reform. There are concerns about livelihood. One rabbi saw speaking and teaching opportunities dwindle following an effusively supportive Facebook post. Another Rabbi (half) jokingly remarked that allyship jeopardizes his job as the head of a religious council. Nevertheless, a handful of rabbinic authorities are public about their support for LGBT persons, activists, and organizations (though they are not fully aligned with Kadag goals, strategies, and rhetoric). Three rabbinic authorities' engagements capture these tensions and the limits of tolerance.

Rabbi Benny Lau often writes and speaks about his interactions with Orthodox LGBT persons in mainstream outlets and on social media. Many consider his final "coming out" a brief speech at an impromptu rally in 2015 following Shira Banki's stabbing where he declared "the closet is death." In 2018, Rabbi Lau briefly attended a same-sex wedding, stopping by to congratulate the couple—Chaim Elbaum and Yair Strauss—*after* the wedding ceremony.[53] In an interview Rabbi Lau distinguished between *religious* same-sex weddings, which he does not support, and committed relationships, which are a lifeline because "living alone is a death sentence and one must do everything possible to avoid such death." His advice to Orthodox persons contemplating whether they should attend an LGBT wedding is grounded in a time-honored Jewish ethical principle: one should honor family and friends.[54]

In May 2017 Rabbi Lau reported, in a Facebook post, about a meeting with parents of Orthodox LGBT persons. Participants shared painful stories about their children's attempts to change, their own journeys of acceptance, and enduring criticism from family, friends, and rabbis. The meeting culminated with the creation of a new "dictionary" to replace the "old, religious language replete with hurting words." The new vocabulary would provide parents, educators, and congregations tools to support LGBT youth.[55] This and other meetings were part of a Kadag initiative that culminated in a December 2019 event (around Hanukkah), in which Kadag's educational arm Shoval launched a series of informative booklets for parents of Orthodox LGBT persons.[56] The booklets were not halachic, instead deploying what Rabbi Lau termed a "new religious language," a combination of sanitized and stripped-down concepts drawn from queer, gender, and sexuality studies, psychological research, and Jewish ethics and philosophy.

In these and other interactions, Rabbi Lau skirted and sidestepped the halacha, but it bears emphasizing that the "old, religious language replete with hurting words" that he sought to cast aside is the language of the Torah and its interpreters. On the flip side, in his interview, the rabbi was not making halacha but rather dispensing guidance. But given his stature and the fact that he was communicating through an Orthodox media outlet, the effect was not far from that. In the fall of 2020 the rabbi released a position paper outlining halachic principles for recognizing (some) same-sex relationships and families, bringing them into the Jewish fold.[57]

Another ally is Rabbanit Malka Puterkovsky, who approaches halachic activism from her perch as an Orthodox feminist trailblazer. Malka Puterkovsky has long been publicly supportive of LGBT persons and their causes. Kadag members praise her as a singularly courageous, compassionate, and wise ally. One Bat Kol member said that while she has some significant disagreements with "Malka," as Puterkovsky is widely known, "Malka is the only one who attempts to bring a comprehensive *religious* worldview, to bring the LGBT community in. . . . She believes in writing a halachic book."

A few days prior to the 2015 Jerusalem Pride Parade, Havruta posted a photo of fourteen activists with Malka Puterkovsky. The post acknowledged that the Rabbanit did not support the parade but she did give them sage advice: "Demand from the rabbis and from the entire Orthodox community answers grounded in doctrine, halacha, and faith. The way to make change is from the bottom up." It is rumored that Malka Puterkovsky herself has developed a systematic halachic solution to some pressing concerns regarding same-sex relationships but is reluctant to release it because she does not believe that Orthodox communities are ready.[58] Surely, pressure from the ground would help move them along.

In November 2016, several dozen cisgender, *hommo* men, a handful of lesbian women, and a few parents gathered in Rabbi Lau's Jerusalem synagogue for a dialogue with Malka Puterkovsky (Rabbi Lau was not in attendance, but his brother, who is gay and a rabbi of a progressive congregation in New York City, was there). The three-hour meeting covered topics including how to engage Orthodox communities and rabbis, pride parades, conversion therapy, family rejection. The tone was respectful, but the conversation grew tense at times; this happens often in meetings with "our rabbis," when attendees express impatience with halachic impasses and rabbinic hesitations. Malka Puterkovsky acknowledged frustrations and admitted that she lacked adequate answers. She offered the Orthodox feminist revolution as a blueprint: move ahead of the rabbis, she deplored, "you have to insist, to fight. There are prices that I paid as a woman, and some of you will be willing to pay. Don't tire!"[59] The session ended with the requisite photo-op featuring some participants and Malka Puterkovsky; making the rounds on social media, the photo, with accompanying posts by participants, reiterated that Kadag was talking to rabbis; they may disagree on some points, but the march toward full recognition continues.[60]

As opposed to Rabbi Lau, whose public work seemingly sidesteps the halacha and is yet imbued with the authority associated with his stature, and Malka Puterkovsky, who emphasizes grassroots-led transformation, other allied rabbis stay within the bounds of the theology of tolerance even as they acknowledge its limitations. Rabbi Madan, a longtime yeshiva head in Har Eztion, was an early ally. His positions, too, evolved. In the early aughts the rabbi encouraged mixed-orientation marriages, but within less than a decade rumors circulated among *hommos* that the rabbi is inclined to (discreetly) offer guidance and support to same-sex couples.[61] The rabbi attended a meeting in 2009, among the first of its genre, with several dozen Havruta activists. (One participant described the meeting as "the coming of the messiah.") Per a contemporaneous journalistic account, Rabbi Madan agreed to attend because he had recently learned that a former student would be in the audience.[62] The rabbi has continued to meet regularly with individuals, couples, families, and organizations and has addressed the topic in the media. He has had no choice: with his yeshiva gaining reputation as a (relatively) gay-friendly haven, some of the most vocal and prolific activists of the late 2010s emerged from its ranks.

By some measures, Rabbi Madan has been a consistent ally. "Homosexuals are not deviants," he wrote in July 2018 in a rebuke to a letter condemning homosexuality signed by two hundred fifty Orthodox rabbis.[63] He has taken some of the most lenient positions to be released publicly on halachic recognition of same-sex relationships and some forms of intimacy.[64] But Rabbi Madan rejects lenient interpretations of the ban on same-sex sexual intimacies: "It is unequivocal, we cannot compromise on Torah bans." As for same-sex marriage, "it is not that Orthodoxy cannot give its blessing—it explicitly condemns."[65] The rabbi has been steadfast in his refusal to release *universal* guidelines for same-sex couples despite the guidance he has provided in private consultations: "There is no singular answer, not a clear list of halacha. We have clear halacha between husband and wife but we have nothing organized for a man and a man. This can work to our advantage, we can be flexible, but we have to address each case individually." Not good enough, admonished an attendee at a 2012 meeting with the rabbi: "You speak of personal guidance but not everyone knows that there are solutions and they don't know that they can go for personal guidance. A seventeen-year-old kid who slashes his wrists because he doesn't understand what's happening to him doesn't get personal guidance."[66]

A decade after Rabbi Madan's historic meeting with Havruta in 2009, many had lost their patience with rabbis' cautious rhetoric and the "old language" of transgression, silence, and dis-ease. When Rabbi Madan met again with Havruta members at their 2019 Shabbat retreat emotions ran high, revealing fracture lines *within* Orthodox *hommo* circles. Some, holding out hope for halachic solutions, requested that the rabbi publicly release guidelines for halachic same-sex relationships; others conceded the halacha's limitations: "You can't erase the halacha, erase the God all mighty. We have a problem . . . but you can't expect rabbis to come and say, all's great, do whatever you want."[67] Others, wary of being branded as transgressors, their families tainted, had tired of waiting for rabbis to "find a way." Rabbis reluctant to make halacha for same-sex couples, one participant observed, are reneging on their public responsibility and contribute to the continued erasure of same-sex couples. Another attendee said he had "lost the last bit of trust [he] had in the rabbinic establishment" upon realizing that Rabbi Madan's support for same-sex coupling was contingent on a promise to refrain from transgressing "the biblical ban. . . . Rabbis don't enter straight couples' bedroom, why enter mine?"

Twenty-five years after Rabbi Lubitch's lone voice called for acceptance, tolerance is no longer a fringe position. Some allies are open to creative interpretive solutions; others are more cautious. Some rabbinic authorities prefer discreet, private consultations; others engage activists in public venues. They all recognize that LGBT persons' plight can no longer be ignored and that old frames of transgression have lost their universal resonance. These rabbinic authorities are willing to engage with and learn from LGBT persons. And, by speaking out publicly, they normalize LGBT matters as legitimate halachic, social, and cultural concerns. To be sure, there are tensions within Orthodox LGBT circles, between Orthodox LGBT persons and rabbinic authorities, and among allied authorities. Where the road would lead is an open question. Meanwhile, LGBT persons expand the circle of sympathizers, if not allies, as they follow the natural course of Jewish life. Discreet, concrete, case-specific consultations further serve to educate rabbis and, consequently, shape the glacial process of halachic change.

Deploying Halacha, Consulting Rabbis

In 2007, a distraught seventeen-year-old high school student asked Rabbi Yuval Cherlow whether the halacha permits suicide. The anonymous writer feared that he would violate "the prohibition." He did not want to live in sin, nor could he fathom letting go of halachic life. But what other options did he have? The rabbi was sincere and empathetic: suicide was not an option, though the path ahead would be challenging, a "life of mission and considerable, unending trial."[68] Rabbi Cherlow invited the writer to meet with him and published the responsum on an online portal.

The anonymous writer was Yehonatan Gill Rossen Maman, who became, a decade after writing this letter, a leading Kadag activist. A gifted public speaker, Yehonatan has appeared at panels along with the rabbi he consulted as a teen. Yehonatan posted this exchange in June 2019 on his Facebook page as part of a coordinated Kadag campaign. The occasion: a conservative Orthodox critic had implied that suicide was a plausible route for same-sex-attracted persons. But when he wrote his original query as a deeply closeted and highly observant seventeen-year old, Yehonatan was not looking to score a win. He was an observant Jew in need rabbinic guidance. The vast majority of Orthodox LGBT persons' encounters with rabbis occur when they reach out to rabbis for ethical, spiritual, or halachic guidance, and here, too, activism has had profound impacts.

Jewish rules of conduct infuse, inform, and direct everyday life. An observant Jew who is unsure about conduct in a specific set of circumstances can turn to a learned expert in Jewish law (typically a male rabbi, though more recently women are beginning to be recognized as experts) for guidance. Yeshiva students questioning their sexual orientation routinely turn to a rabbi-educator to help make sense of their emergent desires; parents seek guidance from community rabbis on existential as well as mundane matters. One mother turned to several rabbis before she received a satisfactory response to her query: how to accommodate a daughter's request to bring a same-sex partner to a Shabbat dinner that included young siblings. In aggregate, such consultations, grounded in the "stuff" of everyday life, produce profound halachic changes because they expose a wide array of rabbis—those who educate the young and lead congregations—to the trials and tribulations, needs, experiences, and desires of LGBT Orthodox persons and their families. Such conversations help disseminate tolerance and may eventually nudge rabbis toward taking further halachic leaps.

LGBT persons' numerous consultations with rabbis can be grouped into two varieties.[69] Some questions are existential or philosophical in nature: interviewees reported private conversations with trusted rabbis involving tears, wise advice, and deep dive into texts. They discussed interpretations of the tradition's supposed ban on same-sex relationships; sought rabbinic advice on how to "mange" their attraction, whether they could change, and what kind of family life they could aspire to; and reflected on their loss of faith. LGBT persons do not always find solace in these consultations.

Questions of the second variety concern conduct. Orthodox LGBT persons seek concrete halachic guidelines to live by: "Am I allowed to go to the *miqveh*? Because I might see things there. Like a heterosexual man who is not allowed to go to women's *miqveh*. Can I study at a yeshiva? It is forbidden to live with girls, so this is allowed? When I dance in a circle I am aroused."[70] Orthodox women cover their hair—should a woman in a committed same-sex relationship cover her hair? Should same-sex-attracted persons observe the laws of *yichud* (prohibition of seclusion, normally applied to opposite-sex contexts)? What kinds of blessings are appropriate for a same-sex couple commitment ceremony? Can same-sex couples sponsor a *kiddush* in the synagogue to mark the birth of a child? These are all real questions asked by, or of, LGBT persons and rabbinic authorities I talked to. Orthodox LGBT persons waiting for a halachic guidebook have these types of questions in mind.

The second variety of questions is notable for what they *do not* do: they do not inquire whether one is "allowed" to be in a same-sex relationship nor whether certain acts are permissible: "No one is going to ask a rabbi for permission to engage in anal sex. We know what the answer will be," one man told me, an observation confirmed by a Rabbi's comment that he is no longer asked whether "the halacha will find us a solution, will permit us to live our orientation as we wish . . . they understand that no one can permit the prohibitions." But it is the concrete nature of questions that solicit guidance in clearly delineated circumstances that bears the potential for far-reaching halachic change. In the past, rabbis almost uniformly responded that since same-sex relationships are prohibited, there was no point in proceeding with the inquiry. One man recounted asking "a rabbi a question regarding saying *shma* when in bed with my partner. He answered, one sentence 'the halacha doesn't recognize same-sex relationships.' But I didn't ask him about the relationship! I asked you about a reality!"

More rabbis are now willing to address these concrete realities head-on. One lesbian couple received a ruling regarding menstrual purity laws. Another received guidance that helped them reconcile with their families. An observant *hommo* spoke highly of a rabbi who helped him navigate the intricacies of dating a nonobservant man. Not all decisions are favorable for *hommos* and lesbians; one ruling imposed strict seclusion laws on same-sex-attracted men,[71] and in keeping with the public/private distinction of halachic ruling,[72] most LGBT-affirming decisions are case-specific and for the most are part kept private. Nevertheless, by focusing on the "small stuff" of everyday life, these rabbis acknowledge the existence of same-sex attraction and relationships: the affirmation of Jewish personhood that had eluded lesbians and *hommos* for so long. Furthermore, stories of such encounters and the existence of such affirming answers are passed among the community. Meanwhile, the first comprehensive guidebooks (or chapters) are being contemplated and published.

The potential impact of these engagements is immense precisely because of the organic and authentic context in which they occur. Those who engage with rabbis in this manner are typically more observant and halachically committed, and as opposed to activist efforts that target a specific subset of established allies, these engagements are dispersed and diffuse. Consulting rabbis do not always provide satisfactory answers, but because these engagements occur in the natural course of living Jewish lives, more authorities are confronted with concrete situations—not over the airwaves or an anonymous Facebook exchange. Jewish theological change works through a dispersed set of such legal experts. Thus, acquainting a growing number of rabbinic authorities with LGBT lives is key to social change. A recent survey of the halachic landscape found an emergent expansive archive,[73] suggesting that the limitations of the theology of tolerance and the injuries inherent in the still dominant "old religious language" notwithstanding, negotiations with religious elites is worthwhile strategy.

Tolerance Is Not Enough: Beit Hillel Policy Paper

In April 2016 twenty-one rabbinic authorities affiliated with the liberal Beit Hillel issued a halachic position paper that called on Orthodox communities to accept *hommos* and lesbians.[74] "The Congregation and People with Homosexual Tendencies" reiterated the prohibition against same-sex relationships but called upon Orthodox communities to treat *hommos* and lesbians per a cardinal Jewish value: love thy neighbor.[75] Signatories, LGBT persons, allies, and critics differed in their assessments whether the opinion represented a significant breakthrough, but its issuing suggested that LGBT issues had arrived on Orthodoxy's center stage; Kadag celebrated the document as a milestone if not a game changer. The document also captured the consensus around the theology of tolerance born of reality: LGBT people were already living within Orthodox communities, albeit without official recognition or halachic guidelines. The rabbis were late to the party.

The opinion began with a declaration: "The prohibition of homo-sexual relations is from the Torah, and since the Torah is eternal and irreplaceable, homosexual relations cannot be condoned." It then dis-tinguished between behavior (forbidden) and orientation, declaring that "there is nothing wrong, morally or halachically, with individuals, men or women, exhibiting homosexual tendencies." It then called on congre-gations "to refrain from adding insult to injury, and find ways to allow these people, who wish to be part of the religious community, to do so. They should not be subjected to any restrictions beyond those that are acceptable in the congregation regarding other types of transgressors." Tolerance was grounded in transgression.

Orthodox conservatives critiqued the document's halachic premises, but Beit Hillel insisted that there was not much by way of halachic inno-vation; "We really did nothing new, just implemented existing halacha," one signatory told me. But Rabbi Kula, who led the effort, conceded three extra-halachic innovations: the document recognized an empirical reality (Orthodox *hommos* and lesbians exist), affirmed that homosexual orientation was not transgressive, and articulated a clear halachic stance: communities were to accept and make space for same-sex-attracted persons.

Kadag activists were split on the episode's implications: some thought the publicity surrounding the document might alleviate prejudice, but others thought that rabbinic authorities were adding insult to injury by issuing an opinion, *in 2016*, premised on transgression, exclusions, and omissions. Some of the document's fiercest critics were LGBT persons and their allies. To Beit Hillel's credit, two of them—Havruta activist Nadav Schwartz and Dr. Hanna Friedman, a Beit Hillel member who was not a signatory—were included on the roster of speakers at a con-ference about the opinion. Schwartz was introduced as bringing "voices from the field," while Dr. Friedman spoke for the Orthodox left. Neither minced words.

First, rather than rejecting the lens of transgression, the entire legal edifice was grounded in parsing out its implications. The opinion's logic was: if congregations allow people who do not abide by halachic prin-ciples such as the Sabbath, kosher laws, or purity laws, to partake fully in its life and rituals, those transgressing the purported ban against homosexuality should not be singled out. Dr. Friedman was troubled by this logic: "Just to read and to hear sinner, sinner, sinner. Can we refrain from judging? . . . Yes, this is the religious language, the language of our scripture. But our inability to free ourselves from this language pains me."

Activists were infuriated by the document's preamble, which explained that "this document addresses the congregation. It deals with the issue of homosexuality, but does not address homosexuals themselves." Nadav Schwartz excoriated this logic:

> With this declaration, did you exclude *hommos* and lesbians from the Orthodox community? Did you put us outside the fence in your attempt to include us? And is this a logical statement? What is this community that you speak to? Our brothers and sisters? Our parents' friends? Are we not going to be directly impacted by this document? . . . Please do not write a document about *hommos* and lesbians and say that it doesn't speak to *hommos* and lesbians.

Schwartz also rejected the core logic of the theology of tolerance— acceptance without legitimacy. It left LGBT persons hanging. Tolerance, he insisted, was not enough; like many observant Orthodox LGBT persons, he was waiting for the halachic guidebook; the time was yesterday he added. Dr. Friedman acknowledged a common refrain among rabbis—"the time has not yet come," but telling *hommos* and lesbians that rabbis have no solution for them "is a tough statement." Dr. Friedman reminded her peers that rabbinic authorities had a *duty* to provide guidance. Eventually, she added, they would be forced to do so: "Reality will produce the solution and halacha and law will follow" after practices and traditions take root. Her comments have indeed proved prescient.

Nevertheless, some activists framed the position paper as a milestone on the road toward recognition and legitimacy. One man appreciated that Beit Hillel declared "that the orientation is not a transgression. And they called on communities to accept *hommos* in no uncertain terms." A semicloseted young woman noted that "the rabbis are starting to understand that this [same-sex attraction] is a real thing that exists. . . . They're talking about it as something that can't be controlled." Activists were also delighted that Beit Hillel countered conservative halachic positions. Citing an opinion by a staunch foe that "said that you can't give *hommos aliya*, they should be banished from ritual, community," one Havruta member marveled: "Beit Hillel said the opposite!" Finally, although the document was narrowly construed (communities' acceptance of same-sex-attracted persons), both foes and the media framed it as a more general opinion about LGBT persons and Orthodoxy, a public relations victory for Kadag.

Another milestone: Kadag activists had a direct say and seat at the table; their refrain "talk with us, not about us" found its way into halachic-making processes. Granted, these rabbis all hail from the liberal wing of Orthodoxy and grounded their decision in the theology of transgression. But the group extended beyond "our rabbis." Moreover, the rabbis listened. An early draft created an equivalency between a same-sex-attracted person who is in "a committed relationship and observes sexual purity with one partner and has children and a family with this partner" and one who "turns to a life of one night stands in the bars." Activists, who were consulted on an earlier draft, could not let this stand. It is in this context that Nadav Schwartz relayed the story of inviting a rabbi for (an educational) night of cruising, an exchange that culminated in the removal of the troubling equivalency.[76] This was no small victory, even if the whole episode was relegated to a distant footnote. The "biggest innovation of all," an activist told me, was that LGBT persons "were involved in the process and had lots of comments and suggestions and many things in the document changed. . . . The published draft is a product of dialogue with us . . . they listened. And one of us was invited to speak at the conference." The experience of *hommos* and lesbians thus served as a source of authoritative knowledge for halachic decisors, with a caveat: the process favored cisgender men with halachic training (Nadav Schwartz had been a student at an elite yeshiva before coming out).

Most of all, Orthodox LGBT persons were relieved to be acknowledged: "This is the first time the rabbis aren't talking about 'whether' [but rather] about 'what.' So I don't care what [the document] says, and that it's not perfect. . . . They started talking about the what." Just having rabbinic authorities talk about LGBT issues "out in the open" was refreshing: "They didn't change halacha. But they gave a sense of openness." The rabbis, another activist said, "took the problem out of the closet."

Likewise, a rabbinic authority not involved in the process observed that "we are moving forward, because now it's on the table, its spoken, you can't dismiss, ignore, put it in the closet." In a community where religious laws and everyday lives are deeply intertwined, this was a win. An activist said that she felt the impact of Beit Hillel's move a few months later, "in the 2016 parade, when Rabbi Levinstein criticized us and it backfired . . . suddenly there was a legitimate discourse of acceptance."

Havruta celebrated the episode with a Facebook post: "We are proud that our position was taken into account in the writing of this historical document, and hope that it will be a basis for dialogue among equals . . . that will bring about, in the end of the process, full recognition in us, our relationships, and our families." The post also lamented "the complete absence of transpeople and their halachic status" but was confident that the "document is just a first step on a long shared journey still ahead."[77] Havruta was offering a bear hug of sorts: the post also acknowledged that the Beit Hillel move was a "courageous step, that will undoubtedly be received with criticism."

Official declarations aside, some Orthodox LGBT persons were angry. They resented Beit Hillel's claim that it had opened up the conversation. At the conference, one speaker framed the document and the conference itself as "an opening for dialogue in our communities" and the document cited a pastoral duty to speak up: "As congregational leaders and rabbis, we must take part in influencing public discourse, especially within our communities. It is up to us dissipate the unease that surrounds this issue, to speak in the spirit of the Torah, and to contribute to shaping its ethical complexity." An activist seethed: "*Rabbis*, perhaps, haven't been talking about this, but *we* have been talking for over a decade." Another activist insisted on clarifying "the order of things. *We* came out of the closet. *We* turned to rabbis because *we* have been encouraging our families to accept us, our families turned to rabbis and as a result the rabbis of Beit Hillel published this document." By the time Beit Hillel finally spoke up, communities were knee-deep into these conversations, and leading the charge were Orthodox LGBT persons already living in their midst, attending synagogue, sending their children to schools, sitting at Shabbat and holiday tables. As rabbinic authorities debated congregations' appropriate responses to same-sex-attracted persons, several dozen Orthodox *hommos* and lesbians had come out collectively through the Our

Faces public visibility campaign (chapter 5). "Of course they had to write about this," one activist cynically remarked. "They understand that they have to talk to the people, really look at them. Otherwise they'll lose us. They already have." That rabbis were scrambling to catch up with reality was in line with Malka Puterkovsky's sage advice: live your lives and the halacha will follow because halachic change emerges from realities on the ground.

Some critics thought the document was too little too late. The women of Bat Kol were particularly wary. One interviewee, upset that the document didn't address "the real halachic issues," said that she did not "care if the rabbis accept me or if they tell me that they hug me. I don't want these hugs. I want answers." Another said, "Like, yeah, accept us, okay, okay, okay, we've heard this before. We want a more serious conversation." She thought that the failure to address gender identity was an "unforgiveable omission." Still others rejected Beit Hillel's theory of social change: "I don't think that in any public issue the change will come from above," one said, while rejecting the idea that social change happens slowly from within the tradition: "evolution revolution is not the way."[78] "Beit Hillel are not the best allies because they're not enough. They're basically where Rabbi Lau was ten years ago. And he has evolved but isn't ideal either," said another. Mostly, they were ambivalent:

> When it was published there was this collective "wow." But it wasn't enough. Their position is irrelevant, not sufficiently grounded in reality. . . . This partial recognition that you are human beings who deserve respect. This is old news. *Because of course you have to respect us!* But what's the next step? There's an expectation here that a person won't have a family. Because that undermines heteronormative social order. If we haven't progressed from there I'm not satisfied. Like, it's nice that they talk about it. They talk to me to create dialogue. But you can't demand that I won't have a family, that I won't be in a relationship. You can't ask this of people. So the bottom line of this discourse is that we will accept you etc. but don't have a family. Not good enough!!

Beit Hillel had planned additional position papers on LGBT issues, but thus far none had materialized. One rabbinic authority suggested to me that Kadag's lukewarm response may have dampened enthusiasm for further dialogue: "[Beit Hillel] knew they'd be criticized by conservatives but they also got a cold shoulder from Kadag because the community wanted more than that. So they were afraid to continue." "The community is angry," told me a young activist, "because [rabbis] aren't advancing fast enough."

Expecting Orthodox LGBT Jews to wait is impractical: halachically committed persons are already in same-sex relationships, raising or planning to raise children in new (un-Orthodox?) family structures. Given this reality, Orthodox leaders are reneging on their pastoral duty: providing structure and guidance to *all* Jews. Intimate, committed, long-term relationships and families are key values in Orthodoxy, and thus excluding an entire category of people from the core of Orthodoxy amounts to an admission of the halacha's limitations. Worse: it might signal that rejecting Judaism is preferable to remaining within its fold, a heretic position. Worse still: if the halacha leaves an entire category of people without adequate answers, how can it claim to be a systematic and comprehensive moral, ethical, legal, and practical guide? Dr. Hanna Friedman thus urged Beit Hillel to address halachic questions that directly pertain to LGBT persons. Doing nothing, she warned, is unethical and unsustainable, an anomaly, a problem not only for LGBT persons but for the entire Orthodox community that exposes the halacha

> in its nakedness. Halacha that doesn't know how to give a response to a person and says to him, "Sit aside. If you can, please leave this issue outside the synagogue. Just come to pray. . . ." It's an anomaly, a test case. An extreme case that reflects something deeper about the halacha. This pains *me . . .* because this halacha is mine, this Torah is mine.[79]

Dr. Friedman suggests a strategy for breaking the impasse of the theology of tolerance: shift the gravity and urgency for finding a solution from LGBT persons' needs to shared and broader concerns about Orthodox viability. But this strategy, too, can backfire, further exposing the inherent limitations of interventions that leave intact systems of power and knowledge.

LGBT and the Future of Judaism

In July 2018 a distinguished panel of rabbinic authorities gathered in Jerusalem to discuss the challenges that LGBTQ identities posed to Jewish law and theology.[80] At stake was no less than the future of Judaism. Per publicity materials and panel organizer Rabbi Malamet's opening remarks, the goal was to consider how Jewish law adapts to modernity; "how Judaism navigates between ancient codes and contemporary values of recognition and dignity"; how Orthodoxy "can navigate the conflict between traditional prohibitions and the reality of people's personal experience"; and whether LGBT persons "usher in a new discourse about God and Jewish theology."

The panel featured the American Rabbi Steven Greenberg, a gay man and longtime LGBT activist; Professor Tamar Ross of Bar-Ilan University, a key architect of the Orthodox feminist movement (and Dr. Hanna Friedman's mother); Rabbi Shlomo Vilk, head of the Machanaim Yeshiva, which is considered by some as gay-friendly; and Rabbi Yoni Rosenweig, a community rabbi in Beit Shemesh who has written about the topic.[81] The panel was rounded off by the organizer, Rabbi Elliott Malamet, a progressive Orthodox rabbi.

The evening got off to a late start as latecomers looked for chairs in adjacent rooms, and by the time the event began there were well over three hundred people in the room, some standing at the door and sitting on windowsills. But the event ran afoul of Kadag's organizing principles: don't talk about us, talk with us, give us a seat at the table. Although Rabbi Greenberg is gay, he did not come up through the ranks of Israeli Orthodoxy, where familial, communal, and national contexts have shaped local debates.[82] Kadag activists were furious, and behind-the-scenes wrangling resulted in a last-minute solution: a second set of panelists composed of Orthodox LGBT persons, chaired by Shoval leader Benjamin Katz. But this panel sat on the auditorium floor with the audience, not onstage with the main panelists, a spatial arrangement that further underscored LGBT persons' marginalized status in the conversation that turned homosexuality into a halachic test case. Unseen and inaudible to the audience, the activist panel had few opportunities to engage the panel of religious authorities. An attendee fumed, "I have a lot of respect for the rabbis and am glad that there is so much interest.

But they are sitting there talking about *our* lives." The most thunderous clapping of the night came when Professor Ross made a similar point. Asked about interpretations of the Leviticus abomination clause, she opined that there were more pressing questions to consider, adding that Orthodox leaders' most important duty was to provide answers to concrete questions about conduct, not engage in theoretical debates about a Bible verse. Social change, she added, was compatible with halacha. In fact, halacha demanded change when out of step with the times.[83]

But Ross's comments were an outlier in a conversation that largely remained true to its intent to interrogate the relationship between halacha and social change. A question about the Bible's prohibition regarding male anal intercourse turned into a discussion of halachic exegeses techniques. Questions about community acceptance, whether LGBT people should even seek halachic guidance, and distinctions between orientation and practice tracked broader debates about halachic interpretive methods and commentary, theories of social change, and relationships between rabbis and their congregation. Rabbi Rosenweig remarked that "you can't legislate against LGBT existence" and pondered whether rabbinic authorities were relevant in this conversation. Rabbi Vilk, representing the Rabbinic establishment, seemed to be biding time as he reflected on the changes that *had* occurred in the past decade. The event thus captured the gamut of responses among Orthodox liberals and their dilemmas: LGBT as the biggest challenge to Judaism of our time (Rabbi Malamet); we are listening and hurting with you but we do not yet have answers (Rabbi Vilk); maybe you should stop asking us and just live your lives (Rabbi Rosenweig); the Orthodox community must find answers (Professor Ross); we do have answers! (Rabbi Greenberg). The event also demonstrated that talking about, rather than talking with, had run its course. The activist panel pressed a different agenda: "This is our story, our challenge, not your challenge." "We are not some phenomenon that you debate about." "You will give us answers because you'll have to."

This episode demonstrates that shifting the urgency from LGBT persons' demand to be seen by the halacha to addressing Orthodoxy's fears about relevance and self-preservation marginalizes LGBT voices. There is a crucial difference between focusing halachic inquiry on the stuff of life and positing "the LGBT question" as a test case through which to work out theoretical principles and halachic dilemmas. LGBT persons are wary: insisting that rabbis *must* find a way, they point out that halachic alternatives are possible, that the guidebook is way overdue, and that rabbinic authorities would do well to let LGBT persons speak for themselves.

The Missing Guidebook and Alternative Paths Forward

How long can the halachic impasse last? How will it be overcome? Many LGBT persons and their allies argue (and some worry) that the theology of tolerance will collapse under the weight of its own inconsistencies. Lack of recognition of same-sex relationships belies a reality: Orthodox persons are living in same-sex unions and raising children within these and other types of families. They post engagement and birth announcements and wedding videos in defiance of expectations that they remain single, celibate, or mum about their personal lives and intimate relationships. The theology of tolerance is not one to live by.

Some allied rabbinic authorities think that the time is not yet ripe for full halachic recognition and beg for patience. Others, like Professor Tamar Ross and the Rabbanit Malka Puterkovsky, encourage activists to keep pressing. Some rabbis fear that they would not be able to provide satisfactory answers. One told me, "Why even risk getting into this business . . . you saw what happened with Beit Hillel. I have given this topic thought but I haven't published anything because I'm afraid that they'll demand more of me." Meanwhile, Orthodox LGBT persons have tired of halachic deliberations that fail to produce full halachic legitimacy. Some think that as in the case of the Orthodox feminist revolution, leadership should emerge from within; a female rabbinic authority told me that LGBT persons "need their own leaders. I can't be a leading public figure." "That's what we want too," an activist told me bitterly, "but they kick us out of the yeshivas when we make too much noise. You heard about what happened to [name], right?"

In the meantime, the halachic wheels are slowly turning, following the halacha's natural course: halacha is written behind the scenes, incrementally, question by question, conversation by conversation, driven by the realities, force, and fabric of everyday life. Notably, these conversations extend beyond "our rabbis" and Kadag activists. A significant portion of this work is done privately, and these responsa exist on people's computers, phones, and servers. In a blink of an eye, they can enter the public domain. Occasionally, they do. Rabbi Avishai Mizrachi's recent mapping of the state of responsa indicates that more rabbis are willing to address halachic questions head-on. Though these responsa do not always provide the answers Orthodox LGBT persons desire, they certainly communicate "you exist."[84] This is one reason that critics grudgingly celebrated the flawed Beit Hillel document as a breakthrough.

Rabbi Steven Greenberg offered one path forward in 2004. In *Wrestling with God*—part halachic tract, part autobiographical confession—Rabbi Greenberg proposed a reading restricting the Leviticus ban to exploitative and humiliating relationships.[85] His interpretation, which provides a halachic route to recognizing same-sex relationships without imposing sexual limitations, has not caught traction in Israel. Some Orthodox *hommos* vociferously reject this reading on interpretive grounds, but others say that centering same-sex halacha on the Leviticus ban on male-on-male anal sex reduces a rich lived experience to one sexual act. These critics say that the halachic conversation should instead focus on recognizing and *celebrating* LGBT personhood. Doing so is not compatible with a lens that continues to view gender and sexual diversity as a problem.

The real obstacles, then, are not halachic. Ultimately, the issue is not whether the halacha can (and should) evolve, but rather whether rabbinic authorities are willing to take an LGBT-centered perspective: a point of departure that not only rejects transgression and embraces tolerance and acceptance, but also values LGBT persons' (Jewish) humanity and views gender and sexual diversity as a net positive. One activist explained,

> If the question is what *hommos* and lesbians are allowed to do, I don't need that book, because the answer is that they can't. Are we allowed this? No. Are we allowed that? No, forbidden. That will be the answer. But if the question is "How do we create a religious life for *hommos* and lesbians?"—that's a book I'm interested in! It's like Shabbat elevator. If the question had been "Can you use the elevator on Shabbat?" The answer is no. But if the question is *how* to use the elevator on Shabbat, then you start finding solutions.

Rabbi Yuval Cherlow agrees: the hard question is not what is forbidden but what is permissible: "What does religion, belief demand of these guys?" He also dismisses the possibility that "this particular issue [is] too big. Just fifteen years ago rabbis all agreed that conversion therapy was the obvious route, [they said] there's 100 percent success and if you didn't succeed it was your fault. But the fallout was awful and no one advocates that anymore."[86]

Professor Tamar Ross points out that the Jewish archive provides ample tools to guide this undertaking; in previous eras decisors had overcome other seemingly intractable biblical prohibitions. Historically plural and internally incoherent, halachic discourse has always adjudicated competing interests and norms; like all legal systems, it is expected to respond to new situations and provide answers in a dynamic and changing world. Consolidation and insistence on one route is the aberration.

Why, then, has the halacha of same-sex attraction been so slow to change? One rabbi pondered whether "there is something about same-sex attraction that is irrational,"[87] but Orthodox LGBT persons think the answer is clear: transphobia and homophobia masquerading as religious decrees. One activist put it this way: "Homophobes use religion, so they can be homophobic but not be called that. 'Oh, I'm not homophobic. It's that it's forbidden in the halacha.'" Resistance to change, then, is less about what is *legally* and theologically possible than about what rabbis (and, by extension, Orthodox communities) believe to be culturally, politically, and religiously desirable and expedient. The missing guidebook tells us less about legal logics and precedents, and more about how the prospect of gender and sexual diversity threatens the existing (Jewish) order of things. This is partly why the halacha remains an activist arena even for those who have long written off its relevance in their own lives: it signifies recognition and legitimacy. Full recognition, in turn, can emerge only from halachic deliberations that center on Orthodox LGBT persons' experiences, concerns, and perspectives and value them for what they are: a variation on the Jewish experience.

Where does this leave those awaiting the halachic guidebook and recognition? Some wait for rabbis to catch up, others shrug them off as irrelevant in the context of a diversifying Orthodoxy where halachic guidance has lost its luster. And while activists see rabbinic interest as strategically beneficial, they are tired of being regarded as a "phenomenon," a challenge of the time. Still others optimistically await the halachic guidebook, written, perhaps, by one of their own. Activist Ziva Ofek put contemporary Orthodox LGBT persons' predicament in historical perspective: "Every desert generation lives with deep conflict vis-à-vis their culture, identity."[88] A desert generation, by definition, is transitional—the historical one led the biblical Israelites to the Holy Land.

Beyond a Theology of Tolerance

At a 2018 conference at the Orthodox-affiliated Bar Ilan University, Havruta activist Chaim Elbaum explained that Kadag was not defiant of the halacha—but rather "asking that it inquire our questions as it inquires other new issues that reality brings about—objectively, without emotions, without prejudice, and without fears of a slippery slope."[89] The goal, he added, was to make room for LGBT persons within Orthodoxy.

Some Orthodox LGBT persons may shrug off the halacha and its gatekeepers as irrelevant, but making room within Orthodoxy cannot bypass the halacha because many Orthodox LGBT persons experience lack of jurisprudence as a spiritual harm. The battle over halacha is a battle over legitimacy because as an aspirational system the halacha is subject making: by providing a framework for conducting one's everyday life the halacha marks and recognizes Jewish subjects, legitimizing and validating their experiences within the Jewish cosmos. On the flip side, lack of jurisprudence is akin to an erasure of personhood, marking those deemed not worthy of halachic recognition with illegitimacy and shame. By making the halacha a battleground LGBT persons force Orthodoxy to confront its self-understanding, boundaries, and future: a battle for Orthodoxy's soul, waged on the backs of a marginalized group who rose up and declared, no more.

The process is not over, but Kadag has won the framing war and laid bare a historical reality: the halacha is always evolving. Conservative Orthodox rabbis may claim that the theology of transgression is timeless, but the historical record suggests it was fairly recently that homosexuality was singled out from other biblical abominations. Nevertheless, Orthodox conservatives have gone to war, using progressively extreme and violent language to claim that homosexuality was not only perverse but also un-Jewish. The dispute is not only, or predominantly, theological: the gulf between tolerance and transgression reflects a deeper chasm between those who view modernity as an existential threat and those who view it as a challenge that will propel Orthodoxy forward. Conservative Orthodox rabbis' stance is part of a broader radicalization—more stringent modesty measures, separation between men and women, condemnations of alternative family forms, and a general disdain for a range of social ills associated with secular, Western culture.[90]

For a while, the theology of tolerance was a sufficient antidote as it restored homosexuality to the domain of the normal, allowing rabbis to communicate: you are just fine. But, ultimately, tolerance was not enough as it left too many questions unanswered, too many categories of Jews outside the camp, thereby revealing the inherent limits of a political strategy of acceptance without legitimacy. In some ways, the limits of tolerance track those of an authenticity discourse that similarly stops short of dismantling existing power structures: there is only so much that can be done while leaving systems of knowledge and power intact.

The controversies covered in this chapter bear a striking resemblance to those in Catholicism and Evangelical Christianity, where allied thought leaders have passed through similar stages: invisibility, erasure, and lack of knowledge; wanting to provide spiritual guidance; acceptance for the community but not much guidance to LGBT people themselves; and later doubting whether tolerance is enough—and if not, what they can do theologically that would be sufficient. In the Christian context, what lies "beyond tolerance" is a queered theology, what sociologist Dawne Moon characterizes as homopositive views that hold not only that it is wrong to shut people out of the community, but that homosexuality can be a good thing—a gift and a calling.[91] Though individuals shared thoughts along these lines with me, Kadag, and certainly "our rabbis," are not quite there.

Nevertheless, the willingness of "our rabbis" to listen and learn does speak to a crisis unique to Jewish Orthodoxy, one that pits a liberal faction that is open to expanding Orthodoxy's ranks and conservatives who prefer more rigid boundaries between traditional Orthodoxy and Judaism's diversifying forms. With the decline of shared meanings, reality, and modes of argumentation, halachic activism also exposes a gap be-

tween halachic producers and consumers. Rulings that do not acknowledge new realities further accelerate these processes—when Orthodox
LGBT persons say that they no longer find the halacha relevant, the
consequences extend far beyond the halachic status of LGBT persons.
Religious elites worry because they know that halachic anomaly cannot stand for long. These dynamics are most prominently felt in liberal
Orthodox circles but extend beyond it.[92] Might this be the path toward
articulating Orthodoxy's version of queered theology?

Rabbis whose eyes are wide open encourage same-sex persons to
come out. But what kind of life does Orthodoxy offer to those who step
out of the homophobic closet but wish to remain within the holy ark?
Will the same-sex-attracted be forever relegated to feeling "blemished,
degenerate, uncouth"? Will they ever find a room of their own in the
Jewish home?

The answer might be in challenging not only halachic formulas but
also (especially) their promulgators:

> I talked to a rabbi and he said we can agree to disagree, "I think that a
> child needs and father and mother." And I said ". . . we're not asking you."
> And if in eight years a kid who has two moms knocks on your door, you
> won't accept them? And he started, "Well, it's a complicated issue." Or if a
> student comes out, "It's a complicated issue." And if a parent calls and says
> I don't want my son to be with him in the same room. "It's complicated."
> I said to him, "Rabbi no one says the issue isn't complicated. So what if it
> is? We close our eyes and close our ears and say it doesn't exist?" (Havruta
> activist)

On the flip side, there is now a thriving scene of LGBT learning communities: literally, a Jewish study hall, *beit midrash*, is a space dedicated
to Torah study, interpretation, and the development of halacha. In 2019,
one of these initiatives, under the direction of Ido Zangen, published a
collection of LGBT halachic writing; contributors included Orthodox
LGBT youth, rabbinic authorities, and activists. One of the themes running through the volume is the idea that homosexuality is not just something to be tolerated but rather a social good, reminiscent of Christian
queer theological writing that posits that gender and sexual variation
can bring individuals, and faith communities, closer to God. A partici-

pant declared this Kadag's Stonewall moment. It is worth pondering that this form of LGBT resistance is marked not by a violent tearing down but rather by contemplative rebuilding from within by young persons whose LGBT identities are consolidated (in part) by debating scripture. The anonymous writer playfully bestowed their leader Ido Zangen, a Talmud student in his twenties, the honorific Admor: a scholarly teacher and leader of a Jewish community.[93]

Activists and rabbis recognize they cannot fully sidestep the halacha, a legal system intended to provide guidance to live by. But as rabbis beg for patience, Orthodox LGBT persons are living their lives and forming communities and families that make their own theology visible. They leave halachic authorities little choice but to address questions that earlier generations of decisors could ignore. Thus, activists remain hopeful. One Bat Kol told me that she had "no doubt that we will be part of the Orthodox community. I don't know how it will happen but I am sure that it will." Professor Tamar Ross is adamant that the halachic fate of *hommos* and lesbians will not be decided by rabbis who consult ancient texts and consider halachic arguments in a vacuum but will rather emerge from lived reality, making Kadag's activism urgent and necessary. The next two chapters turn to consider the peculiarities of an LGBT movement anchored in such politics of authenticity, bringing it in conversation with queer scholars' concerns about complicity (chapter 5) and respectability politics (chapter 6).

5

Telling Stories, Making Space

Politics of Authenticity

"We're not seeking to destroy the institution of the straight family. . . . All we want is a room of our own within the Jewish home," Havruta's Chaim Elbaum told an audience at Bar Ilan University in May 2018.[1] The occasion: a panel hosted by the Orthodox-affiliated university as part of events marking Pesach Sheni (second Passover), the Jewish day of religious tolerance, which occurs a month after Passover. Pesach Sheni had been a fringe folk Hasidic tradition that involved eating a piece of matzah, if anything, until progressive Jewish groups in the United States harnessed its core idea—giving second chances to excluded members of society—to advance a broad vision of social justice centered on the inclusion of marginalized groups. The original idea focused on the formerly incarcerated, those recovering from addiction, and persons struggling with mental health,[2] but in 2009 two Bat Kol members extended the idea to LGBT inclusion, and a tradition was born: an annual celebration of Jewish tolerance.

Kadag uses Pesach Sheni as an occasion to educate Orthodox communities about LGBT Others in their midst. Though some of its programs engage *halachic* questions, most Pesach Sheni events focus on Jewish norms, cultural practices, and ethics. Bat Kol member and a past Pesach Sheni coordinator Or Ellisian explains why: Judaism is lived in a community. "As opposed to my confidence that [God] is okay with me, the fear of rejection by the Orthodox community is still raw. . . . How can I build a home that does not have a community? How can I raise children for Torah and commandments? Will there be a school that accepts them, is there a *minyan* where they could be bar mitzvahed?"[3]

Pesach Sheni is among the dizzying array of initiatives that Kadag deploys to raise awareness about, elicit empathy toward, and make space for Orthodox LGBT persons. While these initiatives differ in strategy and style—some are intimate small gatherings guarded by a code of silence, while others unfold in public forums, on the internet, or through traditional media—they share storytelling as a methodology and Orthodox authenticity as their grounding rhetoric. This chapter discusses three initiatives: Our Faces, a public visibility campaign; Shoval, an educational outreach initiative; and Pesach Sheni, a celebration of Jewish tolerance. Read together, these ethnographic threads reveal how the stories that Kadag activists tell about themselves as individuals, about their collective, and about Orthodoxy tread a tension between homonormative complicity and queer radicalism (homonormativity refers to the incorporation of heteronormative ideals and constructs into LGBT culture and identity).[4]

Storytelling is utilized by many identity movements agitating for political recognition and cultural, social, and attitudinal change.[5] But stories are not created equal; narrative arc, tone, narrator, and register all matter. Persuasive stories are familiar, simple, urgently important, and commonsensical yet sufficiently ambiguous to engage and mobilize listeners. Stories that demonstrate concrete instances of bias and injustice and evoke sympathy for victims are particularly potent. Good stories are told by and about individuals but gesture toward collective struggles. Storytellers, too, are not all equally effective: insiders generally encounter more goodwill than rebels and trailblazers. But even the best stories fall flat without an audience; marginalized narrators need to mobilize sufficient institutional resources and political clout to ensure that they will be heard. Good stories, in short, do not just happen; they are products of strategic and deliberate curation of narrative arcs, storytellers, venues, and messages.

As Kadag mastered the form, it converged on three main messages. First, the demand for making space is rooted in Orthodox LGBT persons' claim to Orthodoxy: "We are *of* you" (not "We are *like* you"). Second, the ethical case for embrace and acceptance is rooted in Jewish traditions, scripture, and philosophy and assumes these to be shared Jewish values. The third message frames Kadag as a moderate movement: Kadag insists that it does not intend to rock (let alone destroy) the Orthodox boat, just to make space for marginalized—and unique— Jews. Together, these compose what I call a politics of authenticity.

On the face of it, the politics of authenticity is a variation on the well-trodden liberal playbook of sameness and equality. As recounted in chapter 4, Kadag has injected into public discourse tolerance and inclusion as alternatives to the once-hegemonic approach that framed homosexuality as transgressive. But this chapter does not tell an unqualified story of progress. Tolerance and inclusion, even for the most privileged Orthodox LGBT persons (those who are cisgender, Ashkenazi, educated), remain contingent and fragile. Moreover, queer scholars and activists are cautious about progress narratives that rest on claims of sameness ("we are like you") and assimilationist politics ("we just want a room of our own") because they leave intact other systems of oppression and inequality.[6] Many (though certainly not all) Orthodox LGBT persons who make a Jewish ethical case for inclusion and tolerance also subscribe to an Israeli nationalism that rests on an inherently illiberal project: the settlement enterprise. The limits of liberal equality come into full view in a discussion of Kadag's inroads in an Orthodox stronghold, the settlements of Gush Etzion at the end of the chapter. The conclusion to the chapter brings these tensions full circle. By the close of the aughts, Kadag foes and allies alike conceded that Orthodox LGBT persons indeed do "exist" in Orthodox spaces. That Orthodox conservatives deemed this presence as an urgent, existential threat reveals the radical potential of Kadag's politics of authenticity.

Visible, Authentic, Disarming: Our Faces Campaign

In December 2015, a few months after the violence at that year's Jerusalem Pride Parade, forty-four *hommos* and lesbians took out ads in Orthodox and mainstream online and print media outlets to announce that they were same-sex-attracted.[7] A few days later, they released a digital photo album. This was the first of a three-phase public visibility campaign, Our Faces.[8] The album included a professional portrait, a vignette, and biographical notes listing profession, family status, military service, and markers of Orthodox identity: high school, yeshiva or *ulpana*, and hometown (many are Orthodox strongholds, including West Bank settlements). Narrators reported how they came to make sense of and embrace their Orthodox LGBT identities. The general narrative arc was uplifting—for every story of pain and hurt another story countered with joy and empowerment, resulting in an overall "it gets better" rhetoric. Ostensibly, participants were speaking to closeted Orthodox brothers and sisters:

> We, *hommos* and lesbians who grew up in Orthodox or Haredi homes, know the feeling of loneliness, alienation, choking. . . . Like you, we were in the yeshiva, ulpana, the youth group, military service, *hesder* [an abbreviated military service path that includes studying in a yeshiva]. Like you, we were afraid to share our stories. But we are here—strong and exposed—inviting you to read a brief story from our lives that may help you feel safer.[9]

The campaign also put the larger Orthodox community on notice—Orthodox *hommos* and lesbians are in your midst. One participant said that the "goal was to raise the topic. Like hello, we are here, we live here. We study in your yeshivas and we do military service with you. We're part of the community." Dan Oziel, who produced the project and was featured in it explained that the campaign sought to "speak to parents, educators, the leaders of religious Zionism, so they understand that this is an empirical fact. . . . LGBT exist. They are here. It's a reality. And they should look reality in the eye."[10]

The collective coming out was no manifesto but rather a collection of individual stories that presented the group as normative, familiar, run-of-the-mill Orthodox. The stories ran the gamut of the Orthodox LGBT journey (discussed in chapters 2–3). Participants recounted painful experiences with families, communities, and rabbis: the pressure to marry heterosexually, conversion therapy, and self-harm. They spoke of the costs of the Orthodox closet (Feigi Stern lists loneliness, depression, self-hatred, and loss of faith in herself and God) and the joys of stepping outside of it—discovering Orthodox LGBT spaces, receiving compassionate pastoral care, and self-acceptance. Activist Chaim Elbaum's entry articulated a distinctly Orthodox self-acceptance journey: "When I entered the yeshiva I knew that I would emerge from it differently, that [God] would make a miracle that I will be like everyone else. But the miracle that happened was much bigger—I emerged *hommo* and Orthodox—one who believes in [God] and how he created me."

References to ritual objects (*kippa*), prayer, holiday gatherings and family Shabbats, rabbis, yeshivas, Jewish values, and connection with

God painted a picture of ordinary Orthodoxy. Many stories revolved around the most quintessential aspect of Orthodoxy sociality: the quest for and achievement of family life. Bat Kol activist Ayala Reifler told a story of family rejection and redemption on the occasion of her daughters' birth. Her intention was to demonstrate that

> we're a typical family. At synagogue they accept us. In the educational institutions, we're accepted. . . . We come to synagogue with the kids and we're there. And they accept us. And they're nice to us. . . . [The synagogue] is typical. With a men's section and a women's section, and a *mechiza* [partition] and arguments about the *mechiza* [debates about gendered separation of space that mark the synagogue within mainstream liberal Orthodoxy].[11]

Dan Oziel, the producer, linked the campaign to Kadag's broader principles of dialogue through visibility and self-determination: "Instead of trying to talk *about* us, talk with us. It's important to us that people will hear our stories, and will know that it doesn't go away." But he struck conciliatory rhetoric: "We come from a place of peace." Reifler explained why Kadag chose this strategy: "When people come with face, names, it's harder to say to them leave, get out of here."

By 2015, Kadag members had participated in, and organized, many public forums, their faces and narratives leaving a trail across the digital media landscape; others were out in more intimate circles of family, friends, and communities. But the public nature of the Our Faces campaign defied any pretense that these stories could be silenced. In LGBT movement lore, coming out, public visibility, is a goal in and of itself,[12] but Our Faces had a second goal: establishing Orthodox authenticity. These stories about Orthodox LGBT lives were framed around the logics of familiarity; visibility was strategic and curated.[13]

The campaign's second phase, Our Faces 2, Together, was released in July 2017, a few weeks before Jerusalem Pride.[14] This campaign featured seventeen Orthodox *hommos*, lesbians, and transgender persons with "the grandmother, the friend from yeshiva, a friend from work, the couple from the synagogue, the *havruta* [study companion]." Building on the previous campaign's themes of authenticity, making space, and acceptance, these snippets conveyed love, respect, and belonging: LGBT persons were not only ordinarily Orthodox but also integral to Orthodox communities. Moreover, the campaign signaled that generational change was possible.

But perhaps the most important message of this campaign was that communities had a duty—a *Jewish* duty—to embrace LGBT persons. Participants were asked, what would it take to make the world a better place? Eliq Oster's grandmother said that "the world is already good. It is just that us humans need to work harder not to ruin it and accept the other." Helen Elbaum, Chaim's mother, is pictured with his partner (now husband), Yair Strauss. Her entry reads, "I want to tell him [Yair] that I'm very happy that he is my son's partner. . . . The world will be a much better place when parents accept our children as they are. Because [God] created them in this way and we have to believe in him and accept this with love because everything is given from God and it's all for the good." Here was a distinctly Jewish case for acceptance: embracing LGBT persons was a matter of *tikkun olam* (literally, repairing the world; metaphorically, a Jewish approach to social justice). The deployment of tikkun olam as an organizing principle—rather than human rights, equity, and fairness—references an alternative Jewish cosmology that recognizes the limitations of halachic discourse and its declining relevance. This language reflects what Dr. Friedman, in her critique of Beit Hillel's position paper, and Rabbi Benny Lau, in his work with Orthodox LGBT persons and their families, call a new religious language around LGBT concerns (see chapter 4).

The third campaign portrayed this just world as a reality. Released piecemeal starting in July 2019, Our Faces 3 included eight brief videos that provided a glimpse into Orthodox LGBT lives, set to a soundtrack that might be characterized as Hasidic pop.[15] This was the most diverse campaign. Featured subjects included same-sex couples, individuals, and families and trans people; Kadag itself was evolving. Most clips centered on stories of acceptance involving ritual Jewish objects (*tallit, kippa*, a *Kiddush* cup), the Jewish calendar (Shabbat dinners, holidays), and family members. Yishai Moskovitz and Micha Yehudi (both male presenting) shared how Yishai's mother signaled her support for their marriage when she surprised them with a gift moments before the wedding ceremony: handknitted kippas. Yishai's mother had gifted her other sons a kippa on the occasion of their weddings, but he had braced himself to be excluded from this family tradition; the gift was doubly redemptive for Micha, who is trans (in the Orthodox tradition women do not wear kippas). Other stories communicated the utter ordinariness of LGBT lives: Eliq and Adam Oster, featured with their young sons, told the story of cookware they had bought with money received from Adam's grandmother as a wedding gift; this secular grandmother had no problem accepting the "*hommo* angle." The punchline was that Eliq's religiosity stumped her.

Together, these campaigns demonstrate Kadag's rhetorical strategies in its quest to make space. First is *familiarity*: Our Faces presented participants as products of and integral to Orthodox Jewish communities, institutions, and families. Second, the campaigns ostensibly did not seek to upend the Jewish world order. As opposed to the queer rallying cry "we're here, we're queer, get used to it!" Kadag's efforts send reassuring messages that it comes "from a place of peace." Such assurances, however, are at odds with the fact that these campaigns target Orthodoxy's heteronormative underpinnings. The Faces campaigns problematized— albeit subtly—Orthodox practices and messages about transgression, heteronormativity, and the very definition of Orthodoxy. When Faces 1 participants spoke about exclusions from families, communal life, and ritual and worship spaces and as they reflected on hurtful messages about their identities, choices, and lives, they implied that the existing Jewish world order inherently compromised its marginalized members. The second and third campaigns, which invited participants to imagine what a better world looked like, made it clear that this world order was due for a major overhaul. Still, the implicit threat to the Jewish world order was tempered by the mobilization of Jewish values, language, sensibilities, and symbols. Such rhetorical strategies—and the tensions surrounding them—are central to the work of Shoval, an educational outreach organization that sends trained volunteers to talk with Orthodox educators, therapists, and communities about LGBT persons.

Shoval's Educational Outreach

In 2007, several *hommos* and lesbians on the Orthodox spectrum launched an outreach organization. The idea was simple yet radical: trained volunteers would meet with staff at Orthodox schools to educate them about sexual and gender diversity. They would not do battle nor argue about halacha. Instead, they would share glimpses from their lives. To do so, they would enlist volunteers willing to identify, publicly, as same-sex-attracted or gender-variant in a community that denied their existence and portrayed homosexuality and gender variance as transgressive, sinful, and deviant.[16] To gain entry, they would need to convince institutions that sexual and gender variance was not just the providence of secular culture. It was a tall order. And it worked.[17]

Shoval was among several Orthodox LGBT organizations and initiatives launched in the mid- to late aughts. By the time its founders had found each other, many were in their late twenties and ex-Orthodox; some were veterans of secular LGBT organizations. Without Orthodox LGBT visibility when they came of age, they had confronted their families and communities alone. Shoval's founders envisioned an intervention that would help others avoid that fate, and honed in on educating the educators. The goal was to confront stereotypes and offer an alternative to the lens of transgression: an affirming stance grounded in Orthodox sensibilities and cosmology. The solution was Shoval, an acronym for "All is created for His glory."[18]

Shoval is a central node of Kadag activism. The organization has provided Kadag with a language and a framework for effective outreach work, and it routinely collaborates with other organizations and initiatives. Shoval volunteers overlap with Havruta and Bat Kol membership, and it has been supported by both organizations.[19] Shoval mostly relies on volunteer labor (it employs one part-time coordinator). Workshop fees, roughly $150, cover costs and can be negotiated down. (When Shoval began operating, its workshops were free, but it moved away from a charity model toward a professional one, thereby marking its workshops as providing essential professional training.) Current volunteers display a broad range of Orthodox identification. Likewise, gender and sexual identities are diverse. Shoval's model of outreach and education is well supported by the literature: face-to-face conversations in small settings can diffuse prejudice toward (and fear of) marginalized and stigmatized groups.[20] As in the Our Faces campaign, Shoval's secret weapon is its (carefully selected and trained) volunteers, whom audiences can imagine as being, as one volunteer put it, "your friend from school, your neighbor, your cousin." Nevertheless, when Shoval was certified by the Ministry of Education in 2018 to provide programming in public schools, Orthodox conservatives protested "the LGBT agenda's" corrupting effects on youth.

A typical Shoval training lasts an hour and a half to two hours and features two volunteers, usually one male-presenting and another female-presenting. Workshops begin with a crash course on terminology, theories, and debates about sex, gender, and sexuality. Volunteers then tell their Orthodox LGBT stories. Like the vignettes of the Our Faces campaigns, these stories run the gamut of the Orthodox experience and are reference markers, milestones, and sensibilities familiar to Orthodox audiences. Workshops end with a Q&A; questions are probing and often insensitive. Originally designed as training for staff at Orthodox educational institutions (this is still the core mission), Shoval also offers workshops and activities tailored for mental health professionals and the broader community.[21] A singular logic motivates Shoval activities: familiarity with Orthodox LGBT persons' experiences will equip educators, mental health professionals, rabbis, and families with tools to support them. Shoval has its eye on the long game: to build an army of sympathizers by working school by school, community by community.

Shoval's work is guided by four principles. First, being at peace with one's gender and sexual identity is key to achieving well-being. Second, LGBT persons should be able to live within Orthodox communities without having to conceal or deny their gender or sexual identities. One volunteer tells audiences, "I want to be able to raise a family in [settlement where grew up] and be able to send my children to the [local] school, with their cousins." Third, communities have a responsibility to preserve the physical and mental well-being of LGBT persons in their midst. "This is not a lifestyle choice . . . for many youths, it's a life and death issue," a volunteer told a group of teachers. Finally, Shoval trainings emphasize that gender and sexual diversity is compatible with Orthodoxy.

Shoval trains and vets its volunteers; novices are typically paired with seasoned volunteers in their first public appearances. Shoval training seminars, offered every couple of years, cover theories, terminology, and the science of sex, gender, and sexuality, as well as halachic issues. Volunteers receive a crash course in public speaking and learn how to effectively respond to an array of questions. Crucially, Shoval seminars teach volunteers how to create a fifteen-minute narrative arc that is the cornerstone of the Shoval program. Volunteers often refer to their "Shoval story"—one that is updated with life events—partnering, parenting, separating, family acceptance. Indeed, many Shoval volunteers experience the training itself as an empowering and therapeutic milestone on their journey toward self-acceptance.

The Shoval story is a distinctly Orthodox LGBT story, and its public retelling communicates Orthodox authenticity. Shoval's website claims that its volunteers "grew up and were educated in Orthodox educational institutions, know firsthand the Orthodox community, and most of us continue to see ourselves as integral to it. Most of us belong to religious communities and observe halacha."[22] Volunteers' stories reference Orthodox institutions (schools, youth movement), milestones (Bar/Bat Mitzvah is a staple in these coming of age stories), calendar (anecdotes tying significant events to Shabbat or Jewish holidays), rituals (a volunteer talked about how donning a ritual garment was a daily painful reminder that he was not a "worthy" Jew), messaging surrounding modesty (a narrative that implies that the speaker did not engage in "prohibited" sexual acts, i.e., male-on-male anal sex), authorities (rabbis figure prominently in these narratives—not always positively), and family expectations ("I fully expect to marry and have children, like my siblings. Our family will just look a little different"). As volunteers name schools and youth groups, talk about large families, reference rabbis, and tell heartbreaking stories about harms inflicted on them in Orthodox spaces—getting thrown out of the yeshiva, being barred from participating in a community ritual, conversion therapy—they come across as ordinary and familiar. Their message: we are *of* you; we *are* you. Shoval workshops also "feel" familiar: Orthodox audiences frequently attend talks and workshops that synthesize Jewish learning, commentary, and engagement with broader social issues. It certainly helps that Shoval workshops are typically offered in familiar settings: school, yeshiva, synagogue, a local community center, or at the home of an Orthodox acquaintance, sometimes at the invitation of or with the blessing of a local community leader.

Shoval's operational strategy emphasizes respectful dialogue. Shoval bills itself as an *educational* organization that promotes tolerance and provides professional training, not an LGBT rights organization. It does not aim to shock, preach, or take a righteous stance. Shoval's model is based on the one successfully used by the secular organization Hoshen, with necessary adjustments to format and rhetoric to make the content palatable to Orthodox audiences.[23] (Its work was also shaped by the groundbreaking work of the Trembling outreach project mentioned in chapter 1.) Shoval's website assures that "the story and dialogue are communicated utilizing a respectful language appropriate for an Orthodox audience." Thus, workshop leaders' sex and gender identities are venue-dependent. Shoval may send cisgender male volunteers, preferably with yeshiva training, to meet with educators at a highly observant yeshiva (by definition an all-male institution). Gender, sexual, and religious identities are more diverse if the training is part of a public conference or is held at the invitation of a more liberal Orthodox group, institution, or community. In all contexts, Shoval's method of choice is dialogue: "We are open to every question, emotion, or opinion" it assures on its website. A volunteer confirmed, "We are not trying to change halacha. We are only interested in dialogue and reducing prejudice." Another explained that Shoval asks audiences just to "listen. We say to the people we meet 'you're talented educators.' I'm excited to talk to them about questions that they have, what's appropriate. We don't come with arguments about how to teach, how community should be lived. . . . Our job is to teach them what they may not know and would help them reach the kids." On one issue Shoval does not budge: Shoval takes an uncompromising stance on conversion therapy.

I saw "respectful dialogue" play out in workshops I attended—though respect was occasionally one-sided. Workshops begin with a brief introduction in which the volunteer declares, "My name is ___ and I am an Orthodox lesbian/*hommo*/transperson." Hearing the speaker utter those words in public, early in the workshop, sets the tone for the program: audiences are alerted that the speaker is comfortable in their own skin. In the workshops I attended volunteers were even-keeled and patient, even as they fielded prying and sometimes hostile questions about their emotional, family, and sex lives. In a workshop with a high school teaching staff, a middle-aged teacher pressed a volunteer about his sexual practices. She was uncomfortable even broaching the topic: "I find it hard to believe that until you were twenty-four you didn't have . . . didn't engage . . . in [pause] intimacy." Without losing his cool, the volunteer confirmed. "I did not have a relationship until I was in my twenties." Audiences challenge public visibility: "I support your decision to live your life but why do you have to march in Jerusalem" is a recurring comment. Confronted with the idea that sexual orientation is largely immutable, some participants push back. In one training a teacher insisted that "sexual orientation can change with the right help," referencing a persistent and simplistic belief in Orthodox circles that same-sex attraction is a "choice." The Shoval volunteer responded with a concise summary of the literature on conversion therapy and the intricacies of sexual desire, then ended with a (rhetorical) question of his own: "Given how difficult the lives of *hommos* are in the Orthodox community, why would anyone ever choose this?" At another training a volunteer responded to claims that the halacha of same-sex attraction was settled with a brief survey of halachic debates; his goal was not to counter, just make a case for ambiguity. Other questions center on concerns that discussing gender and sexual identity with impressionable teens might "give them ideas. . . . It may push them to make a decision prematurely." The volunteer's response: "Regardless if you agree, a certain percentage of your students *are* questioning their identity and they are at higher risk of suicide." Offensive questions that reduce LGBT persons to their sexual and gender identity—"would you tell an employer who you are?," an audience member asked a teacher-in-training—are used to reframe the conversation without admonishing: "I would tell them that I have several years of relevant experience. I don't think that my sexual identity is relevant but in all honesty, I wouldn't seek a job at every cost because it would not be good for my mental health, though it's unfortunate for the closeted teenager who could use a role model." And when asked what their ideal future might look like, volunteers' requests seemed quite reasonable: "to be able to build a home in the neighborhood I grew up in"; "to send my children to an Orthodox school"; "to be able to bring my partner home for a family Shabbat, just like my siblings." Volunteers' patience in the face of ignorant, insensitive, hostile, and unabashed homophobic and transphobic comments was notable. "We have no choice; we have to meet people where they are," one volunteer told me. Pragmatism served the long game: "If we are perceived as too liberal we will lose our target audience. So what will I have achieved?"

Shoval's entry ticket is that their programs serve a communal goal: protecting the physical and emotional well-being of LGBT and questioning youth. Its website reads, "[Shoval's] hope is that Orthodox LGBT youth will feel that their school, community, and home are embracing and supportive spaces, and that they won't have to choose between their gender/sexual and religious identities." Volunteers cite youth well-being as motivation for getting involved with Shoval: "I want to create something that my sixteen-year-old self wished I had." "I want to save lives." "I'm not doing this to rescue the Orthodox world, I'm doing this to ease the lives of students. Only the strong ones stay faithful to themselves and emerge sane from this system that rejects the lesbian or *hommo*."

But motivations extend beyond this lifesaving mission. Some volunteers hope to advocate for an alternative Orthodoxy, one that is more aware and accepting of difference. One volunteer said she views herself not only as "an ambassador of Kadag [but also] an ambassador for a certain type of Judaism," a more nuanced, more accepting Judaism that unconditionally embraces marginalized Others. "I'm working also on behalf of others . . . like single mothers," she added. Indeed, many volunteers speak of their work at Shoval as their tikkun olam, or world repair, a calling. Noga traced this calling to the values instilled in her at the *midrasha* (seminary) she had attended. Her midrasha was far from supportive of LGBT persons, but it did emphasize working toward the greater good. The irony was not lost on Noga, but she insisted that "doing Shoval felt like I was acting on the Orthodox values I had been taught at the midrasha."

Volunteers acknowledged more tangible motivations: by reducing prejudice they were creating space for themselves; "I don't have the luxury not to do this work," explained one volunteer. And the Shoval experience itself was empowering: "Learning to say—out loud!—I'm a lesbian. Wow!" "Writing out my story, going through the training, and now doing these workshops has helped me figure out where I stand on issues, my identity. It was a crucial part of coming out of the closet."

Outreach work, however, can take a toll, some of it benign—"how many times can you tell the same story? It gets boring" (some volunteers joke that they've been paired with particular peers so often that they could tell their workshop partner's story; experienced storytellers proved to be challenging interviewees because their narratives were so well rehearsed). But standing in front of a crowd time and again, professing to embrace a stigmatized and marginalized identity—to *perform* it, repeatedly—requires emotional stamina. "There are parts of me that I cannot bring to Shoval, even if I know that they would be most powerful—the shame, conversion therapy, how close I came to taking my life. That's too painful," one volunteer said. Greeting all questions, including insensitive and aggressive ones, with respect also comes at a cost. I asked one cis male volunteer after a session in which an attendee pushed him several times on the question of "forbidden" intercourse how he kept his cool (the attendee used the biblical phrase *mishkav zachar*, or lying with a man, a common euphemism, to communicate her skepticism that same-sex love could be anything but transgressive); "I can't afford to let them get to me. But it's painful." This is the reason Shoval trains and vets its volunteers. Some Kadag members resent not being chosen for a seminar or being tapped infrequently for workshops, but a veteran activist insisted that Shoval's caution was warranted because "there's no place for broken and hurt people to come tell the story. Yet Orthodoxy breaks and hurts us."

Shoval claims that its workshops are transformative, though it is impossible to separate Shoval's impact from larger processes. One Shoval veteran observed that audience questions have grown less hostile and more knowledgeable. Another volunteer said he knows "many people who changed their minds because we were attentive to them. . . . They sometimes write to me long after a workshop." Another was encouraged by an exchange at a teacher training session. A male co-presenter said he was expecting a child in a shared parenting arrangement and "the school counselor called it perversion. The *school counselor*! But then another teacher said, 'He's telling you that he's expecting a child, how dare you talk to him like that?' I didn't have to say anything!" Though I was told repeatedly by volunteers that they often hear from participants that Shoval workshops had helped them "come out" as allies, one can assume that many minds are probably not changed, even if they are touched. At a meeting I attended a middle-aged female teacher, who presented as highly observant, insisted that sexual orientation was mutable; "Why won't you accept it's a possibility, just because you weren't able to change," she charged in an exchange with Shoval volunteers at the session's end. When she realized that her interlocutors would not budge, she left, fuming.

Perhaps the best indication that Shoval's messaging is effective is that its calendar is busier than ever. Visibility, increased awareness, and the

Ministry of Education's certification have made Shoval's job easier and more challenging. In the past, each booking was a win, but increased demand for workshops is sometimes impeded by a lack of available volunteers (some have aged or burned out; all have busy, full lives as students, parents, employees). Moreover, Shoval has been pushing further into more mainstream and conservative arenas. (Invitations to more conservative spaces are often precipitated by a local incident, such as the coming out of a student or a suicide attempt; educators recognize that they can no longer ignore the issue.)

While educational institutions still represent the bulk of Shoval's work, it also helps plan and coordinate ad hoc training, conferences, and community events. Its volunteers speak at professional conferences and workshops for Orthodox educators, rabbis, and therapists. Shoval also helps recruit volunteers to partake in two adjacent initiatives that stage a series of intimate meetings intended to encourage familiarity and dialogue. I discuss Pesach Sheni below; the second initiative, "Pride in the Living Room," was launched in 2017 by the murdered teenager's parents as part of the response to stabbings in the 2015 Jerusalem Pride Parade.

The entire enterprise is predicated upon getting people through the door and a willing audience. Shoval thus navigates a fine line between its claims to Orthodox authenticity and to ideology-free outreach, and its messaging about gender, sexuality, and family formation, which are inherently transgressive. Shoval's messages (making space), rhetorical strategies (Orthodox authenticity), and messengers (volunteers who come across as "someone they would recognize from the neighborhood") render its volunteers and their sensibilities as legible and disarming. Authenticity is key: here are real people, not caricatures, with familiar appearances, biographies, language, and stories. They are conversant in Orthodoxy and its internal debates. Similarly, while Shoval recognizes the power of public visibility—in recent years it has signed on or taken the lead on some signature public campaigns, such as a video featuring messages of penitence from prominent rabbis ahead of Yom Kippur in 2016[24]—it also recognizes that visibility can impede other goals. Thus, some sessions are not advertised, allowing the organization more freedom when it operates in highly conservative communities. The organization further downplays its radical potential by insisting that it is an Orthodox *educational* organization, not an LGBT one.

Nevertheless, Orthodox conservatives are rattled. Shoval volunteers speak publicly about sexuality, same-sex love, gender identity. They (subtly) question the halacha and rabbinic authority. And being true to one's identity, an emphasis on personal fulfillment, and communal responsibility for mental well-being belie Orthodoxy's historically collectivist religiosity and assumptions that heterosexuality and sex/gender alignments are natural and sanctified. How could naming business as usual as hurtful and marginalizing be perceived as anything other than a demand for radical institutional and cultural changes? The Pesach Sheni initiative, launched at around the same time as Shoval, tackles this question by claiming that inclusivity, tolerance, and acceptance are shared Jewish values. This initiative also demonstrates the type of dialogue made possible when activists have full control of the public narrative.

Pesach Sheni: A Jewish Case for Inclusion

Recognizing that empathy and familiarity are necessary but insufficient messages on the quest to make space, Kadag also makes an ethical case for inclusion. LGBT battles typically mobilize the language of human rights and legal frameworks, but Kadag and its allies reason that *theologically* grounded homophobic and transphobic worldviews are best countered with an alternative *religious* language and rhetoric. Activists thus sought to develop a moral, ethical, and halachically informed framework through which Orthodox communities could think about gender and sexual minorities in their midst. Bat Kol members Dina Berman Maykon and Tamar Gan-Zvi Bick found this language in the Jewish archives, in the biblical story of Pesach Sheni.[25]

Chapter 9 in the book of Numbers tells the story of a group of biblical Jews who had missed out on the first Passover in the desert because they had been in a state of ritual impurity. Biblical purity laws exclude ritually unclean individuals from participating in a variety of rituals, but the individuals at the center of this story acquired impurity through no fault of their own.[26] In the biblical story, the ritually unclean complained to Moses, "Why should we be excluded?" A conference with God yielded a solution: the ritually impure would celebrate the holiday a month later.

The scriptural story rendered Pesach Sheni a quintessential Jewish framework to advocate for tolerance and acceptance: it concerns the exclusion of Jewish persons from one of the religion's foundational holidays and centers on a dialogue between stigmatized minorities, religious elites (Moses), and God. And it was the ritually impure, not God or religious elites, who advocated for this solution. Pesach Sheni, a second Passover, was a second chance at inclusion. Pesach Sheni founders drew on this story to make two claims: inclusion is a Jewish value, and change comes from the bottom up, through a participatory process.

Orthodox LGBT persons have adopted the story as a fitting metaphor for their own predicament: an exclusion based on traits beyond one's control (as discussed in chapters 3 and 4, the prevalent view among Orthodox LGBT persons is that they were "born this way," a rebuke of the conservative Orthodox theory of sexuality as chosen and malleable), a tolerance grounded in Jewish cosmology, and a leadership committed to the marginalized. They also followed ancient Jews' examples, generating a solution from the ground up. It made sense that the women of Bat Kol approached tolerance from an ethical framework rather than a halachic one. More likely to suffer from social derision and ritual exclusion, and under pressure to undergo conversion therapy, hommos, at least in the early years, were more concerned with identifying halachic pathways for acceptance. Bat Kol members, more likely to have children, prioritized social practices and cultural norms. Many were also inspired by Orthodox feminists' social experimentation and theological creativity in other arenas. Or Ellisian, Bat Kol member and Pesach Sheni coordinator at the time, captured these sentiments, writing about a tension between her desire for "a home in which there is a Torah, commandments, and a bookcase filled with holy books in the living room" and a future home composed of two women, one which "some in the Orthodox community would not recognize as a home or a family." Ellisian writes that she became involved with the initiative because while "in the past, questions such as these resulted in LGBT persons leaving the world of Torah . . . today, we refuse this rupture in our souls."[27]

Pesach Sheni rhetorical strategies echo those of Shoval: how can Orthodox communities deny a place for their brothers and sisters "who grew up in the [Orthodox youth] movement as scouts, counselors, leaders"? But unlike Shoval's "get to know us" rhetoric, this initiative, at least initially, outlined an expansive—not LGBT-specific—case for inclusion. Pesach Sheni's rhetoric sought to sidestep thorny questions about the

origins, essence, and malleability of LGBT identities, traits, or disposi-
tions, centering instead on articulating an ethical, cultural, political, and
halachic framework for the treatment of stigmatized and marginalized
Others. In making a seemingly innocuous *Jewish* case for tolerance, acceptance, and inclusion, the Pesach Sheni initiative also tells a story about
communal values and ethics. The original essay from which Pesach Sheni
was born enumerated other groups clamoring for inclusion such as single
women who opt to have children outside the bounds of marriage and
women who cannot obtain a divorce (*aguna*).[28] These excluded groups
share "a sincere and truthful desire to obey the laws of the Torah, out of
a deep understanding of the meaning of belonging to the Jewish people";
they want "to be, in the most basic sense, a part of the fabric of the nation" but are barred from doing so by Orthodoxy's gendered cosmology.

Some activists still portray Pesach Sheni as an expansive intervention
that targets the ethics of "treatment of those who are different, welcoming minorities, and respect for the Other" in Israeli society, including
"the place of LGBT, refugees, the disabled, people who are not Jewish."
But although its conference theme one year centered on ethnicity and
colorism in Israeli society (referencing intra-Jewish ethnicities), in practice Pesach Sheni in Israel has become closely associated with LGBT
acceptance (in the United States the concept has been applied more
broadly).[29] This focus is reflected in Pesach Sheni materials; though
youth programming materials, especially for the younger age groups,
articulate abstract notions of acceptance and tolerance, the materials
in the adult handbook leave no room for doubt about the initiative's
focus on LGBT acceptance. Social justice solidarity—intra-Orthodox
and intra-Jewish, let alone other forms of solidarity—had been hard to
maintain in part because, as I discuss below, claims to Orthodox authenticity are deeply intertwined with nationalism.

Pesach Sheni began in the late aughts as a small gathering where the
(then) nascent Kadag hosted public discussions over the course of an
evening.[30] Within a decade, the little-known date on the Jewish calendar
was recommissioned as a multifaceted celebration of LGBT tolerance
and inclusion. The initiative has expanded into a countrywide effort
that includes, in addition to a main event, outreach meetings hosted
in a variety of communities under the title "Making Space" (2019 saw
several dozen events).[31] Activists have assembled a resource packet that

includes a list of workshops, sources, bibliographies, movie suggestions, and conversation starters, thus lowering the entry bar. "If you volunteer to organize an event for us, it's going to be very easy. We'll send you this PDF and you can choose what's appropriate for your audience." Making Space gatherings vary and may take the form of a shared evening of learning, film screening, and open discussion. Some events are public, others discreet. All formats are guided by two principles: respectful dialogue and Kadag-controlled messaging. Not only are Orthodox LGBT persons the focal point of the conversation, they also set its perimeters as planners, moderators, and participants—the activist slogan "talk with us, not about us" comes to full view here.

The roster of participants in Pesach Sheni events has expanded over time to include, in addition to Orthodox LGBT persons, allied rabbinic authorities and Orthodox and secular academics, lawyers, and therapists. Topics and entry points outpace halachic discourse. In 2016, when the rabbis of Beit Hillel issued a lackluster halachic opinion about acceptance that made no mention of transgender persons (see chapter 4), Pesach Sheni sponsored a discussion of transness in Jewish sources. Meanwhile, a speaker at another panel who made a conservative halachic case for LGBT tolerance came under fire. The Rabbanit Oria Mevorach, a woman halachic authority, denounces feminism and "postmodernity" (a frequent proxy for secular culture).[32] An unlikely ally, she was invited to share her take on LGBT inclusion at the 2016 Pesach Sheni main event. In her remarks at the conference and an accompanying publication, Mevorach made a conservative case for embracing *hommos* and lesbians (not LGBT persons) in committed relationships: such persons, she argued, do not undermine Jewish values but rather strengthen and enhance the spirit of Judaism, specifically its emphasis on nuclear families. Mevorach's qualified support for (some) Orthodox LGBT partnerships and families might have been celebrated in the context of a halachic discourse still struggling to make space for same-sex relationships, but the reaction in Kadag-controlled space was less generous. One Bat Kol member was angry when I met with her a year later: "Sure, she said that LGBT persons don't undermine the family. But what about single people? I'm single so you're throwing me out?" Nevertheless, Mevorach was an effective communicator of another key Pesach Sheni message: here was a homegrown, Jewish, case for tolerance.

It is difficult to gauge Pesach Sheni's impact, although anecdotal evidence suggests that it is an effective voice. Pesach Sheni events appeal to varied audiences that include, per one host of a Pesach Sheni event in the southern city of Yeruham, "a well-known religious figure in our community, who talked about how she and her extended family deal with the *hommo* son and his partner . . . a teacher in a high school yeshiva seeking tools to help students who question their sexual identity, a young Orthodox woman seeking to understand how she can help Orthodox relatives understand, and a male couple who just relocated to Yeruham who sought to know whether they will be accepted." After participating in a Pesach Sheni event, Orthodox journalist Miriam Adler, writing in a popular Orthodox outlet, vowed to refrain from judgment, be empathetic, and make space. "One does not need to agree or disagree, to allow or prohibit. Only to listen."[33] Another participant reflected on the initiative's downstream impacts:

I participated in this evening despite my identity, and in addition because of who I am. "Despite my identity": because I am wholly committed to the Torah and halacha and aspire to live a Torah-inspired life. . . . "Because of who I am"—because the commandment "love thy neighbor" and the prohibition to "stand idly by the blood of your neighbor" are as important to me as other commandments and additions of our Sages—even more so. . . . I understood that evening that none of us are perfect, we all live with conflict—and the job of judging people . . . is not mine but of our creator. Since that dialogue, I have shared the stories I heard and the need to listen, understand, and respect with my wife, my grown children, my friends, and acquaintances.[34]

Like other efforts led by media-savvy young activists, Pesach Sheni events are amplified on social media. Official Pesach Sheni and Kadag accounts and many activists circulate notices and promotional materials in the days leading up to events, followed by post-event reflections by hosts, guests, and volunteers. In 2020, per COVID-19 restrictions, Pesach Sheni went online, landing on a series of fifteen Zoom events that were streamed on Kadag organizations' Facebook feeds. Most of these events were open to the public, and some were cohosted with allied organizations and individuals. The 2020 lineup encapsulated how far Kadag activism had come in the thirteen years since the first, low-key evening in Jerusalem, and provided a glimpse into how Kadag curates messengers, interlocutors, and messages. The weeklong series of events was preceded by a publicity blitz—Facebook posts by activists intended to go viral and write-ups in the media, with contributions from veteran activists as well as younger activists fresh off the latest Shoval training. Event formats varied widely and included panels, dialogues, workshops, and personal stories (mostly by trained Shoval volunteers). Most events were moderated by Kadag activists, and the vast majority featured key activists. Two events focused on gender variance, a majority on the same-sex-attracted, though all were united under the term LGBT.

The lineup also reflected Kadag's role as a bridge between Orthodox and LGBT communities, with some events targeting presumably secular audiences, including a closed event for volunteers of Hoshen, the secular LGBT education organization.[35] However, most events centered on Orthodox audiences' concerns: family, community, religious messaging. A father/daughter duo told their family's LGBT journey, and a moderated conversation among Orthodox mothers of LGBT children communicated: love your children. Three events were hosted by LGBT-affirming congregations, signaling LGBT persons' normalized presence in communities outside Tel Aviv's and Jerusalem's progressive Orthodox bubbles. An event cohosted with Kolech, the Orthodox feminist organization, featured a dialogue between Bat Kol's founder and Kadag visionary Avigail Sperber and Kolech's CEO. The two leaders discussed similarities and divergences in their respective organizations' agendas. Another dialogue (in English) featured activist Nadav Schwartz and Rabbi Nechama Barash, who used the occasion to assess the impact of two decades of Orthodox LGBT activism. The takeaway from the latter two events: we have come a long way and have a long way to go still.

The events cohosted with mainstream Orthodox personalities underscored Kadag's claims to Orthodox authenticity while portraying a battle hard fought and (mostly) won. Cohosts helped publicize the event to their social media followers and streamed it on their Facebook pages, but their stature as Orthodox insiders also lent legitimacy to the conversations. A panel headlined by Oded Revivi, the head of Efrat municipal council (a liberal Orthodox stronghold located in the Gush Etzion area in the West Bank), discussed his municipality's support for LGBT initiatives. Another panel, headlined by Rabbi Raffi Ostroff, the regional rabbi of a neighboring municipal council, interrogated the ethics of choosing to partner heterosexually. (Local religious councils, headed by rabbis, are state authorities that provide religious services to the state's Jewish residents.) The rabbi stunned his co-panelists with a qualified endorsement of same-sex partnerships for "true" homosexuals and lesbians (i.e., not bisexual).[36] A third panel was hosted by Ariel Horowitz, a journalist with the popular Orthodox publication *Makor Rishon*; this conversation veered into a reflection on the legacies of Kadag activism.

In aggregate, the 2020 panels covered a wealth of topics—negotiating closets, family members, and communities; supportive rabbis and skeptical ones; communal pressures to marry heterosexually; leaving the community and recommitting to it; the community's responsibility toward the vulnerable. This breadth, open disagreements between activists and their interlocutors, and the fact that these interlocutors were Orthodox insiders suggested an arrival of sorts: activists were not so much asking for tolerance nor making the case for acceptance as they were describing an Orthodoxy that had already been transformed. Perhaps, pondered journalist Ariel Horowitz, in response to his interviewees' depiction of a polarized Orthodoxy—a tolerant liberal faction and an increasingly intolerant conservative one—the latter were in a state of panic, an indication that the Kadag project had largely been successful. Judging by developments in Orthodox strongholds from which Oded Revivi and Rabbi Ostroff hail, this assessment rang true. Left unsaid, though clearly conveyed, was the fact that Kadag's politics of authenticity were deeply intertwined with—in fact grounded in—a shared nationalist vision.

Pride in the Settlements

In June 2019, hundreds gathered in Alon Shvut, an Orthodox settlement in the Gush Etzion region of the West Bank, for an evening titled "Invisible Among Us."[37] The occasion was somber: a young transgender woman, Netta Hadid, who had grown up in the settlement, had died by suicide. The tragedy was a catalyst for a reckoning about the treatment of LGBT persons in the community. A publicity flyer announced, "The Alon Shvut community listens." Rabbi Ostroff, the head of the local religious council and an event organizer, explained that the evening was about "seeing our sons and daughters, some of whom are invisible among us," although he acknowledged that the event was also born of a new reality. Attendees at Netta Hadid's funeral heard eulogies in which the deceased was referred to as both male and female. They needed context.[38]

The event and publicity preceding it did not abide by Kadag's principle "talk with us, not about us": Alon Shvut's rabbi, a local prominent therapist, and Netta Hadid's father were listed on a publicity flyer that also promised the evening would feature (unnamed) "sons and daughters of the settlement." In the end, only Erez Bruchi, a veteran Kadag activist who had grown up in Alon Shvut, spoke ("I am the son of Yair and Shlomit Bruchi," were his opening remarks). Instead, organizers read letters written by three lesbian women who chose to remain anonymous. Their voices pierced the veil of invisibility with harsh truths: "The social sanctions in the settlements are sophisticated," one of the women wrote, adding that her parents pleaded with her not to come out publicly because they feared their community's response. Interviewees shared similar sentiments with me: "The environment was tough, I couldn't wait to get out," a woman who grew up in a nearby settlement told me. Another letter writer used the occasion to plead with rabbis, "Tell us: you are part of the community. Like everyone." This plea was answered that evening by Alon Shvut's rabbi Weitman who had a request of his own: tone down pride events because there is nothing prideful about being nonnormative.

Alon Shvut, which numbers about three thousand residents, is among the almost two dozen settlements that compose Gush (bloc) Etzion, a cluster of West Bank Jewish settlements in the Judaean Mountains located between Jerusalem and Bethlehem and Hebron. About half of the bloc's seventy thousand Jewish residents are Ultra-Orthodox who reside in Beitar Illit; the rest are scattered among twenty settlements, the largest of which is Efrat, a town of about ten thousand. The roughly thirty-five thousand Orthodox Jews living in the region compose a tiny fraction of religious Zionism, but the area's outsize ideological, social, and cultural role belies this reality. The area is home to progressive educational institutions, and many feminist trailblazers—including Malka Puterkovsky and Dr. Hana Friedman (mentioned in previous chapters)—live or had lived in the area. (Oria Mevorach, mentioned earlier, was also an Alon

Shvut resident.) The Gush is both a potent bellwether of change and a flagship of religious Zionism and the settler project. It is considered illegal under international law.[39]

When I began my research in 2016, I heard rumors about LGBT persons who reside in Gush settlements—a lesbian couple raising children in Efrat; a closeted *hommo* yeshiva student (possibly more) at Har Etzion (in Alon Shvut); under-the-radar Shoval training in one of the smaller settlements. In 2016 I was not able to attend a training because the hosts worried about exposure. By the time Alon Shvut hosted the "Invisible Among Us" event a mere three years later, several Gush communities had hosted Shoval sessions (one session drew several dozen attendees despite—possibly because of—a local rabbi's fierce objection); both Efrat and Alon Shvut had hosted other public events in the summer of 2018; and the closeted yeshiva student—Yehonatan Gill Rossen Maman—had since come out, joined the Havruta board, and helped found a support group for local LGBT young adults. Though Yehonatan had left the yeshiva after coming out, he paved the way for others to remain. The support group he helped found has been operating in the Gush since 2018—initially with support from LGBT organizations (the Jerusalem Open House and IGY), later with local support. More recently, a support group for parents was launched in 2019 with the blessing of Efrat's top elected official. Years of patient work to recruit prominent allies had paid off: elected officials such as Oded Revivi and rabbinic authorities such as Raffi Ostroff have become effective spokespeople for tolerance and helped organize—and legitimatize—Kadag events, conferences, gatherings, and support groups.

The Alon Shvut event in the summer of 2019 was not the first to address LGBT issues publicly, nor was it the first event to feature rabbis and local leaders, but it did break new ground: it was the first event explicitly co-organized by rabbis. Formal recognition matters in Orthodox communities; leaders, and especially religious leaders, can help communities chart ethical and theological paths as they reassess their vision, boundaries, and values. The event was groundbreaking in another sense: it was clear that the center of gravity had shifted. An event held in the same venue just a year earlier featured a rabbi who would not mutter the words *hommo* or LGBT, referring instead to "the tendency." That earlier event took a "both sides" approach to assess the possibility of "overcoming" same-sex attraction. The original plan had been to feature only the conservative Orthodox approach that is grounded in claims of mutability, but residents intervened to ensure a more balanced discussion.[40] A year later, the conservative wing received little airtime. The most conservative remarks came from Rabbi Weitman, who referred to same-sex attraction as nonnormative but did not advocate intervention. His remarks were overshadowed by messages of tolerance, acceptance, and communal self-reflection.

Another groundbreaking event took place in neighboring Efrat in July 2018, following a string of attempted and completed suicides in that settlement. The municipality wanted to provide parents and educators tools to help youth who questioned or struggled with their gender and sexual identities, but the original lineup did not include LGBT persons. Activists and allied residents mobilized to ensure that the panel would feature Shoval volunteers alongside the planned roster of rabbis, educators, and therapists. LGBT persons who had grown up in the town or were still living there inundated Revivi with their personal stories in the lead-up to the event. Revivi emerged from this episode reliable ally. A youth and parent support group operates in the area with his blessing; when Rabbi Yigal Levinstein, of "perverts speech" fame (see chapter 6), was invited to speak at a synagogue in Efrat, Revivi issued a press release distancing the municipality from the controversial rabbi.

The 2018 Efrat panel outraged Orthodox conservatives; "LGBT terrorism continues," declared a headline in an Orthodox outlet, observing that Kadag organizations were supported by the much-reviled New Israel Fund (a philanthropy that takes a critical stance toward the settlement project). Revivi was accused of legitimizing "abnormal phenomena" and sowing confusion,[41] but he was not deterred because, he later explained, he had a responsibility as an elected official to listen to and protect *all* members of his community, including the disabled, immigrants, and LGBT persons: "We are not going to lose our children . . . not on my watch." Echoing Pesach Sheni logic, Revivi's cases for tolerance and inclusion were grounded in Jewish cosmology, in his case in the Passover story that tells of four sons who are very different from one another. The moral of the story, he writes, is that "we don't know how our children are going to turn out . . . [but] they are all ours. We didn't choose. It is our duty to embrace them and see how we can protect them. That's family." Rabbi Ostroff's similarly grounds his tolerance in the Jewish tradition; the Torah, he reminded his audience at the "Invisible Among Us" event, is rife with examples of communal responsibility toward marginalized groups.

Herein lies the paradox. On the one hand, a seismic shift. Religious and civic leaders have embraced Kadag's vision of a tolerant, accepting Judaism that listens to and strives to protect the vulnerable.[42] Even Rabbi Weitman, who held the conservative line at the "Invisible Among Us" event, professed unconditional support for LGBT persons. In contrast to yesteryear's rabbis who insisted that "there is no such thing a religious homosexual," Rabbi Weitman said that communities must do all in their power to keep LGBT persons within the fold. He also echoed Kadag's longtime stance that reducing LGBT persons to their sexual identity undermines their full Jewish humanity.

And yet this support is not unconditional because embrace, tolerance, and acceptance of the vulnerable do not amount to normalization. As we saw in the previous chapter, tolerance does not address the root cause of marginalization: an uncompromising cis and heteronormative social order. Rabbi Weitman's "love thy neighbor" logic leaves the theology of transgression intact, homosexuality outside the bounds of the normal. Revivi, for his part, skirts the question of normalization, emphasizing instead Jewish values such as harm avoidance—but the comparison of disabled and LGBT persons is tone-deaf. Likewise, in 2020 Rabbi Ostroff went on record with qualified support of same-sex partnerships during a Pesach Sheni event. Nicole Gil Chen, a Bat Kol member and a co-panelist, was deeply moved: the rabbi's words were "cold water for a tired soul. I am sure that if I had heard such pronouncements [when I was younger] I would have experienced less misery in my life." But Ostroff's recognition of same-sex partnerships was far from unequivocal: it excluded those who engaged in "mishkav zachar," a sanitized, biblical reference to anal sex, and referred only to those who were "unable" to partner heterosexually, an imprecise and ambiguous definition of homosexuality that, among other things, erases bisexuality. As with the Mevorach case, a stance that might have received a more forgiving reception within a purely halachic discourse earned only qualified praise in Kadag controlled space; moderator Yehonatan Gill Rossen Maman pushed back on bisexual erasure.

Tolerance keeps hitting its limits because as a political strategy, tolerance leaves intact dominant power structures that separate the normative (marked tolerant) from the marginalized (marked tolerated), what queer scholar Gayle Rubin calls the "charmed circle" of sexual practices that distinguishes between good/natural and bad/unnatural behaviors.[43] Reflecting similar developments in Evangelical circles in the United States, this charmed circle lends legitimacy to some same-sex acts, identities, and partnerships but not others.[44] A tolerance premised on continued marginality avoids harder conversations about normalization; "embracing the vulnerable," claiming that "we love all of our children," can live in peace with a cis and heteronormative Jewish world order in ways that approaches that affirm and celebrate difference cannot.

Finally, for all the talk of tolerance, acceptance, embrace of the Other, for all the reaching into the vaults of Jewish thought and philosophy, the "Other" deemed deserving of protection is privileged—Jewish, those who are "among us," "our children," preferably those who are in monogamous relationships and want to have children. And there is a layer of irony—hypocrisy, really—of speaking about tolerance and pride *in the settlements*, and, more generally, of a tolerant Orthodoxy, without addressing politics, geography, and history. Is it even possible to speak of tolerance and inclusion in this irredeemably illiberal setting? "The Jewish home" that we have heard about throughout this chapter is not an abstract notion—it was also the name of a right-wing religious-nationalist Zionist party that supported annexation and enjoyed popular support in Orthodox circles; that party is now defunct, but its vision lives on.

* * *

This chapter has recounted how Kadag enlisted storytelling about the Orthodox community and those who compose it to assert belonging, in the process challenging dominant values, beliefs, ideologies, frames, public discourses, social practices, norms, and institutional logics. Though it benefited from extraneous processes outside of its control, Kadag's successes are certainly the direct result of carefully crafted rhetorical strategies—authenticity, familiarity, anodyne agenda. These messages are premised on a logic of assimilation and tolerance that leaves intact Judaism's gendered and sexual social order, not to mention ethnic, political, and national ones. I engage these critiques in the conclusion, but I end this chapter by pointing out these rhetorical strategies' radical potential: "making space" expands the house of Torah, to use the words of feminist trailblazer Professor Tamar Ross.[45]

In a 2020 Peach Sheni event Zehorit Sorek reflected on her daughter's Bat Mitzvah at the inclusive Orthodox synagogue Yachad she helped found. It is customary for the prayer leader to bless the child on this occasion, a ritual that includes naming the child's parents. Zehorit wondered whom the prayer leader would name—the child's father or her mother's longtime wife who raised her. The prayer leader, Aviad Friedman, named all three parents: "Nowhere this is written. He made space for everyone."[46] Naming three parents in a synagogue ritual in Tel Aviv is not innocuous; Friedman challenged seemingly intractable foundational categories in Jewish thought: Who is a parent? What constitutes a family?

The battle over making space is far from over. Orthodox persons still report feeling rejected, marginalized, and stigmatized. Shoval volunteers are still told, often directly and in no uncertain terms, that their interlocutors would not hire them, rent them a home, accept their families in their synagogues and schools, or attend their weddings. And though most Orthodox LGBT persons would rather shy away from politics and just live their lives, they have inadvertently become embroiled in a culture war over Orthodoxy's boundaries. The next chapter considers these struggles in the context of a polarized Orthodoxy and Kadag's efforts to navigate this polarization as it balances respectable, playful, and provocative forms of public visibility.

6

The Battle for Judaism's Straight Soul

Queer Antics, Religious Restraint, and Respectability Politics

In 2016, Moshe Argaman (then Grossman), a college student in his early twenties and Havruta activist, hung a Jewish pride flag, with a Star of David superimposed on the rainbow stripes, outside his childhood home in Shilo, an Orthodox West Bank settlement. This was the second flag to hang outside his home; the first flag was torn down in a brazen act that involved trespassing and scaling the house.[1] The second flag, too, caused a stir, but controversy was part of the plan; pride flags, like other forms of visibility, double as political tools of protest.

The controversy reached far beyond this small West Bank settlement. In December 2016 Moshe and his flag were one of the three subjects of a Channel 10 piece about Orthodoxy and LGBT acceptance.[2] As a series of images moved across the screen—a landscape alluding to its West Bank location, a synagogue, men engaged in male-coded religious rituals, women with a baby, and then sudden, stark darkness—Moshe is heard saying, "Orthodox people usually live in communities and they want to stay in their communities. And when a community is not willing to accept . . . acknowledge and hear about it at all, you find yourself pushed out." As Moshe, *kippa* on his head and the flag in the background, finally appears in the frame, he explains that he did not discuss his secret with his rabbis—he surmised (correctly) that they would not understand. But he struck an optimistic note: "Today it is much easier."

The piece featured two other activists. Daniel Jonas, then Havruta's CEO, was interviewed along with his husband Uri Arman in their Jerusalem home. Uriel Tehila Levi, then a Bat Kol member and Jerusalem Open House activist who now identifies as nonbinary, was interviewed in a nondescript Jerusalem rental alongside a straight Orthodox roommate, an ally. Visuals, including a synagogue, communal prayer, ritual objects, and Orthodox-presenting people at the Jerusalem Pride Parade, telegraphed the activists' Orthodox credentials and normalized their presence in Orthodox spaces.

The hook to the story was a declaration by a prominent rabbi that "the proud community must be killed,"[3] and the narrator referenced Rabbi Levinstein, whose "perverts speech" is credited with bolstering turnout at the 2016 Jerusalem Pride Parade.[4] In a playful exchange, the reporter jokes with Daniel Jonas and Uri Arman, "You should bring Rabbi Levinstein a large bouquet of flowers." Daniel agreed: "Rabbi Levinstein deserves a huge *yishar koach* [well done] for the service he did for us."

The story, which aired on Saturday evening (after the Sabbath), capped a busy week for Kadag activists: a public dialogue about tolerance in a Jerusalem neighborhood on Tuesday; a conference about LGBT youth organized by the liberal Orthodox Religious Kibbutz movement on Wednesday;[5] and a conversation with the Rabbanit Malka Puterkovsky, one of "our rabbis," in a Jerusalem synagogue on Thursday.[6] The conference made national news, while the requisite photo with Malka Puterkovsky, featuring only a fraction of the dozens in attendance, was duly posted on Havruta's Facebook feed and shared widely. The Channel 10 story echoed Kadag talking points: visibility promotes dialogue; LGBT persons were already living in Orthodox communities; Orthodoxy was transforming; intolerance and hatred were a minority stance.[7]

But as it normalized the presence of LGBT persons in Orthodox spaces, the story did not mention that many, perhaps most, same-sex-attracted Orthodox persons were making other choices—partnering heterosexually, seeking conversion therapy, contemplating celibacy, struggling with their identity. It also did not mention the relative privileges of those aligned with Kadag's vision, nor ponder the merits of a tolerance campaign waged on occupied land. As it lauded rabbinic support for LGBT persons, the piece skirted the fact that even Kadag's most progressive allies were behind the curve. At the educators' conference, the Religious Kibbutz movement's CEO referred to *hommos* and lesbians as "those with inverse tendencies," an archaic phrase that many in the Kadag circle consider offensive. That same week, Rabbanit Malka Puterkovsky reiterated that she considered pride parades, including the one in Jerusalem, to be incompatible with Orthodox values. No matter: the Channel 10 story was a major win in the context of an intensifying political and cultural battle over Orthodoxy's essence.

Kadag's claims of legitimacy and authenticity, along with demands for tolerance and acceptance, gained traction in the soul-searching aftermath of the violence at the 2015 Jerusalem Pride Parade. So did conservative rabbis' vilification of Orthodox LGBT persons. Public discourse in the murder's aftermath laid bare the widening chasm between conservative and liberal Orthodox factions, forcing previously silent Orthodox persons to take sides. There was another plot twist to Moshe's flag that went unmentioned in the Channel 10 story. Shilo is home to Rabbi Arale Harel, a conservative Orthodox Rabbi who had been associated with the now-defunct conservative *hommo* men's organization Kamoha. While Kadag normalizes LGBT lives and holds that same-sex relationships are compatible with Orthodoxy, Kamoha promoted celibacy and heterosexual marriage (see chapter 1). Kadag activists relished the flag as a symbolic affirmation of their vision as well as a personal affront to this rabbi and his allies.

This chapter considers the role of public visibility and protest in Kadag's activism against the background of increasing polarization between conservative and liberal Orthodox factions, on the one hand, and disagreements, within activist ranks, about the limits and limitations of Orthodox authenticity, on the other. The chapter engages debates about the politics of respectability, a concept that refers to rhetoric and strategies that marginalized groups deploy as they seek to advance an inoffensive, nonthreatening picture of themselves guided by the belief that doing so will increase support for their causes.[8]

Many LGBTQ+ movements tread a tension concerning the presentation of self in the public sphere. Activists weigh the benefits and drawbacks of public stunts and outrageous queer antics that may draw public attention to their cause but also alienate potential allies (think AIDS-era public stunts in the United States such as the funeral at the White House that culminated in the hurtling of bags of ashes on its lawn or the "stop the Church" protests at St. Patrick's Cathedral).[9] Respectability politics also applies to the framing of a movement's messages; a prime example is the American marriage equality's campaign slogan "love is love," which replaced earlier campaigns' rights-based claims for inclusion with an emphasis on love and commitment. Some LGBTQ+ activists and scholars view campaigns grounded in respectability as a capitulation to dominant norms and a strategy that benefits more privileged LGBTQ+ constituencies. Others point out that "respectability," which is premised on a dissonance between public and private lives and the association of identity traits with sin and transgression, results in grave emotional, psychological, and spiritual harms. Empirical analyses of the efficacy of respectability strategies are inconclusive, perhaps a reflection of the simultaneously generative and constraining power of social conformity: as this chapter shows, respectability can concurrently destabilize and reproduce social hierarchies.[10]

Focusing on three episodes, this chapter considers how activists take their cause to a polarized public sphere. The analysis demonstrates how Kadag's take on the politics of respectability, which mobilizes authenticity not so much as a tactic but rather as an essence, complicates the tension between respectable visibility and normalization on the one hand, and queer, disruptive protest and playful theatrics on the other.[11] These strategies converge in the sense that Orthodox LGBT persons' very existence in the public sphere threatens to undo the Orthodox world order—queer it?—from within.

Orthodox Drag

On July 17, 2017, Zehorit Sorek, a prominent Kadag activist, attended a women's conference in Jerusalem. Titled "And Thou Shall Be Holy," the conference sought to provide educators and spiritual leaders with tools to deal with LGBT issues within the Orthodox community. Zehorit was undercover: she donned a headcover and modest shirt and skirt for the occasion (she registered and paid for the conference using her real name). Sitting among the more than two hundred other women, Zehorit heard rabbis, therapists, educators, and spiritual leaders, the majority of them men, discuss LGBT persons' struggles. No LGBT persons were invited to speak. The closest the conference came to giving LGBT persons a voice was a play that dramatized the trials and tribulations of a young woman whom queer activists would call "questioning," but in the Orthodox vernacular is branded as "confused." The play's outcome was predictable; after some plot twists, including the revelation that the young woman's father had been an absent workaholic, she acknowledges her "confusion" and marries a man.

Zehorit's low profile was warranted. In April 2017, just before Passover, several Havruta activists were barred from entering a similar conference for men because organizers suspected that the activists planned to disrupt the day's proceedings.[12] The activists were indignant that a conference about Orthodox LGBT persons did not give them a voice but insisted that they were there to listen. They remained outside, their registration fees refunded. The dispute spilled onto the Facebook pages of Havruta activists and rabbis and onto mainstream media, finally arriving at an impasse with mutual accusations of silencing.[13]

Throughout the day, Zehorit shared anecdotes from the conference with her hundreds of Facebook followers via status updates and videos. The audience, she remarked in one video, was eerily familiar; she was "surrounded by people I know, that I recognize, people . . . women who look exactly like my mom's friends, like those I grew up with."[14] But this was no friendly home crowd, and Zehorit's updates gave a taste of the day's homophobic atmosphere. She was particularly enraged by a narrative that reduced orientation and attraction to behavior—coming, no less, from psychologists who claimed to work with same-sex-attracted persons (none of these therapists are considered to be LGBT allies). She then polled her followers: should she confront the speakers?

A lively conversation ensued on Facebook, with some encouraging Zehorit to disrupt, others advising caution. One Facebook friend was concerned that speaking out would "give them ammunition and reason to hate" and advised Zehorit to "show them what it means to love thy neighbor through personal example." Zehorit did speak up during the closing session. She summarized the day and the conference's messages in a Facebook post:

> You may falter and we will help with therapy. You will be healed. We have dozens of cases. And if you say that you cannot [be healed] then you are *choosing* to live this way, a life of sin from the Torah. . . . At the end of the conference, Rabbi Shmuel Eliyahu [chief rabbi of Safed and a central figure in conservative Orthodox circles] took the stage. Spoke in almost messianic passion and condemned the phenomenon of reviled lifestyle. Boasted about success in making change. And in the end said that he would like to use the actual word: abomination! The phenomenon is an abomination.

Zehorit stood up. Drawing on language, imagery, and rhetoric from the Jewish tradition, she denounced conversion therapy and Orthodoxy's mischaracterization of same-sex attraction. Her choppy two-minute video captured the rest of the exchange: "Rabbi, in the *Gemara* there is a story about a rabbi who studied a lot of Torah and was very satisfied with it. The rabbi met an ugly man and said to him 'what an ugly man you are.' The ugly man responded: 'go to the artist who made me [i.e., God] and tell him what an ugly vessel you created.'" Zehorit indicted the speakers: "I have been sitting here all day and heard you calling me ugly, ugly, ugly."

Zehorit's point was that people are God's creation, and therefore sexual orientation is divinely ordained. Attacking same-sex-attracted persons for *who they are* represents a challenge to God's (handi)work. Rabbi Eliyahu objected, "We said that we love each and every one.[15] We did not call you ugly. We said that the *phenomenon* is ugly. Don't put words in our mouths." Zehorit did not relent: "This is a paraphrase on how I live my life." A woman in the audience asks, "Why an ugly vessel?" "If it is not ugly," Zehorit retorts, "why do you want to change me?"

Throughout the brief exchange, the rabbi attempted to shut Zehorit down; she is heard politely requesting to finish her remarks, but the rabbi admonishes, "You will not silence us. We are saying that the phenomenon is ugly. And it remains so even after your words. Thank you very much." With clapping in the background Zehorit gets the last word: "Love thy neighbor is an important principle in the Torah."

The irony of Rabbi Eliyahu's choice of words—silencing—while yelling into a microphone onstage was not lost on social media. A summary of the day's proceedings compiled by a participant and posted on the conservative *hommo* organization Kamoha's website and an official press release did not mention Zehorit's intervention. But Rabbi Amichai Eliyahu (a conservative Orthodox rabbi with a large social media following and Rabbi Shmuel Eliyahu's son) articulated his camp's views in an op-ed published on an online Orthodox outlet. In the op-ed, the rabbi asserted his camp's exclusive hold on Orthodoxy and vowed to counter those who "speak lies" and attempt to silence the Torah. He also denied the very plausibility of Orthodox LGBT existence, referring to Zehorit as a political hack, not an Orthodox LGBT activist.[16] He ended with a sense of urgency: "We are committed to supporting normal family life.

We cannot let these people confuse the youth and tell him that life with members of his sex is normal. Places that did not try to address this social ill have paid a dear social price."[17]

As we have seen throughout this volume, denial of Orthodox LGBT persons' claims to Orthodox authenticity and the sense of urgency around such claims are common tropes. Per the report of the day's proceedings, Rabbi Arale Harel said that "one cannot be half Orthodox" and that "Orthodoxy must battle organizations that threaten the wholeness of the Torah, be they Orthodox people who desecrate the Sabbath or Orthodox *hommos*." There is an irony when the powerful cry "foul," while silencing their critics, but conservatives' intense responses indicate that they are aware that their boundaries around Orthodoxy no longer hold. A year later, these ideas made their way onto billboards plastered in strategic locations in Tel Aviv and Jerusalem proclaiming that "father and mother = family" and promoting "the courage to be normal."

As Zehorit's post circulated in Orthodox feminist and LGBT networks, it generated lively discussions about the role of public performance and antics in social movement struggles.[18] Zehorit was mostly celebrated as a queen, a hero, and an inspirational role model, but some questioned her tactics. One commentator cautioned that public stunts could prove counterproductive. An activist told me that dialogue is better pursued through cautious, curated visibility campaigns, slow and steady outreach, and *halachic* conversations. "How does this confrontation help an orthodox gay kid in a settlement whose mother might be in the audience?" Zehorit pushed back: "Real dialogue is one in which *both* sides are willing to change . . . unfortunately Rabbi Eliyahu asks of [those who cannot change] to live a life of loneliness, at home, and quietly."[19] Kadag, she implied, will not remain silent because silence cedes too much ground.

On the one hand, Zehorit's protest takes many pages from the queer protest playbook. It was theatrical, playful, daring. She dressed up. She took a risk, went undercover, and reported from the belly of the beast. She may have acted alone, but her action involved an army of followers to whom she gave voice and hope. She challenged authority on its own turf. Her intervention conveyed the pain of exclusion and demanded a legitimate, rightful place for the marginalized. She called out conversion therapy's high-stakes game. And she practiced what Kadag activists preach: "Don't talk about us, talk with us." As opposed to the carefully curated Faces campaign (chapter 5), whose main goal was to claim Orthodox authenticity through dialogue, with activists insisting that they "come in peace," Zehorit engaged in confrontational theatrics.

But there is irony in a queer discourse where the hero is dressed in Orthodox drag and grounds the demand to make space in the Jewish tradition's language, logics, and scripture—not in the language and frameworks of science, gender and sexuality studies, or human rights. Viewing these acts of protest as acts of "disidentification"—a strategy that, per queer theorist José Esteban Muñoz, recognizes the importance of local context, locates resistance in everyday lives, works on and against dominant ideology, and seeks to transform cultural logics from within—eases this irony.[20] As we saw in previous chapters, Kadag's activism is grounded in the Jewish tradition—fighting fire with fire, they draw on the master's (Judaism's) tools (rhetoric, sensibility, language)—but their goal is not to dismantle the master's house, currently hostile to LGBT persons, but rather to expand it. To do so they need to embody and claim it—physically, metaphorically, and spiritually.

The argument is not that Kadag's use of Jewish imagery and sensibilities is merely strategic (though it certainly is to an extent) but rather that Kadag's brand of queer protest is thoroughly and fundamentally Orthodox: it is shaped by Jewish logic and thought and reflects activists' identities, backgrounds, and core demand that they be recognized *as they are*. They lay claim to their rightful place within Orthodox communities *as LGBT persons*. Thus, their brand of queer protest is continuous with more carefully curated politics of respectable visibility: both draw on Orthodox logic and sensibilities in the quest to make space for LGBT persons within Orthodoxy.

Protest and visibility campaigns are also inextricably linked. Zehorit's intervention circulated beyond conference attendees and Facebook denizens. The post and video went viral and onto mainstream media, and within forty-eight hours from Zehorit's three minutes of fame, she and Rabbi Amichai Eliyahu (the son) were seated at a mainstream media outlet's studio for a joint interview.[21] Rabbi Eliyahu said that the conference was groundbreaking and that it had sought to bring "comfort" to same-sex-attracted Orthodox Jews. Such Jews, he said, wanted their community to recognize their struggles and embrace them, but what they were really after was a "righteous" way forward.[22] In their joint interview, Zehorit ceded one point: the conference indeed broke new ground, though she saw a different breakthrough; "ten years ago one would not encounter a rabbi admitting that Orthodox LGBT persons exist." That was the extent of common ground they could muster. The rabbi framed same-sex attraction as a flaw and deficiency and invited those struggling with same-sex attraction to seek "help." The visibly appalled interviewers joined Zehorit in denouncing conversion therapy. Less than two weeks after this confrontation, the 2017 Jerusalem Pride Parade indicated where the winds were blowing. For the second year in a row, the parade drew a record-breaking number of Orthodox allies, confirming Rabbi Eliyahu's sense of urgency. This urgency was also on display in guerrilla-war-like altercations between Kadag activists and operatives of the Noam political party, which burst into the public sphere in 2019 with an unapologetically homophobic tagline: "a normal nation in its country."

Protest and the Politics of Normality

In July 2019 the new political party Noam joined a crowded field of right-wing parties identified with the religious-Zionist camp. Noam means "pleasantness," but most observers perceived it as anything but pleasant. The party traded in homophobic, transphobic, and antifeminist rhetoric that decried religious pluralism and touted normalcy and "traditional values,"[23] waging what the left-leaning *Haaretz* newspaper called a holy war against the LGBTQ community with a platform as something "out of a Margaret Atwood novel."[24]

Nominally a political novice, Noam had ties to previous hard-right religious campaigns, most notably that of the Hazon (vision) movement, whose billboards and stickers announcing "the courage to be normal" had been circulating for over a year and a half. Both organizations asserted a narrow field of normativity, one premised on a "natural," divinely ordained heteronormative and cisnormative social order. A video set the tone for the brief campaign. Warning that "an entire country is undergoing conversion therapy, the time has come to stop it," the video features a family on its way to the polling station. The family is coded normative—a father, mother, and son—and secular—the mother wears jeans and no head covering; the father and son do not wear a kippa. On their brief drive, the family hears a report on the radio that streets around the Kotel (Wailing Wall)—Judaism's most holy site—are closed for a post-pride-parade event. The mother (inexplicably) beams at her son. But as they make their way into the polling station, they are accosted by protesters coded as LGBT and reform; one is holding a sign that reads "because children don't need a mother." The family literally fights its way into the polling station, where they encounter hip poll workers dressed in LGBT merch (one sports a Brooklynite beard and a "love is love" T-shirt) or coded "non-Jewish" (a clownish Clint Eastwood–esque cowboy). The distressed parents ditch the traditional ballot, instead writing in their vote: the mother's ballot reads, "let my son marry a woman"; the father writes in, "let my grandson be Jewish." This change of heart apparently came too late to warrant redemption: when they arrive back in their car, their tires have been slashed.[25]

Noam was not a serious political contender at the time. As expected, the party dropped its bid before the election to avoid fragmenting the Orthodox Zionist right. But its messaging captures the larger battle for Orthodoxy's soul waged on the backs of LGBT persons. Noam's campaign featured a conservative Orthodoxy that brands itself as the sole and valiant protector of "the family" and "normalcy," both under siege in a culture dominated by a coalition of hostile and dangerous Others: Reform Jews, secular Jews, non-Jews, feminists, and (especially) LGBT persons. Yet, like Evangelicals in the United States, whose claims of persecution belie an outsized political power and wherewithal,[26] as these events were unfolding the secular left had been out of power for years, and amid shifting political alliances and efforts to oust then–prime minister Benjamin Netanyahu, Ultra-Orthodox and Zionist Orthodox parties solidified their status as his core political allies. A post on the Confessions Page captured the irony of a political group claiming to be under siege while in fact residing close to the seat of power: "Following Noam on Facebook is the light of my life at the moment. With all the anti-LGBT rhetoric around, it is awesome to discover that Shoval's and other organizations' workshops and lesson plans are everywhere . . . that children are exposed to this content in preschool."[27] A young bisexual interviewee marveled, "We are so threatening to them they need a whole political party directed at us." Kadag activists also pointed out that Noam's messaging was anything but new, and drew connections between its fierce anti-LGBT rhetoric and that of establishment figures.

It was tempting to dismiss Noam as a distracting sideshow in the circus of never-ending election cycles, yet Noam's run marked a turning point: Orthodox responses to LGBT issues were no longer just an intra-Orthodox battle but a matter of *national* urgency. Many Orthodox LGBT persons, especially those vulnerable due to age and closet status, experienced Noam's presence during the raucous weeks leading up to the elections as hostile, violent, and threatening. Despite its doomed candidacy, Noam had an outsize presence in Orthodox spaces, especially in Jerusalem; its online visibility spilled into Orthodox homes, communities, and synagogues. One young interviewee said, "They're everywhere. I mean I know they're not *everywhere*. But if you live in Jerusalem you just can't get away. . . . I see their booths, then they're on Facebook, I see my friends liking their posts. It's discouraging. I'm terrified." A flood of messages on the Confessions Page reflected the depth of angst, anger, and distress: "Seventeen years old. In the closet. And in these very moments, there is a Noam meeting at my house."[28] Another wrote that she would like to confront Noam activists when she passes their Jerusalem booth but is too scared to do so because "my brothers volunteer with you and on my parents' home hangs a huge Noam sign and what if they find out and I'm so deep in the closet."[29]

Most disheartening for Orthodox LGBT persons was the fact that this was an in-house affair; Noam criticized secular culture but targeted its messaging at Orthodox LGBT persons' brothers and sisters, their neighbors and schoolmates—not "the folks dancing in bikinis on floats in the Tel Aviv parade. These folks don't know who you are, half of them think that you're a parody or trolls. The other half shrug and think '*nu, shoyn* [Yiddish for oh well], LGBT phobia isn't new.'"[30] "Noam activists broke me to pieces," one interviewee told me. "They tell me that I don't belong here [Jerusalem], in the city where I grew up! They tell me that the heart that my God—OUR God gave me, is not appropriate." Another anonymous post pleaded, "Noam: Please know you are hurting *me*. . . . When you talk, hang signs, lecture in the yeshivas—please think about me."[31]

The party's outsize public presence, combined with its offensive messaging and comical lack of nuance, was fodder for campy protest. Within twenty-four hours of Noam's launch, rogue "Noam gays" Facebook and

Twitter accounts began to troll the campaign. Zehorit Sorek reported on her Facebook feed picking up a call that led to the following exchange:

"Hi, this is Miriam, from the Noam party. Have you heard about us?" "Hello Miriam, yes, I have heard about you. You put up a sign on *Ayalon* highway [major thoroughfare in the Tel Aviv area] that calls for protecting family structure, that family is only fathers and mothers." Miriam (happily), "oh I'm so glad you've heard about us. I can send you some materials about the party. Maybe you will join us?" "Well, the campaign didn't quite speak to me . . . I'm an Orthodox lesbian, and if you add me to your proud group so that I can bring both my religious and lesbian identities into being that would be great." She hung up.[32]

Kobi Handelsman, a relentless activist who takes delight in trolling Orthodox conservatives, wrote on his feed about a meeting with a Noam representative:[33]

For a whole hour, he sat and lectured on how "reverse tendencies" are the embodiment of all that's awful in Western society. How the organizations of the "reverse" are the embodiment of everything that is bad in Israeli society, and how the infiltration of the "reverse" into the education system is the mother of all sins. . . . During the questions, when everyone in the audience attacked him, [saying] that the party will waste right-wing votes, his justification was "yes, you're right, but the house is burning." When I had the chance to speak I introduced myself in front of everyone as *hommo*, and I said, "I'm Kobi. *Hommo*. And I'm the one you've just attacked for a full hour." The speaker was quiet for a minute and then said, "No, no, it wasn't you who I attacked. We don't attack individuals. You, I love."

Protestors also took to the public sphere, turning Noam's distressing presence into a golden opportunity to elevate Orthodox LGBT visibility. As responses to Noam started flooding the anonymous Confessions Page, Michal Schonberg, the moderator, distributed a printout of their reflections in Noam booths.[34] Kobi Handelsman and Nadav Schwartz, sometimes joined by others, also protested Noam booths, standing beside them with clothing or props that marked their LGBT status.[35]

Photos of their protest, standing with their pride flags alongside Noam slogans, made for jarring images.

Ido Zangen, then a counselor with the LGBT youth organization IGY's religious groups, protested a Noam booth strategically located outside Jerusalem's busy Machne Yehuda market. Over two days, Ido and a group of fifteen- to twenty-five-year-olds braved the sun, heat, and unsympathetic passers-by, as they held pride flags and rainbow signs reading "religious and proud," "love thy neighbor," "LGBT proud," "you're fine as you are." Zangen explained that this peaceful protest aimed to communicate to LGBT youth that they were not alone in the public space.[36] While the group endured violent and vile reactions, it also elicited spontaneous messages of support, along with offerings of cold water and ice cream. The protestors also engaged in genuine dialogue with unlikely interlocutors, like a group of Haredi young men.

The vulnerable youth these protestors strove to reach appreciated this support:

> I went to the Machne Yehuda market . . . next to Noam, I see pride flags and a kippa in pride colors. . . . I started to shiver. And then cry in the middle of the market. . . . I was filled with joy. I wanted to hug you all. This moment was more meaningful to me than all pride parades ever. Where I did not expect the beautiful flag, I saw sweet people holding it. So if you see this, thank you. You are amazing.[37]

Noam's visibility also emboldened and mobilized rank-and-file Orthodox LGBT persons and allies into action; its presence in the public sphere provided them with opportunities to enact smaller acts of resistance, taking joy in acts such as tearing down and defacing Noam stickers, posters, and signs or burying them behind LGBT-friendly stickers. A waitress at a restaurant frequented by Noam activists reported throwing away the flyers they left behind. A young woman stood alone next to a Noam booth in Jerusalem holding a large pride flag. An anonymous post wished the ultimate curse on Noam: that its signs be defaced by "tons of pink *with sparkles*."[38] Subversive action was cathartic:

> My pious sister and I knocked down Noam's sign in our neighborhood. You might say that because of people like us the community gets blamed

for silencing, yadda, yadda, yadda. But to see that crumpled sign is a message to the fourteen-year-old closeted lesbian and her likes who every day are beating themselves up and wish upon themselves horrible things . . . that instead of waking up tomorrow morning and thinking "shit I'm really surrounded by these horrible people" to give them some hope and they can see that there are people around them who reject this evil and there are accepting and loving people in their environment. Oh, and also to annoy those who hung the flag.[39]

Two threads run through these acts of protest, public and anonymous, campy and restrained. First, activists come to the table not as LGBT activists but as *Orthodox* LGBT activists. Second, from the perspective of some conservatives, no form of LGBT visibility would meet the high bar of "respectability." Thus, the ultimate act of resistance is beating Noam at its own game: denying its status as the guardian of normality, Jewish values, and piety, thereby (re)claiming ownership of defining what it means to be Orthodox. "I want to yell at them that the Temple was destroyed because people like them, that they are doing nothing but . . . [filling] the streets of Jerusalem with messages of hatred. There is no greater desecration of God."[40] Activists claimed to have the upper hand not only because the public was with them but also because, one activist said, Noam was on the wrong side of *Jewish* history. "We are advancing towards heaven, and you are running towards the place where people who shame others in public are sent" (a reference to hell), read another anonymous contribution to the Confessions Page.[41]

In the March 2021 parliamentary elections, Noam united with other factions to form the Religious Zionist Party. One of its representatives was elected to the Knesset. With Noam's rhetoric encroaching upon Orthodox LGBT persons in their homes, families, schools, communities, and places of worship, in the public square, and in Parliament, the mood turned dark. Kadag organizations and activists were among a coalition of organizations who converged outside the Knesset during the swearing-in ceremony to protest the election of unapologetic sexist, racist homophobes. The election also forced a reckoning about the limitations of a politics of authenticity and respectability. Michal Schonberg said at the rally that when Noam first ran she laughed, but she ceased laughing when she realized how many of her friends, family, and neighbors supported the party.[42] Another Kadag activist posted a message on Facebook saying he had felt "punched in the stomach" by an Orthodox community that allowed a party, whose sole essence was negating LGBT normativity and inclusion, to be elected. "Am I still part of this community? Where will I have space," he wondered.[43]

As in other episodes recounted throughout this book, activists mourning the violence of exclusion stopped short of comprehensively interrogating the dangers of melding a militant nationalism, a fervent Orthodoxy, and conservative gender and sexual ideology. I return to this point in the conclusion, where I ponder the limitations of a politics of authenticity that does not challenge other forms of oppression. For now, I point out that Noam's campaigns provided opportunities for bold and visible action as well as small moments of resistance and pushed to the limit the logics of respectability. Some of the activism Noam spurred was taken right out of the queer activist playbook—activists proudly and unapologetically took their messages to the streets, making their case to the court of public opinion. Yet their language was not so much one of rights, radical queer politics, or antinormativity but one of authenticity. One of the rainbow-themed signs carried at the rally protesting Noam's newly minted membership in the Knesset was a play on the Talmudic story of the ugly vessel and its creator mentioned earlier in the chapter: "go tell the artist who made me what a fabulous outcome." But the escalating public rhetoric also allowed—forced?—activists to take a different approach, less complacent, more publicly raucous and critical. Ido Zangen wrote that his group's plan had been to "be silent and beautiful and present. But maybe it's time to stop being silent." The breaking of the silence, in modes both campy and restrained, happens every year at Jerusalem Pride.

Pride and Prejudice in the Holy City

On the eve of the 2016 Jerusalem Pride Parade, longtime Havruta activist Yivnia Kaplahon pleaded with his friends and followers to join the marchers:

> This coming Thursday you can do something for me and for all the women and men and those in between, in whom something was murdered a year ago; you can do something for the young people, from Jeru-

salem and across the country who still do not dare march in a parade that is all about life and a celebration of folks who were created in the image [of God] and dare stand proudly even though so many others would prefer that they decay in the dark closet, in the obscurity of the cellar. Don't be fooled—this is a battle. Only that in this battle there are many good and a few bad. The rest are all fools, or they hold prejudices and they need to see you marching with pride in the cities of Yehuda and in Jerusalem's streets, to crack this ignorance and empower their loved ones who hide from them in fear, sometimes hiding from themselves.

My friends, the Jerusalem Pride Parade is an unapparelled opportunity for each and every participant to meet the beautiful Israeli; joining the parade is a powerful way for each and every one of you to do something for your sisters and brothers, for your colleagues and neighbors, for numerous sons of Adam and daughters of Eve, who were fortunate enough to have been born with an identity that is different and invisible in dark and violent times. True, there have been darker and more violent times and much progress has been made, but to those who smell the stale air of a dark closet, this fact changes nothing. He needs your [gendered male] declaration, she needs your [gendered female] declaration. You don't need to be lesbian or transgender to come and march with me and my brave community; you don't need to be *hommos* or bisexual to respect, with your presence, the sweet memory of Shira Banki may she rest in peace; you don't need to identify with each and every of the proud community's goals in Israel to convey: "in this struggle, my heart is in the right place"; you don't have to feel comfortable with every sign or every performance of each and every of the marchers to make sure that your loved ones will know that you are marching this year in the pride parade and that they will always be embraced, no matter what.

When you enter Gan Pa'amon [the parade's staging area] this coming Thursday at 5:00 PM, you will see me and my friends from the proud community, but also many other world-repairing citizens, women and men with a huge heart and historical awareness, those who remember that significant changes always begin with a deep breath and a small step. Men and women like you and me partook in each historical drama, from (the Egypt) Exodus to the suffragists, from the Blacks in South Africa to Stonewall—they woke up one morning, looked in the mirror, and said, "This has to do with me."[44]

Another Kind of Pride

Jerusalem city center on a hot summer day. Families. Balloons. Love thy neighbor stickers (theme: rainbow). Kids in strollers. Kids in pride T-shirts. Men in kippas and women in headgear. Men (and a few women) in rainbow kippas. Women wearing shirts advertising "free mom hugs." Somewhere there are dad hugs too. Some pink hair in the background. A group of Orthodox-presenting persons in matching "Allied Orthodox Community" shirts (also, a sign: "Religious. Straight. Ally"). Groups of excited youth decked in their movement uniforms. Police in uniforms. A handful of Haredi-presenting men patiently waiting to get through the security checkpoint, though some will be barred entry for being suspected of wanting to disrupt the parade. A *minyan*. Alternative *minyans*! Prayers. Face painting. People gather around Havruta and Bat Kol booths, some sporting their respective organizations' merch; hesitant onlookers, including the author, are welcomed with warm smiles. A young woman in tears. This is her first time marching; she's frightened and relieved to be here. Some are holding signs advertising the yeshivas and *ulpanas* they attended. A massive sign: "Religious Proud Community." In the background, outside the security checkpoints, young Orthodox men protest.

Onto the parade path. Thousands of people, casually dressed, marching, through the streets of Jerusalem. And the flags; so many rainbow flags, in people's hands, hanging from balconies across the route. Some bear the Star of David, others are run-of-the-mill pride flags. Walk with Kadag, and you'll be treated to Hasidic/Orthodox/Jewish music blasting from boomboxes in shopping carts and horah circles; the dancing is cathartic, joyous, and very "Jewish." "The only time during the year I dance horah is at the Jerusalem parade, and at the occasional wedding," tells me a young hip woman who identifies as lesbian and ex-Orthodox ("but I always march with our block"; to the author: "You seem bewildered. Must be your first Jerusalem parade"). Those holding signs that name the yeshivas and *ulpanas* they attended line up for the ultimate photo op, with Jerusalem's Great Synagogue as the background (a yearly ritual). An onlooker, a young man wearing a rainbow kippa, said he suffered too harshly at his yeshiva to participate in this ritual, but he relishes the sight: "This is a parade highlight . . . it feels so good to show them that we are not afraid." Since 2016, there has also been a makeshift memorial for the teen murdered at the 2015 parade. Many stop to reflect and pay respects with flowers and silent prayers. Bands of Orthodox protestors beyond the parade's "secure parameter" are barely visible or audible along the route, but their presence is well known. (A woman in her twenties, a week after the parade: "I wanted to march but was too scared . . . my brothers were out there protesting.") At the end of the route: thousands sitting quietly on the grass waiting for speeches. The next day, Kadag hosts a communal Shabbat dinner at a local park.

These are snapshots from the Jerusalem Pride Parade, an event that even liberal rabbinic authorities view as un-Orthodox and strategically misguided at best, and conservative Orthodox rabbis view as flirting with the wrath of God. "Desecration of Jerusalem . . . one of the worst transgressions in the Torah" announced a Jerusalem chief rabbi on the eve of the 2016 parade.[45] Since its inauguration in 2002, the Jerusalem March for Pride and Tolerance has been the focal point of fierce debates, political machinations, doomsday warnings about divine retaliation, and violence.[46] Opponents have petitioned the legislator, public officials, the police, and the courts to block funding and otherwise circumvent the event; most of these attempts have failed to pass judicial muster. Objections to holding World Pride events in Jerusalem in 2006 produced a rare truce that united Christian, Muslim, and Jewish religious leaders. Postponed due to national security concerns (some attributed the war with Lebanon that thwarted the event's original date as a divine signal), World Pride was eventually canceled due to credible threats of domestic violence. In 2005 and 2015, the parade was the site of actual violence, inconceivably perpetrated by the same man, Yishai Shlisel. Liberal Orthodoxy had done much soul-searching since 2015, but hard-liners have been emboldened.

Unable to stop the parades, conservative Orthodox groups convene counterprotests and conferences, like the one Zehorit Sorek attended in 2017. And like a well-choreographed dance, every year in the weeks and days leading up to the event conservative rabbis can be relied on to provide what Kadag activists view as free advertising: condemnations so vile that they ensure widespread media coverage and bigger turnout. In 2016, it was Rabbi Levinstein's "perverts speech." In 2018, more than one hundred rabbis signed a letter denouncing the parade, LGBT organizations, and LGBT acceptance as "media brainwash" that makes "perverts into heroes."[47] A counter-letter, organized within days by fast-thinking activists, garnered an equal number of signatories.[48] Jerusalem Open House (JOH), the local LGBT nonprofit that stages the event, remains undeterred. When protestors petitioned the police to cancel the parade in 2018, JOH responded, "We will not give in to your violence . . . everyone who opposes your extremism and supports pluralism, love, tolerance [will march]."[49] In 2019, when a chief rabbi opposed the hanging of Pride flags throughout the city, JOH removed flags from the vicinity of the Great Synagogue and launched a flags campaign: volunteers made home deliveries. Meanwhile, participation swelled even as security tightened after 2015. In recent years the event has attracted 15,000 to 20,000 participants, dwarfed by the better known Tel Aviv parade (2019 estimate: 250,000), but significant in a city where *30 percent* of residents are Ultra-Orthodox Jews.

Pride parades are multivalent events.[50] Party, carnival, protest, and political speech in one, a central node of LGBT visibility. The Tel Aviv parade sometimes makes lists of the best pride parades worldwide: with floats, music, outrageous outfits, a celebration of all modes of sexual displays, and a weeklong carnivalesque atmosphere, it offers a fine show. Such images are a rare exception at Jerusalem Pride. In the bastion of Orthodoxy, the event is cerebral and muted by design: a tame, desexualized, family-friendly affair, a political statement, not a party. But for those who relish the sight of Orthodox-presenting persons in a pride parade, a horah circle of LGBT persons and signs in front of the Great Synagogue, the Star of David rainbow flags taking over the streets of the Holy City, this is quite the party indeed: a coming out and coming to terms party that announces, we are here, we deserve to be here, deal with it.

Thus, while Kadag organizations are present on the national pride circuit (June and July 2019 saw a record two dozen events around the country; most 2020 events were canceled due to the COVID-19 pandemic, and a more muted lineup returned in 2021), the Jerusalem parade holds a special place; "That is 'our' day," one activist told me. Indeed, some secular LGBT persons resent the event's restrained format and prominent religious presence.[51] But this "family-friendly," "sanitized" parade serves a larger political purpose: by distancing the Jerusalem pride parade from other forms of LGBT visibility, the organizers celebrate the many faces of queerness, including the peculiarities of Orthodox LGBT identities. This is an important talking point in Kadag's outreach to Orthodox communities and leaders. In another sense, the Jerusalem pride parade is the most ordinary parade of all: the debates that engulf it anew every year serve as a reminder of the precarity of LGBT gains as well as of unresolved tensions between competing visions of political goals and tactics, sexual ethics, and belonging.

Competing Visions of Activism, Sexual Ethics, and Orthodox Authenticity

The Jerusalem Pride Parade has long been the subject of fierce debates among Orthodox same-sex-attracted persons, their representative organizations, and their allies. Some of the tensions that plagued the first public forums for Orthodox *hommos* and lesbians and bubbled up again within Havruta resurfaced as Orthodox LGBT persons debated participation in pride parades. One faction holds that participating in parades is a misguided strategy because pride parades are inherently un-Orthodox (the now-defunct Hod and Kamoha held these views). Kadag dismisses this stance as plagued by internalized homophobia and a narrow vision of Orthodoxy. The stakes are high: who can claim an Orthodox identity, and what are its boundaries? Kadag's vision seems to have won the day, with Orthodox allies and, most recently, a handful of liberal rabbis increasingly heeding their stance.

The factions disagreed on activism goals, rhetoric, tactics, and strategies: should Orthodox LGBT activism be public and aligned with secular LGBT organizations, or should Orthodox organizations maintain a "respectable" conversation with rabbis behind closed doors? Should the struggle center on tolerance and acceptance or also demand halachic accommodations for same-sex relationships? In his decade of activism at the helm of Hod, Rabbi Ron Yosef was steadfast: marching in the streets is not the appropriate solution to Orthodox *hommos'* plight (Hod focused primarily on homosexuality). Part of the problem is that marching and public protest are premised on frameworks such as human rights rather than Jewish theology and sensibilities; real change, this faction argues, can come only from working from *within* Orthodoxy, enlisting its sensibilities and appealing to its authority structures.[52] I heard variations on this theme. Orthodox LGBT visibility should be directed toward study groups, communities, and synagogues, one interviewee claimed. Another was concerned that parades, including the ones in Jerusalem, are inextricably linked to larger LGBT causes and agendas that are not only foreign to but also downright hostile to "authentic" Jewish values. A man in his late twenties who said he was attracted to men (but did not identify as *hommo*) said that it was impossible to dissociate the parade from the liberal, secular context in which it was embedded: "I reject a lot of the goals of the liberal LGBT organizations and their reasoning. For them, the basis for recognition is human rights; or this vague claim to 'a right to love.' That comes too close to promiscuity. I say that to love and be loved, to be in a relationship, is a *Jewish* value. It is not good to be alone. Rabbi Benni [Lau] has said this as well."

A closeted lesbian was similarly ambivalent, saying she did not "believe in defiance. I call it a provocation, not a parade, there's something very provocative about the whole thing, even though in Jerusalem they call it a tolerance parade. . . . I believe in outreach like Pesach Sheni, I think that's the best way to communicate our messages respectfully, modestly. I believe in humility, not in pride."

Kadag activists and their allies reject these positions. They concede that public visibility initiatives, including pride parades, are insufficient interventions, but insist that visibility plays a key role in their overall campaign. As one activist put it, "The critics speak as if the parade is ALL that we do. But that's misleading. The parade is one of many avenues of struggle. They're all important, together they send a comprehensive political message: we are here." A lesbian in her twenties said that visibility was not just about politics—it was self-affirming: "People ask 'why do you need this day of pride parade' and it's a ridiculous question. It's as if you don't feel for the rest of the 364 days you have to keep quiet about a part of yourself." A Havruta activist explained that the main goal is "visibility. To show that we are not ashamed and not apologetic about who we are. . . . What bothers me most is that some Orthodox *hommos* are opposed to the parade. Just like our biggest foes, they say that it's not Orthodox, they see the parade as glorifying sex and promiscuity. Sex???? We dance to Jewish music and carry signs."

Kadag activists and their allies also claim that unapologetic public visibility is a powerful statement and take issue with the distinction between "Jewish" and other frameworks for achieving social change: "Yes, we're Orthodox. We base our activism on this idea of *veahavta* [and you shall love]. But we *also* march for our rights. This is the essence of democracy." Another activist was frustrated by critics from within Orthodox LGBT circles who still believed that "we should just be talking to rabbis. Sure, that's important. But really, not enough. And we've been talking to rabbis. *A lot!* So being visible in public, out in the streets, having all sorts of community events, and yes!—pride parades!—are important for changing public opinion."

Kadag activists and their critics also disagree on whether it is appropriate to collaborate with groups and organizations premised on paradigms, values, and ideas that they may not fully share. Kadag claims that one does not need to fully identify with secular LGBT organizations' goals and strategies to convey messages of love, embrace, and support— the real essence of the parade. A Bat Kol activist had tired of these debates by the time I interviewed her in 2018: "There are so many reasons to march, why can't they [the critics from within] accept that when we [Kadag] march, we infuse the parade with our vision, *our* meaning?" As discussed in chapter 1, Bat Kol envisions itself as a bridge between LGBT and Orthodox communities. Where critics see provocation, Kadag and their allies see dialogue. "The goal of the parade in Jerusalem is to encourage dialogue in the Israeli public, and no locale is more fitting for this purpose than Jerusalem." "So many people hate Jerusalem but they ignore the beauty, so many people from all walks of life coming together." "They don't see the difference between Tel Aviv and Jerusalem parades. It's very frustrating. But really, even if there's 'sex,' it doesn't mean that that's what it's all about, that you agree with everything, and that there aren't other reasons to be there."

For some, the real issue *is* sex. Though the conservative *hommo* organizations Hod and Kamoha are now defunct, their view that the parade is a hedonistic, overly sexualized affair lives on. Echoing rabbis of all stripes, in-house critics argue that parades "externalize" sexuality. As one of them put it, "Originally, pride parades were about protest and anger and taking up the public sphere. No more. Now it's a 'happening.' A celebration of sexiness. Of sex. This is not Orthodox!" Even putting sex aside, the parade "gives legitimacy to a lifestyle that's not Orthodox, embraces things that undermine Orthodoxy. The issue is the public aspect. The parade says: anyone can live their life according to how she or he sees fit."

Kadag activists point out that this characterization of the Jerusalem parade is grossly inaccurate ("Other than a couple of provocateurs who show up in thongs you won't see naked men in the streets," one interviewee told me), but disagreements about movement tactics and goals, about whether the critics' characterization of the Jerusalem parade was fair, and about collaborating with secular organizations rest on deeper theological and ideological disputes about Orthodox authenticity and its limitations: Should the same-sex-attracted refer to themselves as gay, as same-sex-attracted, as *hommo*/lesbian, or as having reverse tendencies? Is theological recognition of their love and relationships possible, or is tolerance the best they can hope for? Can Orthodox LGBT ever be sufficiently "respectable"—and if so, at what cost?

Hod, Kamoha, and their allies had claimed that participation in the parade is un-Orthodox because LGBT rights, same-sex attraction, and sex are inextricably connected. Kadag activists and their allies are perturbed by such claims. There is a vast gulf between LGBT identity, demanding rights, and "sex." One activist resented claims about "externalization" because they reduced LGBT existence to sex. Another could not see any connection between halacha and marching in a parade: "The Torah forbids something very specific, and our march isn't about that, it's about recognition, and rights, equality. There's no connection between the halachic prohibition and marching. . . . No one marches in the parade with a sign proclaiming 'I engage in forbidden sex.'" A third pointed to the crux of the matter—who can claim to be Orthodox: "They say that marching in the parade is not Orthodox even when we dance to Jewish music because they think that even talking about same-sex attraction in public is un-Orthodox. But you know what their real issue is? That we are not ashamed of who we are. They think *that* is un-Orthodox." For another activist, the case was easy: "We are marching to remind people that we have a right to exist, we were legitimately created by God."

For a long time "our rabbis" did not support Kadag's stance, but the needle seems to be moving, ever so slightly. None have attended the parade, and their public statements and writing about the parade are less forgiving than their stance on acceptance. These allies raise a variety of concerns but center on the un-Orthodox nature of parades: conversations about sexuality are inherently immodest, and the ethical frameworks within which they are grounded are secular.[53]

Regardless, Orthodox communities are increasingly receptive to Kadag's messages. Ariella Matar, an LGBT ally, founded "Allied Orthodox Community" in 2014 and has seen the group grow from year to year. In 2017 she urged her Facebook followers to join the parade "so that no Orthodox young woman will have to live in a closet because of us. Our brothers and sisters don't deserve it. No one deserves this. And so long that we are silent and don't support our LGBT brothers and sisters—we are part of the problem."[54] In the lead-up to the 2017 parade, Ariella launched a #whyImarch campaign. An anonymous Orthodox lesbian appreciated the effort:

> You have no idea what it means to me to see you at the parade. I couldn't explain why seeing a married Orthodox couple or a group or straight Orthodox women marching with us touched me to this extent. Perhaps because it reminded me that Orthodox women in my life not there with me. Or perhaps it reminded me of my adolescent years when I was surrounded primarily by Orthodox women—teachers, counselors, neighbors [all gendered female]. I walked around in the ulpana, lost, but I knew that I couldn't talk about it with any of the adult figures in my life. . . . [Now I think about] the youth, when they start reflecting about their sexual identity and often feel that they will have to give up all that they know and belonging to the Orthodox community. . . . And maybe for them seeing adult Orthodox people in the parade qualms some of the alienation. . . . Now it seems that other people care, that I can feel free and comfortable in the world. That the battle over tolerance and freedom is not ours alone.[55]

Jerusalem Pride is a microcosm of visibility and protest campaigns. It captures the tension between multitude of allegiances and ideologies: a human rights framework seen through the lens of Jewish values and sensibilities, and one that Kadag claims to be authentically Orthodox; a desire to assert their right to exist in a community that frowns upon public discussions of sexuality. The parade both celebrates and empowers Orthodox LGBT persons and is an occasion to assert, in the public square, "we exist," "we are part of your communities," "acknowledge us, talk to us," and "this is what an Orthodox Jew looks like." In this, the parade serves as a rebuttal to conservatives who vilify LGBT lives in general and Orthodox ones in particular. But it also highlights tensions within LGBT Orthodox circles vis-à-vis competing visions of the repaired world, and how to best achieve it. In taking charge, insisting on their own meanings, interpretations, tactics, and alliances, Kadag activists signal that they are no longer willing to wait for their community and their leaders. Finally, the parade highlights the complexity of LGBT activism in conservative communities: campaign tactics may be grounded in queer antics and theatrics (signs, stickers, and dancing), but their particular brand of queer antics is steeped in Jewish theology, language, and sensibilities—a religious restraint that many in the broader LGBT community in Israel find distasteful. Ariella Matar's anonymous interlocutor captures the gist of the battle: while it may center on tolerance toward LGBT persons and sexual ethics, the real battle is about what it means to be Orthodox. Orthodox LGBT persons are remaking Orthodoxy in part by being visible out in the streets.

At a 2020 Pesach Sheni event Daniel Jonas explained why he continues to insist on the Orthodox label even though the pluralistic religious landscape in Jerusalem affords him easy access to more affirming Jewish communities: "If I stop defining myself as Orthodox we will allow the Orthodox community to say what used to be true, 'that [LGBT persons] don't exist here.' Now they can no longer say that . . . we insist on our place within the Orthodox community, so that we feel comfortable. It's also about not letting them feel comfortable without us." It is a small wonder, then, that Orthodox conservatives consider Orthodox LGBT persons as an existential threat. A group that had been marginalized, maligned, then offered a partial acceptance only if they assume a narrative of victimhood emerged as a consensus-defying agent of change.

* * *

In the chronicles of LGBT activism, revolutionary antics and disruptive, outrageous, mirthful public performances are often in tension with campaigns that center on normalization and respectability.[56] Kadag enlists

THE BATTLE FOR JUDAISM'S STRAIGHT SOUL | 219

both strategies. On the one hand, educational outreach and dialogue with rabbinic authorities center on creating a safe space for marginalized Others and opening up a public dialogue about acceptance and tolerance. On the other hand, visibility campaigns such as the Channel 10 story and the Faces campaign discussed in the previous chapter may seem to be carefully planned and highly curated, but their message is provocative: Orthodox LGBT persons already inhabit Orthodox spaces. Kadag also deploys more combative forms of protest. But protests are continuous with the activist strategies discussed throughout this volume, not least because they are all premised on activists' willingness to emerge from the safety of anonymity and thrust themselves into the public sphere. Visibility, protest, and outreach initiatives are often continuous with and complement one another; the signifiers travel from one sphere to another. Moshe Argaman's flag may have marked a safe space and provoked dialogue in a particular locale, but by 2016 the pride flag had become a potent symbol of cultural warfare. In addition, as befitting an LGBT social movement that emerged in tandem with social media and is spearheaded by young activists, both types of Kadag initiatives seamlessly traverse the online and physical world and are often laden with theatrics, drama, and witty playfulness. Even subdued forms of visibility—a photo of activists with rabbinic authorities, an awareness campaign that narrates sanitized stories about Orthodox LGBT lives— take on a measure of playful subversion as they travel from the physical world and go viral online.

Like the outreach initiatives discussed in chapter 5, the mobilization of Orthodoxy's registers, values, language, and sensibilities and the claim to authenticity both temper and fuel a politics of disruption. Thus, while some acts of protest and visibility may seem quite benign and restrained—really, how threatening are photos of smiling young *hommos* and lesbians and their friends, neighbors, and grandmothers, as in the Faces 2 campaign?—they are *religiously* subversive, which is why Kadag's claims of peaceful dialogue are perceived by its adversaries as an all-out, urgent, and frontal assault. To a community attempting to maintain its boundaries, threats are everywhere: a sign at a pride parade announcing the marcher's religious institutional affiliation, a young woman standing quietly with a pride flag next to a homophobic and transphobic campaign slogan, staging a counter-lesson outside a hall where a homophobic rabbi is lecturing, a queer safe-zone sticker in a yeshiva study hall.

In June 2017, Moshe Grossman, of flag infamy, married his boyfriend Eran Ashkenazi. Both men were well-known activists, and they exchanged vows before hundreds of family, friends, and fellow Orthodox LGBT persons. Their declaration of love symbolized the dawn of new possibilities for LGBT persons of faith. The wedding looked and felt Jewish: it featured a huppah, the Jewish wedding canopy, and a broken glass (two, one for each groom to crush), among other Jewish rituals, and both grooms—and many of their guests—presented as Orthodox in their choice of clothing and ritual garments. This was not a normative Orthodox Jewish wedding in the sense that there were two grooms and no bride, and the wedding was officiated by a yeshiva-trained transgender woman, not an ordained male rabbi. But the impressions that circulated on social media (videos and photos of the wedding went viral) were clear: this was an authentic Jewish wedding because the partners identified as Orthodox and their community recognized them as such. At the heart of Kadag activism, then, is a politics of visibility of persons legible at times as queer, Orthodox, or both. By occupying public space, they challenge ideas about what it means to be Orthodox (cisgender and heterosexuality can no longer be assumed), what it means to be LGBT (secularity and resistance to the settlement project can no longer be assumed), and the spaces in between, thereby blurring the boundaries between subversion and normalization.

Conclusion

Queering Orthodoxy

> We cannot say "our hands did not spill this blood."
> Anyone who has ever sat at a Shabbat table, in a school classroom, in
> a synagogue, on a soccer field, at a club or at a community center, who
> heard those racist jokes, the homophobic jokes, the crude language and
> did not stand up to stop it, he too is an accomplice to this bloodshed. . . .
> It all begins with our words. . . .
> We must take responsibility.
> It is not permissible for anyone to live in a closet. A closet is death! . . .
> And you should choose life
> —Rabbi Benny Lau

A lone perpetrator was responsible for the violence at the 2015 Jerusalem Pride Parade, but Rabbi Lau, speaking at an impromptu rally in its
bloody aftermath, indicted an entire social system. The parade marked
a turning point. Here was a highly respected rabbi publicly embracing
LGBT persons, giving voice to their plight, and calling out the community and its leaders for pushing people into closets—and to their deaths,
whether at the hands of a mentally ill fanatic, through suicide, or to a
metaphoric, spiritual death.

Shira Banki's violent death yielded a year of firsts: a collective coming-
out (Our Faces campaign, December 2015), a groundbreaking *halachic*
position paper (Beit Hillel, April 2016), rabbinic leaders' public penitence (October 2016),[1] a conference for Orthodox educators (November 2016). Turnout for the Jerusalem Pride Parade in August 2016 was
the largest on record and included thousands of new religious allies.[2] A
pride flag hung outside Havruta activist Moshe Argaman's (then Grossman) home in Shilo, a conservative Orthodox settlement in the West
Bank. Meanwhile, people just continued living: they came to terms and

came out, got married, had children, remained in Orthodox yeshivas, attended services in neighborhood synagogues, and so on.

The violence and its soul-searching aftermath hastened processes a decade and a half in the making. That the ground was ripe was a testament to Kadag's relentless activism but also reflected favorable social conditions. Social movements do not operate in a vacuum, and Orthodoxy itself was experiencing seismic shifts: as it fractured and polarized, liberalizing forms of Orthodoxy that emphasize self-determination and prioritize individuals' well-being over rabbinic authority proliferated.[3] These processes had accelerated with the expansion of social media platforms that provided openings for marginalized groups and voices to enter the conversation.

At the turn of the twenty-first century, same-sex-attracted Orthodox persons had launched and found their way into anonymous chatrooms and then took the leap into other digital and physical spaces, where, sheltered from prying eyes, they recast their identities and developed a collective consciousness. Together, they articulated a vision of what it meant to be a religious LGBT person. Realizing that to achieve real change they would need to confront a community that wrote them out of existence, pathologized them, and labeled them as transgressors, they coalesced around the goal of making space. They told stories about themselves to their families, friends, Orthodox communities, and rabbinic leaders and leaned into Jewish scripture, values, ethics, and theology to make a *Jewish* case for tolerance, acceptance, and inclusion.

By 2015 thousands of LGBT persons from Orthodox homes had gone through harsh journeys. They had seen their paths to normative Orthodox adulthood rupture and disintegrate. Now, as they rewrote their stories, they also reimagined Orthodoxy. Religious elites played a supporting, mostly reactive, role. By the time Rabbi Lau gave his speech in 2015, thousands of Orthodox LGBT persons had come out. By the time he had attended a same-sex wedding, in 2018,[4] images of Orthodox attendees at such weddings had lost their shock value. Even his groundbreaking position paper charting a path for recognizing (some) same-sex unions and families was preempted by a young Havruta member, Rafael J. Kelner Polisuk, whose halachic roadmap made its debut on social media several months earlier.[5] Still, religious leaders' public speech matters. Rabbi Lau is a descendant of a rabbinic dynasty, and in 2015 he led a popular liberal Orthodox congregation in Jerusalem.

The wars of words have escalated since 2015, suggesting that the story was never about LGBT acceptance, inclusion, halachic roadmaps, or a Leviticus clause. At stake were Orthodoxy's essence and future. Thus, though Kadag did not set out to start a revolution, the modest request— "make space"—earned conservatives' wrath. "What defines where you are within the Orthodox community is how you relate to the question of *hommos*," observed Kadag ally Rabbi Raffi Ostroff.[6]

Rabbi Lau has been consistent: "And you should choose life." But what does "choosing life" mean when the still-dominant theological stance views gender and sexual diversity as transgressive, sinful, and perverted and "the LGBT question," a proxy for an internecine struggle, serves as a constant reminder of one's marginal status? What kind of life can one make in a community that denies LGBT existence? And whose life is worthy of choosing and protecting? When Beit Hillel rabbis published their position paper on tolerance in April 2016, Kadag's tepid response caught them off guard; the paper was the most affirming public document released by religious leaders at the time. "They should have seen it coming," an activist told me, "what did they expect with a document that offered no guidance for *hommos* and lesbians and ignored transgendered and bisexual people?" Similar critiques were directed at Rabbi Lau's 2020 document affirming (some) same-sex relationships. At any rate, a large swath of the Orthodox population did not view either Rabbi Lau or Beit Hillel as spiritual leaders. A young man was bitter: Kadag's celebratory dance excluded those who, like him, hailed from the geographic and cultural periphery, who did not attend Orthodox elite institutions, and whose families viewed Rabbi Lau as "irrelevant." Kadag, he maintained, had created its own pink Ashkenazi neighborhoods in hip Jerusalem bubbles. And then there is the question about Kadag's alliance with illiberal projects: can a movement that does not stand in solidarity with victims of gross injustice and violence—Israel's Palestinian citizens and those living in its occupied territories—claim to be promoting social justice? That I have said little about this question is not an oversight but rather an honest ethnographic report. Most of my respondents criticized Orthodoxy's cis and heteronormative universe but were aligned with its nationalist vision, if they addressed the issue all.

It is hardly surprising that Kadag's case for awareness, inclusivity, tolerance, and acceptance had its blinders and limitations. LGBTQ+ battles for livable lives are shaped and constrained by local context. Still, Kadag is both a destabilizing and a productive force. As one camp ascended to claim its rightful presence within Orthodoxy, foes have redoubled their normalizing messaging, framing acceptance and embrace as an existential threat. The personal became literally political in March 2021, when several right-wing parties, including Noam, merged to form the Religious Zionist Party. Reeking of religiously inspired homophobia, transphobia, racism, sexism, and xenophobia, the party's platform now challenges Orthodox LGBT persons' silence on larger questions of justice and solidarity. Where this might lead is an open question.

In what follows I provide an analytical summary and the key takeaways from this volume, lessons from a religious LGBT movement that occupies a liminal space between radical queer politics, religious authenticity, and nationalist belonging.

The Lessons of Proud Religious Activism

How did same-sex-attracted Orthodox Jews in Israel, within the space of a decade and a half, forge new identities, create a Proud Orthodox community, and win over (some) Orthodox families, communities, educators, and leaders? How did a dominant stance—one that pathologizes and silences homosexuality, and which had been so taken for granted that it hardly needed to be articulated—come to play defense? And what to make of a deradicalized LGBT movement that leans into respectability politics, subscribes to heteronormative frameworks, and embraces a homonationalist stance in defiance of queer solidarity?

The Many Faces of LGBT Activism

This volume has described a dizzying array of organizations, activist programs (inner looking, community education and outreach, visibility campaigns), modalities (digital vs. physical), strategies (radical, disruptive, and "respectable") that coalesced around the rhetoric of Orthodox authenticity.

Kadag was born of digital and physical safe spaces that served as a lifeline for those who had previously thought that they were alone in the world. Its trajectory reads like a textbook case on how internal safe spaces can result in collective action. Safe spaces, where stigmatized persons can let down their guard, provide respite; access to mentors, role models, and a peer group; and a context for generating new rituals, symbols, rhetoric, shared history, destiny, and needs. It is here that marginalized persons reframe traits that distinguish them from the majority as positive, articulate new legible social and political categories, develop networks of trust, and mobilize on behalf of the collective.

It is in such safe spaces that early Kadag activists articulated and expanded their field of vision along with their social circle; they dared to dream big. With a newfound community providing support, solace, and a source of pride and empowerment, some decided to remove the veil of anonymity by launching and joining organizations. New sensibilities, visuals, and visions gave rise to previously inconceivable categories ("I am a religious lesbian," "I am a religious transgender person," "I am a religious *hommo* and this is my husband").

But the political impact of inward-looking safe spaces that shelter the stigmatized is limited. Upending existing social structures hinges on *public* visibility. Activists knew that to achieve full, meaningful lives they would need to step out of these spaces: the goal was not to create a gay-friendly ghetto ("they would be happy to ship us all out to Tel Aviv," said one early activist—Tel Aviv serving as the metaphoric foil to authentic Orthodoxy) or "attend some gay-friendly synagogue in Tel Aviv"; the goal was to "bring my husband home [to a community where interviewee grew up]," to live in Orthodox neighborhoods, and to send their children to Orthodox schools. Orthodox LGBT persons were seeking acceptance and inclusion. Activists realized that challenging Orthodoxy's hetero and cisnormative order hinged on changing hearts and minds; they would need to engage, educate, mobilize, and, when necessary, rattle. Thus, *inward-looking* initiatives intended to empower individuals through the collective articulation of positive LGBT identities gave rise to *community engagement* initiatives, aimed at creating space for LGBT persons within Orthodoxy, and *public-facing* initiatives, some of them campy and transgressive, directed at Orthodox messaging surrounding gender, sexuality, and family life. While community engagement sought to create space for LGBT persons within Orthodoxy, transgressive initiatives challenged the system's foundations. Kadag's success can be partially traced to how this range of initiatives complemented and fed off one another.

Kadag initiatives have been multifaceted and shape-shifting in other ways: a strategic interplay between visibility and discreetness; targeting both religious and secular spaces and practices; diverse forms of activism, including public demonstrations and online presence in both friendly and hostile spaces; an activist network inhabited by "professional" activists and people just going about their daily lives, many loosely connected through personal ties, social networks, and movement organizations; and the simultaneous deployment of slow-paced, consensus-building dialogue along with the more disruptive tactics of political theater. Kadag comprises a vibrant, rich, and nuanced hodgepodge of initiatives, activities, and spaces: from movie nights and hiking groups that seemingly have little to do with religion, through covert meetings with religious leaders, to LGBT community Shabbats and public visibility campaigns that walk a fine line between claiming authentic Orthodoxy and transgressive LGBT campiness.

The organizations and initiatives worked both separately and through broad coalitions as their constituencies have expanded from a focus on *hommos* and lesbians to a movement aware of the full suite of needs of LGBT—and, increasingly, Q—persons. The coalition approach meant that each organization could focus on its core constituents and causes while working with a collective toward common goals. Collaboration was not seamless; organizations' visions and goals both competed against and complemented one another; rogue activists sometimes defied agreed-upon modes of action; and disagreements occasionally resulted in the departure of key activists.

Turning from the organizations to those who populate them, Kadag's successes can be traced to its expanding ranks of activists. Early Kadag activists may have started a movement from scratch, but they came armed with experience gained at established LGBT and feminist organizations. It also helped that some Kadag activists, and certainly early activists, hail from relatively privileged Orthodox backgrounds.[7] These privileged activists had much at stake while their cultural capital, including family and other connections and the ability to speak with rabbis in their own language, meant that they became the movement's public face. It is small wonder that Ashkenazi, cisgender men from educated backgrounds are still the movement's most visible faces. Finally, the movement also benefitted from media savvy, gen Y and gen Z activists who took full advantage of the digital media landscape.

Over the years, the circle of activists has expanded. Though at any particular moment a relatively small number of activists who work across initiatives, groups, organizations, and platforms composed the movement's prominent public face, numerous others provide support in small and large ways. Some are one-issue activists, others are seemingly everywhere, but the movement has been propelled by the actions of "small-time activists"—those who day in and day out answer anonymous Facebook posts; organize social events, outings, and support groups; provide mentorship and advice; reach out to rabbis; and document their lives for the world to read and see on Facebook. The distance between formal, contentious politics and everyday lives is not as large as the scholarship on social movement activism would have us believe (more on this below).

A final piece of the puzzle resides in Kadag's target audience. As an Orthodox Jewish LGBT movement, Kadag has directed most of its efforts at Orthodox communities rather than at state actors and institutions (conversion therapy has been a notable exception). Accordingly, Kadag's activism has drawn on Jewish values, language, sensibilities, premises, and teachings, simultaneously affirming and challenging what it means to be an "authentic" Orthodox Jew. However, while Kadag disrupts heteronormative Orthodox images, it does so while leaning into assimilationist, homonormative, and homonationalist rhetoric, imagery, and messaging.

Using the Master's Tools to Expand the House of Torah

Kadag's goals evolved over the past two decades. The goal at the turn of the twenty-first century was modest—activists asked to be seen and acknowledged. Within a few years, the emphasis had shifted to fomenting tolerance and acceptance, then further expanded to coalesce around a vision of full inclusion in Jewish life, theology, congregations, and rituals.

In its quest to "make space" and create livable spaces *within* Orthodoxy, Kadag has relied on a tried-and-true social change strategy: telling stories.[8] Kadag activists tell stories in Shoval public engagements, on social media, and in their everyday lives as they rewrite lifecycle, religious, and familial scripts. These stories cover the gamut: what it's like to grow up as LGBT and Orthodox; how to make sense of one's life; how to engage rabbis and families; how to put together a Jewishly meaningful same-sex wedding. Storytelling happens in a variety of venues, intimate and public: Shoval outreach programs; public visibility campaigns; meetings with rabbis; conferences and symposia, organized by the Orthodox LGBT community, academic institutions, and other Orthodox bodies.

The connective thread running through these stories is what I have called a politics of authenticity.[9] Kadag activists speak to their target audience—Orthodox nationalist Zionist communities—using their language, symbols, and frameworks. Shoval narrative arcs are organized around legible Orthodox milestones and geographies: the yeshiva, the military unit, the youth group, the neighborhood. Our Faces campaigns evoke stories about family gatherings and holiday celebrations. The very category *hommo* (as opposed to gay) distances Kadag from secular culture (though both terms are used in secular LGBT circles). Demands for tolerance, acceptance, and space are grounded in the language and imagery of the Torah ("love thy neighbor"; "and you should choose life"), not only the secular language of human rights. Even public spectacles "feel" Jewish: a rainbow kippa; two Orthodox-presenting grooms performing Jewish wedding rituals; a Jewish pride flag. The premier parade on Kadag's calendar is the family-friendly Tolerance Parade in Jerusalem, not the carnivalesque party scene in Tel Aviv. Far from the rallying cry of U.S. gay liberation, "we're here, we're queer," a celebration of radical difference, Kadag's message is: we are *of* you; we *are* you; we are educated in your schools, synagogues, youth groups, products of and integral to Orthodox Jewish communities, institutions, and families. See but do not fear us.

Kadag's rhetoric of authenticity seems like a strategically prudent choice, but it reflects an essence: Kadag seeks to expand, rather than dismantle, the master's house. The house, of course, is not only metaphorical (as in how broad Orthodoxy's tent can be) but also physical. Many of the communities in which Kadag seeks to make space are deep in the occupied territories. Claims to Orthodox authenticity thus demand that Orthodox LGBT persons take a stance on the Jewish state-making project. But Kadag's silence on the injustices and violence suffered by Palestinians residing within Israel and its occupied territories is less of a strategic choice and more of a reflection of the extent to which religious affiliation (i.e., authentic Orthodoxy) and nationalist sentiments are deeply intertwined. The result is a demand for inclusion that is disassociated from attempts to bestow equality for *all* marginalized groups.

Queering Orthodoxy? The Radical Potential of Assimilationist Politics

Black feminist and critical race scholar Audre Lorde famously observed that the master's tools cannot dismantle the master's house.[10] But when a movement seeks to expand, rather than destroy, the master's house, those tools may work just fine. This is one of this book's key insights. The house, in our case, is the house of Torah,[11] to which Orthodox LGBT persons lay claim, and the tools are Orthodoxy's logics, frameworks, sensibilities, and language. Orthodox LGBT persons lean heavily into the master's tools, but in doing so they inevitably shake the master's house. Hence the five-star alarm raised by Orthodox conservatives.

The third Our Faces campaign, released in the summer of 2019, featured Orthodox LGBT couples, individuals, and families who reflected on religious (or religious-adjacent) objects and practices in two-minute videos. One couple, Zehorit and Limor Sorek, proudly displayed the wine glasses used only on holidays; the backdrop is a story of acceptance by the religious partner's parents. Eliq Oster and his partner Adam, filmed with their preschool-aged twin boys, shared a seemingly innocuous story about wedding presents; the punchline, to state the obvious: here was a photogenic LGBT family.

On the face of it, Kadag's demands are not only benign ("a room of our own within the Jewish home") but conservative. But dismissing these scenes of respectable gay domesticity as assimilationist, complicit, and homonormative misses their subversive and provocative undertone: those laying claim to blissful domesticity mark themselves as Orthodox. Normalizing LGBT persons' relationships and emotional lives *is* a leap of faith for those schooled in the theology of transgression. As Our Face clips were released piecemeal online, Noam, the homophobic political party, was hanging billboards around the country declaring heteronormative and cisnormative families as natural and timeless, while marking LGBT domestic scenes, couples, and families as nonnormative, anti-Jewish, and un-Orthodox. What worries Noam are not only, or even primarily, flag-waving parades but also such blissful ("boring," as some respondents called them) moments of domesticity. Kadag's peaceful dialogue is perceived by its adversaries as an all-out, urgent, and frontal assault. A religious conservative rabbi reportedly responded to one Kadag campaign (Our Faces, Together, which featured Orthodox LGBT persons with a friend or family member) with the following remarks:

> My fellow rabbis have been telling me: "family acceptance will become community acceptance." I didn't think so, but when I see Havruta's campaign, of family members accepting same-sex relationships, I realized I might be wrong. I may have been naïve.
>
> That is why I say now: when someone comes and turns family acceptance into communal acceptance, we will not accept him into the family. It is hard because it's our son, but if that's what they do with it then they have to stop with family acceptance. If you do not disturb us we will not disturb you. If he lives with a partner, it's his problem, not mine. Once he waves it like a flag, we cannot accept him.[12]

New lines in the sand are drawn: Kadag's insistence that they come in peace is belied by conservatives, who see *any* departure from a cis and heteronormative social order—including just coming to a Shabbat dinner with one's life partner—as an existential threat. But those portrayed to be "disturbing us" are not intruders but those born and raised within the community. Their insistence to live a life that honors their sexual orientation and gender identity, in other words, is the source of disruption.

There is another paradox to public visibility campaigns grounded in the politics of respectability: LGBT struggles are typically associated with more blatant performative initiatives premised on disruption, theatrics, in-your-face politics—a far cry from the messages and rhetoric of Our Faces campaigns. And yet the rabbi's response above indicates that depending on context, seemingly respectable public visibility initiatives can be campy and confrontational. At times mere existence in the public sphere suffices. As one activist put it, "When people start coming out, their religious friends and families have to learn to accept them. Suddenly you get this straight religious cloud around religious *hommos*." This religious cloud—one that can imagine different kinds of love, families, and sexual practices—is deeply destabilizing. "How can you be Orthodox and gay?," asked an exasperated educator at one Shoval training I attended. Those working to create space from within Orthodoxy, those who claim a both/and identity, say the answer is easy: by expanding the bounds of Orthodoxy itself. Kadag may indeed come in peace—but to Orthodox conservatives the very presence of Orthodox LGBT persons means an all-out war.

To lay claim to authentic Orthodoxy, LGBT activists contend that long-standing practices, interpretations, ideologies, and theologies are exclusionary, homophobic, and transphobic. What the average Orthodox person views as business as usual—seeing only opposite-sex unions as legitimate, rejecting the plausibility of alternative family forms, viewing gender identity as inborn and immutable—Orthodox LGBT activists deem a heteronormative and cisnormative universe. LGBT families, romantic lives, embrace of same-sex desires defy Judaism's cis and heteronormative social order. Making space entails upending social norms, creating a new social context and a new set of identities—two brides under a wedding canopy? A child with two dads? LGBTQ+ families in synagogue?

But the disruption, subversion—the *queering*—that this book identifies reaches beyond demands for visibility, embrace, tolerance, or legitimacy of same-sex couples. Making space, claiming Orthodox authenticity, arguing that the Jewish tradition is tolerant and embracing of LGBTQ+ persons and families hinges on mobilizing theology, a reordering of values, expanding Judaism's legitimate languages, and challenging traditional authority structures. "It's very problematic that the rabbinic establishment chooses solutions that they haven't breathed, and lived," one man told me, suggesting that religious traditions, practices, sensibilities, and authority structures emerge at the murky intersection between "tradition" and everyday life. "To be an Orthodox *hommo*," the anonymous Facebook poet claims, "is . . . to understand that you don't need some rabbi who will approve of you; that to be Orthodox is your own decision." No wonder Orthodox conservatives cry foul: a queered Orthodoxy threatens (and exposes) foundational categories, mythology, and authority structures.

The heart of the transgression, then, resides not in the image of smiling same-sex couples but rather in the fact that they lay claim to Orthodoxy. These claims, even in their most nonconfrontational iterations, unsettle traditional visions of Orthodoxy precisely because they mobilize, mine, and harness the Jewish tradition. It is this grounding in Judaism that is the most transgressive act of all. As the previously marginalized insist that they belong, they also—sometimes inadvertently—rethink, challenge, reorder Jewish values, cosmologies, concepts, values, theologies, and authority structures. The battle goes to the heart of orthodoxy: who is Orthodox and who gets to decide the bounds of Orthodoxy? As one man put it—with a wink and a nod—his own journey led him to conclude that he is a queer Orthodox—"queer" referring not to gender or sexual categories but rather to religious ones. What is queerer than blowing up categories?

The point is that assimilationist politics can produce potentially revolutionary, radical, transgressive outcomes. Havruta activist Avichai Abarbanel observes that "a new generation is emerging here. . . . It is not a revolutionary generation but it is a revolution. They are not looking to transform or rebel against the values on which they were raised and educated, they want their tradition. But it is a revolution because this generation isn't giving up . . . it's holding both ends, Torah and Pride."[13]

I have traced Kadag's success in opening up livable place for LGBT persons to claims of authenticity. The conservative rabbi's dismissal notwithstanding—"we cannot accept him"—a growing portion of Orthodox families and communities *are* accepting—or at least not wholesale rejecting—their sons, daughters, and, increasingly, nonbinary, genderqueer, and trans persons. "Of course they are angry. It was much more convenient for them when we just quietly slinked away and they could ignore us. We are now in the synagogue, in the yeshiva, and we plan to stay," one interlocutor told me. As they make good on their promise (or threat?), more Orthodox people are being confronted with the possibility of a queered orthodoxy.

Where does this leave Kadag as an LGBT movement? Kadag's rhetorical strategy strives to normalize LGBT existence. At the same time, by making a moral, ethical, and theological case for inclusion for insiders, one articulated in the language and cosmology of Judaism, Kadag replicates membership rules drawn on nationalist (and ethnic) lines. Making space within the Jewish home leaves this home's existence and modes of operation unexamined.

•

Making Space in the "Jewish Home"

On June 29, 2020, during a pride event in Tel Aviv's Rabin Square, two women protesting pinkwashing, one of them holding a Palestinian flag, were attacked by a gay man who had been holding a pride flag. A human rights lawyer and activist, whose portfolio includes advancing ethnic and racial justice and supporting asylum seekers, women's rights, poverty, and LGBT rights, bore the majority of the violence. Pride events were canceled or pared down in 2020 due to COVID-19, and the typically carnivalesque Tel Aviv parade was replaced by a more somber gathering. Some speakers addressing the crowd reminisced about fraying solidarity and divisions within LGBT communities. Reportedly, the attack took place as Itai Pinkas, the CEO of Israel's largest LGBT organization, the Aguda, was speaking. The Aguda later condemned the violence in a Facebook post but did not name "solidarity" as a key concern, centering instead on violence as an affront to LGBT values. A Havruta post about the incident did address solidarity, noting that without solidarity equality is reserved "to those who are like us." Havruta's post also called for addressing systemic hatred and oppression at their root.[14]

Critics have been arguing for decades that Israeli LGBTQ+ organizations' lackluster stance on the Palestinian question has irreparably compromised the movement. Critics also blast pinkwashing, a political strategy that uses the embrace of gay rights to conceal violations of Palestinians' human rights, as a fig leaf for Israeli democracy.[15] And yet many LGBTQ+ persons and their allies subscribe to the state's self-branding as the most gay-friendly nation in a homophobic region—a villa in the jungle per former prime minister Ehud Barak.[16] Endorsing this narrative helped Kadag gain a foothold in both secular LGBTQ+ and Orthodox spaces.

For example, Havruta's reflections on solidarity mentioned above did not profess solidarity with the Palestinian cause but instead referenced gender equality and violence against women. "How is it possible that even this post can't talk about the occupation," wondered one commentator on the thread, while another observed that "it is not possible to talk about the LGBT battle for equality without talking about millions of Palestinians living under military occupation without rights for decades." A third respondent pushed back: "Solidarity itself is the problem. The fact that a person is attracted to members of his own sex doesn't mean that he is necessarily left-wing, secular, supports [racial justice protests] . . . a Palestinian state. . . . We are here for equality for the LGBT community. Nothing else."[17]

A week later, another controversy erupted, this time involving an Arab-owned food manufacturer, Tahini El-Erez. The company announced that it would fund a dedicated hotline for Arab LGBT persons, to be operated by the Aguda. The reaction within Israel's Arab Christian and Muslim communities was swift, with calls for a consumer boycott of the company, accompanied by death threats.[18] An Aguda press release praised Tahini El-Erez's move as a "testament to the welcome change in the Arab community towards LGBT persons," and invited its followers to signal solidarity by adding their names to a petition. Kadag issued its own brief statement supporting the company, the Arab LGBTQ community, and the hotline initiative. This response may seem inconsistent coming at the heels of the Tel Aviv incident, but solidarity here was easier to profess, since the Arabs in question were Israeli citizens. But the "villa in the jungle" rhetoric carried through. Kadag ally Rabbi Ostroff had attested in an interview a couple of years earlier that, though he was critical of some of Kadag's public stunts, he was "proud to live in a country where there is such a parade and not in a country where LGBT people are thrown off a high-rise building."[19] This homonationalist sentiment is precisely what has enabled this idea of a tolerant Judaism, one that can stretch its limits as it draws on Jewish ethics while remaining legibly in line with Orthodoxy's broader cosmology.

Social movements of all stripes debate solidarity and arrive at strategic and ethical decisions about building alliances and coalitions. In the Kadag case, this debate captures the potential and limitations of a rhetorical strategy centering on authenticity. As noted, the absence of solidarity with Palestinians is not a strategic choice but a substantive one: Kadag's battle focuses on making space *in the Jewish home*—which, for many of its members, (naturally and unapologetically) includes West Bank settlements like Shilo, where Moshe Argaman's pride flag flew high in defiance of conservative Orthodox neighbors.

In a heated political environment in which the national question is the best predictor of one's political affiliation, and where religiosity and nationalism are deeply intertwined, Kadag activists try to stay out of the fray. Many told me they deliberately avoid engaging larger political battles. But these larger battles routinely flare up, each time underscoring the tensions that inhere when a movement that works toward inclusion and equality remains tethered to a political bloc whose imagery and leanings have grown increasingly violent and supremacist.

The entry, in 2021, of the homophobic and ultranationalist Noam party to the Israeli Parliament brought a new moment of reckoning, with one prominent activist writing that he had felt "punched in the stomach" by an Orthodox community that allowed a party whose sole essence was negating LGBT normativity and inclusion to be elected. Where this moment of reckoning of the dangers of melding a militant nationalism, a fervent Orthodoxy, and conservative gender and sexual ideology will take Kadag remains to be seen, though it has exposed a plain truth: sexual and gender progressivism do not map onto political progressivism.[20]

Will Kadag come to embrace the critique that only radical visions of justice, ones that claim that all systems of oppression are linked and work to identify and end all forms of violence and exclusion, may be deemed queer? Can a queer worldmaking enterprise provide real safety for a minority in its metaphorical, privatized "home" while refusing to interrogate larger social structures that do not guarantee safety and justice for all? The history of LGBT activism is not promising on this front—as Orthodox LGBT persons are finding out. I am skeptical that in the current political environment a broader vision of social justice is possible.

So, What Is It Like to Be an Orthodox *Hommo*? Lessons from the Front Lines of Identity Conflict

"So, what's it like to be an Orthodox *hommo*," asks an anonymous writer in a post shared on a Facebook page popular among Orthodox LGBT persons and allies.[21] His thousand-plus-word response breaks down a narrative arc familiar to Orthodox LGBT persons: shame, secrecy, fear of ostracization, family dramas, a desire to be normal, and a shattered life plan. Religion looms large on this journey: the anonymous poet navigates religious texts, leaders, communities, and lifecycle events as he strives to discern what it means to be an Orthodox *hommo* and how to fill haunting "black holes of uncertainty." By the poem's end, the poet articulates a new script for living as an Orthodox *hommo*, one that includes a husband, children, a supportive family, and a newfound community. It turns out that religion is not *only* an obstacle for LGBT persons of faith to overcome but also a source of knowledge, self-understanding, and new scripts for living. One of the key findings of this book is that Jewish traditions, symbols, sensibilities, language, and mythologies—intertwined with nationalist sentiments—figure in Orthodox LGBT persons' attempts to reframe, reimagine, and rewrite stories of self and community to achieve "psychological well-being" (in social scientists' parlance) or "livable lives" (queer theory's take).

Despite decades worth of evidence to the contrary, dominant social science paradigms continue to center on so-called identity conflicts as the core religious LGBTQ+ experience. In Judeo-Christian contexts, the conflict is traced to several verses, most prominently Leviticus 18:22, which includes the abomination clause. LGBT persons of faith can resolve this conflict, this literature suggests, by integrating their religious and LGBT identities, though many individuals fail to do so, landing instead on suboptimal solutions such as compartmentalization or rejection of one's religious or sexual identity.[22] The literature further suggests that integrated identity, when achieved, is *despite* religious messaging.

The stories recounted in this volume bear witness to such conflicts. Like LGBT persons of faith from other religious traditions, many same-sex-attracted Orthodox Jews pass through a period when they are convinced that their sexuality, romantic desires, practices, attachments, and realities are incompatible with Jewish teachings, theology, doctrine, and norms, regardless of whether they act on their desires. Initially, the identity conflict frame and categorical schema made sense: I identified integrators, rejecters, celibates; the religiously affiliated and the ex-Orthodox. But as the stories mounted I realized that some "integrators" defied the identity conflict frame's emphasis on conflict as a core experience as well as its categorical schema of stable solutions and neatly bounded categories. So-called identity conflicts, this volume has shown, do not emerge in a vacuum but rather are products of the marking of LGBT persons as sinners, deviants, transgressors, and inauthentic. That is, interior dramas such as theological angst and crises of faith, often cited as evidence for identity conflict, were a product of the broad cosmology of Jewish life, dramas of exclusion, and hegemonic theological traditions beyond their control.

Thus, while the lives of LGBT persons of faith are certainly marked by conflict, as a conceptual framework this lens misses the dynamic, lived, and culturally and historically contingent process by which religious and sexual identities are made (and remade). In addition, the Jewish tradition introduced much more than "conflict" to my interviewees' lives; they mobilized to write new life scripts and enlisted Jewish rhetoric, language, sensibilities, and frameworks to speak to religious elites, theological traditions, and communities. Even transgressive action mined the Orthodox tradition. In short, this book has shown how religious sensibilities, frameworks, communities, and education can be a productive force in the lives of same-sex-attracted persons of faith. Jewish authenticity operates here not only as political rhetoric but also as an orienting framework that helped pour meaning into and guide everyday decisions of how to live and how to love. Religious LGBT identity was possible because of—not in spite of—the Jewish tradition.

The case thus suggests a corrective on a scholarly and popular narrative that views religion as a predominantly detrimental force in the lives of LGBT persons of faith, demonstrating instead how religion facilitates a productive journey into unchartered territory. This journey draws on Jewish philosophy, concepts, and messages to reflect on what it takes to be Orthodox and who can rightfully claim this label. Paying attention to journeys and exclusions, silencing and shattering old pictures, and writing new scripts suggest an alternative to the identity conflict and reconciliation frame, one that emerges from lived experience. Interlocutors who figured out how to be orthodox and gay did not so much "integrate" these identities but rather, through trial and error, and in conversation with their fellow travelers and an expanding army of allies, created new ones.[23]

The conflict frame seems to assume that the conflict—and therefore its resolution—resides within individuals; many studies of "the conflict" pay little attention to social and, ultimately, political dynamics. But if the core experience is one of exclusion from existing norms and a struggle to write new ones, a focus on the personal drama of conflict, integration, and redemption is misplaced. Even the crisis of faith—one that leads many LGBT persons of faith to disaffiliate—is social: "Everything they say, they're not saying to you. Because if they knew, they wouldn't be willing to talk to you," writes the heartbroken anonymous Facebook poet. When they say, as many of my interlocutors did, that "God loves me, it's society that needs to change," they imply that their predicament was not so much a psychological obstacle that one could resolve on their own but rather an entire universe of meanings attached to Orthodoxy.

Accordingly, the remedy to pain, depression, striving to be "normal," turmoil, and angst hinged on articulating new scripts. When Bat Kol activist Nicole Gil Chen told Kadag ally Rabbi Ostroff that her goal was to live 100 percent, she was not referring to resolving some internal moral incongruence: she wanted the rabbi to lead the way and take a stance in support of same-sex unions, thereby supporting her community's efforts to normalize these scripts. Hadar in chapter 3 suggested that some dilemmas cannot be resolved and one must learn to live with ambiguity and that it is precisely here where the Jewish tradition was at its best: providing guidance through chaos. The dilemma, then, is this: how to be true to oneself in the face of social stigma, a lack of role models, and lifelong messages of vilification and erasure. The outcome hinges not on "integrating" preexisting categories but rather on creating a new social reality. To do this, Orthodox LGBT persons dialogue with the very categories that challenge them: What does it mean to be Orthodox? What does it mean to be LGBT?

The conflict frame's categorical schema of potential outcomes ("integrators," "celibates," "disaffiliated") also implies that ambivalence and movement across categories are indicative of an integration not yet achieved (or gone awry), but my study belies this claim. Ambivalence was ubiquitous among my interlocutors, and many had moved across categories; sworn celibates eventually sought relationships, the heterosexually married got divorced, the disaffiliated remained tied to Orthodoxy. These ambiguities are far from paradoxical: people are complicated. Fluidity does not indicate a failure to arrive at a resolution, just as "integration" does not imply a life free of ambivalence. Rather, fluidity and ambivalence are intrinsic to the experience of those who had been raised amid hurtful Orthodox messaging and were now trying to transcend these messages. The lived religion tradition reminds us that life is messy, chaotic, rife with ambivalence, ambiguities, and convoluted paths. Why expect the experiences of LGBT person of faith to coalesce around a neat set of categories?

Moreover, the categories "religious" and "gay" are not static. The identity conflict frame rests on nondynamic identity categories that defy scholarship about sexual and gender identity, the history of homosexuality, and poststructuralist theories that reject the idea of a stable, discoverable, core self. Whereas the categorical schema presents "integration" as an arrival vis-à-vis fixed categories of "gayness" and "religiosity," Orthodoxy itself is (and always has been) up for grabs. My interlocutors were not only telling new stories of self—theirs was *also* a story of a different kind of Orthodoxy, one that existed on a spectrum, responsive to the experiences of the faithful. Their journey is one of reframing and creating rather than one of reconciling.

In sum, while the identity conflict frame assumes a natural and insurmountable divide between LGBTQ+ persons and religion, this lens fails to account for how religion is lived, and how religious identities, institutions, and doctrines emerge and evolve from seemingly conflictual encounters. This book has documented the numerous ways in which Orthodox LGBT Jews harnessed, mined, and mobilized the tradition's own logics, language, and sensibilities first to make sense of themselves, then to demand that communities "make space." In the process, they produced a theology that worked from the ground up. My interlocutors did not so much "reconcile" a conflict as they uncovered and challenged societal controlling images, norms, and interpretive traditions—and learned how to live with and through ambivalence. Religion, in other words, was not only an obstacle and a source of angst but also a source of solace, support, providing tools to make sense of oneself and one's place in the world and articulate new traditions, practices, sensibilities, and scripts. While the new stories and scripts are, first and foremost, personal narratives of self and new scripts for living, essential for achieving psychological well-being and livable lives, they also envision an alternative Orthodoxy.

The battles of LGBT persons of faith are at once religious and LGBT: they seek a path that will allow them to be true to their religious *and* sexual selves. Rather than "integrating" these parts of their identities (take Orthodoxy, take homosexuality, and stir), this book argues that LGBTQ+ persons of faith actively construct new categories. Just as we should be wary of imposing a priori definitions of what it means to be Orthodox premised on homonormative and cisnormative assumptions, we should be wary of imposing definitions of "how to be gay" that do not account for religiosity.[24] In other words, we must pay attention, *simultaneously*, to both religious and gender/sexual identities, while keeping in mind that identity categories themselves are unstable, constructed, co-constitutive, and contingent. Identities are not an amalgam of constituent parts—but rather coproduced through the drama of being both/and: they are intersecting, rather than conflicting.

This productive process is less about coming to terms with oneself vis-à-vis an *existing* social order and more about constructing a new story, picture, vision of self that is rooted in the Jewish tradition. The story is less about individuals who navigate hateful faith traditions and more about how they reshape these traditions as they live them. Thus, the story *Queer Judaism* tells is about what it means to be Orthodox. Somewhat ironically, concepts drawn from queer theory—livable lives and queer worldmaking—help shift the emphasis from individual experiences to larger social dynamics that structure and constrain them. These concepts suggest that making LGBTQ+ lives "livable" entails the transformation of everyday spaces, practices, and discourses: precisely the political work that Orthodox LGBT persons and Kadag activists are engaged in.

Lessons on Social Change and the Subversions of Everyday Lives

Early in my research, I ran into what I initially thought of as a methodological problem: separating activists from other interviewees. It was easy enough to identify the "real" activists and activist spaces: founders, leaders, and key volunteers of organizations and other initiatives, parades, meetings with lawmakers, interviews in the press. But then things got murky. Does speaking at an occasional outreach workshop count? How about an impromptu meeting with a group of teenagers in town? What about writing fiction, a blog post, or Torah commentary that is later published on a Kadag organization's website? A Facebook post that goes viral? Patrolling social media of homophobic groups or public figures and intervening in the comments? Giving interviews to the media (or to a sociologist?) Testifying at a hearing in the Parliament about pro-LGBTQ+ legislation? Disrupting a homophobic rabbi's lesson? Posting a "safe space" sticker in a yeshiva (and posting the image to Facebook)? What about launching a study group for Orthodox LGBT persons? Or an anonymous Facebook page that serves as a community meeting space? Dropping off promotional materials for a Kadag event at a community center in a peripheral town (outside gay-friendly bubbles)? Walking in the Jerusalem Pride Parade? Attending a meeting with a rabbi? Being willing to be photographed at the meeting? Posting about the meeting? Just attending the local synagogue with one's same-sex partner? Living in a mostly Orthodox neighborhood, sending one's kids to a local school? And so on. The people I met did all this—and much more, defying a clear distinction between "activism" and "life."

One remarkable feature of the challenges to the hegemonic Jewish world order documented here is the extent to which these challenges are rooted in small practices of everyday life. In June 2020, activist Ayala Reifler spoke at an outreach event. Reflecting on her two decades of activism, Reifler said that much of it came down to just residing with her family in Orthodox spaces—going to synagogue, sending her children to school, being visible in the community.

These remarks challenge research on contentious politics and political action, which often removes these arenas from everyday life, with tales of social change typically centering on activists', organizations', and movements' goals, strategies, tactics, and engagement with countermovements. Above I traced Kadag's successes to some of these traditional arenas of social movement activism (and scholarship), but here I highlight how social change emerges from the seemingly mundane "stuff" of everyday life. The case demonstrates that contentious politics and political action are continuous with everyday life: to understand Kadag's profound impacts we must think beyond the usual subject matter of social movement activism (goals, visions, tactics, frames, strategies, recruitment) and interrogate the connection between lived realities and politics. Collective action, after all, is rooted in social relations—

joint struggle often begins with and is embedded in the mundane structures of everyday life.

While social movement scholarship tends to focus on collective action in the public sphere, queer scholars suggest that making LGBTQ+ lives "livable" begins with and is rooted in transforming everyday spaces. The process of queer worldmaking implies that in addition to formal routes of collective action in the political sphere, LGBTQ+ persons resist and reshape hegemonic institutions, discourses, practices, and identities through a bottom-up engagement with the everyday, involving any number of places, spaces, and people. Per queer theorist José Esteban Muñoz, queer worldmaking is a "mode of being in the world that is also inventing the world."[25] Queerness, Muñoz observes, "is not yet here. Queerness is an ideality . . . [a] warm illumination of a horizon imbued with potentiality."[26] This potentiality has been at the center of this volume.

In 2008 Yael Mishali, a writer, journalist, life coach, mother of *hommos*, and bellwether of liberal Orthodoxy, encouraged Orthodox LGBT persons to "come out of the holy ark, start families, fill the synagogues," and just live their lives, predicting—correctly—that religious authorities and communities (at least, the liberal among them) would follow.[27] Mishali was providing a blueprint not for how to live LGBT lives but rather for how to live *religious* ones, suggesting that in the case of LGBT persons of faith, queer worldmaking hinges on understanding the intricacies of how religion is embodied, lived, experienced, and negotiated vis-à-vis everyday spaces, institutions, and relationships.

By claiming Orthodox authenticity, Orthodox LGBT persons have inadvertently become conduits of religious change. As the anonymous Facebook poet writes, to be an Orthodox *hommo* does not require some rabbinic stamp of approval but is rather one's own decision, with a stroke of a keyboard questioning not only the boundaries of Orthodoxy but an entire social order premised on rabbinic expertise and guidance. Likewise, a lesbian in her twenties told me that she chose not to live her life as a problem, in defiance of messages from (some) religious elites that same-sex attraction (and those who harbor such attractions) is indeed a problem.

The fortunes of Orthodox LGBT persons have turned in large part on the accumulated impact of the actions of individuals who decided not to live their lives as a problem; who recalibrated their dreams; who demanded their families, friends, religious leaders, and congregations recognize that they exist and make space for them. The battle may not seem radical or queer enough for some, but given that the battle for Orthodoxy's straight soul is waged on the backs of people who just want to live their lives as Orthodox (or Orthodox-adjacent) persons who happen to *also* identify as LGBT, what else can we expect?

Since the battle of LGBT persons of faith is not just an LGBT battle but also a religious one—Orthodox LGBT persons seek a path that will allow them to be true to their religious *and* sexual selves—their battle complicates how other LGBT and Orthodox groups (and scholars who study them) define what it means to be Orthodox and what it means to be gay. I read these paths as acts of queering because they are inherently transgressive. Choosing not to live one's life as a problem exposes the fact that despite its claims to timelessness, Orthodoxy is constructed, malleable, and historically contingent.

Some argue that the conservative obsession with LGBT persons is a byproduct of them losing the framing war. Others see it as a byproduct of radicalization and polarization. Both claims are correct—if partial. The shift from invisibility to visibility, from a beleaguered minority to a set of politically salient identities, from lonely individuals to a vibrant community has undoubtedly radicalized conservatives. But it has been more of a dance, and the LGBT issue is at once an emblem, a cause, and a product of broader changes within Orthodoxy. Liberalizing and conservative voices co-construct one another, with radicalizing voices facilitating the emergence of a coherent set of counter-identities. It seems that Orthodox conservatives have themselves to blame for the queering of Orthodoxy as they denied the obvious: Orthodox LGBT persons do, in fact, exist, and they live joyous, fulfilling, meaningful lives.

ACKNOWLEDGMENTS

The strange thing with intellectual products is that author credits inadequately capture the contributions, large and small, of our interlocutors. First and foremost, I am indebted to the dozens of Orthodox LGBT persons and their allies who entrusted me with their stories. Most of them remain anonymous, but the following activists are named in the text at their request. I am forever in your debt for meeting with me (in some cases more than once), introducing and vouching for me, adding me to your social networks, and helping me make sense of the organizations and initiatives you are involved in: Avichai Abarbanel, Eran and Moshe Argaman, Hadas Benayahu, Or Ellisian, Kobi Handelsman, Daniel Jonas, Yehonatan Gill Rossen Maman, Michal Schonberg, Nadav Schwartz, Ze'ev Shvidel, and Zehorit Sorek. I do not know if this is the story you wanted me to tell, but I hope that my admiration for your work comes through. A special thanks to Ben Katz—friend, confidante, collaborator. Your support at every step of the process, relentless critique, and assurances that I could and must tell this story helped me get to the finish line.

Large research projects are expensive endeavors, and I was fortunate to have earned the trust of several organizations. The Memorial Foundation for Jewish Culture, the Hadassah-Brandies Institute, the Association for the Sociology of Religion, and the Society for the Scientific Study of Religion, supplemented by Fordham Research Grants, provided funds for travel and research assistance. Perhaps more than money, scholars yearn for time off their normal faculty duties to focus on their research. A Fordham Faculty Fellowship helped get this research off the ground. A course buyout from the E. Rhodes and Leona B. Carpenter Foundation, and a Global Religion Research Initiative Book Leave Fellowship provided the focused writing time when I needed it.

I have been blessed with an expansive network of colleagues, many turned friends. Elazar Ben Lulu opened doors, has been a critical sounding board, and read most of the volume. Kelsy Burke, Jonathan Coley, Carl Fischer, Katie Gaddini, Golshan Golriz, Ronit Irshai, and Brenna Moore read parts of this volume and provided invaluable feedback. Melissa Wilde was an early believer. Gilly Hartal helped me grasp Israeli LGBTQ+ activism. Ben Kasstan generously offered to read and give feedback (the quickest turnaround ever!), although we had never met. Tanya Zion-Waldoks's brilliant observations and her extensive knowledge of Israeli Orthodoxy are all over this manuscript. Dawne Moon— where do I begin? I cannot thank you enough for believing, pushing, challenging, and then coming back for more. Everyone deserves a friend with a sharp eye like Dawne's. My editor, Jennifer Hammer, thanks for taking this project on, for your feedback, and gracious patience as I missed one deadline after another. Who knew that writing through a pandemic would be so challenging? At Fordham, I am honored to count Patrick Hornbeck as a friend and collaborator. Thanks for throwing opportunities and challenges my way. Ayala Fader: I literally could not have done this without you. Thank you for believing, reading (and then rereading), hashing out, pointing out sources and potential pitfalls, and most of all, for encouraging me to believe in myself. Last but not least, Lyron Bentovim, my life partner of twenty-five years who still cannot figure out why we academics are so slow to produce but supported me through a six-year journey anyway.

NOTES

PREFACE

1 Such queries are hardly restricted to those conversant in religious texts. Andrew Yip's study of British LGBT Christians and Muslims found that LGBT critics with little theological knowledge often used clichés such as "the Bible says so" to justify their stance against homosexuality. Yip, "Queering Religious Texts," 49. I frequently encountered such claims as well.

2 Rabbi Aviner has repeated this stance on multiple occasions. For one instance, see "There is No Such Thing as a Religious Homosexual," *NRG Maariv*, December 12, 2004, www.makorrishon.co.il.

3 Document shared in personal communication.

INTRODUCTION

1 "Rabbi Raffi Peretz Revealed That He Partook in Conversion Therapy," *Kipa*, July 13, 2019, www.kipa.co.il. "Conversion therapy" is an umbrella term that refers to interventions intended to change a person's sexual orientation, gender identity, or gender expression. The ethics and efficacy of conversion therapy have been central to LGBT activism in Israel and elsewhere. Conservative Orthodox factions in Israel have been resistant to efforts to curb the practice through legislation, though in February 2022 the Israeli Ministry of Health instituted a long-sought policy shift that effectively bans conversion therapy by licensed health care and mental health professionals. The impacts of this policy change remain to be seen, but it should be noted that many practitioners of conversion therapy such as rabbis and other religious figures are not licensed by the state to begin with. Nevertheless, Kadag has framed this policy shift as a major win.

2 "Rabbi Amar Attacks Religious LGBTQ Persons: 'They Should Throw Away Their Kippa,'" *Kipa*, July 23, 2019, www.kipa.co.il.

3 "Rabbi Levanon: I Have Not Seen a Male on Male Beast Relationship," *Kipa*, July 22, 2019. www.kipa.co.il. Most Orthodox conservatives claim that same-sex attraction is not innate.

4 The pamphlet is available for download at www.boi-haruach.com/our-family-book.

5 Arik Bender, "Noam Party Asks the Public: Report to Us Content Related to 'Proud Organizations,'" *Maariv*, August 7, 2019, www.maariv.co.il.

6   Yehonatan Klein, "Anger at the Rabbis' Anti-LGBT Statement: 'An Unhealthy Obsession,'" *Kipa*, July 23, www.kipa.co.il.

7   Bat Kol, "The Rabbi's Authority," Facebook, July 23, 2019, www.facebook.com.

8   Commemorating the murder of a teenager in the 2015 Jerusalem Pride Parade, an organization founded by the teen's parents hosts a series of outreach events promoting tolerance titled "Pride in the Living Room."

9   Bat Kol, "The Kids of the Cna'an Family," Facebook, July 30, 2019.

10 A community reader who read this manuscript observed that such occurrences were so common that if it hadn't been Peretz, it would have been someone else. The reader added that during their activist days they would worry that program launches would "miss the wave" until they realized that the next wave was always just three or four months away.

11 Englander and Sagi, *Sexuality and the Body*; Ettinger, *Undone*; Sagi, "Does Religious Zionism Still Exist?"

12 Michal Schonberg, "Yesterday We Protested," Facebook, April 7, 2021.

13 Butler, *Precarious Life*.

14 Chaim Elbaum, "The Orthodox LGBT Battle," Facebook, May 2, 2018.

15 For an excellent overview, see Hartal, "Israel's LGBT Movement."

16 Duggan, "New Homonormativity."

17 Berlant and Warner, "Sex in Public." As originally suggested by Berlant and Warner, queer worldmaking privileged gender and sexuality, but in subsequent revisions of the concept scholars suggested that to achieve their full impact, projects of sexual and gendered normalization should be considered alongside other axes of difference, such as gender, race, class status, age, able-bodiedness, and so on. Religion has largely been left off the radar screen. For a recent overview of the concept, see Otis and Dunn, "Queer Worldmaking."

18 Yuval-Davis, "Belonging and the Politics of Belonging"; Zion-Waldoks, "Orthodoxy's Politics of Belonging."

19 Religious acceptance movements across faith traditions share these goals. For parallels among Catholic LGBT activists in Poland, see Mikulak, "Between the Market and the Hard Place."

20 Kadag also works in collaboration with other LGBTQ+ organizations on shared goals.

21 Cohen, "Straight Gay Politics"; Warner, *Trouble with Normal*.

22 Cohen, "Punks, Bulldaggers, and Welfare Queens," 438.

23 For a good summary of the debate, see Ghaziani, Taylor, and Stone, "Cycles of Sameness."

24 Duggan, "New Homonormativity"; Halperin, "Normalization of Queer Theory." For a recent take that nuances these debates in the context of the United Kingdom, see Mowlabocus, *Interrogating Homonormativity*.

25 Puar, *Terrorist Assemblages*.

26 Taylor and Bernstein, *Marrying Kind?*

27 McQueeney, "'We Are God's Children'"; Sumerau, "'That's What a Man Is Supposed to Do.'"

28   For a good summary of the debate, see Ghaziani, Taylor, and Stone, "Cycles of
     Sameness." See also Cohen, "Punks, Bulldaggers, and Welfare Queens"; Gamson,
     "Must Identity Movements Self-Destruct?"; Ghaziani, *Dividends of Dissent* and
     "Post-Gay Collective Identity Construction"; Taylor and Bernstein, *Marrying
     Kind?* Some queer geographers argue that the sorting of queer politics into a
     radical versus assimilationist binary is insufficiently nuanced: Browne and Bakshi,
     Ordinary in Brighton?; Hartal and Sasson-Levy, "Being [in] the Center"; Misgav,
     "With the Current, Against the Wind"; Oswin, "Critical Geographies."
29   Ghaziani, Taylor, and Stone, "Cycles of Sameness." For a contrasting view, see
     Murib, "Trumpism, Citizenship, and the Future of the LGBTQ Movement," which
     argues that the Trump era may have altered the advantages of assimilationist
     agendas.
30   For a good summary, see Amenta and Polletta, "Cultural Impacts of Social Move-
     ments."
31   For parallels among Catholic LGBT activists in Poland, see Mikulak, "Between
     the Market and the Hard Place."
32   Puar, *Terrorist Assemblages*. Puar later clarified in "Rethinking Homonationalism"
     that homonationalism is not an identity (there are no homonationals) but rather
     an ideology, framework, regime that emerges at the intersection of political, so-
     cial, economic forces and marks new forms of inclusions (gays and lesbians) and
     exclusions (transgender persons and foreigners).
33   Puar, *Terrorist Assemblages*; Raboin, "Exhortations of Happiness."
34   Franke, "Dating the State"; Gross, "Politics of LGBT Rights"; Hartal, "Israel's
     LGBT Movement"; Stelder, "'From the Closet into the Knesset.'"
35   Hartal, "Israel's LGBT Movement"; Hartal, "Touring and Obscuring"; Hartal and
     Sasson-Levy, "Progressive Orient"; Yacobi, *Israel and Africa*; Ziv, "Performative
     Politics."
36   Amir Ben David, "Gush Etzion Faces the LGBT Struggle for the First Time,"
     Zman Israel, June 27, 2019, www.zman.co.il.
37   Jagose, *Queer Theory*.
38   In "Israel's LGBT Movement," Hartal argues that Israel has entered a post-
     homonationalist moment, one deeply involved in the economy and local
     politics. For other calls to nuance homonationalism, see Franke, "Dating the
     State"; Freude and Waiters, "Analysing Homophobia"; Hartal and Sasson-Levy,
     "Re-reading Homonationalism"; Ritchie, "Pinkwashing, Homonationalism, and
     Israel-Palestine"; Zanghellini, "Are Gay Rights Islamophobic?" For a summary
     of the development of the concept, see Winer and Bolzendahl, "Conceptualizing
     Homonationalism."
39   In *Out in Africa*, Currier documents how Namibian activists adapt their messag-
     ing and rhetoric in an environment where homosexuality is viewed as inherently
     "un-African." Anthropologist Tom Boellstorff coined the term "state straightism"
     to capture national heteronormative and cisnormative sentiments that define
     citizens as heterosexual and normatively gendered, thereby excluding LGBT per-

sons from national belonging despite their formal citizenship. See "Against State Straightism."

40 Mikulak, "Between the Market and the Hard Place."

41 Hartal and Sasson-Levy, "Re-reading Homonationalism."

42 Savci, *Queer in Translation*; Moussawi, *Disruptive Situations*.

43 Muñoz, *Disidentifications*, 11–12.

44 Oswin, "Critical Geographies"; Oswin, "End of Queer."

45 Secularism refers to a dominant discourse that deems secularization as the progressive alternative to religion, implies that "the religious" and "the secular" are mutually exclusive categories, and claims that secularism is the best position from which to articulate rights and freedoms, while religion is a space of censure, control, and oppression. For an introduction to these debates, see Berlinerblau, *Secularism*. For treatments, see Asad, *Formations of the Secular*; Mahmood, *Religious Difference in a Secular Age*.

46 Jakobsen, *Sex Obsession*; Page and Shipley, *Religion and Sexualities*; Wilcox, *Queer Religiosities*.

47 For coverage of the fallout, see "For and Against: Jerusalem Pride Parade Theme Religion and LGBT," *Ynet*, May 22, 2017, www.ynet.co.il. See JOH reflection in Jerusalem Open House, "We Are Proud of the Theme," Facebook, May 25, 2017. In *Dividends of Dissent*, Ghaziani discusses a similar dynamic that unfolded as a response to the 2000 March on Washington organized by the Human Rights Campaign.

48 The injuries are much broader when we consider that purportedly secular heteronormative institutions are deeply embedded in religious histories, theologies, and rhetoric; see Jakobsen and Pellegrini, *Love the Sin*.

49 U.S. organizations include Affirmation, which serves Mormon LGBTQ persons (https://affirmation.org); Dignity, which serves LGBTQI Catholics (www.dignityusa.org); Q Christian Fellowship, an Evangelical organization (www.qchristian.org); and MASGD, a Muslim organization focusing on gender and sexual diversity (www.themasgd.org). For scholarly treatments of the Evangelical case in the United States, see Vines, *God and the Gay Christian*; Moon, Tobin, and Sumerau. "Alpha, Omega, and the Letters in Between"; Moon and Tobin, "Sunsets and Solidarity." Coley, *Gay on God's Campus*, considers religious LGBT students' activism. See Golriz, "'I Am Enough,'" for Muslims in Canada.

50 See Savci, *Queer in Translation*; Page and Shipley, *Religion and Sexualities*.

51 Currier, *Out in Africa* and *Politicizing Sex in Contemporary Africa*; Munro and Pérez-Sánchez, "Introduction"; Thoreson, *Transnational LGBT Activism*.

52 Savci, *Queer in Translation*; Moussawi, *Disruptive Situations*.

53 Mowlabocus, *Interrogating Homonormativity*.

54 Crenshaw, "Mapping the Margins."

55 Halperin, *How to Be Gay*.

56 I attribute this lack of utilization to several factors. First, gender, sexuality, and queer studies have a secularist bias. Second, in feminist studies, where the concept

originated, intersectionality has historically been used to study minorities, domination, and power. Some question whether this lens should be utilized to study dominant actors with nonemancipatory agendas, but such use of intersectionality as an orienting lens divorced from its original political agendas is emerging; see Avanza, "Using a Feminist Paradigm," and Yuval-Davis, "Situated Intersectionality." Finally, as Courtney Irby and I have shown in "Bifurcated Conversations," research practices of the sociology of religion tend to remain disengaged from interdisciplinary gender scholarship. Page and Shipley, *Religion and Sexualities*, and Wilcox, *Queer Religiosities*, also call for more meaningful engagement with critical studies of identity and intersectionality. Some sociologists of religion have begun to use what Melissa Wilde calls a "Complex Religion" lens, which holds that religion is part and parcel of racial, ethnic, class, and gender inequality and that research that focuses on inequality or religion would be better off taking those intersections into account more explicitly. This research, however, does not engage critical frameworks of intersectionality nor dynamic processes of identity construction.

57 The assumption of incompatibility is grounded in studies on the psychological well-being of religious LGBTQ+ persons: affiliation with traditions that stigmatize homosexuality and nonnormative gender identities is associated with diminished mental health outcomes such as depression and increased risk for suicide: see Anderton, Pender, and Asner-Self, "Review of the Religious Identity / Sexual Orientation Identity Conflict Literature"; Cragun and Sumerau, "Last Bastion of Sexual and Gender Prejudice?"; Ganzevoort, van der Laan, and Olsman, "Growing Up Gay and Religious"; Sowe, Brown, and Taylor, "Sex and the Sinner." However, relationships with other LGBTQ+ persons of faith, membership in an accepting congregation, and disaffiliation can lessen or buffer these negative effects. See Coley, *Gay on God's Campus*; Fuist, "'It Just Always Seemed Like It Wasn't a Big Deal.'" For a psychological assessment of well-being, see Craig et al., "Fighting for Survival"; Cravens, "Identity-Affirming Religious Experience"; Dehlin et al., "Navigating Sexual and Religious Identity Conflict"; and Stuhlsatz et al., "Spirituality and Religious Engagement." However, the problem is often not so much with "religion" in and of itself but rather with heteronormativity, gender binarism, and a general homophobic environment (Taylor and Cuthbert, "Queer Religious Youth"). Studies of LGBTQ+ students on college campuses have found that increased religious conservatism of a college was associated with higher depression and greater internalized homophobia; see Heiden-Rootes et al., "National Survey on Depression." Likewise, in "Coming Out vs Staying Safe," Katz finds that decisions to disclose one's LGBT status are contingent on societal attitudes.

58 Reform and Conservative congregations are marginalized in the Israeli religious landscape. See Michael Lipka, "Unlike U.S., Few Jews in Israel Identify as Reform or Conservative," Pew Research Center, March 15, 2016, www.pewresearch.org.

59 Ammerman, "Lived Religion as an Emerging Field"; Ammerman, "Rethinking Religion"; Knibbe and Kupari, "Theorizing Lived Religion."

60 In "New Theoretical Directions," Wulff, Bernstein, and Taylor argue that the study of gender and sexuality movements expands the definition of contentious politics. See also Linneman, *Weathering Change*.

61 Muñoz, *Cruising Utopia*, 121.

62 For queer worldmaking, see note in 17 this chapter.

63 In "'Family Resemblance' and Its Discontents," Zion-Waldoks argues that the term "Orthodox" did not catch on in the Israeli context outside scholarly discourse and remains most prevalent in elite intellectual circles.

64 Orthodox LGBT persons are not alone in this battle; other examples in the Orthodox Jewish context include the Orthodox women's movement (Irshai and Zion-Waldoks, "Orthodox Feminism") and Mizrachi Jews' claims to authenticity (Leon, "Ethnic Structuring of 'Sepharadim'").

65 Batnitzky, *How Judaism Became a Religion*. Per historian Joshua Shanes, Orthodoxies emerged in eighteenth- and nineteenth-century Europe as Jews negotiated a transformation from a shared traditional culture to a voluntary religious identity. Orthodoxy was one of several modern options of Jewish identity. In Western Europe the term was originally introduced by progressive Jews as an epithet to mark old-style Jews, but the latter embraced the term to mark their opposition to Enlightenment; the *denominational* label opposed to reform in religious practice followed later. In Eastern Europe the term served as a marker of differentiation from Zionism.

66 Sagi, "Orthodoxy as a Problem"; Zion-Waldoks, "'Family Resemblance' and Its Discontents." On the one-dimensional paradigm, see Keren-Kratz, "Contemporary Study of Orthodoxy." For a mapping of such cases, see Avishai and Fader, "Introduction to the Theme."

67 On the particularities of Israeli modern Orthodoxy, see Schwartz, *Religious Zionism* and essays in Shalmon et al., *Jewish Orthodoxy*. For a more general treatment of Jewish modern Orthodoxy, See Brill, "What Is 'Modern' in Modern Orthodoxy?"

68 For an overview and assessment of these processes and context, see Ettinger, *Undone*, esp. chap. 1. See also Caplan, "Studying the Orthodox Jewish Community in Israel"; Ferziger, "Israelization and Lived Religion"; Sheleg, *From Kosher Inspector to the Driver's Seat?* Students of American political culture are now observing a similar process in the United States: "Evangelical" is increasingly becoming a political rather than a religious label, with some non-Protestant and non-Christians self-identifying as Evangelical. See Ryan Burge, "Why 'Evangelical' Is Becoming Another Word for 'Republican,'" *New York Times*, October 26, 2021.

69 Ettinger, *Undone*; Sagi, "Does Religious Zionism Still Exist?"; Zion-Waldoks, "'Family Resemblance' and Its Discontents."

70 Similar dynamics seem to be playing out in other religious traditions; both the Anglican and Methodist churches have experienced tensions over LGBTQ acceptance that threatened to tear the traditions apart.

71 See the special issue of the journal *Deot* on the end of the rabbinic era (vol. 73, December 2015).

72 On the general process see Ettinger, *Undone*; Irshai, "Public and Private Rulings in Jewish Law." For these dynamics in the context of sexuality, see Englander and Sagi, *Sexuality and the Body*.

73 Compton, Meadow, and Schilt, *Other, Please Specify*; Sumerau, Cragun, and Mathers, "Contemporary Religion and the Cisgendering of Reality."

74 Realities on the ground are quickly changing. As I discuss in chapter 1, following several years of contentious negotiations, Bat Kol changed its name and mission in 2021 to include queer and trans women. As this book went to press in July 2022, Havruta was engaged in similar discussions, with emotions running high. See Havruta, "Lack of Fit," July 19, 2022.

75 I alternated several periods of intense fieldwork with periods focused primarily on digital ethnography. The data are mostly in Hebrew: I am a native speaker and translated all excerpts. Most interviews were recorded and transcribed verbatim (some interviewees declined to be recorded). All data were evaluated according to methods of grounded qualitative analysis, proceeding from an open coding phase to a structured coding system following Emerson, Fretz, and Shaw, *Writing Ethnographic Fieldnotes*, and Charmaz, *Constructing Grounded Theory*.

76 I identified some participants through publicly available information and Kadag organizations. I asked respondents for referrals, and information about the research was disseminated through organizations' newsletters and websites, social media, and public message boards. About three dozen interviewees are activists: founders, spokespeople, and current and past board members of Orthodox LGBT organizations and organizers of social and ritual gatherings (some were interviewed more than once). Fifty-five interviewees are Orthodox LGBT persons. This sample was purposeful and heterogeneous in age (18–42), sexual and gender identities, religiosity, life history, family status, geographical location, and closet status. Interviews covered personal history, self-acceptance journey, coming out, religiosity, navigating life as an Orthodox LGBT person, theology, and engagement with Kadag and other LGBT organizations and initiatives. Interviews with activists additionally covered pathways into activism and goals, strategies, and involvement.

77 For a similar mixed-methods approach, see Fader, *Hidden Heretics*. On virtual ethnographies, see Boellstorff, *Coming of Age in Second Life*; Miller, "Digital Anthropology."

1. MAKING A SOCIAL MOVEMENT

1 "We Are Here Thanks to Him," Kamoha, February 2, 2015, www.kamoha.org.il.

2 "Avigail Sperber," Kamoha, August 8, 2008, www.kamoha.org.il.

3 This was not the first online forum: it was preceded by other chat rooms in IOL, nana, and tapuz, all similarly lost to history. See the report about the forum on

Kamoha's website, "A Peek into Walla's Religious Gays," February 2, 2015, www. kamoha.org.il.

4 The piece is preserved on Bat Kol's website, Vered Kelner, "Coming Out of the Holy Ark," Bat Kol, June 20, 2003, www.bat-kol.org.

5 For a recent comprehensive overview, see Hartal, "Israel's LGBT Movement." For an early celebratory take on Israel's gay decade, see Kama, "From 'Terra Incognita' to 'Terra Firma.'" For a more critical analysis, see Engelstein and Rachamimov, "Crossing Borders and Demolishing Boundaries."

6 The Aguda's website lists over two dozen affiliated organizations and initiatives.

7 Hartal, "Gay Tourism to Tel-Aviv"; Schulman, *Israel/Palestine and the Queer International*.

8 Gamson, "Must Identity Movements Self-Destruct?"

9 Hartal, "Israel's LGBT Movement."

10 Gross, "Politics of LGBT Rights"; Puar, *Terrorist Assemblages*.

11 For critical analysis of these dynamics, including observations on how claims of homonationalism take shape in Israel, see Gross, "Politics of LGBT Rights" and "Israeli GLBT Politics"; Hartal, "Gendered Politics of Absence"; Hartal and Misgav, "Queer Urban Trauma"; Schulman, *Israel/Palestine and the Queer International*; Ziv, "Performative Politics." In the aughts Israel began to brand itself as a gay-friendly nation in a homophobic region: the villa in the jungle, per then-prime minister Ehud Barak. See Machtei Samov and Yishai, "Fragmented Citizenship"; Yacobi, *Israel and Africa*. For some pushback on critiques of homonationalism and pinkwashing, see Harel, "Rise and Fall of the Israeli Gay Legal Revolution."

12 A recent overview noted that there are over thirty LGBT organizations in Israel.

13 There was one redeeming factor to the proliferation of organizations, interests, and agendas: excluded groups challenged the normative gay hegemony, including in language: *lahatab* (LGBT; sometimes *lahatbaq*, LGBTQ) began to replace "gay" as the dominant referent.

14 Shared in private communication.

15 Rabbi Aviner has repeated this stance on multiple occasions. For one instance, see "There Is No Such Thing as a Religious Homosexual," *NRG Maariv*, December 12, 2004, www.makorrishon.co.il. For a theological analysis of this stance of erasure, see Mizrachi, "Between Denial and Recognition of Homosexuality."

16 Englander and Sagi, *Sexuality and the Body*.

17 Engelstein and Rachamimov, "Crossing Borders and Demolishing Boundaries."

18 Lubitch, "Judaism's Position on Same-Sex Relationships" and "Disgust or Permissiveness."

19 Social movements thrive in response to fierce critics; see Fetner, *How the Religious Right Shaped Lesbian and Gay Activism*.

20 Parliamentary Committee on Women's Status, "Protocol no. 184," May 31, 2005, www.nevo.co.il.

21 Other forums continued into the early 2010s but were by then far less popular.

22 Entry to the first Our Faces campaign, Havruta, "Our Faces," Facebook, December 13, 2015.

23 Havruta left the JOH in part as a result of internal politics, but also because the organization sought financial independence.

24 In September 2008 Ron Yosef remained anonymous (Tal Guttman, "A Peek into the World of a Gay Rabbi from Netanya," *Makor Rishon*, September 4, 2008, www.makorrishon.co.il/nrg), but by April 2009 he was out with an op-ed, Ron Yosef, "Until You Are in His Place," *Kipa*, April 23, 2009, www.kipa.co.il.

25 Throughout his career, Ron Yosef was referred to as rabbi; in 2016 questions emerged about his ordination. I refer to him as rabbi since this is the public persona that was recognized during his public life and activism.

26 Koren, *Closet within a Closet*. See a retrospective positive book review posted to the conservative Kamoha's website in 2018, Nofar Kedar, "Queer in the Holy Land," Kamoha, February 20, 2018, www.kamoha.org.il.

27 In July 2019, Vardi spoke at a book launch for Eyal Zack's *Between the Creator and Desire*.

28 Ze'ev Dror and Ruth, "I am an Orthodox Lesbian, I am an Orthodox *Hommo*," *Makor Rishon*, December 13, 2004, www.makorrishon.co.il/nrg.

29 Shvidel, "Others Within."

30 The document had evolved over time. One version was posted on Bat Kol's website: Ofek, "Lesbians and *Halacha*," Bat Kol, June 4, 2013. Though they make some of the same observations about the dearth of materials and come to some of the same conclusions in *Sexuality and the Body*, Englander and Sagi do not cite Ofek.

31 Rabbi Raffi Ostroff made a comment to this effect at a Pesach Sheni 2020 event discussed in chapter 5. See also Lau, "On Same-Sex Couples."

32 Padva, "Gay Martyrs."

33 Moshe Vistoch, "Why I Participated in a Wedding of *Hommos*: Rabbi Lau Explains," *Kipa*, January 18, 2018, www.kipa.co.il. The ideas were later incorporated in Lau's "On Same-Sex Couples," a groundbreaking opinion on recognizing some same-sex relationships.

34 Legally binding same-sex marriages cannot be conducted in Israel, but since 2006 the state has registered as married same-sex couples who wed in jurisdictions where such marriages were legal. Registration has little impact on same-sex couples' legal status since it serves predominantly statistical purposes.

35 Browne, Munt, and Yip., *Queer Spiritual Spaces*; Seitz, *House of Prayer*.

36 Danny Zak, "The Proud Minyan—Five Years to a Home That Connects the Community to Judaism," *Mako*, September 12, 2013, www.mako.co.il.

37 The Tel Aviv Pride Center opened in 2008 and quickly became an important power broker. For analysis of the center's politics, see Gross, "Politics of LGBT Rights"; Hartal and Sasson-Levy, "Being [in] the Center"; Misgav, "With the Current, Against the Wind."

38 Yochanan Azriel's entry to the first Our Faces campaign, Havruta, "Our Faces," Facebook, December 13, 2015.

39 Such liturgical and ritual updates are more common with Reform and Conservative Judaism; see Ben-Lulu, "'Who Will Say Kaddish for Me?'"
40 Karmit Sapir Weiss, "The Woman Who Makes Synagogue Accessible to *Hommos*," *Makor Rishon*, April 16, 2015, www.makorrishon.co.il.
41 Other inclusive congregations include Sod Siach in Jerusalem, Be'erot in Beer Sheva, and a nascent community in Zur Hadassah.
42 In Hebrew there is a gendered play on words: a board or committee, *va'ad*, is gendered male; an executive or management committee, *va'ada menahelet*, is gendered female.
43 www.bat-kol.org/takanon.
44 Bat Kol members more frequently mention women *halachic* figures, including the religious authorities Estie Rosenberg, Tami Bitton, Malka Puterkovsky, and Dr. Friedman.
45 In a 2019 interview, Bat Kol's CEO characterized the organization as serving women on the religious and feminine spectrum, emphasizing that it was not just a lesbian organization but one that included transwomen. At a public event in 2020 she implied that the organization was moving toward billing itself as one that caters to queer women. The organization indeed added the word "queer" to its organizational identity in 2021.
46 The tension made its way to mainstream media; see Tamar Rotem, "This Is No Way to Be Orthodox *Hommo*," *Haaretz*, February 18, 2011, www.haaretz.co.il.
47 Aliana Shefer, "We Are Not Alone," *Makor Rishon*, November 29, 2011, www.makorrishon.co.il.
48 Havruta did not publicly endorse the Minyan until 2011 due to objections on the part of some of its board members.
49 Yosef also sought to document this experience. Hod claimed to have collected demographic information from more than 6,000 men who had turned to it for advice, support, and referrals. I cannot asses the data's reliability, but Yosef's general claim—that Orthodox *hommos* emerge from all strata of Orthodoxy and Ultra-Orthodoxy, certainly holds.
50 The document is archived here: www.news1.co.il/uploadFiles/937313258647919.pdf.
51 A similar document, signed by a hundred rabbis, was published in the United States. See Englander and Sagi, *Sexuality and the Body* for comparisons between the documents.
52 Tal Guttman, "Hod's Principle Document," *Makor Rishon*, October 8, 2009, www.makorrishon.co.il/nrg.
53 Hod also brought early attention to conversion therapy. Ron Yosef was interviewed about the topic by one of Israel's most respected investigative journalists in 2009. His appearance on the show *Uvda*, which took on unregulated therapists and organizations, doubled as a public coming out. In a 2011 position paper, the Israeli Psychological Association's ethics committee declared that conversion therapy was an ideologically driven and unethical intervention, noted that success

rates are low, and enumerated the harms these interventions inflicted, but without legislative action, the document was largely symbolic. I have not been able to verify Hod's role in producing the document, though the organization seems to have been instrumental in calling attention to conversion therapy's harms through private consultations with professional and parliamentary committees and public conferences that brought together psychologists, therapists, and rabbis.

54 This is a common occurrence in social movements; see Tindall, "Networks as Constraints and Opportunities."

55 Hod and Kamoha had a contentious relationship: both organizations claimed to represent *halachically* committed Orthodox *hommos*. Hod favored same-sex relationships (without anal sex) and rejected conversion therapy, while Kamoha supported conversion, celibacy, or heterosexual marriage. A history of sharp exchanges between the organizations culminated in accusations that surfaced following Ron Yosef's arrest that he had not been ordained.

56 Rabbi Yuval Cherlow reportedly was upset when he heard that Havruta cofounder Benni Elbaz had gotten married. One member remembered that "that was a halachic red line. He broke ties with us [Havruta] for a while." The break with the ally was reported in a popular sectorial media outlet: Yishai Fridman, "Rabbi Cherlow to Havruta: Don't Use My Name," *Srugim*, January 13, 2011, www.srugim.co.il.

57 Daniel Ochayon, "A Rupture in the Proud Religious Community," *Makor Rishon*, January 25, 2011, www.makorrishon.co.il.

58 This is a well-documented phenomenon; see Tindall, "Networks as Constraints and Opportunities."

59 Tensions arose when the theme chosen for the Jerusalem parade in 2017 was religion and LGBTQ. For coverage of the fallout, see "For and Against: Jerusalem Pride Parade Theme Religion and LGBT," Ynet, May 22, 2017, www.ynet.co.il, and JOH reflection in Jerusalem Open House, "We Are Proud of the Theme," May 25, 2017. In July 2018 one of the largest LGBTQ rights demonstrations, loosely focused on the exclusion of single men (and gay couples) from accessing surrogacy in Israel, was scheduled on Tisha Be'av, a ritual fast. Kadag activists were enraged, but many activists participated despite fasting.

60 "Bat Kol—Parade," YouTube, June 6, 2013, www.youtube.com/watch?v=4Wg_NyWnro8&feature=youtu.be.

61 The speech is available on YouTube: Kehilat Ramban, August 1, 2015, www.youtube.com/watch?v=d3bYDVMggNI.

62 The wave of Orthodox *hommos* and lesbians who came out in 2015 reflected the relative privileges of some Orthodox LGBT closets. The Our Faces campaign (discussed in chapter 5) skewed Ashkenazi, male, highly educated. Likewise, Orthodox LGBT came to prime-time television in the form of a *hommo* character in the popular, award-winning TV drama *Srugim*, which aired from 2008 to 2012 and centered on the lives of young Orthodox Jews living in Jerusalem's Orthodox educated and hip bubble. The actor, Uri Lachmi, had also played the protagonist in Chaim Elbaum's film about the *yeshiva* student struggling with same-sex attraction,

Thou Shalt Love. Closing a circle, Lachmi came out after Shira Banki succumbed to her wounds, issuing an apology for having previously cooperated with "contorted and deceitful" social norms. "The Actor Uri Lachmi Asks for Shira Banki's Forgiveness," *Maariv*, August 4, 2015, www.maariv.co.il.

63 Featured rabbis included the Rabbanit Malka Puterkovsky, Dr. Hanna Friedman, and Rabbi Benny Lau. Shoval, "Penitence," Facebook, October 8, 2016, www. facebook.com/shovalsovlanut/videos/1121817944567079.

2. UNLIVABLE LIVES

1 Religious LGBTQ Confessions, "#5590," Facebook, June 17, 2019.

2 See the collection of essays in Slomowitz and Feit, *Homosexuality, Transsexuality, Psychoanalysis and Traditional Judaism*, the most comprehensive treatment to date of the circumstances and contextualizing forces affecting Orthodox LGBTQ+ Jews and their communities.

3 For Jewish citizens of the state, military service in Israel is compulsory. It is a waypoint in many young people's coming-of-age narratives.

4 On suicidal ideation and well-being among LGBTQ+ persons, including those from religious backgrounds, see Haas et al., "Suicide and Suicide Risk;" Gibbs and Goldbach, "Religious Conflict"; King et al., "Systematic Review"; Plöderl and Tremblay, "Mental Health of Sexual Minorities."

5 Confession Page readers thanked the poet for putting words to their own experiences: "Exhausting but on point," one reader wrote; "Connected to every word," wrote another.

6 Berlant and Warner, "Sex in Public"; for a recent overview of the concept, see Otis and Dunn, "Queer Worldmaking."

7 On the concept of sacramental shame in the Evangelical context, see Moon and Tobin, "Sunsets and Solidarity."

8 This is beginning to change in large part thanks to the efforts of feminist critics, scholars, and thought leaders. See Yahal Center for Family Life, https://merkazyahel.org.il, founded by Dr. Michal Prins.

9 This message board is publicly available, though it takes some sleuthing to find. Several people who were concerned about inviting unwanted attention to this resource asked me not to name it.

10 Heiden-Rootes, Hartwell, and Nedela, "Comparing the Partnering, Minority Stress and Depression"; Meyer, "Resilience in the Study of Minority Stress" and "Prejudice, Social Stress, and Mental Health."

11 Individuals raised in environments that reject homosexuality and use concepts such as abomination and sin experience more prejudice and report higher rates of internalized homophobia and minority stress than individuals raised in more accepting environments: Anderton, Pender, and Asner-Self, "Review of the Religious Identity / Sexual Orientation Identity Conflict Literature"; Sowe, Brown, and Taylor, "Sex and the Sinner."

12 Jewish menstrual laws regulate the intimate lives of married heterosexual couples and are considered an important marker of observance. The practice has long been a source of anger and anxiety, and in recent years Orthodox feminists have paved the way not only for public discussion of the ritual but also for a creative re-thinking of this ritual domain. Some Orthodox lesbian couples are seeking similar creativity to adapt this and other rituals to their circumstances. On menstrual laws as a ritual domain, see Avishai, "'Doing Religion' in a Secular World." On emergent sex education, see Yahal Center for Family Life, https://merkazyahel. org.il; Prins, *To Simply Want*; and Taragin-Zeller and Kasstan, "'I Didn't Know How to Be with My Husband.'" The entire April 2014 issue of the journal *Deot* focused on innovations in *niddah* practices.

13 Kadag activists have focused on what scholars call "mixed orientation marriage" for a long time, but rabbinic leaders have now taken up the issue as well—e.g., Rabbi Mordechai Vardi's highly regarded documentary, *Marry Me, However*. For background on mixed orientation marriages in Orthodox communities, including messages that advise same-sex-attracted persons, and especially men, to marry heterosexually, see Itzhaky and Kissil, "'It's a Horrible Sin'"; Kissil and Itzhaky, "Experiences of the Marital Relationship"; Slomowitz and Feit, *Homosexuality, Transsexuality, Psychoanalysis and Traditional Judaism*; Zack and Ben-Ari, "'Men Are for Sex and Women Are for Marriage'"; Zack, *Between the Creator and Desire*. For more general scholarship, see Benack and Swan, "Queer People Who Enter 'Straight' Marriages." For comparison with the Mormon case, see Legerski et al., "Mormon Mixed-Orientation Marriages."

14 See note 4 above.

15 Fertility norms, rooted in religious and Zionist ideals, are persistent; see Taragin-Zeller, "Towards an Anthropology of Doubt" and "Conceiving God's Children."

16 Religious LGBTQ Confessions, "#6256," Facebook, September 16, 2019.

17 Englander and Sagi, *Sexuality and the Body*.

18 Lau, "On Same-Sex Couples."

19 The story of the ugly vessel and the craftsman appears in the Babylonian Talmud, Ta'anit 20a–b. The story is understood to be a meditation on the concept of humankind being made in the image of God. See chapter 6 on how Kadag uses this story subversively.

20 Zack, *Between the Creator and Desire*.

21 See chapter 4. This is the solution proposed by Rabbi Stav.

22 Rabbi Benny Lau was so moved by the 2020 documentary *Marry Me, However* that he released a groundbreaking *halachic* position paper on monogamous same-sex relationships, a step for which he was praised and pilloried. Lau, "On Same-Sex Couples."

23 For a recent overview, see Alempijevic et al., "Statement on Conversion Therapy."

24 For parallels with the Mormon case, see Dehlin et al., "Sexual Orientation Change." The practice is ubiquitous in Orthodox circles, and Kadag activists have

focused on this issue intensively in recent years. Benjamin Katz, Hadas Benayahu, Nadav Schwartz, and Ze'ev Shvidel have been instrumental to studying, documenting, and communicating conversion therapy's harms. In 2021 their efforts consolidated into the Center for Information about Conversion Therapy, a support and advocacy organization focused on ending conversion therapy. Started as an independent initiative by Gil Friedman and Nadav Schwartz, it has been taken up by Havruta. A Facebook Confessions page for conversion therapy survivors has operated since 2020. Conservative Orthodox factions in Israel have been resistant to efforts to curb the practice through legislation, though in February 2022 the Israeli Ministry of Health instituted a long-sought policy shift that effectively bans conversion therapy by licensed health care and mental health professionals. Whether this policy change will have real-world impacts is not clear, however, because many practitioners of conversion therapy such as rabbis and other religious figures are not licensed by the state to begin with. Nevertheless, this policy represents a major win for Kadag and its allies.

25 Dr. Eyal Zack, a clinician social worker who works with such couples and has published on the topic, argues that in some cases such marriages can be successful, though he too acknowledges that maintaining the marital bonds requires hard work and "success" is qualified. See Zack and Ben-Ari, "'Men Are for Sex and Women Are for Marriage'"; Zack, *Between the Creator and Desire*. See also Adler and Ben-Ari, "'How We Stay Together Without Going Crazy.'" For a comparison with the Mormon case, see Legerski et al., "Mormon Mixed-Orientation Marriage."

26 Though individual rabbis who were consulted came up quite consistently and are well known in the community, I was advised to refrain from including their names in this volume because, as more than one activist told me, "they will come after you with lawsuits."

3. ORTHODOX QUEER WORLDMAKING

1 Eran Argaman, "Sixth Candle," Facebook, December 16, 2020.

2 Heiden-Rootes, Hartwell, and Nedela, "Comparing the Partnering, Minority Stress and Depression"; Meyer, "Resilience in the Study of Minority Stress" and "Prejudice, Social Stress, and Mental Health"; Wolff et al., "Sexual Minority Students."

3 Avishai, "Religious Queer People."

4 In work with Benjamin Katz, we articulated this idea focusing more specifically on the psychological dimension of rewriting one's narrative (Katz and Avishai, "Visions and Revisions").

5 See an account of the wedding: "I Didn't Need the Tissue Because Mom Is Mom," *WDG*, January 19, 2018, https://wdg.co.il.

6 Or Ellisian, "I Am an Orthodox Lesbian and God Is with Me," *Mako*, May 10, 2017, www.mako.co.il.

7 Until 2022, surrogacy in Israel was available only to opposite-sex couples, a point of much contention within LGBTQ+ activism.

8 Browne, Munt, and Yip, *Queer Spiritual Spaces*; Seitz, *House of Prayer*.
9 Yochanan Azriel's entry to the first Our Faces campaign, Havruta, "Our Faces," Facebook, December 13, 2015.
10 For more information about these spaces, see chapter 1.
11 Browne and Ferreira, *Lesbian Geographies*; Quinan, "Safe Space."
12 Irshai, "Homosexuality and the 'Aqedah Theology.'" This view is not unique to Judaism.
13 Some same-sex-attracted Orthodox Jews identify as "strugglers"—they accept their same-sex attraction as a reality but believe that their religious commitment entails "struggling" rather than living this reality. The defunct organizations Hod and Kamoha (see chapter 1) supported versions of this stance.
14 For parallels to Christian queer theology, see Althaus-Reid, *Indecent Theology* and *Queer God*; Cheng, *Radical Love*; Lightsey, *Our Lives Matter*.
15 For a good overview of the science and debates about the science, see Bailey et al., "Sexual Orientation, Controversy, and Science."
16 In "Beyond the Dichotomy," Dawne Moon argues that such assumptions temper the radical potential of seemingly radical theological moves. Moon distinguishes between two homopositive approaches to the negotiation of religion and sexuality based on their stance on human volition. Per Moon, a truly queer approach, which she terms "Godly calling" (1232), fully embraces human volition, showing that same-sex practices and transgender identities can be righteous choices not despite of being nonnormative but precisely because of it.
17 Zack, *Between the Creator and Desire*.
18 Most recently, guided by this logic, Dr. Rabbi Benny Lau issued guidelines intended to help observant LGBTQ+ Jews manage their family lives within religious communities. For a report about the document, see Tzvi Joffre, "Rabbi Lau Releases Guide for Religious LGBTQ+ Jews: Not Good to Be Alone," *Jerusalem Post*, October 12, 2020. For the Hebrew version, see Benny Lau, "It's Not Good to Be Alone," Facebook, October 10, 2020. For an English translation, see Lau, "On Same-Sex Couples."
19 Rafael J. Kelner Polisuk, "Intersectionality," Facebook, April 16, 2021.
20 Rewriting the narrative draws on many other resources, including surrounding oneself with a supportive community, fellow travelers, mentors and role models, and therapists (and weeding out unsupportive people from their lives); a changed social environment; and financial independence that allows one to distance oneself from family and community.
21 Muñoz, *Cruising Utopia*, 121.

4. EDUCATING OUR RABBIS

Epigraph: Benny Lau, "The Religious Community and Homosexuality," a recording available on Eshel's website, www.eshelonline.org (my edits). Rabbi Lau was set on the path to allyship when, as a young rabbi, he was tapped by his parents for support when his younger brother, now a rabbi in New York, came out as gay.

1 Eyal Liebermann, "Something Happened This Past Shabbat," Facebook, November 13, 2016.
2 Abarbanel's entry to Our Faces campaign, Havruta, "Our Faces," Facebook, December 13, 2015.
3 Benny Lau, "It's Not Good to Be Alone," Facebook, October 10, 2020.
4 For a Catholic take, see Martin, *Building a Bridge* and two volumes edited by Hinze and Hornbeck, *More Than a Monologue*. For Evangelical writing, see Gushee, *Changing Our Mind*, and Brownson, *Bible, Gender, Sexuality*.
5 Brown, *Regulating Aversion*. See also Jakobsen and Pellegrini, *Love the Sin*.
6 For an overview of queer theology, see Cheng, *Radical Love*; Tonstad, *Queer Theology*. See also Althaus-Reid, *Queer God* and *Indecent Theology*. In "Beyond the Dichotomy," Moon offers a categorical schema that maps homonegative positions that view homosexuality as sinful (theology of transgression), moderate positions that emphasize inclusivity but are ambivalent toward homosexuality (theology of tolerance), and homopositive positions that do not see homosexuality and connection with God as incompatible (queer theology).
7 Religious LGBTQ Confessions, "#6256," Facebook, September 16, 2019.
8 Englander and Sagi, *Sexuality and the Body*; Ettinger, *Undone*; Irshai, "Public and Private Rulings in Jewish Law." See Yuval Cherlow's reflection on the topic of homosexuality in an interview, a snippet of which is preserved on Havruta's website as Leeor Shapira, "Rabbi Cherlow: I'm Making a Change," Havruta, July 13, 2010, https://havruta.org.il.
9 Englander and Sagi, *Sexuality and the Body*.
10 Irshai, "Homosexuality and the 'Aqedah Theology'"; Mizrachi, "Between Denial and Recognition of Homosexuality."
11 For a critical assessment, see Knust, *Unprotected Texts*.
12 See Jordan, *Rewritten Theology*. For a roadmap on early Christianity, see Dunning, *Oxford Handbook*.
13 Knust, *Unprotected Texts*.
14 See Englander and Sagi, *Sexuality and the Body*; Kosman and Sharbat, "'Two Women.'"
15 Ben Naeh, "Judaism and Jews on LGBT"; Boyarin, *Unheroic Conduct*; Satlow, "'They Abused Him Like a Woman.'"
16 Irshai, "Homosexuality and the 'Aqedah Theology.'"
17 Ben Naeh, "Judaism and Jews on LGBT"; Boyarin, *Unheroic Conduct*; Satlow, "'They Abused Him Like a Woman.'"
18 Ben Naeh, "Judaism and Jews on LGBT" and "Moshko the Jew and His Gay Friends." These divergences reflect differences across Jews' respective host cultures throughout Europe and the Middle East.
19 Lubitch, "Disgust or Permissiveness"; Shvidel, "Others Within."
20 Irshai, "Homosexuality and the 'Aqedah Theology.'"
21 Bleich, "Homosexuality."
22 See discussion in Irshai, "Homosexuality and the 'Aqedah Theology.'"

23 Mizrachi, "Between Denial and Recognition of Homosexuality."

24 Rabbi Aviner has repeated this stance on multiple occasions. For one instance, see "There Is No Such Thing as a Religious Homosexual," *NRG Maariv*, December 12, 2004, www.makorrishon.co.il. See also Aviner, "Same-Sex Abomination," *Jewish Information*, March 12, 2002, http://moreshet.co.il.

25 See overviews in Irshai, "Homosexuality and the 'Aqedah Theology'"; Mizrachi, "Between Denial and Recognition of Homosexuality."

26 One such example is Rabbi Elon, as discussed in Mizrachi, "Between Denial and Recognition of Homosexuality."

27 The Talmud states that women who engage in practices that the text terms *mesolelot* with one another are disqualified from marrying a priest. Although the term *mesolelot* is not clear, later interpreters claimed that it referenced lewdness and immoral acts associated with foreigners ("the doings of the land of Egypt . . . against which we have been warned"). Englander and Sagi, *Sexuality and the Body*; Kosman and Sharbat, "'Two Women.'"

28 Englander and Sagi, *Sexuality and the Body*.

29 Irshai, "Homosexuality and the 'Aqedah Theology'" and "Public and Private Rulings in Jewish Law."

30 This is reminiscent of the Christian "love the sinner, hate the sin" formulation. See, for example, Haim Navon, "Empathy Is Not Legitimacy."

31 Mizrachi, "Between Denial and Recognition of Homosexuality."

32 Lubitch, "To Strive so as to Not Drown."

33 Ronen Lubich, "The Approach to LGBT (and Specifically to Homosexuals)," March 15, 2015. The transcript of this talk is available on Kamoha's website, www. kamoha.org.il/?p=29278.

34 Lecture given at a Beit Hillel conference on January 5, 2019, www.facebook.com.

35 These responses appeared in volume 12 of *Deot*.

36 It has been suggested to me, though I have not been able to confirm this, that this reader was Bat Kol founder Avigail Sperber.

37 *Deot* 12 (2001): 46–47.

38 "Principles Document for Persons with Homosexual Tendencies in the Orthodox Community," April 17, 2008. The document is archived here: www.news1.co.il/uploadFiles/937313258647919.pdf.

39 The document "released" same-sex-attracted men from the obligation to marry.

40 Englander and Sagi, *Sexuality and the Body*.

41 The parallels with the Catholic case are striking. The Hod document echoes a similar breakthrough document, *Always Our Children: A Pastoral Message to Parents of Homosexual Children and Suggestions for Pastoral Ministers*, published in 1997 by the U.S. Conference of Catholic Bishops, Committee on Marriage and Family. The bishops were responding to a 1986 Doctrine of the Faith letter, *On the Pastoral Care of Homosexual Persons*, that was seen as inflicting much harm on Catholic LGBTQ persons and their congregations (the 1986 letter newly characterized homosexuality as an "objective disorder"). I do not know whether the

Israeli rabbis were aware of these Catholic documents, but their American counterparts surely would have been familiar with the controversy that roiled Catholic thinkers on this issue.

42 Hod claims that over 160 rabbis endorsed the document, but the number of public endorsements is much smaller, though the list includes prominent rabbis such as David Bigman, Yuval Cherlow, Benny Lau, Ronen Lubitch, Haim Navon (http://archive.is/LigvS), and Benny Perl (http://archive.is/4JSyZ); see Yair Ettinger, "Dozens of Orthodox Rabbis Wrote a Principles Document That Calls to Recognize *Hommos* and Lesbians, *Haaretz*, July 29, 2010. A similar document, endorsed by 100 rabbis, was published in the United States at around the same time. See Englander and Sagi, *Sexuality and the Body*, for comparisons between the documents.

43 Irshai, "Homosexuality and the 'Aqedah Theology.'"

44 Yuval Cherlow, "*Hommos* in Theological Discourse," *Ynet*, January 1, 2009, www.ynet.co.il.

45 Eliq Oster, "Religious *Hommos*? There Is No Such Thing," Havruta, May 6, 2010, https://havruta.org.il.

46 Hanna Friedman, "Remarks, Beit Hillel Conference," YouTube, April 14, 2016, www.youtube.com/watch?v=BUQosM-M464.

47 This was a hypothetical. Nadav Schwartz, "Remarks, Beit Hillel Conference," YouTube, April 14, 2016, www.youtube.com/watch?v=4FrYBjnFARQ&t=22s.

48 Meir Kula, "Remarks, Beit Hillel Conference," YouTube, April 14, 2016, www.youtube.com/watch?v=RPB5t4YpNXY.

49 Ettinger, *Undone*.

50 Mainstream Orthodoxy does not recognize women's ordination, but the feminist Orthodox revolution of the past two decades has ushered in a new class of learned women who fulfill many rabbinic functions, especially in terms of providing spiritual guidance and halachic decisions, and in some progressive pockets women are ordained and serve as spiritual leaders. Orthodox conservatives challenge the halachic legitimacy of these developments. See Ferziger, "Sanctuary for the Specialist"; Raucher, "Rabbis with Skirts"; Ross, *Expanding the Palace of Torah*.

51 The names most commonly mentioned within Orthodox LGBT networks when I conducted my research (the list keeps growing) include Rabbanit Malka Puterkovsky; Dr. Hanna Friedman; Estie Rosenberg, rabbis Beni Lau, Yuval Cherlow, and Elkana Cherlow; and Professor Tamar Ross. Other allied rabbis include Ronen Lubitch, Raffi Ostroff, Ilai Ofran, Yaaqov Madan, and David Bigman. These rabbinic authorities differ on the bounds of acceptance but share a commitment to viewing homosexuality and gender divergence as part of the natural variety of human nature.

52 Observers have assumed that rabbinic theological stances on acceptance emerged from such interactions (see, for example, Englander and Sagi, *Sexuality and the Body*; Irshai, "Homosexuality and the 'Aqedah Theology'"; Ross, "Halacha as Event"), but this is the first study to document the phenomenon.

Examples include the following: Speaking at a 2019 Beit Hillel conference, Rabbi Lubitch said that his positions were a product of conversations with young men who had sought his counsel. Rabbi Vardi's indictment of the pressure to marry heterosexually captured in the film *Will You Marry Me* (see chapter 1) was based on his experience guiding a former student through a marriage gone sour due to undisclosed same-sex attraction. Rabbi Yuval Cherlow said in 2019 that rabbis are "in a fog" when it comes to LGBT matters and that interactions breed knowledge, understanding, and empathy. (The latter two shared these insights in July 2019 at a launch event for Dr. Eyal Zack's book.) Rabbi Yuval Cherlow went on record in the early aughts about being set on a path to acceptance through his work providing online responses; see Ze'ev Shvidel, "Can an Orthodox *Hommo* Go to the Miqveh," *Makor Rishon*, February 27, 2005, www.makorrishon.co.il. Dr. Hanna Friedman said in an interview with an Orthodox online publication that her allyship began with friendships she forged when she moved to Tel Aviv with her family; see Karmit Sapir Weiss, "The Woman Who Makes Synagogue Accessible to *Hommos*," *Makor Rishon*, April 16, 2015, www.makorrishon.co.il.

53 Moshe Vistoch, "Why I Participated in a Wedding of *Hommos*: Rabbi Lau Explains," *Kipa*, January 18, 2018, www.kipa.co.il.

54 The more conservative Rabbis Stav have also ruled on the topic, arriving at a similar stance; David Stav and Avraham Stav, "Participation in a Wedding That Counters *Halacha*," *Zohar*, 2016, www.kamoha.org.il.

55 Benny Lau, "A New Religious Language," Facebook, May 11, 2017. In September 2018 (around the High Holidays) Rabbi Lau wrote about another meeting where Orthodox LGBT persons and their parents talked about pain, courage, and spiritual journeys. That link has been removed, but an invitation to the meeting is available: Rabbi Lau, "A Reminder," Facebook, September 13, 2018.

56 Benny Lau, "We Are Filling the World with Light," Facebook, December 30, 2019.

57 Lau, "On Same-Sex Couples."

58 In the interim, Rabbi Lau has published his take on the matter. Lau, "On Same-Sex Couples." The original piece in Hebrew was posted to Facebook on October 10, 2020.

59 See a summary of the event posted by Eyal Liebermann, "Ramban Synagogue in Jerusalem," Facebook, December 2, 2016.

60 There is a subtext here that's worth noting: the alliance between newly recognized women authority figures and LGBT persons, both marginalized by hegemonic visions of Orthodoxy. At a Pesach Sheni event on May 6, 2020, Bat Kol founder Avigail Sperber and the CEO of Kolech (the Orthodox women's feminist organization) discussed synergies and divergences.

61 Yehuda Shlezinger, "Love Thy Neighbor," *Israel Hayom*, March 15, 2012, www.israelhayom.co.il.

62 Avishai Ben-Haim, "Rabbi Madan Supports Coming Out of the Closet," *Makor Rishon*, February 21, 2009, www.makorrishon.co.il.

63 "Rabbi Madan: 'The Rabbis Who Signed the Rabbis' Letter Violated the Prohibition to Humiliate Others,'" *Srugim*, August 7, 2018, www.srugim.co.il.

64 Irshai, "Homosexuality and the 'Aqedah Theology,'" 30.

65 Remarks shared with Havruta members at their 2019 retreat, private communication.

66 Yehuda Shlezinger, "Love Thy Neighbor," *Israel Hayom*, March 15, 2012, www.israelhayom.co.il.

67 Religious LGBTQ Confessions, "#6679," Facebook, December 4, 2019.

68 "Ask the Rabbi," Moreshet, December 29, 2009, http://shut.moreshet.co.il.

69 In "Between Denial and Recognition of Homosexuality," Rabbi and educator Avishai Mizrachi identifies six key areas of questions: romantic relationships, family relationships, sexuality, social acceptance, authenticity, and psychological wellbeing.

70 Remarks shared at a 2019 Beit Hillel conference. Ronen Lubitch, "The Orthodox Community and the LGBT Community," Beit Hillel, January 5, 2019. The recording is available on Facebook.

71 See Mizrachi, "Between Denial and Recognition of Homosexuality," for a discussion of Rabbi Stav's ruling.

72 Irshai, "Public and Private Rulings in Jewish Law."

73 Mizrachi, "Between Denial and Recognition of Homosexuality."

74 A rabbi not involved with the document told me, "I don't know what a rabbinic policy paper is. Rabbis are writing it so its halacha. Calling it position paper just makes it more palatable."

75 Beit Hillel, "The Congregation and People with Homosexual Tendencies," April 9, 2016. Unless noted otherwise, the quotations are taken from the executive summary of the document, which was published in English (I could not find the full document in English, so other translations are my own): https://eng.beithillel.org.il.

76 Nadav Schwartz, "Remarks, Beit Hillel Conference," YouTube, April 14, 2016, www.youtube.com/watch?v=4FrYBjnFARQ&t=22s. This, of course, was a hypothetical.

77 "Beit Hillel Document," Havruta, April 11, 2016, www.facebook.com.

78 On this idea, see Ross, *Expanding the Palace of Torah*.

79 Dr. Hanna Friedman alluded to these tensions and concerns in her remarks at the Beit Hillel Conference; "Remarks, Beit Hillel Conference," YouTube, April 14, 2016, www.youtube.com/watch?v=BUQosM-M464.

80 "LGBT and the Future of Judaism," YouTube, September 13, 2018, www.youtube.com/watch?v=mch8MvlzRBY.

81 Mizrachi, "Between Denial and Recognition of Homosexuality."

82 Rabbi Greenberg has been an important figure in Orthodox LGBT persons' struggles for recognition in both the United States and Israel; he played a central role in the launching of both Israeli and American Orthodox gay organizations and was one of the subjects of the *Trembling Before G-D* documentary on the tensions between homosexuality and Orthodoxy.

83 She made similar arguments in Ross, "Halacha as Event."

84 A father and son duo, the Rabbis Stav, published a ruling that recognized *hommos'* distinct halachic status, which expanded the rules concerning modesty (see overview in Mizrachi, "Between Denial and Recognition of Homosexuality").

85 Greenberg, *Wrestling with God and Men*. See also Knust, *Unprotected Texts*.

86 The rabbi reportedly shared these remarks at a conference for rabbis and therapists focusing on same-sex attraction in 2009. "Can a Religious *Hommo* Go to the Miqveh?," Havruta, September 25, 2009, https://havruta.org.il.

87 Rabbi Ostroff, "Remarks, Beit Hillel Conference," YouTube, April 14, 2016, www.youtube.com/watch?v=_sauIaMaY-s&t=8s.

88 Ziva Ofek, "Observations," Facebook, May 11, 2017.

89 Chaim Elbaum, "The Orthodox LGBT Battle," Facebook, May 2, 2018.

90 Ettinger, *Undone*.

91 Moon, "Beyond the Dichotomy."

92 Dr. Hanna Friedman alluded to these tensions and concerns in her remarks at the Beit Hillel Conference; YouTube, April 14, 2016, www.youtube.com/watch?v=BUQosM-M464.

93 Religious LGBTQ Confessions, "#7001," Facebook, April 10, 2020, www.facebook.com/ReligiousLGBTQconfessions/posts/899442070505064.

5. TELLING STORIES, MAKING SPACE

1 Chaim Elbaum, "The Orthodox LGBT Battle," Facebook, May 2, 2018.

2 Alan Brill, "*Pesach Sheni* as a Therapeutic Holiday," *Book of Doctrines and Opinions*, April 25, 2018, https://kavvanah.blog.

3 Or Ellisian, "I Am an Orthodox Lesbian and God Is with Me," *Mako*, May 10, 2017, www.mako.co.il.

4 Duggan, "New Homonormativity"; Halperin, "Normalization of Queer Theory." For a recent take that nuances these debates in the context of the United Kingdom, see Mowlabocus, *Interrogating Homonormativity*.

5 For an overview of the use of stories in social movements, see Polletta and Gardner, "Narrative and Social Movements." On the use of stories in LGBTQ+ activism, see Plummer, *Telling Sexual Stories*.

6 Brown, *Regulating Aversion*.

7 Some of those featured in the album were well-known activists, but others were not public figures. Havruta, "Our Faces," Facebook, December 13, 2015. The campaign was covered by mainstream and Orthodox media. See, for example, Zvika Klein, "The Rabbi Said: You Won—Orthodox *Hommos* Is a Reality," *Makor Rishon*, December 24, 2016, www.makorrishon.co.il.

8 In 2022 filmmaker Moran Nakar produced a seven-part docuseries, *The Holy Closet*, featuring Orthodox LGBT lives, expanding on this genre. Avigail Sperber helped produce the series.

9 "Dozens of Orthodox LGBT Persons Come Out on the Internet: We Are Comfortable with Ourselves," *Ynet*, December 13, 2015, www.ynet.co.il.

10 Radio interview with Keren Noybach on December 17, 2015, https://soundcloud.com.
11 Radio interview with Noybach.
12 Orne, "'You Will Always Have to "Out" Yourself.'"
13 Currier, *Out in Africa*; Ayoub, *When States Come Out*. On the complexities of visibility in hostile environments, also see Moussawi, *Disruptive Situations*.
14 Shoval, "Our Faces, 2," Facebook, July 13, 2017.
15 Shoval, "Our Faces, 3," Facebook, July 15, 2019.
16 In Hebrew, Shoval refers to activists, not volunteers, but I used the term "volunteer" to distinguish between this educational intervention and other dissent and abolitionist forms of Kadag activism.
17 I attended nine Shoval sessions. My discussion also draws on the perusal of organization documents and interviews with founders, activists, and volunteers.
18 The following played a role in getting the initiative off the ground: Erez Bruchi, Tzachi Mezuman, Avigail Sperber, and Ziva Ofek (there were others). The first training session took place in April 2007, and to date there have been six more. Benjamin Katz led the organization for several years after the 2015 Jerusalem Pride Parade.
19 Shoval operated under the auspices of Bat Kol until 2021, when it became legally independent.
20 Thornicroft et al., "Evidence for Effective Interventions."
21 Shoval actively participates and sometimes takes the lead in the planning of conferences directed at mental health professionals. Notable recent examples include a conference at Bar Ilan University in January 2019 and another held at Hebrew University in September 2019. Both were co-organized by Shoval leaders and clinical psychologists Benjamin Katz and Hadas Benayahu.
22 www.shovalgroup.org.
23 The same was true for IGY, an LGBT youth organization, and the religious groups run by the Jerusalem Open House.
24 Shoval, "Penitence," Facebook, October 8, 2016.
25 The two outlined their intervention in Dina Berman and Tamar Gan-Zvi Bick, "Pesach Sheini," *Tirzvah: A Community of Frum Queer Women*, May 5, 2009, https://tirtzah.wordpress.com. This history is also recounted in *Osim Makom* (Making Space), a booklet produced and distributed by the Pesach Sheni initiative.
26 Berman Maykon and Gan-Zvi Bick did allow that perhaps ritually unclean individuals were negligent or poor planners, neither reason enough to prevent them from fulfilling a mitzvah.
27 Or Ellisian, "I Am an Orthodox Lesbian and God Is with Me," *Mako*, May 10, 2017, www.mako.co.il.
28 In Israel marriage and divorce are governed by Jewish law. Jewish divorce laws effectively grant men veto power and are the target of activism by both secular and Orthodox feminists. See Zion-Waldoks, "Politics of Devoted Resistance."

29 Alan Brill, "*Pesach Sheni* as a Therapeutic Holiday," *Book of Doctrines and Opinions*, April 25, 2018, https://kavvanah.blog.

30 The first conference received enthusiastic coverage in Jewish feminist and queer venues in and outside Israel. Elana Sztokman, "A Month after Passover, Eating Matzoh to Promote Inclusion," *Forward*, April 28, 2010, https://forward.com.

31 In 2020 this expanded to include a similar outreach campaign during Sukkot. Kadag activist and Shoval coordinator Hadas Benayahu led the expansion effort.

32 Mevorach, "LGBT and the Institution of the Family."

33 Miriam Adler, "Do You Want to Celebrate *Pesach Sheni* with Me?," *Kipa*, May 9, 2017, www.kipa.co.il.

34 Pesach Sheni, "A Touching Message," Facebook, April 25, 2018.

35 These were intended for participants in IGY's support groups for LGBT youth and participants in JOH support groups.

36 Pesach Sheni, "A Jewish Home—at Any Price," Facebook, May 12, 2020.

37 A recording is available at https://youtu.be/lL_3Eyo5JII.

38 Some of the eulogies, including those by Netta Hadid's family, referred to Netta by her dead/birth name Itzik; other speakers referred to her as Itzik Netta, using female pronouns.

39 Ferziger, "Role of Reform"; Hirschhorn, "Origins of the Redemption"; Morrison, *The Gush.*

40 The event featured two Orthodox psychologists, Rabbi Benni Lehman and Muli Grossman, and two Orthodox men experiencing same-sex attraction, Gilad (a pseudonym) and Yehonatan Gill Rossen Maman, a key Havruta activist. The panel proceeded in a debate-like fashion. Yehonatan and Rabbi Benni Lehman criticized conversion therapy, while Gilad and Muli Grossman presented the once-dominant view: most people experiencing same-sex attraction can partner heterosexually; Gilad had claimed to have overcome his attraction to men with Grossman's help (Gilad's wife and baby were in the audience). Muli Grossman emphatically denied that his treatment amounted to conversion therapy, arguing instead that his intervention is premised on the idea that most people are rated as neither Kinsey 0 (exclusively heterosexual) nor Kinsey 6 (exclusively homosexual) and can therefore be content in heterosexual marriages. Critics contend such "softer" interventions are as harmful as other forms of conversion interventions.

41 Similar critiques were leveled at organizers of other events; Rabbi Rimon hinted at "fireworks" prior to the 2018 Alon Shvut evening.

42 Tomer Aldobi, "Eleven Influences," *Mako*, June 19, 2020, www.zman.co.il.

43 Rubin, "Thinking Sex."

44 The same process is unfolding in Evangelical Christianity. See, for example, Gushee, *Changing Our Mind.*

45 In *Expanding the Palace of Torah*, Ross argues that the feminist revolution expanded, rather than threatened, Jewish traditions.

46 The panel took place on May 10, 2020.

6. THE BATTLE FOR JUDAISM'S STRAIGHT SOUL

1 Imri Levi Sadan, "Between Flag Dancing and Pride Parade: When the Answer to Homophobia Comes from the Orthodox," *Walla*, June 6, 2019, https://news.walla.co.il.

2 Amichai Stein, "Religious Pride," YouTube, December 4, 2016, www.youtube.com/watch?v=OMUQvraI61c.

3 Zvi Shaiman, "Freedom of Speech? The Left Calls for Rabbi Amar's Firing," *Srugim*, November 17, 2016, www.srugim.co.il. Rabbi Amar created another maelstrom in 2019, this time honing in on Orthodox LGBT persons: "Rabbi Amar Attacks Religious LGBTQ Persons: 'They Should Throw Away Their Kipa,'" *Kipa*, July 23, 2019, www.kipa.co.il.

4 Gili Cohen, "A Senior Rabbi: The IDF Has Lost Its Values, Educates to Recognize the Proud Community—Perverts," *Haaretz*, July 18, 2016, www.haaretz.co.il.

5 The conference was titled "Acceptance of Same-Sex Attracted LGBT Youth in the Community." Havruta, "The *Kibbutz Dati* Movement," November 17, 2016.

6 For more information about this meeting, see chapter 4.

7 Rabbi Ronen Lubitch made a similar claim in an April 25, 2018, interview as part of a media blitz surrounding that year's Pesach Sheni events. www.facebook.com.

8 Dazey, "Rethinking Respectability Politics."

9 Petro, *After the Wrath of God.*

10 The concept was first suggested by Evelyn Brooks Higginbotham, in *Righteous Discontent*, as a tool for assessing Black women's civil rights activism. For a recent general summary, see Dazey, "Rethinking Respectability Politics." For assessments of respectability politics in the LGBTQ+ context, see Ghaziani, Taylor, and Stone, "Cycles of Sameness," and essays in Taylor and Bernstein, *Marrying Kind?* Yuvraj Joshi, "Respectable Queerness," proposes a theoretical framework. Philip Edward Jones, "Respectability Politics and Straight Support," has recently called into question the assumption that "respectable" members of marginalized groups can effectively change public opinion.

11 Warner, *Acts of Gaiety.*

12 The group included Daniel Jonas, Kobi Handelsman, Nadav Schwartz, and Avichai Abarbanel.

13 The activists and the rabbi wrote about the conference on their Facebook feeds. For one report about the fallout, see Moshe Vistuch, "Confrontation in LGBT Conference of the Community Rabbis' Association," *Kipa*, April 18, 2017, www.kipa.co.il.

14 Zehorit Sorek, "And Thou Shall be Holy," Facebook, July 17, 2017.

15 The day's transcript as it appears on Kamoha's website suggests that this was indeed the case, though note that "we love everyone" is a common trope that does not signal acceptance or tolerance but rather references a framework that views homosexuality as a transgression (see chapter 4). "Conference Summary," Kamoha, www.kamoha.org.il.

16 Zehorit had been a candidate for Israel's Parliament for Yesh Atid, a centrist party that supports LGBTQ+ rights and religious pluralism.

17 Amichai Eliyahu, "Rabbi Eliyahu Responds to the Religious LGBT Person: Struggle and Win," *Srugim*, July 18, 2017, www.srugim.co.il.

18 A particularly extensive conversation unfolded on the page of a now defunct Orthodox feminist group, "I'm an Orthodox Feminist with No Sense of Humor."

19 Zehorit Sorek, "And Thou Shall Be Holy," Facebook, July 17, 2017.

20 Muñoz, *Disidentifications*, 11–12.

21 Kobi Nachshoni, "Confrontation in the Studio: The Religious Lesbian versus the Rabbis," *Ynet*, July 19, 2017, www.ynet.co.il.

22 See Rabbi Eliyahu's op-ed above. Dr. Shulamit Ben Sha'ia said at the women's conference, per a summary of the day's proceedings, "We have undergone a revolution in our approach to the topic. Five years ago those gathered here would not have thought that we should speak about it in the educational system." "Conference Summary," Kamoha, www.kamoha.org.il.

23 Jeremy Sharon, "Anti-LGBT Noam Party Set to Run in September Election," *Jerusalem Post*, July 17, 2019, www.jpost.com.

24 Allison Kaplan Sommer, "Meet the Israeli Political Party Waging a Holy War Against the LGBTQ Community," *Haaretz*, August 30, 2019, www.haaretz.co.il.

25 Links have been removed from YouTube and Facebook, but the video can be accessed through the nationalist-Orthodox affiliated Channel 7: Tal Polon, "Watch: New Religious Zionist Party's First Campaign Video," *7 Israel National News*, July 19, 2014, www.israelnationalnews.com.

26 Stewart, *Power Worshippers*.

27 Religious LGBTQ Confessions, "#6071," Facebook, August 13, 2019.

28 Religious LGBTQ Confessions, "#6158," Facebook, August 28, 2019; Religious LGBTQ Confessions, "#6159," Facebook, August 28, 2019.

29 Religious LGBTQ Confessions, "#6166," Facebook, August 26, 2019.

30 Religious LGBTQ Confessions, "#6166," Facebook, August 26, 2019.

31 Religious LGBTQ Confessions, "#6164," Facebook, August 29, 2019.

32 Zehorit Sorek, "Noam Party," Facebook, July 18, 2019.

33 Kobi Handelsman, "Noam Party," Facebook, August 9, 2019.

34 Religious LGBTQ Confessions, "#6139," Facebook, August 27, 2019.

35 Nadav Schwartz, "Noam Party," Facebook, August 29, 2019.

36 Roee Alman, "This Is What Happened to Jerusalem Residents Who Decided to Stand with a Pride Flag at the *Machne Yehuda* Market," *Ynet*, September 7, 2019, https://jerusalem.mynet.co.il.

37 Religious LGBTQ Confessions, "#6221," Facebook, September 9, 2019.

38 Religious LGBTQ Confessions, "#5937," Facebook, July 19, 2019.

39 Religious LGBTQ Confessions, "#6136," Facebook, August 22, 2019.

40 Religious LGBTQ Confessions, "#6162," Facebook, August 29, 2019.

41 Religious LGBTQ Confessions, "#6166," Facebook, August 26, 2019.

42 Michal Schonberg, "Yesterday We Protested at the *Knesset* during Its Swearing in Ceremony," Facebook, April 7, 2021.

43 Eliq Oster, "Where Will I Have Space?," Facebook, March 24, 2019.

44 Yivniya Kaplahon, "Come March with Me," Facebook, July 15, 2016.

45 Shlomo Puterkovsky, "Rabbi Amar: Netanyahu's Support for the Parade Is an Embarrassment," *Channel 7*, July 21, 2016, www.inn.co.il.

46 For background, see Adelman, "Politics of Gay Pride in Jerusalem."

47 Yaki Admor, "Zionist Rabbis' Letter: 'The Perverts Have Been Turned into Heroes,'" *Walla*, July 26, 2018, https://news.walla.co.il.

48 Moshe Vistoch, "A Counter Reaction: Rabbis in Support of the LGBT Community," *Kipa*, July 31, 2018, www.kipa.co.il.

49 Jerusalem Open House, "We Will Not Be Deterred," Facebook, July 25, 2018.

50 Bruce, *Pride Parades*.

51 When the Jerusalem Open House announced the 2017 parade's theme—LGBT and religion—its page was flooded with critical responses. For coverage of the fallout, see "For and Against: Jerusalem Pride Parade Theme Religion and LGBT," *Ynet*, May 22, 2017, www.ynet.co.il, and "We Are Proud of the Theme," Jerusalem Open House, May 25, 2017.

52 Ron Yosef, "Why We Won't March Proudly," *Ynet*, June 11, 2010, www.ynet.co.il.

53 Even allies such as the Rabbanit Malka Puterkovsky and Rabbi Benny Lau have publicly criticized participation in parades. Kobi Nachshoni, "Liberal Rabbi to Orthodox *Hommos*: 'No to Pride Parades,'" *Ynet*, June 12, 2014, www.ynet.co.il.

54 Ariella Matar, "Why I, a Straight Woman, Will March in the Pride Parade," *Kipa*, August 1, 2017, www.kipa.co.il. The group garnered mainstream coverage; Atila Shompalby, "The Straight Orthodox Persons Marching in the Parade to Avoid Another Shlisel," *Ynet*, August 3, 2017, www.ynet.co.il.

55 Ariella Matar, "I Appreciate the Support," Facebook, June 29, 2017.

56 Ghaziani, Taylor, and Stone, "Cycles of Sameness"; Warner, *Acts of Gaiety*.

CONCLUSION

Epigraph: The full speech is available on YouTube: Kehilat Ramban, YouTube, August 1, 2015, www.youtube.com/watch?v=d3bYDVMggNI.

1 Shoval, "Penitence," Facebook, October 8, 2016, www.facebook.com.

2 Chapters 4 and 5 recount other prominent events that year.

3 Taragin-Zeller, "A Rabbi of One's Own?"; Ettinger, *Undone*.

4 Moshe Vistoch, "Why I Participated in a Wedding of *Hommos*: Rabbi Lau Explains," *Kipa*, January 18, 2018, www.kipa.co.il.

5 Published on his Facebook Page on July 20, 2020, under the title "For the Torah."

6 Amir Ben David, "Gush Etzion Faces the LGBT Struggle for the First Time," *Zman Israel*, June 27, 2019, www.zman.co.il.

7 For example, Bat Kol founder Abigail Sperber's father is a well-known and highly regarded progressive Orthodox rabbi; her mother was also instrumental in launching Tehila's support for Orthodox parents.

8 A large literature considers how familiarity and positive interaction with marginalized, stigmatized groups can substantially reduce prejudice among individuals and shape societal attitudes. See the overview in Polletta and Gardner, "Narrative and Social Movements."

9 In *Out in Africa*, Currier discusses a similar dynamic in the case of South African and Namibian LGBT activists who encounter claims that homosexuality is un-African and therefore deny their existence. Like Kadag activists, these African activists assert themselves to be proud and Namibian by leaning into context-specific (as opposed to secular or Western) terms, in effect insulating an African imaginary from Western cultural and political incursions.

10 Lorde, *Master's Tools*.

11 On this idea, see Ross, *Expanding the Palace of Torah*.

12 A summary of Rabbi Harel's comments at the And Thou Shall Be Holy conference, "Conference Summary," July 17, 2017, as reported on Kamoha's website, www.kamoha.org.il. I heard similar critiques from other rabbis I interviewed.

13 Avichai Abarbanel, "A New Generation," Facebook, February 16, 2019.

14 Havruta, "Solidarity," Facebook, July 2, 2020.

15 Gross, "Politics of LGBT Rights" and "Israeli GLBT Politics"; Hartal, "Israel's LGBT Movement"; Hartal and Misgav, "Queer Urban Trauma"; Schulman *Israel/ Palestine and the Queer International*; Ziv, "Performative Politics."

16 Yacobi, *Israel and Africa*.

17 See responses to the thread: Havruta, "Solidarity," Facebook, July 2, 2020.

18 Aguda, "In Support," Facebook, July 9, 2020.

19 Amir Ben David, "Gush Etzion Faces the LGBT Struggle for the First Time," *Zman Israel*, June 27, 2019, www.zman.co.il.

20 See Lockhart, "Gay Right."

21 Religious LGBTQ Confessions, "#5590," Facebook, June 17, 2019.

22 Compartmentalization implies a temporal separation (a heterosexually married man claims a heterosexual identity and pursues occasional extramarital same-sex liaisons), while integration hinges on combining identities (a same-sex wedding performed by a clergy member). In this schema, identity integration is the most desirable outcome because it alleviates conflict and integrates religiosity and sexual orientation identity into a single, positive identity. See Wedow et al., "'I'm Gay and I'm Catholic.'"

23 Previous scholarship has documented how LGBT persons of faith respond to their religious tradition from within, but few studies have considered how these responses result in such new categories. For some exceptions, see Bates, *Religious Despite Religion*; Wilcox, "Religion of One's Own" and *Queer Religiosities*; and, more recently, Golriz, "'I Am Enough.'"

24 Halperin, *How to Be Gay*.

25 Muñoz, *Cruising Utopia*, 121.

26 Muñoz, *Cruising Utopia*, 2.

27 Yael Mishali, "*Hommos*, Don't wait for the Rabbi," *Ynet*, December 29, 2008, www.ynet.co.il.

BIBLIOGRAPHY

Adelman, Madelaine. "The Politics of Gay Pride in Jerusalem." In *Jerusalem: Conflict and Cooperation in a Contested City*, edited by Madelaine Adelman and Miriam Fendius Elman, 233–60. Syracuse, NY: Syracuse University Press, 2014.

Adler, Adir, and Adital Ben-Ari. "'How We Stay Together Without Going Crazy': Reconstruction of Reality among Women of Mixed-Orientation Relationships." *Journal of Homosexuality* 65, no. 5 (2018): 640–58. https://doi.org/10.1080/00918369.2017.1333807.

Alempijevic, Djordje, Rusudan Beriashvili, Jonathan Beynon, Bettina Birmanns, Marie Brasholt, Juliet Cohen, Maximo Duque, et al. "Statement on Conversion Therapy." *Journal of Forensic and Legal Medicine* 72 (2020): 101930. https://doi.org/10.1016/j.jflm.2020.101930.

Althaus-Reid, Marcella. *Indecent Theology: Theological Perversions in Sex, Gender and Politics*. London: Routledge, 2010.

———. *The Queer God*. London: Routledge, 2003.

Amenta, Edwin, and Francesca Polletta. "The Cultural Impacts of Social Movements." *Annual Review of Sociology* 45, no. 1 (2019): 279–99. https://doi.org/10.1146/annurev-soc-073018-022342.

Ammerman, Nancy T. "Lived Religion as an Emerging Field: An Assessment of Its Contours and Frontiers." *Nordic Journal of Religion and Society* 29, no. 2 (2016): 83–99. https://doi.org/10.18261/issn.1890-7008-2016-02-01.

———. "Rethinking Religion: Toward a Practice Approach." *American Journal of Sociology* 126, no. 1 (2020): 6–51. https://doi.org/10.1086/709779.

Anderton, Cindy L., Debra A. Pender, and Kimberly K. Asner-Self. "A Review of the Religious Identity / Sexual Orientation Identity Conflict Literature: Revisiting Festinger's Cognitive Dissonance Theory." *Journal of LGBT Issues in Counseling* 5, nos. 3–4 (2011): 259–81. https://doi.org/10.1080/15538605.2011.632745.

Asad, Talal. *Formations of the Secular: Christianity, Islam, Modernity*. Stanford, CA: Stanford University Press, 2003.

Avanza, Martina. "Using a Feminist Paradigm (Intersectionality) to Study Conservative Women: The Case of Pro-life Activists in Italy." *Politics & Gender* 16, no. 2 (2020): 552–80. https://doi.org/10.1017/S1743923X18001034.

Avishai, Orit. "'Doing Religion' in a Secular World: Women in Conservative Religions and the Question of Agency." *Gender & Society* 22, no. 4 (2008): 409–33. https://doi.org/10.1177/0891243208321019.

————. "Religious Queer People beyond Identity Conflict: Lessons from Orthodox LGBT Jews in Israel." *Journal for the Scientific Study of Religion* 59, no. 2 (2020): 360–78. https://doi.org/10.1111/jssr.12650.

Avishai, Orit, and Ayala Fader. "Introduction to the Theme." *AJS Review* 46, no. 1 (2022): 1–11. https://doi.org/10.1017/S0364009421000076.

Avishai, Orit, and Courtney Ann Irby. "Bifurcated Conversations in Sociological Studies of Religion and Gender." *Gender & Society* 31, no. 5 (2017): 647–76. https://doi.org/10.1177/0891243217725244.

Ayoub, Phillip M. *When States Come Out: Europe's Sexual Minorities and the Politics of Visibility*. London: Cambridge University Press, 2016.

Bailey, J. Michael, Paul L. Vasey, Lisa M. Diamond, S. Marc Breedlove, Eric Vilain, and Marc Epprecht. "Sexual Orientation, Controversy, and Science." *Psychological Science in the Public Interest* 17, no. 2 (2016): 45–101. https://doi.org/10.1177/1529100616637616.

Bates, Aryana F. *Religious Despite Religion: Lesbian Agency, Identity, and Spirituality at Liberation in Truth, Unity Fellowship Church, Newark*. Sunnyvale, CA: Lambert, 2011.

Batnitzky, Leora Faye. *How Judaism Became a Religion: An Introduction to Modern Jewish Thought*. Princeton, NJ: Princeton University Press, 2011.

Benack, Suzanne, and Thomas Swan. "Queer People Who Enter 'Straight' Marriages: The Academic Community's Struggle to Understand an Anomalous Choice." *Journal of Bisexuality* 16, no. 3 (2016): 312–38. https://doi.org/10.1080/15299716.2016.1167152.

Ben-Lulu, Elazar. "'Who Will Say Kaddish for Me?' The American Reform Jewish Response to HIV/AIDS." *Journal of Modern Jewish Studies* 20, no. 1 (2021): 70–94. https://doi.org/10.1080/14725886.2020.1763070.

Ben Naeh, Yaron. "Judaism and Jews on LGBT: A Historic Overview." In *LGBTQ Rights in Israel: Gender Identity, Sexual Orientation and the Law*, edited by Alon Harel, Einav Morgenstein, and Yaniv Lushinsky, 117–55. Jerusalem: Nevo, 2016. (Hebrew)

————. "Moshko the Jew and His Gay Friends: Same-Sex Sexual Relations in Ottoman Jewish Society." *Journal of Early Modern History* 9, nos. 1–2 (2005): 79–105.

Berlant, Lauren, and Michael Warner. "Sex in Public." *Critical Inquiry* 24, no. 2 (1998): 547–66.

Berlinerblau, Jacques. *Secularism: The Basics*. New York: Routledge, 2022.

Bleich, J. David. "Homosexuality." In *Judaism and Healing: Halakhic Perspectives*, 69–73. New York: Ktav, 1981.

Boellstorff, Tom. "Against State Straightism: Five Principles for Including LGBT Indonesians." *E-International Relations*, March 21, 2016. https://www.e-ir.info.

————. *Coming of Age in Second Life: An Anthropologist Explores the Virtually Human*. Princeton, NJ: Princeton University Press, 2015.

————. *The Gay Archipelago: Sexuality and Nation in Indonesia*. Princeton, NJ: Princeton University Press, 2005.

Boyarin, Daniel. *Unheroic Conduct: The Rise of Heterosexuality and the Invention of the Jewish Man*. Berkeley: University of California Press, 1997.

Brill, Alan. "What Is 'Modern' in Modern Orthodoxy?" In *Yitz Greenberg and Modern Orthodoxy: The Road Not Taken*, edited by Adam S. Ferziger, Miri Freud-Kandel, and Steven Bayme, 172–92. Brookline, MA: Academic Studies Press, 2019.

Brown, Wendy. *Regulating Aversion: Tolerance in the Age of Identity and Empire*. Princeton, NJ: Princeton University Press, 2008.

Browne, Kath, and Leela Bakshi. *Ordinary in Brighton? LGBT, Activisms and the City*. London: Routledge, 2016.

Browne, Kath, and Eduarda Ferreira, eds. *Lesbian Geographies: Gender, Place and Power*. London: Routledge, 2018.

Browne, Kath, Sally R. Munt, and Andrew Kam-Tuck Yip. *Queer Spiritual Spaces: Sexuality and Sacred Places*. London: Routledge, 2020.

Brownson, James V. *Bible, Gender, Sexuality: Reframing the Church's Debate on Same-Sex Relationships*. Grand Rapids, MI: W.B. Eerdmans, 2013.

Bruce, Katherine McFarland. *Pride Parades: How a Parade Changed the World*. New York: New York University Press, 2016.

Butler, Judith. *Precarious Life: The Powers of Mourning and Violence*. London: Verso, 2006.

Caplan, Kimmy. "Studying the Orthodox Jewish Community in Israel: Achievements, Missed Opportunities, and Challenges." *Megamot* 17 (2017): 267–90. (Hebrew)

Charmaz, Kathy. *Constructing Grounded Theory*. Thousand Oaks, CA: Sage, 2014.

Cheng, Patrick S. *Radical Love: An Introduction to Queer Theology*. New York: Seabury Books, 2011.

Cohen, Cathy J. "Punks, Bulldaggers, and Welfare Queens: The Radical Potential of Queer Politics?" *GLQ: A Journal of Lesbian and Gay Studies* 3, no. 4 (1997): 437–65. https://doi.org/10.1215/10642684-3-4-437.

———. "Straight Gay Politics: The Limits of an Ethnic Model of Inclusion." *Nomos* 39 (1997): 572–616.

Coley, Jonathan S. *Gay on God's Campus: Mobilizing for LGBT Equality at Christian Colleges and Universities*. Chapel Hill: University of North Carolina Press, 2018.

———. "Reframing, Reconciling, and Individualizing: How LGBTQ Activist Groups Shape Approaches to Religion and Sexuality." *Sociology of Religion* 81, no. 1 (2019): 45–67. https://doi.org/10.1093/socrel/srz023.

Compton, D'Lane R., Tey Meadow, and Kristen Schilt, eds. *Other, Please Specify: Queer Methods in Sociology*. Oakland: University of California Press, 2018.

Cragun, Ryan T., and J. E. Sumerau. "The Last Bastion of Sexual and Gender Prejudice? Sexualities, Race, Gender, Religiosity, and Spirituality in the Examination of Prejudice Toward Sexual and Gender Minorities." *Journal of Sex Research* 52, no. 7 (2015): 821–34. https://doi.org/10.1080/00224499.2014.925534.

Craig, Shelley L., Ashley Austin, Mariam Rashidi, and Marc Adams. "Fighting for Survival: The Experiences of Lesbian, Gay, Bisexual, Transgender, and Questioning Students in Religious Colleges and Universities." *Journal of Gay and Lesbian Social Services* 29, no. 1 (2017): 1–24. https://doi.org/10.1080/10538720.2016.1260512.

Cravens, Royal G. "Identity-Affirming Religious Experience and Political Activism among LGBT People." *Journal of Contemporary Religion* 36, no. 3 (2021): 501–24. https://doi.org/10.1080/13537903.2021.1975942.

Crenshaw, Kimberlé. "Mapping the Margins: Intersectionality, Identity Politics, and Violence against Women of Color." *Stanford Law Review* 43, no. 6 (1991): 1241. https://doi.org/10.2307/1229039.

Currier, Ashley. *Out in Africa: LGBT Organizing in Namibia and South Africa.* Minneapolis: University of Minnesota Press, 2012.

———. *Politicizing Sex in Contemporary Africa: Homophobia in Malawi.* New York: Cambridge University Press, 2018.

Dazey, Margot. "Rethinking Respectability Politics." *British Journal of Sociology* 72, no. 3 (2021): 580–93. https://doi.org/10.1111/1468-4446.12810.

Dehlin, John P., Renee V. Galliher, William S. Bradshaw, and Katherine A. Crowell. "Navigating Sexual and Religious Identity Conflict: A Mormon Perspective." *Identity* 15, no. 1 (2015): 1–22. https://doi.org/10.1080/15283488.2014.989440.

Dehlin, John P., Renee V. Galliher, William S. Bradshaw, Daniel C. Hyde, and Katherine A. Crowell. "Sexual Orientation Change Efforts among Current or Former LDS Church Members." *Journal of Counseling Psychology* 62, no. 2 (2015): 95–105. https://doi.org/10.1037/cou0000011.

Duggan, Lisa. "The New Homonormativity: The Sexual Politics of Neoliberalism." In *Materializing Democracy,* edited by Russ Castronovo and Dana D. Nelson, 175–94. Durham, NC: Duke University Press, 2002.

Dunning, Benjamin H., ed. *The Oxford Handbook of New Testament, Gender, and Sexuality.* Oxford: Oxford University Press, 2019.

Emerson, Robert M., Rachel I. Fretz, and Linda L. Shaw. *Writing Ethnographic Fieldnotes.* 2nd ed. Chicago: University of Chicago Press, 2011.

Engelstein, Gil, and Iris Rachamimov. "Crossing Borders and Demolishing Boundaries: The Connected History of the Israeli Transgender Community 1953–1986." *Journal of Modern Jewish Studies* 18, no. 2 (2019): 142–59. https://doi.org/10.1080/14725886.2019.1593696.

Englander, Yakir, and Avi Sagi. *Sexuality and the Body in the New Religious Zionist Discourse.* Brighton, MA: Academic Studies Press, 2015.

Erzen, Tanya. *Straight to Jesus: Sexual and Christian Conversions in the Ex-Gay Movement.* Berkeley: University of California Press, 2006.

Ettinger, Yair. *Undone: The Controversies Tearing Religious-Zionism Apart.* Jerusalem: Zemorah Bittan, 2019. (Hebrew)

Fader, Ayala. *Hidden Heretics: Jewish Doubt in the Digital Age.* Princeton, NJ: Princeton University Press, 2020.

Ferziger, Adam S. "Israelization and Lived Religion: Conflicting Accounts of Contemporary Judaism." *Contemporary Jewry* 40, no. 3 (2020): 403–30. https://doi.org/10.1007/s12397-020-09324-4.

———. "The Role of Reform in Israeli Orthodoxy." In *Between Jewish Tradition and Modernity: Rethinking an Old Opposition: Essays in Honor of David Ellenson,* edited by David Harry Ellenson, Michael A. Meyer, and David N. Myers, 51–66. Detroit: Wayne State University Press, 2014.

——. "Sanctuary for the Specialist: Gender and the Reconceptualization of the American Orthodox Rabbinate." *Jewish Social Studies* 23, no. 3 (2018): 1–37. https://doi.org/10.2979/jewisocistud.23.3.01.

Fetner, Tina. *How the Religious Right Shaped Lesbian and Gay Activism*. Minneapolis: University of Minnesota Press, 2008.

Franke, Catherine. "Dating the State: The Moral Hazards of Winning Gay Rights." *Columbia Human Rights Law Review* 44, no. 1 (2012): 1–46.

Freude, Leon, and Matthew Waites. "Analysing Homophobia, Xenophobia and Sexual Nationalisms in Africa: Comparing Quantitative Attitudes Data to Reveal Societal Differences." *Current Sociology* (2022). https://doi.org/10.1177/00113921221078045.

Fuist, Todd Nicholas. "'It Just Always Seemed Like It Wasn't a Big Deal, Yet I Know for Some People They Really Struggle with It': LGBT Religious Identities in Context." *Journal for the Scientific Study of Religion* 55, no. 4 (2016): 770–86. https://doi.org/10.1111/jssr.12291.

Gamson, Joshua. "Must Identity Movements Self-Destruct? A Queer Dilemma." *Social Problems* 42, no. 3 (1995): 390–407. https://doi.org/10.2307/3096854.

Ganzevoort, R. R., M. van der Laan, and E. Olsman. "Growing Up Gay and Religious: Conflict, Dialogue, and Religious Identity Strategies." *Mental Health, Religion & Culture* 14, no. 3 (2011): 209–22. https://doi.org/10.1080/13674670903452132.

Ghaziani, Amin. *The Dividends of Dissent: How Conflict and Culture Work in Lesbian and Gay Marches on Washington*. Chicago: University of Chicago Press, 2008.

——. "Post-Gay Collective Identity Construction." *Social Problems* 58, no. 1 (2011): 99–125. https://doi.org/10.1525/sp.2011.58.1.99.

Ghaziani, Amin, Verta Taylor, and Amy Stone. "Cycles of Sameness and Difference in LGBT Social Movements." *Annual Review of Sociology* 42, no. 1 (2016): 165–83. https://doi.org/10.1146/annurev-soc-073014-112352.

Gibbs, Jeremy J., and Jeremy Goldbach. "Religious Conflict, Sexual Identity, and Suicidal Behaviors among LGBT Young Adults." *Archives of Suicide Research* 19, no. 4 (2015): 472–88. https://doi.org/10.1080/13811118.2015.1004476.

Golriz, Golshan. "'I Am Enough': Why LGBTQ Muslim Groups Resist Mainstreaming." *Sexuality & Culture* 25, no. 2 (2021): 355–76. https://doi.org/10.1007/s12119-020-09773-x.

Greenberg, Steven. *Wrestling with God and Men: Homosexuality in the Jewish Tradition*. Madison: University of Wisconsin Press, 2004.

Gross, Aeyal. "Israeli GLBT Politics between Queerness and Homonationalism." *Bully Bloggers*, July 3, 2010.

——. "The Politics of LGBT Rights in Israel and Beyond: Nationality, Normativity, and Queer Politics." *Columbia Human Rights Law Review* 46, no. 2 (2015): 81–152.

Gushee, David P. *Changing Our Mind: A Call from America's Leading Evangelical Ethics Scholar for Full Acceptance of LGBT Christians in the Church*. Canton, MI: Read the Spirit Books, 2014.

Haas, Ann P., Mickey Eliason, Vickie M. Mays, Robin M. Mathy, Susan D. Cochran, Anthony R. D'Augelli, Morton M. Silverman, et al. "Suicide and Suicide Risk in Lesbian, Gay, Bisexual, and Transgender Populations: Review and Recommendations." *Journal of Homosexuality* 58, no. 1 (2010): 10–51. https://doi.org/10.1080/0091 8369.2011.534038.

Halperin, David M. *How to Be Gay*. Cambridge, MA: Harvard University Press, 2012.

———. "The Normalization of Queer Theory." *Journal of Homosexuality* 45, nos. 2–4 (2003): 339–43. https://doi.org/10.1300/J082v45n02_17.

Harel, Alon. "The Rise and Fall of the Israeli Gay Legal Revolution." *Columbia Human Rights Law Review* 31 (1999): 443–71.

Hartal, Gilly. "Gay Tourism to Tel-Aviv: Producing Urban Value?" *Urban Studies* 56, no. 6 (2019): 1148–64. https://doi.org/10.1177/0042098018755068.

———. "The Gendered Politics of Absence: Homonationalism and Gendered Power Relations in Tel Aviv's Gay-Center." In *Lesbian Geographies: Gender, Place and Power*, edited by Eduarda Ferreira, 91–112. Farnham, UK: Ashgate, 2015.

———. "Israel's LGBT Movement and Interest Groups." In *Oxford Research Encyclopedia of Politics*, October 27, 2020. https://doi.org/10.1093/acrefore/9780190228637.013.1295.

———. "Touring and Obscuring: How Sensual, Embodied and Haptic Gay Touristic Practices Construct the Geopolitics of Pinkwashing." *Social & Cultural Geography* (2020). https://doi.org/10.1080/14649365.2020.1821391.

Hartal, Gilly, and Chen Misgav. "Queer Urban Trauma and Its Spatial Politics: A Lesson from Social Movements in Tel Aviv and Jerusalem." *Urban Studies* 58, no. 7 (2021): 1463–83. https://doi.org/10.1177/0042098020918839.

Hartal, Gilly, and Orna Sasson-Levy. "Being [in] the Center: Sexual Citizenship and Homonationalism at Tel Aviv's Gay-Center." *Sexualities* 20, nos. 5–6 (2017): 738–61. https://doi.org/10.1177/1363460716645807.

———. "The Progressive Orient: Gay Tourism to Tel Aviv and Israeli Ethnicities." *Environment and Planning C: Politics and Space* 39, no. 1 (2021): 11–29. https://doi.org/10.1177/2399654419862819.

———. "Re-reading Homonationalism: An Israeli Spatial Perspective." *Journal of Homosexuality* 65, no. 10 (2018): 1391–1414. https://doi.org/10.1080/00918369.2017.1 375364.

Heiden-Rootes, Katie, Erica Hartwell, and Mary Nedela. "Comparing the Partnering, Minority Stress, and Depression for Bisexual, Lesbian, and Gay Adults from Religious Upbringings." *Journal of Homosexuality* 68, no. 14 (2021): 2323–43. https://doi.org/10.1080/00918369.2020.1804255.

Heiden-Rootes, Katie, Ashley Wiegand, Danielle Thomas, Rachel M. Moore, and Kristin A. Ross. "A National Survey on Depression, Internalized Homophobia, College Religiosity, and Climate of Acceptance on College Campuses for Sexual Minority Adults." *Journal of Homosexuality* 67, no. 4 (2020): 435–51. https://doi.org/10.1080/0 0918369.2018.1550329.

Hershkowitz, Isaac. "Rabbi Yosef Hayyim's Halakhically and Kabbalistically Based Approaches to Homosexuality: A Spatial-Traditional Study." *Jewish Studies Quarterly* 20, no. 3 (2013): 257–71.

Higginbotham, Evelyn Brooks. *Righteous Discontent: The Women's Movement in the Black Baptist Church, 1880—1920.* Cambridge, MA: Harvard University Press, 2003.

Hinze, Christine Firer, and J. Patrick Hornbeck II, eds. *More Than a Monologue: Sexual Diversity and the Catholic Church.* New York: Fordham University Press, 2014.

Hirschhorn, Sara Yael. "The Origins of the Redemption in Occupied Suburbia? The Jewish-American Makings of the West Bank Settlement of Efrat, 1973–87." *Middle Eastern Studies* 51, no. 2 (2015): 269–84. https://doi.org/10.1080/00263206.2014.941821.

Irshai, Ronit. "Homosexuality and the 'Aqedah Theology': A Comparison of Modern Orthodoxy and the Conservative Movement." *Journal of Jewish Ethics* 4, no. 1 (2018): 19–46. https://doi.org/10.5325/jjewiethi.4.1.0019.

———. "Public and Private Rulings in Jewish Law (Halakhah): Flexibility, Concealment, and Feminist Jurisprudence." *Journal of Law, Religion and State* 3, no. 1 (2014): 25–50. https://doi.org/10.1163/22124810-00301002.

Irshai, Ronit, and Tanya Zion-Waldoks. "Orthodox Feminism in Israel: Between Nomos and Narrative." *Law and Governance* 15, nos. 1–2 (2013): 233–327. (Hebrew)

Itzhaky, Haya, and Karni Kissil. "'It's a Horrible Sin. If They Find Out, I Will Not Be Able to Stay': Orthodox Jewish Gay Men's Experiences Living in Secrecy." *Journal of Homosexuality* 62, no. 5 (2015): 621–43. https://doi.org/10.1080/00918369.2014.9885 32.

Jagose, Annamarie. *Queer Theory: An Introduction.* New York: New York University Press, 1996.

Jakobsen, Janet R. *The Sex Obsession: Perversity and Possibility in American Politics.* New York: New York University Press, 2020.

Jakobsen, Janet R., and Ann Pellegrini. *Love the Sin: Sexual Regulation and the Limits of Religious Tolerance.* New York: New York University Press, 2003.

Jones, Philip Edward. "Respectability Politics and Straight Support for LGB Rights." *Political Research Quarterly* (2021). https://doi.org/10.1177/10659129211035834.

Jordan, Mark D. *Rewritten Theology: Aquinas after His Readers.* Malden, MA: Blackwell, 2006.

Joshi, Yuvraj. "Respectable Queerness." *Columbia Human Rights Law Review* 43, no. 2 (2012): 415–67.

Kama, Amit. "From 'Terra Incognita' to 'Terra Firma': The Logbook of the Voyage of Gay Men's Community into the Israeli Public Sphere." *Journal of Homosexuality* 38, no. 4 (2000): 133–62. https://doi.org/10.1300/J082v38n04_06.

Katz, Ben A. "Coming Out vs Staying Safe: Modeling the Distinct Roles of Interpersonal and Systemic Contexts in Sexual Minority Identity Disclosure." PsyArXiv, February 15, 2022. https://doi.org/10.31234/osf.io/2rpxb.

Katz, Ben A., and Orit Avishai. "Visions and Revisions: Narrative-Building among Israeli Orthodox LGB Activists." Presentation at the 126th Annual Convention of the American Psychological Association, San Francisco, 2018.

Keren-Kratz, Menachem. "The Contemporary Study of Orthodoxy: Challenging the One-Dimensional Paradigm." *Tradition: A Journal of Orthodox Jewish Thought* 49, no. 4 (2016): 24–52.

King, Michael, Joanna Semlyen, Sharon See Tai, Helen Killaspy, David Osborn, Dmitri Popelyuk, and Irwin Nazareth. "A Systematic Review of Mental Disorder, Suicide, and Deliberate Self Harm in Lesbian, Gay and Bisexual People." *BMC Psychiatry* 8, no. 1 (2008): 70. https://doi.org/10.1186/1471-244X-8-70.

Kissil, Karni, and Haya Itzhaky. "Experiences of the Marital Relationship among Orthodox Jewish Gay Men in Mixed-Orientation Marriages." *Journal of GLBT Family Studies* 11, no. 2 (2015): 151–72. https://doi.org/10.1080/1550428X.2014.900659.

Knibbe, Kim, and Helena Kupari. "Theorizing Lived Religion: Introduction." *Journal of Contemporary Religion* 35, no. 2 (2020): 157–76. https://doi.org/10.1080/13537903.2020.1759897.

Knust, Jennifer Wright. *Unprotected Texts: The Bible's Surprising Contradictions about Sex and Desire.* New York: HarperOne, 2012.

Koren, Irit. *A Closet within a Closet: The Stories of Religious Homosexuals and Lesbians.* Tel Aviv: Yediot Achronot, 2003. (Hebrew)

Kosman, Aadmiel, and Anat Sharbat. "'Two Women Who Were Sporting with Each Other': A Reexamination of the Halakhic Approaches to Lesbianism as a Touchstone for Homosexuality in General." *Hebrew Union College Annual* 75 (2004): 37–73.

Lau, Benny. "On Same-Sex Couples in the Orthodox Jewish Community." *Times of Israel,* December 11, 2020.

Lefevor, G. Tyler, Edward B. Davis, Jaqueline Y. Paiz, and Abigail C. P. Smack. "The Relationship between Religiousness and Health among Sexual Minorities: A Meta-Analysis." *Psychological Bulletin* 147, no. 7 (2021): 647–66. https://doi.org/10.1037/bul0000321.

Legerski, Elizabeth, Anita Harker, Catherine Jeppsen, Andrew Armstrong, John P. Dehlin, Kelly Troutman, and Renee V. Galliher. "Mormon Mixed-Orientation Marriages: Variations in Attitudes and Experiences by Sexual Orientation and Current Relationship Status." *Journal of GLBT Family Studies* 13, no. 2 (2017): 186–209. https://doi.org/10.1080/1550428X.2016.1159163.

Leon, Nissim. "The Ethnic Structuring of 'Sephardim' in Haredi Society in Israel." *Jewish Social Studies* 22, no. 1 (2016): 130–60.

Lightsey, Pamela R. *Our Lives Matter: A Womanist Queer Theology.* Eugene, OR: Pickwick, 2015.

Linneman, Thomas John. *Weathering Change: Gays and Lesbians, Christian Conservatives, and Everyday Hostilities.* New York: New York University Press, 2003.

Lockhart, Jeffrey W. "The Gay Right: A Framework for Understanding Right Wing LGBT Organizations." *Journal of Homosexuality.* https://doi.org/10.1080/00918369.2022.2086749.

Lorde, Audre. *The Master's Tools Will Never Dismantle the Master's House.* London: Penguin, 2018.

Lubitch, Ronen. "Disgust or Permissiveness: Judaism's Approach to Homosexuality." *Deot* 11 (2001): 9–15. (Hebrew)

———. "Judaism's Position on Same-Sex Relationships and Guidelines for Applying It in Education." *Mayim Me-Dalyav* 6 (1995): 233–51. (Hebrew)

———. "To Strive so as to Not Drown: Treatment of Orthodox Homosexuals: The Challenge for Us." *Deot* 50 (2010). (Hebrew)

Machtei Samov, Itay Chay, and Yael Yishai. "Fragmented Citizenship in a Religious-National Democracy: Homosexuals in Israel." *Citizenship Studies* 22, no. 1 (2018): 70–85. https://doi.org/10.1080/13621025.2017.1414154.

Mahmood, Saba. *Religious Difference in a Secular Age: A Minority Report.* Princeton, NJ: Princeton University Press, 2016.

Martin, James. *Building a Bridge: How the Catholic Church and the LGBT Community Can Enter into a Relationship of Respect, Compassion, and Sensitivity.* Rev. ed. New York: HarperOne, 2018.

McQueeney, Krista. "'We Are God's Children, Y'All': Race, Gender, and Sexuality in Lesbian- and Gay-Affirming Congregations." *Social Problems* 56, no. 1 (2009): 151–73. https://doi.org/10.1525/sp.2009.56.1.151.

Mevorach, Oria. "LGBT and the Institution of the Family." *Deot* 75 (2016).

Meyer, Ilan H. "Prejudice, Social Stress, and Mental Health in Lesbian, Gay, and Bisexual Populations: Conceptual Issues and Research Evidence." *Psychological Bulletin* 129, no. 5 (2003): 674–97. https://doi.org/10.1037/0033-2909.129.5.674.

———. "Resilience in the Study of Minority Stress and Health of Sexual and Gender Minorities." *Psychology of Sexual Orientation and Gender Diversity* 2, no. 3 (2015): 209–13. https://doi.org/10.1037/sgd0000132.

Mikulak, Magdalena. "Between the Market and the Hard Place: Neoliberalization and the Polish LGBT Movement." *Social Movement Studies* 18, no. 5 (2019): 550–65. https://doi.org/10.1080/14742837.2019.1598353.

Miller, Daniel. "Digital Anthropology." In *Cambridge Encyclopedia of Anthropology*, 2018. https://www.anthroencyclopedia.com/entry/digital-anthropology.

Misgav, Chen. "With the Current, Against the Wind: Constructing Spatial Activism and Radical Politics in the Tel-Aviv Gay Center." *ACME: An International Journal for Critical Geographies* 14, no. 4 (2015). www.acme-journal.org.

Mizrachi, Avishai. "Between Denial and Recognition of Homosexuality: Analysis of Orthodox Zionist Rabbinic Rulings." Thesis, Bar Ilan University, 2020.

Moon, Dawne. "Beyond the Dichotomy: Six Religious Views of Homosexuality." *Journal of Homosexuality* 61, no. 9 (2014): 1215–41. https://doi.org/10.1080/00918369.2014.926762.

Moon, Dawne, and Theresa W. Tobin. "Sunsets and Solidarity: Overcoming Sacramental Shame in Conservative Christian Churches to Forge a Queer Vision of Love and Justice." *Hypatia* 33, no. 3 (2018): 451–68. https://doi.org/10.1111/hypa.12413.

Moon, Dawne, Theresa W. Tobin, and J. E. Sumerau. "Alpha, Omega, and the Letters in Between: LGBTQI Conservative Christians Undoing Gender." *Gender & Society* 33, no. 4 (2019): 583–606. https://doi.org/10.1177/0891243219846592.

Morrison, David. *The Gush: Center of Modern Religious Zionism*. Jerusalem: Gefen, 2018.

Moussawi, Ghassan. *Disruptive Situations: Fractal Orientalism and Queer Strategies in Beirut*. Philadelphia: Temple University Press, 2020.

Mowlabocus, Sharif. *Interrogating Homonormativity*. New York: Springer, 2021.

Muñoz, José Esteban. *Cruising Utopia: The Then and There of Queer Futurity*. 10th anniv. ed. New York: New York University Press, 2019.

——. *Disidentifications: Queers of Color and the Performance of Politics*. Minneapolis: University of Minnesota Press, 1999.

Munro, Brenna, and Gemma Pérez-Sánchez. "Introduction: Thinking Queer Activism Transnationally." *S&F Online* 14, no. 2 (2017).

Murib, Zein. "Trumpism, Citizenship, and the Future of the LGBTQ Movement." *Politics & Gender* 14, no. 4 (2018): 649–72. https://doi.org/10.1017/S1743923X18000740.

Navon, Haim. "Empathy Is Not Legitimacy." *Shabbat*, 2013.

Orne, Jason. "'You Will Always Have to "Out" Yourself': Reconsidering Coming out through Strategic Outness." *Sexualities* 14, no. 6 (2012): 681–703.

Oswin, Natalie. "Critical Geographies and the Uses of Sexuality: Deconstructing Queer Space." *Progress in Human Geography* 32, no. 1 (2008): 89–103. https://doi.org/10.1177/0309132507085213.

——. "The End of Queer (as We Knew It): Globalization and the Making of a Gay-Friendly South Africa." *Gender, Place & Culture* 14, no. 1 (2007): 93–110. https://doi.org/10.1080/09663690601122358.

Otis, Hailey N., and Thomas R. Dunn. "Queer Worldmaking." In *Oxford Research Encyclopedia of Communication*, 2021. https://doi.org/10.1093/acrefore/9780190228613.013.1235.

Padva, Gilad. "Gay Martyrs, Jewish Saints and Infatuated Yeshiva Boys in the New Israeli Religious Queer Cinema." *Journal of Modern Jewish Studies* 10, no. 3 (2011): 421–38. https://doi.org/10.1080/14725886.2011.608558.

Page, Sarah-Jane, and Heather Shipley. *Religion and Sexualities: Theories, Themes and Methodologies*. New York: Routledge, 2020.

Petro, Anthony Michael. *After the Wrath of God: AIDS, Sexuality, and American Religion*. Oxford: Oxford University Press, 2015.

Plöderl, Martin, and Pierre Tremblay. "Mental Health of Sexual Minorities. A Systematic Review." *International Review of Psychiatry* 27, no. 5 (2015): 367–85. https://doi.org/10.3109/09540261.2015.1083949.

Plummer, Kenneth. *Telling Sexual Stories: Power, Change, and Social Worlds*. London: Routledge, 1995.

Polletta, Francesca, and Beth Gharrity Gardner. "Narrative and Social Movements." In *The Oxford Handbook of Social Movements*, edited by Donatella Della Porta and Mario Diani. Oxford: Oxford University Press, 2015. https://doi.org/10.1093/oxfordhb/9780199678402.013.32.

Prins, Michal. *To Simply Want: A Guide for Marital Intimacy*. Self pub., 2021. (Hebrew)

Puar, Jasbir K. "Rethinking Homonationalism." *International Journal of Middle East Studies* 45, no. 2 (2013): 336–39. https://doi.org/10.1017/S002074381300007X.

———. *Terrorist Assemblages: Homonationalism in Queer Times*. Durham, NC: Duke University Press, 2007.

Quinan, Christine. "Safe Space." In *Critical Concepts in Queer Studies and Education*, edited by Nelson M. Rodriguez, Wayne Martino, Jennifer C. Ingrey, and Edward Brockenbrough, 361–68. New York: Palgrave Macmillan, 2016.

Raboin, Thibaut. "Exhortations of Happiness: Liberalism and Nationalism in the Discourses on LGBTI Asylum Rights in the UK." *Sexualities* 20, nos. 5–6 (2017): 663–81. https://doi.org/10.1177/1363460716645802.

Raucher, Michal. "Rabbis with Skirts: Orthodox Female Clergy Embodying Religious Authority." *AJS Perspectives*, Fall 2019, 48–50.

Ritchie, Jason. "Pinkwashing, Homonationalism, and Israel-Palestine: The Conceits of Queer Theory and the Politics of the Ordinary." *Antipode* 47, no. 3 (2015): 616–34. https://doi.org/10.1111/anti.12100.

Ross, Tamar. *Expanding the Palace of Torah: Orthodoxy and Feminism*. 2nd ed. Waltham, MA: Brandeis University Press, 2021.

———. "Halacha as Event: The Halachic Status of Homosexuals Today as a Test Case." In *The Halacha as Event*, edited by Avinoam Rosenak. Jerusalem: Magnus, 2016. (Hebrew)

Rubin, Gayle. "Thinking Sex: Notes for a Radical Theory of the Politics of Sexuality." In *Deviations*, 137–81. Durham, NC: Duke University Press, 2012. https://doi.org/10.1215/9780822394068-006.

Sagi, Avi. "Does Religious Zionism Still Exist?" In *Religious Zionism: History, Ideas, Society*, edited by Dov Schwartz, 13–49. Ramat Gan, Israel: Bar Ilan University, 2021. (Hebrew)

———. "Orthodoxy as a Problem." In *Jewish Orthodoxy: New Perspectives*, edited by Yosef Shalmon, Aaviezer Reviski, and Adam S. Ferziger, 21–54. Jerusalem: Magnus, 2006. (Hebrew)

Salmon, Yosef, Aviezer Ravitsky, and Adam S. Ferziger, eds. *Orthodox Judaism*. Jerusalem: Magnus, 2006.

Satlow, Michael L. "'They Abused Him Like a Woman': Homoeroticism, Gender Blurring, and the Rabbis in Late Antiquity." *Journal of the History of Sexuality* 5, no. 1 (1994): 1–25.

Savci, Evren. *Queer in Translation: Sexual Politics under Neoliberal Islam*. Durham, NC: Duke University Press, 2021.

Schulman, Sarah. *Israel/Palestine and the Queer International*. Durham, NC: Duke University Press, 2012.

Schwartz, Dov. *Religious Zionism: History, Thought, Society*. Ramat Gan, Israel: Bar Ilan University, 2021.

Seitz, David K. *A House of Prayer for All People: Contesting Citizenship in a Queer Church*. Minneapolis: University of Minnesota Press, 2017.

Shalmon, Yosef, Aaviezer Reviski, and Adam S. Ferziger, eds. *Jewish Orthodoxy: New Perspectives.* Jerusalem: Magnus, 2006. (Hebrew)

Sheleg, Yair. *From Kosher Inspector to the Driver's Seat? Religious Zionism and Israeli Society.* Jerusalem: Israel Democracy Institute, 2019. (Hebrew)

Shvidel, Ze'ev. "The Others Within: On the Place of Religious Homolesbians in the Orthodox Community." *Akademot* 17 (2006): 81–110. (Hebrew)

Slomowitz, Alan, and Alison Feit, eds. *Homosexuality, Transsexuality, Psychoanalysis and Traditional Judaism.* New York: Routledge, 2019.

Sowe, Babucarr J., Jac Brown, and Alan J. Taylor. "Sex and the Sinner: Comparing Religious and Nonreligious Same-Sex Attracted Adults on Internalized Homonegativity and Distress." *American Journal of Orthopsychiatry* 84, no. 5 (2014): 530–44. https://doi.org/10.1037/ort0000021.

Stelder, Mikki. "'From the Closet into the Knesset': Zionist Sexual Politics and the Formation of Settler Subjectivity." *Settler Colonial Studies* 8, no. 4 (2018): 442–63. https://doi.org/10.1080/2201473X.2017.1361885.

Stewart, Katherine. *Power Worshippers: Inside the Dangerous Rise of Religious Nationalism.* New York: Bloomsbury, 2021.

Stuhlsatz, Greta L., Shane A. Kavanaugh, Ashley B. Taylor, Tricia K. Neppl, and Brenda J. Lohman. "Spirituality and Religious Engagement, Community Involvement, Outness, and Family Support: Influence on LGBT+ Muslim Well-Being." *Journal of Homosexuality* 68, no. 7 (2021): 1083–1105. https://doi.org/10.1080/00918369.2021.1888585.

Sumerau, J. E. "'That's What a Man Is Supposed to Do': Compensatory Manhood Acts in an LGBT Christian Church." *Gender & Society* 26, no. 3 (2012): 461–87.

Sumerau, J. E., Ryan T. Cragun, and Lain A. B. Mathers. "Contemporary Religion and the Cisgendering of Reality." *Social Currents* 3, no. 3 (2016): 293–311. https://doi.org/10.1177/2329496515604644.

Taragin-Zeller, Lea. "'Conceiving God's Children': Toward a Flexible Model of Reproductive Decision-Making." *Medical Anthropology* 38, no. 4 (2019): 370–83. https://doi.org/10.1080/01459740.2019.1570191.

———. "A Rabbi of One's Own? Navigating Religious Authority and Ethical Freedom in Everyday Judaism." *American Anthropologist* 123, no. 4 (2021): 833–45. https://doi.org/10.1111/aman.13603.

———. "Towards an Anthropology of Doubt: The Case of Religious Reproduction in Orthodox Judaism." *Journal of Modern Jewish Studies* 18, no. 1 (2019): 1–20. https://doi.org/10.1080/14725886.2018.1521182.

Taragin-Zeller, Lea, and Ben Kasstan. "'I Didn't Know How to Be with My Husband': State-Religion Struggles over Sex Education in Israel and England." *Anthropology & Education Quarterly* 52, no. 1 (2021): 5–20. https://doi.org/10.1111/aeq.12358.

Taylor, Verta A., and Mary Bernstein, eds. *The Marrying Kind? Debating Same-Sex Marriage within the Lesbian and Gay Movement.* Minneapolis: University of Minnesota Press, 2013.

Taylor, Yvette, and Karen Cuthbert. "Queer Religious Youth in Faith and Community Schools." *Educational Review* 71, no. 3 (2019): 382–96. https://doi.org/10.1080/00131 911.2017.1423279.

Thoreson, Ryan Richard. *Transnational LGBT Activism: Working for Sexual Rights Worldwide.* Minneapolis: University of Minnesota Press, 2014.

Thornicroft, Graham, Nisha Mehta, Sarah Clement, Sara Evans-Lacko, Mary Doherty, Diana Rose, Mirja Koschorke, Rahul Shidhaye, Claire O'Reilly, and Claire Henderson. "Evidence for Effective Interventions to Reduce Mental-Health-Related Stigma and Discrimination." *Lancet* 387, no. 10023 (2016): 1123–32. https://doi.org/10.1016/ S0140-6736(15)00298-6.

Tindall, David B. "Networks as Constraints and Opportunities." In *The Oxford Handbook of Social Movements,* edited by Donatella Della Porta and Mario Diani. Oxford: Oxford University Press, 2015. https://doi.org/10.1093/ oxfordhb/9780199678402.013.34.

Tobin, Theresa W., and Dawne Moon. "The Politics of Shame in the Motivation to Virtue: Lessons from the Shame, Pride, and Humility Experiences of LGBT Conservative Christians and Their Allies." *Journal of Moral Education* 48, no. 1 (2019): 109–25. https://doi.org/10.1080/03057240.2018.1534088.

Tonstad, Linn Marie. *Queer Theology: Beyond Apologetics.* Eugene, OR: Cascade Books, 2018.

Vines, Matthew. *God and the Gay Christian: The Biblical Case in Support of Same-Sex Relationships.* New York: Convergent Books, 2015.

Warner, Michael. *The Trouble with Normal: Sex, Politics, and the Ethics of Queer Life.* New York: Free Press, 1999.

Warner, Sara. *Acts of Gaiety: LGBT Performance and the Politics of Pleasure.* Ann Arbor: University of Michigan Press, 2013.

Wedow, Robbee, Landon Schnabel, Lindsey K. D. Wedow, and Mary Ellen Konieczny. "'I'm Gay and I'm Catholic': Negotiating Two Complex Identities at a Catholic University." *Sociology of Religion* 78, no. 3 (2017): 289–317. https://doi.org/10.1093/ socrel/srx028.

Wilcox, Melissa M. *Queer Religiosities: An Introduction to Queer and Transgender Studies in Religion.* Lanham, MD: Rowman & Littlefield, 2021.

———. "A Religion of One's Own: Gender and LGBT Religiosities." In *Gay Religion,* edited by Scott Thumma and Edward R. Gray, 203–20. Walnut Creek, CA: AltaMira Press, 2005.

Wilde, Melissa J. "Complex Religion: Interrogating Assumptions of Independence in the Study of Religion." *Sociology of Religion* 79, no. 3 (2018): 287–98. https://doi. org/10.1093/socrel/srx047.

Winer, Canton, and Catherine Bolzendahl. "Conceptualizing Homonationalism: (Re) Formulation, Application, and Debates of Expansion." *Sociology Compass* 15, no. 5 (2021). https://doi.org/10.1111/soc4.12853.

Wolff, Joshua R., Heather L. Himes, Sabrina D. Soares, and Ellen Miller Kwon. "Sexual Minority Students in Non-affirming Religious Higher Education: Mental Health,

Outness, and Identity." *Psychology of Sexual Orientation and Gender Diversity* 3, no. 2 (2016): 201–12. https://doi.org/10.1037/sgd0000162.

Wulff, Stephen, Mary Bernstein, and Verta Taylor. "New Theoretical Directions from the Study of Gender and Sexuality Movements." In *The Oxford Handbook of Social Movements*, edited by Donatella Della Porta and Mario Diani. Oxford: Oxford University Press, 2015. https://doi.org/10.1093/oxfordhb/9780199678402.013.59.

Yacobi, Haim. *Israel and Africa: A Genealogy of Moral Geography*. New York: Routledge, 2019.

Yip, Andrew Kam-Tuck. "Queering Religious Texts: An Exploration of British Non-heterosexual Christians' and Muslims' Strategy of Constructing Sexuality-Affirming Hermeneutics." *Sociology* 39, no. 1 (2005): 47–65. https://doi.org/10.1177/0038038505049000.

———. "When Religion Meets Sexuality: Two Tales of Intersections." In *Religion and Sexuality: Diversity and the Limits of Tolerance*, edited by Pamela Dickey Young, Tracy J. Trothen, and Heather Shipley. Vancouver: University of British Columbia Press, 2015.

Yuval-Davis, Nira. "Belonging and the Politics of Belonging." *Patterns of Prejudice* 40, no. 3 (2006): 197–214. https://doi.org/10.1080/00313220600769331.

———. "Situated Intersectionality and Social Inequality." *Raisons politiques* 58, no. 2 (2015): 91. https://doi.org/10.3917/rai.058.0091.

Zack, Eyal. *Between the Creator and Desire: The Secret Lives of Religious Gay Men Married to a Woman*. Tel Aviv: Resling, 2019. (Hebrew)

Zack, Eyal, and Adital Ben-Ari. "'Men Are for Sex and Women Are for Marriage': On the Duality in the Lives of Jewish Religious Gay Men Married to Women." *Journal of GLBT Family Studies* 15, no. 4 (2019): 395–413. https://doi.org/10.1080/15504 28X.2018.1506374.

Zanghellini, Aleardo. "Are Gay Rights Islamophobic? A Critique of Some Uses of the Concept of Homonationalism in Activism and Academia." *Social & Legal Studies* 21, no. 3 (2012): 357–74. https://doi.org/10.1177/0964663911435282.

Zion-Waldoks, Tanya. "'Family Resemblance' and Its Discontents: Towards the Study of Orthodoxy's Politics of Belonging and Lived Orthodoxies in Israel." *AJS Review* 46, no. 1 (2022): 12–37. https://doi.org/10.1017/S0364009421000076.

———. "Politics of Devoted Resistance: Agency, Feminism, and Religion among Orthodox Agunah Activists in Israel." *Gender & Society* 29, no. 1 (2015): 73–97. https://doi.org/10.1177/0891243214549353.

Ziv, Amalya. "Performative Politics in Israeli Queer Anti-occupation Activism." *GLQ: A Journal of Lesbian and Gay Studies* 16, no. 4 (2010): 537–56.

INDEX

Abarbanel, Avichai, 130, 232, 245, 270n12, 273n13

activism: Bat Kol and, 2, 27, 36, 40, 44, 49, 61, 111–12; beginnings of, 28; and Beit Hillel policy paper, 150–56; defining, 240–41; diversity of, 224–27; engagement with rabbis, 142–43; establishing a movement (2009–15), 44; everyday living as a form of, 7, 9, 110–12, 121–22, 127, 148–50, 165, 197, 229–33, 240–43; Havruta and, 40, 54, 61, 198; in hostile Orthodox settings, 197–200; in Israel, 29–32; Kadag and, xii, 2, 4, 65, 165, 173, 185–87, 195, 201, 203, 207–8, 211, 214–16, 218–20, 222, 225–27, 234, 241; legal and cultural achievements of, 29–30; moderate/complicit vs. transformative, 5–9, 30–32, 200–201, 212–19, 229–33, 235; Pesach Sheni initiative and, 183–84; prominent role of gay cis men in, 4, 30, 132, 153, 227; and right-wing politics, 205–8; Shoval and, 66, 173, 268n16; tensions within, 30–31; visibility as a form of, 215, 219–20, 225, 230–31. *See also* Kadag; outreach/education

Adler, Miriam, 185

Africa, 8, 249n39, 273n9

Aguda (Association for LGBTQ Equality in Israel), 30–31, 32, 34, 233, 234

Alexander, Ilil, 41

aliya (ritual), 88, 112, 132, 153

Alon Shvut (settlement), 187–89

Amar (rabbi), 247n2, 270n3,

Aqedah (theology of binding), 121, 140

Argaman (formerly Ashkenazi), Eran, 200, 245, 260n1

Argaman (formerly Grossman), Moshe, 66, 194, 219, 220, 221, 235, 245

Ariel, 105

Arman, Uri, 194–95

Ashkenazi, Eran. *See* Argaman (formerly Ashkenazi), Eran

Ashkenazim: allied rabbis as, 132; and homosexuality, 136; in LGBT organizations, 29, 32, 60, 64, 227; in Our Faces campaign, 257n62; privileged status of, 29, 32, 47, 223, 227

Attias, Tehila, 49–50

authenticity. *See* politics of authenticity

Aviner, Shlomo, xi, 33–34, 36, 42, 94, 136

Azat Nefesh, 33, 35–36, 39, 42–45, 54, 69, 90, 97

Banki, Shira, 44, 61, 65, 143, 221, 258n62

Barak, Ehud, 8, 233

Barash, Nechama, 186

Bar/Bat Mitzvahs, 69, 79, 111, 112, 166, 175, 193

Bar Ilan University, 157, 162, 166

Bar Noar shooting, 31, 46, 55

Bat Kol: activism of, 2, 27, 36, 40, 44, 49, 61, 111–12; and Beit Hillel policy paper, 155; as bridge between Orthodox and LGBT communities, 51–52, 215; expansion of mission of, 49, 53, 253n74, 256n45; and feminism, 49, 52, 265n60; finances of, 49, 51; founding and early years of, 27, 28, 37–38; goals of, 49–50;

JOH. *See* Jerusalem Open House
Jonas, Daniel, 59, 63, 130, 194–95, 218, 245, 270n12
Journey into Manhood, 97

Kadag: activism of, xii, 2, 4, 65, 147, 165, 173, 185–87, 195, 201, 203, 207–8, 211, 214–16, 218–20, 222, 225–27, 234, 241; and Beit Hillel policy paper, 150–51, 153, 155–56; as bridge between Orthodox and LGBT communities, 63–64, 126, 186; characteristics of leaders of, 29, 47, 226–27; as complicit vs. transformative, 4, 5–8, 10–11, 212–19, 229–33; and conservative organizations, 196; constituent organizations of, 61, 226; conversion therapy opposed by, 60, 98, 259n24; criticisms of, 223–24, 235; demographics of, 64; engagement with rabbis by, 140–45; goals/values of, 4, 5, 131, 167, 201, 227; and issues of sexual and gender identity, 21; and Jerusalem Pride Parade, 212–13, 216, 228; and Jewish tradition, xii, 172, 201, 227–29; LGBTQ+ organizations' collaboration with, 45, 62–64, 215–16; and marriage advocacy, 96; nationalist alignment of, xii, xiii, 4, 6, 8, 11, 229, 233–35; and Noam, 203–4, 207–8; origins of, 61; and Orthodoxy, xiii, 2, 10, 57, 63, 162, 167, 201, 212–13, 217, 223, 227–29; outreach activities of, 4, 40, 140, 147, 157, 166–93, 225–26; and politics of authenticity, xiii, 2, 5–9, 167–93, 228–29, 232, 234; and respectability politics, 196–97, 201; rhetorical strategies of, 4, 5, 172, 181, 192–93, 228, 232–33, 234; ritual spaces supported by, 45, 47; and sexuality, 123–25, 137, 139, 150–51; social context for, 14; storytelling as method used by, 167, 228; support provided by, 114; tactics and outcomes of, xii–xiii, 2–4, 7, 61,

67, 122, 167, 170, 172, 192, 226; tensions within, 29
Kamoha, 54, 57–59, 66, 70, 196, 199, 213, 215–16, 257n55, 261n13
Kaplahon, Yivnia, 208–9
Katz, Benjamin (Ben), 157, 245, 260n24, 268n18, 268n21
Keep Not Silent (documentary), 41
Kelner, Vered, 28
ketubah (marriage contract), 108, 109
Kibbutz movement, 130
kiddush (ceremony), 45, 77, 110, 149
kippas (yarmulkes), 1, 2, 15, 106, 108, 122, 169, 171–72, 194, 203, 206, 210, 228
Kolech, 186, 260n65
Kook, Abraham Isaac, 17
Koren, Irit, 41
Kula (rabbi), 151

Lachmi, Uri, 257n62
Lau, Benny, 35, 39, 43, 63, 65, 86, 91, 123, 129, 130, 132, 140, 143–45, 155, 171, 214, 221–23, 255n33, 258n63, 259n22, 261n(epigraph), 261n18, 264n42, 264n51, 265n55, 272n53
Lehman, Benni, 269n40
lesbians: as couples/families, 50–51, 80–82, 88, 107, 109, 110–12, 182, 184, 229, 268n27; *halacha* and, 42, 90, 110–11, 137, 263n27; media portrayals of, 41; personal stories of, 34, 36, 38, 50, 68–69, 72–75. *See also* Bat Kol; Orthodox LGBT people
Levi, Uriel Tehila, 194
Levinstein, Yigal, 65, 190, 195, 211; *Family Values in the Face of Postmodernism*, 1–2
Leviticus abomination clause, 46, 54, 78, 89, 91, 112, 118, 158, 160, 236
LGBT people. *See* Orthodox LGBT people
LGBTQ+ people: collaboration of, with Orthodox LGBT, 45, 62–64, 215–16; feminist alignment with, 265n60; liv-

Sephardim, 47, 136
settlement enterprise, 168, 187–92
sexuality: blunting of, by conversion
therapy, 98; dynamic vs. born/made
theories of, 98–99, 102, 123–25, 177, 179,
182, 189–90, 261n16, 269n40; everyday theologies of, 123–26; fluidity of,
98–100; *halacha* and, 133; Hod and,
55; in Jewish tradition, xii; Kadag
and, 123–25, 137, 139, 150–51; legitima-
tion/delegitimation of practices of,
192; menstrual rules and, 75, 134, 149,
259n12; Orthodox Judaism's guidance
on, 33–35, 72, 75, 94; pride parades
and, 212, 214–16, 218; repression of, 76,
100. *See also* homosexuality
Shabbat: family observance of, 79–80,
82, 148; LGBT people's observance of,
2, 45, 50, 52, 56, 57–58, 61, 78, 87, 211;
rules and rituals connected with, 45,
52, 63, 82
shame, 27, 71–73, 89–90
Shilo (settlement), 194–96, 235
Shlisel, Yishai, 61, 211
Shoval: activism of, 66, 173, 268n16; Bat
Kol and, 173, 268n19; effectiveness of,
173, 179–80; founding of, 35, 37, 40,
172–73, 268n18; Havruta and, 55, 173;
and Kadag, 61; meaning of the name,
173; mission, principles, and goals of,
173–78; non-educational settings for
the work of, 180; outreach activities of,
xi, 35, 37, 40, 143, 172–81; in the settlements, 189, 190; volunteer characteristics, 173, 175; volunteers' experiences
in, 178–79; volunteer training in, 174–
75, 179, 268n16; workshops conducted
by, 173–76
Shulchan Aruch, 16
Shvidel, Ze'ev, 28, 41–42, 43, 245, 260n24
social and institutional power structures:
persistence of, 4, 131, 156, 163, 168,
191–92

social change. *See* activism
social death. *See* loneliness and social
death
social media, 18, 110, 185–86, 199, 220, 227.
See also Facebook; Facebook Confessions Page for Religious LGBTQ;
online forums and chatrooms
sodomy laws, 29
solidarity, against injustice, 6, 8, 23, 32,
183, 223–24, 233–34
Sorek, Limor, 45, 229
Sorek, Zehorit, 38, 45–46, 49, 61, 193, 197–
201, 205, 211, 229, 245, 271n16
Sperber, Avigail, 27, 28, 35, 37–38, 51, 186,
265n60, 268n18, 272n7
spirituality. *See* faith and spirituality
Srugim (television show), 72–73, 257n62
Stern, Feigi, 169
storytelling: Kadag's use of, 167, 228; Our
Faces campaigns, 168–72; Shoval's use
of, 174, 175, 178; types of stories, 167.
See also Orthodox LGBT people: personal stories of; *Trembling Before G-d*
Stav (rabbi), 259n21, 265n54, 267n84
Strauss, Yair, 43, 107, 143, 171
strugglers, 66–67, 73, 97, 261n13
suffering, 101–2, 120–23
suicidal ideation/suicide, 70, 102, 105, 123,
147, 177, 187, 190
surrogacy, 32, 111, 257n59, 260n7

Tahini El-Erez, 234
Talmud, 98, 124, 208, 263n27
Tehila, 37, 61, 86
Tel Aviv: gay community in, 7–8, 31, 38,
44, 45, 48, 90, 225; LGBT ritual spaces
in, 45–48; Pride Center, 255n37; Pride
Parade, 29, 30, 31, 50, 64, 212, 215, 233;
Proud Minyan prayer group in, 37
theology. *See* faith and spirituality
therapy, sought by LGBT people, 115–16
tikkun olam (world repair), 120–22, 171,
178, 218

ABOUT THE AUTHOR

ORIT AVISHAI is Professor of Sociology and Women's, Gender, and Sexuality Studies at Fordham University. She is affiliated with the Center for Jewish Studies.